MW00629989

明慧

For our family and friends—and yours.

May our humble service open a door for you
to establish a bright future
for yourself and your loved ones.

Witness, be a part of, and record
this significant period of history in the making.

Minghui Report:
The 20-Year Persecution of Falun Gong in China

First English Edition

Original English edition first published on mhpublishing.org in July 2019

First English edition printed in October 2019 by Minghui Publishing in Hackensack, New Jersey, the United States of America

---

Library of Congress Control Number: 2019913369
ISBN 978-1-7334819-0-8 (hardcover)

MINGHUI REPORT

The 20-Year Persecution of Falun Gong in China

BY THE MINGHUI GROUP

CONTENTS

About This Report

About This Report

世界需要真善忍

From bloody political purges like the Cultural Revolution to the Tiananmen Square Massacre, the Chinese Communist Party (CCP) has a long history of demonizing select groups as threats to the country and mobilizing China's people to attack these groups. This way, the Party effectively diverts attention from its own crises.

In the late 1990s, then CCP leader Jiang Zemin turned his sights on the increasingly popular spiritual and meditation discipline of Falun Dafa, also known as Falun Gong. What followed was a brutal campaign that has led to thousands of confirmed deaths, hundreds of thousands of documented torture cases, and tens of millions of peaceful meditators being deprived of their most basic freedoms.

A group of North American volunteers launched Minghui.org on June 25, 1999, shortly before the suppression in China officially began on July 20. Since then, Minghui, with the courageous and selfless support of Falun Gong practitioners in China, has reported a massive volume of firsthand information about the violent suppression campaign, covered practitioners' worldwide efforts to counter the persecution, and provided a platform for the community of Falun Gong cultivators to share experiences and informational materials.

Over the past twenty years, Minghui has also published more than ten periodicals. Every Friday, practitioners in China who volunteer to run "material production sites" download, print, and distribute these materials in their local areas. Minghui publications help practitioners in China to learn how to protect their rights, progress in their self-cultivation, and counter the persecution. These magazines, booklets and video programs also equip practitioners to help their neighbors and friends better understand Falun Gong.

Despite the CCP's internet censorship and overwhelming propaganda attacking Falun Gong, people in China can still access truthful information and updates on Falun Gong because of practitioners' perseverance even while being persecuted themselves. Among those who have come to understand that "Falun Dafa is good" and identify with its principles of Truthfulness-Compassion-Forbearance (真善忍), some have started practicing Falun Gong. Others have found improved health and better relationships with family.

By publishing Falun Gong news reports and experience-sharing articles every day, producing radio programs, and hosting an annual online conference for all practitioners in China, Minghui's free platform allows practitioners to inspire each other to continually elevate their moral character and strive toward spiritual perfection.

With the biggest network of volunteers in China, Minghui has been the only media organization in the world that can overcome online censorship to report firsthand information amid the ongoing persecution. So far, Minghui has built up a database of more than 112,000 persecution cases and 105,500 perpetrators. Without any external funding and relying entirely upon volunteers' dedication and contribution of time, knowledge, and expertise over the years, Minghui has established itself as the official source of Falun Gong information.

The CCP's campaign to eradicate Falun Gong has fundamentally failed, and the perpetrators will be held to account. Despite its unprecedented cruelty and complexity, the persecution has proven futile from the start, and it will eventually bring about the collapse of the CCP itself.

Minghui's thorough documentation of the persecution in real time enables the international community to respond in a timely manner to alleviate and ultimately end this atrocity. As 2019 marks the twentieth year of practitioners' efforts to counter the persecution, we present this milestone report to help decision-makers better understand the human rights violations perpetrated against Falun Gong practitioners, and find ways to support the universal principles of Truthfulness-Compassion-Forbearance (真善忍).

Executive Summary

Executive Summary

世界需要真善忍

Falun Dafa, also known as Falun Gong, is an ancient meditation practice and spiritual discipline based on the universal values of Truthfulness-Compassion-Forbearance (真善忍). First taught to the public in 1992 by Mr. Li Hongzhi, Falun Gong became a household name in China in just a few years after its practitioners experienced profound improvements in their health and well-being and introduced it to their friends and families.

Though the Chinese government initially promoted Falun Gong for many of the same reasons, fear and distrust began to set in at the top levels of the Communist Party a few years later. Both Falun Gong's surging popularity and its values, which were deemed incompatible with those of the Party's doctrine of violence and struggle, were perceived as potential threats to the regime's authoritarian rule.

Violent Repression Built on Incitement to Hatred

In 1996, state-controlled media began to attack Falun Gong in coordinated campaigns. Falun Gong exercise sites in public parks around the country—filled to the brim with people quietly meditating to serene music—came under surveillance by government agents and plainclothes police officers. The publication of Falun Gong books—national bestsellers at the time—was suddenly banned.

In April 1999, Falun Gong practitioners gathered outside a magazine office to discuss errors in a recently published article attacking

Falun Gong, only to be assaulted and arrested. After officials told other practitioners to appeal to the central government in Beijing to seek their release, around 10,000 stood quietly outside the national appeals office as instructed. Their concerns were met that evening after a discussion with then Premier Zhu Rongji. This event became known as the "April 25th Appeal" (explored in more detail in Appendix 1).

However, the Party leadership later characterized the peaceful appeal as a “siege” of the central government compound and used it to justify the launch of an all-out campaign to eradicate Falun Gong nationwide on July 20, 1999. Volunteer coordinators of exercise sites were arrested overnight, with others being taken into custody in the coming days.

To petition the government for their constitutional right to practice their faith, practitioners traveled to Beijing by the hundreds of thousands, congregating at the national appeals office and holding up banners on Tiananmen Square, only to be arrested en masse. Those who revealed their identities were turned over to local authorities in their hometowns. Some refused to do so in order to protect their families and colleagues from the CCP’s policy of implication, and many of these practitioners were transferred elsewhere and have since disappeared.

A sophisticated propaganda campaign soon followed, with state-controlled media making false claims that practicing Falun Gong had led to 1,400 deaths. As public support for the suppression was initially lackluster, the regime later staged a spectacle on Tiananmen Square in which several people claiming to be Falun Gong practitioners set themselves on fire. Though the “self-immolation” event was quickly debunked as a hoax, the damage was done: much of the Chinese population were now firmly prejudiced against Falun Gong and had tacitly accepted the Communist Party’s violent suppression of the group.

Campaign of “Transformation” Through Torture

At its core, the persecution of Falun Gong revolves around a campaign of “transformation,” or forcing practitioners to renounce their belief. The methods range from gentle persuasion to systematic brainwashing to physical and psychological torture. Practitioners who agree to write "guarantee statements" to renounce Falun Gong are offered early release, though many are then made to participate in the transformation of other practitioners.

This campaign is coordinated by Jiang Zemin's Gang through the 610 Office, an extralegal agency created by the central Communist Party leadership specifically to eradicate Falun Gong. To carry out this task, 610 Office has been given control over the judiciary, law enforcement, the penal system, and other authorities at all levels of government.

Falun Gong practitioners throughout China are systematically monitored, arrested, and taken to brainwashing centers (known officially as "legal education centers"), black jails, forced labor camps (until they were shut down in 2013), prisons, detention centers, drug rehabilitation facilities, and mental hospitals. While in custody, they are routinely abused and tortured by both guards and inmates who are instigated to do so by the authorities. Common methods of torture include beating, force-feeding, physical constraint in excruciating positions, sensory bombardment, electric shocks, waterboarding and suffocation, solitary confinement, and sexual assault. In addition, practitioners are often deprived of basic needs, including sleep, food, water, and access to toilets.

More than 4,300 practitioners have been confirmed to have died as a result of the persecution, and many more have been killed on demand to supply China's organ transplant industry. Many survivors of torture are left with permanent injuries, disabilities, paralysis, mental trauma, and in the most extreme cases, insanity. Families of practitioners have been torn apart, with relatives and children living in constant fear of the authorities who continue to harass them.

In addition to suffering physical harm, practitioners have also been denied employment, education, housing, and economic security. Practitioners routinely face fines and extortion by the police, as well as suspension of their pensions. Many have been fired from their jobs or expelled from their schools simply for their belief. This discrimination has also been extended to their family members, with authorities in some areas openly threatening their children's education and careers to force practitioners to renounce their faith.

The persecution has been extended to all children in China. Starting in elementary school, students are indoctrinated with anti-Falun Gong propaganda in their textbooks and mandatory denunciation activities. Some practitioners' children died young after being forcibly separated from their parents, and some were abused or even tortured to death by the authorities for practicing Falun Gong. Some were orphaned after losing their parents in the persecution, and others were driven insane after being forced to watch their parents being tortured.

Because the prosecution of Falun Gong practitioners for their belief has no legal basis, legal procedures are sidestepped or openly violated at every step, from arrest through imprisonment. Police ransack practitioners' homes without search warrants. Courts hold show trials and hand down predetermined sentences while denying lawyers' ability to access case files, meet with their clients, and defend them at trial. Attorneys routinely face intimidation and even assault and torture for defending the rights of Falun Gong practitioners. Even after serving their terms, some practitioners are taken directly to a brainwashing center for further abuse instead of being released.

The communist regime has also extended its persecution campaign outside mainland China. It has carried out and instigated physical attacks against Falun Gong practitioners working to raise awareness of the persecution. The regime has also pressured foreign governments and police forces to illegally obstruct, arrest, or deny entry to Falun Gong demonstrators while Chinese officials are visiting. Organizations and individuals connected with the CCP have also harassed practitioners and intimidated Chinese tourists to prevent them from learning about the persecution.

Falun Gong Gains Support and Newcomers Despite Persecution

To resist the persecution and raise awareness of its brutality despite censorship and surveillance, Falun Gong practitioners in China have worked tirelessly to inform the public through word of mouth, distributing pamphlets and other keepsakes, displaying posters in public areas, writing letters to officials, making phone calls, and sending messages online. Particularly noteworthy are the small but ubiquitous material production sites practitioners have set up in their homes to produce informational materials for the public using designs downloaded from Minghui.org.

Practitioners outside of China have complemented these efforts by making phone calls to dissuade perpetrators involved in the persecution in China, producing censorship-circumvention software to allow people in China to access information freely, and setting up information booths at tourist destinations around the world. In addition to meeting practitioners at community events, the public has learned about Falun Gong through art exhibitions and documentary films on the subject.

Human rights organizations, public officials, and legislative bodies around the world have also spoken out and passed resolutions to call for an end to the persecution in China. Courts in Spain and Argentina have indicted top CCP officials for torture and genocide. The U.S. Department of State and Congressional-Executive Commission on China (CECC) have highlighted the persecution of Falun Gong in their annual reports and called for an end to the persecution.

As a result of these combined efforts, many Chinese citizens have begun to educate themselves and adopt a renewed perspective on Falun Gong. Some police officers and government officials in China have stopped participating in the persecution and even started protecting practitioners within their power. The number of arrests and sentences of practitioners in China has decreased in recent years. The ban on the publication of Falun Gong books was quietly lifted in 2011, though practitioners in China have printed their own books throughout the persecution to meet the demand. Nevertheless, the regime's overall persecution policy and machinery continue to operate.

When former Chinese Communist Party leader Jiang Zemin first launched the persecution, he vowed to "defeat" Falun Gong in three months. However, the spiritual practice has only continued to flourish over the past 20 years. Practitioners in China have persisted in their faith despite pressure and torture, and many who were forced to sign renunciations in detention later recanted their statements when they were released. A steady stream of newcomers has started practicing Falun Gong through instructional workshops and self-study. Today, people in over 80 countries practice Falun Gong, and its books have been translated into more than 40 languages.

More International Leaders Taking Action

Many recent developments have focused on holding accountable the perpetrators of the persecution. Since 2015, more than 200,000 Falun Gong practitioners have filed criminal complaints against Jiang Zemin with China's highest court, and petitions to bring Jiang to justice have garnered millions of signatures.

In 2019, the United States government announced more stringent vetting of visas for human rights violators, including Chinese officials who have participated in the persecution of Falun Gong. Minghui.org has begun to compile information about such perpetrators, including their identities, family members, and assets, to be submitted to the U.S. government.

At the Second Ministerial to Advance Religious Freedom held by the U.S. Department of State on July 16-18, 2019, current and former legislators discussed human rights violations in China, including how Western companies work with the Chinese regime to develop technologies used in its repression of faith groups, such as mass surveillance technology and artificial intelligence. President Trump met with survivors of religious persecution, including a Falun Gong practitioner whose husband remains imprisoned in China.

On July 20, 2019, which marks the 20th year of the persecution, the U.S. CECC issued a statement urging the Chinese Communist Party to stop the "appalling and unacceptable human rights abuses" it has perpetrated against Falun Gong practitioners. In addition, 22 U.S. Senators and Representatives sent letters commending practitioners' efforts over the past two decades. The German Federal Foreign Office also issued a statement calling for the end of the persecution and for independent investigations into the regime's harvesting of organs from Falun Gong practitioners.

Introduction

Introduction

Jiang Zemin's Genocidal Policy

On July 20, 1999, former CCP General Secretary Jiang Zemin launched the persecution of Falun Gong and vowed to "annihilate Falun Gong in three months." He issued an order to "ruin their reputation, cut them off financially, and destroy their physical bodies."

Falun Gong practitioners in China have not only been denied their constitutional rights to freedom of belief, speech, and assembly, but they have also been denied residence, employment, education and the right to life. As soon as someone acknowledges that they practice Falun Gong, they lose their foothold in society, and their lives and property are jeopardized. Falun Gong practitioners are subject to arbitrary detention, extortion, confiscation of property, expulsion from work or school, denial of pensions, home ransacking, and shutoff of utilities. Many have been detained and tortured in prisons, labor camps, brainwashing centers, detention centers, drug rehabilitation centers, or mental hospitals, resulting in death, disability, or mental disorder. Some practitioners have also been raped or sexually assaulted while in custody.

Over the past two decades, Jiang Zemin and his gang have instigated hatred of Falun Gong practitioners by defaming them and intimidating, bribing, and infiltrating the general public. The CCP has almost a century-long history of choosing a group to persecute every ten years on average to ease its own crises and paranoia. Jiang Zemin followed the same playbook and started by labeling Falun Gong an "evil cult" to justify the persecution. This label is not factually or legally supported. Nevertheless, the CCP's campaign has made Falun Gong practitioners the most oppressed group in Chinese society.

Overview of the Persecution

According to information collected by Minghui.org, between July 20, 1999 and July 10, 2019, there have been at least 2,500,000 to 3,000,000 arrests of Falun Gong practitioners (some have been arrested multiple times).

These arrests fall into four categories: 1) administrative detention based on Public Security Administration Punishment Law of the People's Republic of China; 2) illegal detention in brainwashing centers, which are usually labeled "legal education centers" and designed to conduct "thought reform" of Falun Gong practitioners; 3) detention in now-defunct labor camps; 4) criminal detention based on the Criminal Procedure Law of the People's Republic of China.

In addition, up to ten million unnamed Falun Gong practitioners have been arrested for appealing for their belief and taken to secret concentration camps, where they become guinea pigs in the CCP's scientific research and sources of involuntary organ donations. An unknown number have died, their bodies cremated without their families' knowledge.

These practitioners are unnamed because they refused to reveal their identities upon arrest in order to protect their families, neighbors, or employers. We do not have information about these practitioners, so the facts of whatever persecution they were subjected to are not included in our summary of human rights violations. We trust that after the genocide comes to an end, more insiders will step forward to testify against the CCP. We are also working to collect and compile cases of Falun Gong practitioners who have been subjected to organ harvesting and human testing in clinical trials.

The persecution of Falun Gong is carried out by the Communist Party, the government, military, health system, law enforcement, procuratorate (a state organ for legal supervision and prosecution), and judiciary working together. In order to protect their vested interests, each of these entities attempts to cover up its crimes and censor information. Therefore, the information Minghui.org is able to collect is only the tip of the iceberg. Even so, Minghui.org has managed to collect a large amount of firsthand data over the past twenty years. Due to space limitations, this report covers only a small portion of the website's vast collection of persecution cases.

The cases covered in this report indicate that the persecution of Falun Gong is nationwide and covers both urban and rural areas. Practitioners have been persecuted in every one of China's 31 provinces and centrally controlled cities, including Anhui, Beijing, Chongqing, Fujian, Gansu, Guangdong, Guangxi, Guizhou, Hainan, Hebei, Heilongjiang, Henan, Hubei, Hunan, Inner Mongolia, Jiangsu, Jiangxi, Jilin, Liaoning, Ningxia, Qinghai, Shaanxi, Shandong, Shanghai, Shanxi, Sichuan, Tianjin, Tibet, Xinjiang, Yunnan, and Zhejiang.

Victims of the persecution come from all walks of life, including government employees, military personnel, police officers, judges, prosecutors, lawyers, professors, teachers, students, scholars, entrepreneurs, engineers, artists, health workers, business managers, journalists, service workers, homemakers, farmers, retirees, the self-employed, the unemployed, monks, and Taoists.

They work in education, the sciences, government, agriculture, forestry and animal husbandry, hardware, lighting, ceramics, plastics, crafts, textiles, transportation, finance, insurance, utilities, automobiles, steel, electronics, food and beverage, postal service, media, aviation, military, energy, mining, entertainment, literature and art.

Victims also include people of all ages and genders, from infants to seniors in their 90s. Neither pregnant women nor the disabled have been spared. From the accounts it has accumulated, Minghui.org has summarized more than 100 methods of torture used on Falun Gong practitioners, including beating; shocking with electric batons; force-feeding; sleep deprivation; hanging practitioners up in different postures; starvation; denial of toilet access; forced abortion; burning and scalding with hot water, irons, or hot oil; dragging; sexual assault; whipping; forced labor; and solitary confinement.

The persecution has caused tremendous loss of life and property. As of September 10, 2019, Minghui.org has confirmed 4,343 cases of practitioners being persecuted to death. This is far fewer than the actual death toll, as many cases—especially those concerning live organ harvesting—have remained hidden. The bodies of many deceased practitioners have also been forcibly cremated to destroy evidence.

Minghui.org has also confirmed that, as of July 10, 2019, at least 86,050 practitioners have been arrested at one point or another; 28,143 have spent time in labor camps; 17,963 have been sentenced to prison; 18,838 have been taken to brainwashing centers; and 809 have been confined in mental hospitals. It has also documented 519,040 cases of torture. Untold numbers have suffered discrimination, termination of employment, loss of income, mental trauma, broken families, injury, disability, or death over the past two decades of persecution.

Part 1: Persecution of Falun Gong

世界需要真善忍

Part 1: Persecution of Falun Gong

Key Highlights

Falun Gong practitioners have been systematically held in prisons, brainwashing centers, forced labor camps, mental hospitals, and other detention facilities for their faith. While incarcerated, practitioners are subjected to brainwashing, forced labor, and torture. China's rubber-stamp judicial system hands down predetermined sentences even though practicing Falun Gong does not violate any laws.

Outside of detention, practitioners have been denied employment, education, housing, and economic security solely on the basis of their faith. Authorities have extorted money from practitioners, suspended their pensions, and seized their assets at will. Practitioners have also been denied identification cards and passports, and they are constantly monitored through facial recognition, telecommunications, and other surveillance technology.

Children of practitioners have been denied schooling, employment, and parental care. Some have been orphaned, assaulted by police, or driven insane after being made to watch their parents being tortured. Brainwashing campaigns have been extended into mandatory school activities and textbooks, instilling hatred of Falun Gong in a whole generation.

Torture of practitioners has led to more than 4,300 confirmed deaths and countless lives shadowed by injury, disability and mental trauma. Common methods include beatings, force-feeding, constraining victims in excruciating positions, sensory bombardment, restricting basic needs, electric shocks, waterboarding and suffocation, long-term solitary confinement, and sexual torture.

The Chinese regime has extended the persecution outside mainland China. It has used its embassies and CCP-linked organizations to disrupt practitioners' efforts to raise awareness around the world, instigated violence against practitioners on the streets, recruited informants to spy on practitioners, and pressured foreign governments into unlawfully restricting practitioners' right to peacefully demonstrate during visits by Chinese officials.

Chapter 1: Detention Facilities

The Chinese communist regime has used prisons, labor camps, brainwashing centers, and other facilities to detain Falun Gong practitioners since it launched its nationwide campaign against Falun Gong in July 1999.

The formal prison system is used to incarcerate Falun Gong practitioners who have been convicted for upholding their faith after trial. There were 681 prisons across China as of 2012, according to a report by China's Ministry of Justice. It is worth noting that China's court system has served as a rubber stamp in the persecution of Falun Gong: it merely goes through the motions to put on show trials before handing down predetermined sentences.

The now-defunct labor camp system allowed authorities to detain practitioners for up to four years without trial. In a 2009 UN Human Rights Council report, the Chinese delegation described its system of re-education through labor as "similar to that of correctional services in other countries" that was "applied to persons who have committed crimes that do not warrant criminal sentence." The report estimated that there were 320 labor camps holding 190,000 people across the country.

Because labor camps were, in fact, used to detain prisoners of conscience who had not committed any crimes, the Chinese regime faced mounting pressure from the international community and shut the system down in late 2013. The detention of Falun Gong practitioners didn't stop, however, as the regime has since intensified the use of extrajudicial brainwashing centers instead.

§1.1 Brainwashing Centers[1]

To be precise, no detention facility in China is explicitly labeled a brainwashing center; rather, they are officially labeled "legal education centers" or "drug rehabilitation centers." Unlike labor camps (an administrative punishment system) and prisons (a formal criminal punishment system), brainwashing centers are not legally obligated to follow any administrative or criminal procedures. The 610 Office, an extralegal agency established on June 10, 1999, specifically to persecute Falun Gong, created brainwashing centers in 2001, and all subordinate 610 Offices throughout China followed suit.

When brainwashing fails to shake Falun Gong practitioners' faith, the CCP resorts to torture, causing many to suffer irreparable physical injury and mental trauma or lose their lives.

§§1.1.1 An Extrajudicial Branch of China's Multi-Tentacled Detention System

Brainwashing has long been a tactic used by the CCP in its attempt to reform political dissidents and other groups of citizens that it deems a threat to its rule. The persecution of Falun Gong has centered around brainwashing practitioners who live by the principles of Truthfulness-Compassion-Forbearance (真善忍), in an effort to force practitioners to renounce their faith. Under the directive of the 610 Office, any level of government, neighborhood committee, business, or even school can set up brainwashing centers in any location, even in hotels or private residences. Formal detention facilities such as police stations, detention centers, labor camps, and prisons often have their own brainwashing centers.

From their inception to their operation, these brainwashing centers exist outside the law. Some officials claim it is a type of house arrest. However, a house arrest must be approved by a court of law, while no legal procedure or documentation is needed to detain someone in a brainwashing center.

In addition, officers and guards in these facilities have more authority than ordinary law enforcement officers. They can arrest, detain, and release practitioners at will. Nor is there a limit to how long a person can be held. Those in charge closely monitor basic human needs—talking, eating, sleeping, and access to a toilet—and deprive their detainees of them at will. They can beat, force-feed, and shock their charges with electric batons with no repercussions.

Brainwashing centers exist throughout China in almost every city and county and many communities. Their longevity ranges from days to years. It is thus difficult to ascertain the exact number of brainwashing centers, nor is there an official tally. However, Minghui.org has collected data on the number of practitioners sent to brainwashing centers.

Though extrajudicial and extralegal in nature, brainwashing centers have been well-funded by the government. Many law enforcement officers, employers, and residential communities have been incentivized to set up their own brainwashing centers or send practitioners to existing centers. The massive network of brainwashing centers has become a critical component of the Chinese regime's multi-tentacled system to detain Falun Gong practitioners. This chapter discusses its scale, severity, and devastation.

§§1.1.2 A Massive, Well-Funded Network

A keyword search of Minghui.org from 1999 to 2019 returned about 65,000 articles in which the words "brainwashing center" appeared more than 210,000 times in total. After removing those brainwashing centers without exact locations and consolidating redundant entries with varied names, we estimate that there are about 3,640 such establishments across China.

These confirmed brainwashing centers were distributed across 30 provincial-level administrative units, including 26 provinces and 4 centrally controlled municipalities (Beijing, Tianjin, Shanghai, and Chongqing). Hebei Province had the most brainwashing centers (439), followed by Shandong (383), Hubei (336), Sichuan (301), and Jilin (272). Eight other administrative units also had hundreds of brainwashing centers, while 15 units had dozens. Qinghai and Ningxia were the only provinces with fewer than ten brainwashing centers reported.

The real number could be much higher, given the secretive nature of these facilities and the censorship and persecution that persist in China. Furthermore, after the labor camp system was abolished in 2013, many practitioners were redirected to prisons and brainwashing centers, both existing ones and those newly created.

While brainwashing centers are initiated by different levels of the 610 Office, they are largely driven by financial incentives and partially funded by money paid by practitioners' employers or extorted from practitioners. Minghui published a white paper in 2014 on the scale of brainwashing centers:

> *We estimate that over the past 15 years, fees charged to detainees' employers totaled approximately 3.37 billion yuan. Government incentives for each "successfully transformed" detainee brought in a further 226 million yuan. This is in addition to government appropriations of an estimated 1.18 billion yuan dedicated to the construction and remodeling of brainwashing facilities.*

§§1.1.3 Tactics Used to Destroy Practitioners' Faith

While prisons and labor camps existed prior to the persecution of Falun Gong, brainwashing centers are unique in that their sole purpose is to force practitioners to forsake their belief. To achieve this goal, brainwashing centers often employ the following tactics:

› 1.1.3(a) Arbitrary Terms of Detention

Because no legal procedures must be followed to incarcerate someone in a brainwashing center, practitioners can be detained simply for not renouncing their faith and held for an indefinite period of time.

Ms. Li Xihui, a former employee of the Sichuan Radio Station, was arrested in 2006 and detained in the Xinjin Brainwashing Center in Chengdu City, Sichuan Province, for seven years. The authorities secretly transferred her to Er'ehu Brainwashing Center in Ziyang City in 2013 and continued to try to brainwash her. It wasn't clear if she had been released at the time of writing.

Another practitioner in Guangdong Province, Ms. Xie Yu, 32, was taken to a brainwashing center in January 2019, right after she finished serving two years in prison for distributing Falun Gong materials. Her family learned that the authorities had decided to send her to the brainwashing center because she still refused to renounce her faith by the time her prison term ended.

› 1.1.3(b) High Degree of Secrecy

The extrajudicial nature of brainwashing centers makes their operations highly arbitrary and secretive. For instance, after the labor camp system was abolished in 2013, many brainwashing centers in Wuhan City, Hubei Province, removed all visible signs and logos on their facilities to avoid liability and to keep from being traced. Occasionally, some facilities were closed while new ones were established elsewhere.

One practitioner in Hubei Province was arrested in October 2018 for not renouncing her faith. After she was detained for 15 days, the police took her to a mental hospital for five days before moving her to a secret brainwashing center. The officers covered her head with a hood and tied her hands during the transfer so she didn't know where she was being taken.

Her family learned of her whereabouts and went to the brainwashing center to try to see her. Before they got close to the door, they heard an automated voice issue a warning: "Do not approach. Lasers are being activated." Lasers suddenly surrounded them from all directions. The lights followed them as they moved, eventually forcing them to leave.

The practitioner's family then heard she'd been moved to another place, which they found to be an abandoned residence with no signs or plate on the door. The metal door was closed. No one answered when they called the practitioner's name.

The practitioner later told her family after she was released that she was in the second location when they went there. The staff got nervous when they heard her family outside and wouldn't let her make a sound or signal to her family that she was there.

› 1.1.3(c) Administration of Unknown Drugs

In addition to torture and around-the-clock monitoring, the forcible administration of unknown drugs is also common in brainwashing centers. Mr. Xie Deqing, a healthy retiree, died about 20 days into his detention at Xinjin Brainwashing Center in Chengdu City, Sichuan Province. He was emaciated, incontinent, and in extreme pain before his death. His skin was gray. These symptoms are consistent with those of other practitioners who have been confirmed to have been given unknown drugs. Over 100 police officers were later dispatched to take his body from the funeral home in the middle of the night to be cremated.

› 1.1.3(d) Intensive Brainwashing

Besides physical confinement, practitioners are also forced to watch propaganda videos slandering Falun Gong and write down their thoughts afterward. Their written reports are often analyzed by psychologists, who then take advantage of any weaknesses they discover to devise new strategies to destroy their faith. Very often, coworkers and family members are called in to try to coerce practitioners to give up their belief.

In brainwashing centers in Wuhan City, Hubei Province, the authorities installed three cameras in each room. Pieces of paper with sentences defaming Falun Gong printed on them were posted on the tables, chairs, and floor. With the exception of time allotted for sleep, the television in the room showed only programs defaming Falun Gong or other programs aimed at weakening practitioners' willpower. High-volume speakers broadcast propaganda slandering Falun Gong and its founder all day long.

The practitioners were prohibited from doing the Falun Gong exercises, and the guards also set strict restrictions, such as limiting the time to finish a meal and where and how they washed their dishes. Within three days of being taken to Haikou Brainwashing Center on August 9, 2018, Ms. Dai Juzhen was in life-threatening condition with high blood pressure and high blood sugar.

› 1.1.3(e) Misrepresentation and Deceit

Another distinctive aspect of brainwashing centers is that they misrepresent themselves as "legal education centers" and are located in unremarkable locations.

Officials deceive family members who do not support Falun Gong into helping to convince practitioners to go to these centers. This happened to Ms. Tang Xiaoyan in Guilin City, Guangxi Autonomous Region. Her family believed 610 Office officials who said that the center was a favorable, voluntary study place, but once Ms. Tang arrived there, officials beat her, tortured her, kept a bright light in front of her eyes at all times, and deprived her of sleep and water. This led to life-threatening conditions for Ms. Tang on at least two occasions.

§§1.1.4 Deaths in Brainwashing Centers

The physical and mental abuse at brainwashing centers has also contributed to deaths of Falun Gong practitioners. Among the 3,653 confirmed deaths of Falun Gong practitioners between 1999 and 2014, 746 (20.4%) were related to torture in brainwashing centers and 367 (10%) of the deaths took place in brainwashing centers.

Ms. Xu Huizhu, a retired teacher in Guangdong Province, was arrested in late July 2016 and taken to Huangpu Brainwashing Center. She died in August shortly after she was released.

While we do not have data on how many practitioners have been detained in brainwashing centers, we observe a largely positive correlation between the number of brainwashing centers and the number of deaths in various regions. (See chart on page 400.)

Even though we cannot draw definitive conclusions regarding how brainwashing centers have contributed to the deaths of Falun Gong practitioners, the positive correlation at least validates the role of brainwashing centers in the persecution of Falun Gong.

§§1.1.5 Examples in Hubei Province: "What I Say Is Law"[2]

Mr. Lu Yougen, a Falun Gong practitioner in Hubei Province, witnessed something that he would never forget. When another practitioner protested being force-fed while he was detained, three guards grabbed him: one pulled his head backward, one restrained his shoulders, and the third forcibly struck his lower jaw.

"With a crack, the practitioner's lower jaw was dislocated and hung down at an odd angle. As the guards force-fed him, the practitioner was motionless, as if he were dead," recalled Mr. Lu.

This happened in September 2009 at a brainwashing center in Wuhan City, Hubei Province. Labeled the "Hubei Law Education Center," at least 1,200 Falun Gong practitioners have been detained there since February 2002 under orders from the Hubei Province 610 Office. For refusing to renounce their faith, they have been subjected to isolation, deception, brainwashing, humiliation, threats, and torture.

When Mr. Zhang Sifeng from the Hanyang District was confined there, he pointed out that he was being illegally detained. An officer replied that he only cared about brainwashing, not laws. "What I say is law!" shouted the officer. "If you don't believe it, I can take out one of your kidneys right now!"

› 1.1.5(a) Arbitrary Detention and Torture

Like other brainwashing centers, Hubei Law Education Center is dedicated to forcing practitioners to give up their belief. The facility has been praised numerous times by the Political and Legal Affairs Committee, a government agency that oversees the persecution of Falun Gong.

Officials in Hubei Province can arrest any practitioner in the province and detain him or her in this facility without following any official procedures or providing documentation. This includes practitioners who have just finished prison terms. In one case, a surgeon was operating on a patient in a hospital when he was arrested and taken to the center.

Kept in cells behind metal bars, practitioners are watched 24/7 and subjected to brainwashing from 7 a.m. until 10 p.m. or later every day. Officials confiscate their watches so that they lose track of time and block cell phone signals to cut them off from the outside world. They are not allowed to write home or have family visits. The lights are always on, even at night.

Ms. Cui Hai, who used to work at the Wuhan Chemical Import & Export Co., was detained for 70 days in the facility following her arrest in October 2012. "As a result of the torture, I was severely emaciated, and several times, my lower jaw almost fell off." Her hair turned gray, she suffered memory loss, her entire body shook, and her limbs swelled.

Ms. Cui was later sentenced to five years in prison for her faith. She survived torture and abuse during her incarceration, only to die on January 1, 2018, less than three weeks after she was released.

› 1.1.5(b) Beaten and Drugged

Mr. Zhang Su, a tennis coach from Wuhan, talked about how he was mistreated at the Hubei facility. "Several plainclothes officers approached me at a train ticket retail site near my home in May 2011. They sprayed something in my face so I couldn't breathe, knocked me down, and handcuffed me. No one ever showed their identity or explained why I was being arrested," he wrote.

Later that day, Mr. Zhang was taken to Hubei Law Education Center. When he protested the brainwashing, guards beat him, slapped him in the face, and threatened to shock him with electric batons. This went on for about two months, and his blood pressure was often as high as 120/230 mmHg.

After three months, Mr. Zhang noticed that what he ate gave him diarrhea, palpitations, and tightness in his chest. This lasted for three months, during which time he fainted twice. When he was examined, he was found to have heart damage, gallstones, and other symptoms similar to heart disease. The doctor said he had to be hospitalized, and Mr. Zhang also requested it.

But officials dismissed their concerns and continued the brainwashing sessions. Jiang Lili, one of the staff members, said there was no need to discuss "laws" since all the branches of the justice system—the police, the procuratorate, and the courts—work closely with the Political and Legal Affairs Committee, which supervises the 610 Offices.

"The Party can crush you like an ant. You could be executed tomorrow and it would be deemed a suicide. Your family will only get a box of ashes," Jiang smirked. "Or, they could take you to a hospital and remove your organs to save other people—just like at Sujiatun. You will then be cremated, and your family may not get your ashes. There is nothing you can do about it."

› 1.1.5(c) Brainwashing Centers: Funding and Operation

Hubei Law Education Center, also referred as Banqiao Brainwashing Center, was established in February 2002 by the Hubei 610 Office. The first list of arrestees was in the office's document 2002-No. 6, issued by its director at the time, Huang Zhaolin. The brainwashing center was eventually relocated to its current location in Mahu Village.

Funding for the center comes from both the national government budget and extortion from locals, namely employers and village or street neighborhood groups. The government allocation is said to be three million yuan per year, and extortion from locals comes to about 20,000 yuan a person per session (about 40 days). Besides this basic "expense," 610 Office agents also extort wages from locals for two "minders" who accompany the practitioner to be brainwashed. With about 20 rooms in the center, this amounts to about three million yuan per year, a lucrative incentive for officials.

As mentioned above, despite being labeled "law education" facilities, these centers primarily focus on brainwashing for several reasons. First, "transforming" a practitioner is linked to bonuses for the staff members. Second, officials can report their "successes" to the sponsoring 610 Offices to justify the continuation or expansion of the center. Third, with more practitioners being "transformed" and providing detailed information about their activities, more practitioners can be arrested to sustain the operation of the brainwashing centers.

› 1.1.5(d) Worse Than Concentration Camps

Brainwashing centers that target Falun Gong practitioners share many similarities with concentration camps in Nazi Germany and the Soviet Union in the 20th century.

State within a state. The brainwashing centers are extrajudicial entities under the direction of the 610 Offices. Officials are not bound by law, and no other government agencies are allowed to intervene.

Loss of dignity. Like prisons and forced labor camps, practitioners are often physically and mentally abused. They are force-fed, administered unknown drugs against their will, deprived of sleep, deprived of access to a toilet, and humiliated.

Secrecy. The brainwashing centers operate solely under the 610 Office. Family members are not allowed to visit, and the buildings are often unmarked, especially after the labor camp system was abolished in 2013.

Functionaries. Once officials manage to force some practitioners to give up their belief, they coerce these practitioners to "transform" other practitioners, using force, threats, or financial incentives.

Detainees are often forced to sing songs praising the Communist Party. When Mr. Lu Songming from Huangshi City refused to yield, he was forced to say, "Sir, I want to eat food provided by the Party" before given anything to eat or, "Sir, I want to use the toilet provided by the Party" before being allowed to use the toilet. This also happened to other practitioners.

› 1.1.5(e) Systematic Abuse of Body and Soul

Mr. Zhang Weijie was arrested at work on May 5, 2011 and taken to the Hubei Law Education Center. A guard, Deng Qun, told him the brainwashing center's schedule: Stand motionlessly for a long time, get beaten, be deprived of food, get force-fed, be deprived of sleep, get hung up high, be drugged, and get shocked with electric batons. Force-feeding alone took place twice a day, during which guards kept inserting and pulling the feeding tubes in and out to increase the pain. Practitioners were fed two buckets at a time, twice as much as the stomach can hold. "As the liquid food came back up and spilled all over the floor, guard Hu Gaowei sopped it up with newspaper and spread it all over my face and head while beating me. By then, everyone there was laughing at the show," recalled Mr. Zhang.

When Ms. Wang Yujie's labor camp term expired on March 11, 2011, the Xintao 610 Office took her to the Hubei Law Education Center. Within two months, she was often in a trance and mentally disordered. She died several months later on September 3, at the age of 24.

§1.2 Forced Labor Camps

Re-education through labor started in 1957 as a form of punishment for counterrevolutionaries. It was later expanded to detain people accused of petty crimes, political dissidents, and petitioners. ("Petitioners" in China are citizens who visit government appeals offices to protest unfair and/or unpopular policies.) When the persecution of Falun Gong began in 1999, re-education through labor became a widely used form of punishment for practitioners.

The forced labor system was an administrative punishment that was carried out by police, not the court system. Forced labor terms typically ranged from one to three years, with the possibility of a one-year extension. The Standing Committee of the National People's Congress abolished the re-education through labor system on December 28, 2013. However, many Falun Gong practitioners who were released from labor camps found themselves taken straight to brainwashing centers or sentenced to prison. In addition to torture and other abuses, slave labor was a major tactic used to weaken Falun Gong practitioners' willpower even as the authorities profited.

§§1.2.1 Slave Labor Violates Chinese Laws and the Universal Declaration of Human Rights

Slave labor in China's forced labor camps, detention centers, and prisons violates both the Chinese Constitution and the following laws of the People's Republic of China (PRC):

- PRC Constitution, Articles 17, 35, 42, 43, 44
- PRC Law on Work Safety—2002
- PRC Law on the Prevention and Cure of Occupational Diseases—2001
- PRC Law on Trade Unions—1992, amended 2001
- PRC Labor Law—1994
- Regulations on Labor Protection in Workplaces Where Toxic Articles Are Used—2002
- Regulations on Enterprise Minimum Wage—1994
- PRC Regulations Governing the Settlement of Labor Disputes in Enterprises—1993
- Constitution of the Trade Unions of the People's Republic of China—1998

For brevity, we list only Articles 42 and 43 from the Chinese Constitution:

Article 42. Citizens of the People's Republic of China have the right as well as the duty to work. Using various channels, the state creates conditions for employment, strengthens labor protection, improves working conditions and, on the basis of expanded production, increases remuneration for work and social benefits. Work is the glorious duty of every able-bodied citizen. All working people in state enterprises and in urban and rural economic collectives should perform their tasks with an attitude consonant with their status as masters of the country. The state promotes socialist labor emulation, and commends and rewards model and advanced workers. The state encourages citizens to take part in voluntary labor. The state provides necessary vocational training to citizens before they are employed.

Article 43. Working people in the People's Republic of China have the right to rest. The state expands facilities for rest and recuperation of working people, and prescribes working hours and vacations for workers and staff.

Furthermore, Article 4 of the Universal Declaration of Human Rights states, "No one shall be held in slavery or servitude; slavery and the slave trade shall be prohibited in all their forms."

The forced labor system not only violates the basic human rights of the detainees, but also encourages the prison and labor camp systems to persecute the detainees because of the huge profit in products made by forced labor. In addition, it shakes the stability of international labor and trade market when these cheap products are dumped on the international market.

§§1.2.2 "Sanitary" Chopsticks Expose Conditions Inside Labor Camps[3]

In China's small roadside restaurants, the widely used disposable chopsticks are referred to as "sanitary" chopsticks. They are also commonly seen in Chinese restaurants overseas. They are placed together in a container or packaged separately and labeled "Sanitized for Your Safety!"

According to a survey in China, over 80% of these chopsticks have never been sanitized. Fierce market competition has made it impossible to cover all the costs, so some businesses have omitted the sanitizing process. Others bleach the chopsticks using fumes from burning sulfur even though they know it could make the chopsticks toxic. In order to minimize costs and increase profit, some manufacturing jobs are subcontracted out to prisons and forced labor camps, where there are no controls put on sanitary conditions.

› 1.2.2(a) Production of "Sanitary" Chopsticks in Beijing's City Labor Education Bureau

There is evidence that the Department of Dispatch of Beijing's City Labor Education Bureau, a forced labor camp located in Daxing County, Beijing, forced detainees to work long hours to make "sanitary" chopsticks from 6 a.m. to 9 p.m.; sometimes the work continued past midnight.

With dozens of inmates squeezed into one small room, the chopsticks to be packed were simply dumped in a pile on the floor and the inmates often stepped on them. Their job was to put the chopsticks into paper coverings labeled by the Department of Sanitary and Epidemic Prevention, even though they had not been provided sanitary conditions themselves. Many inmates had skin diseases, there were scabies outbreaks, and some were drug addicts or had been diagnosed with sexually transmitted diseases. The income generated by the contracted forced labor went into the pockets of the guards at the labor camps.

Falun Gong practitioner Mr. Yu Ming, former head of a clothing manufacturer in Liaoyang City of Liaoning Province, wrote:[4]

In the Tuanhe Forced Labor Camp in the Daxing District of Beijing, the Department of Dispatch forced everyone to work from early morning to midnight to make money for the guards. Most of the work was packaging disposable 'Sanitary' or 'Convenient Chopsticks' in paper wrappers. They were then regarded as meeting the 'Sanitary Quality Standard' and sold to small roadside restaurants. The profit for one box of chopsticks is about 6 yuan. Each inmate finishes about 3 boxes per day, and there are about 160 people per unit. You can imagine how much money one unit can make for those guards each day.

The 'workshops' were the inmates' dormitories. They were very crowded to begin with, and now the chopsticks were thrown all over the floor. Sometimes they were dropped into an open toilet. They would just pick the chopsticks up and put them in the paper wrappers. The guards watched the inmates carefully on the numbers, but inmates were never required to wash their hands.

The majority of the inmates were drug addicts or prostitutes, yet there were no formal medical exams, regardless of whether a person was carrying hepatitis or sexually transmitted diseases. Any inmate still breathing was forced to work. Even those who had scabies all over their bodies were forced to work, and they grabbed the chopsticks with hands covered in scabies infections.

Anyone behind schedule or failing to complete the quota was beaten by the guards and other inmates, forced to stand still outside for long periods, or deprived of sleep. Every unit and every cell was crawling with lice, and the inmates were not allowed to take showers for long periods. Guards patrolled with electric batons and handcuffs. Many inmates never dared to raise their heads to look at the sky after being here for months.

Mr. Gong Chengxi was a senior in college majoring in administration and management at the Changping Campus of Beijing Political and Law University. Once the chairman of the student association and head of his class, he was regarded as an honest and kind student with excellent academic integrity. Due to the persecution of Falun Gong, he was summarily expelled from school and taken to a forced labor camp when he would not renounce his belief.[5] Below is Mr. Gong' testimony:

In order to maximize the profits from the inmates' work, the Department of Dispatch bordered on madness. The quota for each person per day was 7,500 to over 10,000 pairs of chopsticks. Even working from 6 a.m. to midnight, it was impossible to meet the quota. Besides the unbearable back pain, we also had to endure verbal abuse and beatings from the guards and their aides. During my month in the Department of Dispatch, every day was like that. Several elderly Falun Gong practitioners, Dao Wanhui, Yang Juhai, Li Xieliang, Chen Jingjian and Jia Lin, worked as fast as they could but still could not finish the quota, so the unit head ordered them to sit on the cement floor outside to work for several hours in icy weather. If they still failed to complete the quota, they were only allowed to sleep 3 to 4 hours a night.

› 1.2.2(b) "Sanitary" Chopsticks and BBQ Picks Made in Tianjin City Shuangkou Forced Labor Camp

In a letter to Minghui.org, a Falun Gong practitioner who was once detained in Tianjin City Shuangkou Forced Labor Camp wrote:

Because of the terrible living conditions in the forced labor camp, 90 percent of the inmates developed scabies. At that time, my legs, chest, and hands were all infected. Still, we were forced to work.

› 1.2.2(c) The Only Sanitary Standard for Chopsticks Made in Dalian Forced Labor Camp: No Hair Mixed in Bag

Dalian Forced Labor Camp in Dalian City, Liaoning Province, also did the same work and exported chopsticks to Japan. It was said that the only sanitary standard was that no hair should be in the package.

Besides chopsticks, Dalian Forced Labor Camp produced other low-cost items, including embroidered products, dried flowers, hand-knit hats, cell phone cases, seaweed knots, plastic flowers, popsicle sticks, coffee straws, handmade wool coats, and buttons. The Shibali Forced Labor Camp in Xuchang City, Henan Province, made wigs, tapestries, decorative vases, and embroidery. Inmates were forced to work long hours each day. Those who failed to finish the quota were tortured.

§§1.2.3 More Abuses in Labor Camps[6]

› 1.2.3(a) Henan Province No.3 Labor Camp Specialized in Hair Products

Henan Province No.3 Labor Camp, also known as Xuchang City Labor Camp, was where most Chinese hair products were made. When the labor camp was short of funds and was about to be shut down, many Falun Gong practitioners were abducted and forced to make hair products, which revived the labor camp's business. Qu Shuangcai, director of the No.3 Labor Camp, actively persecuted Falun Gong practitioners and was favored by his superiors. In May 2003, he was transferred to head up the Shibalihe Women's Labor Camp in Zhenzhou City. Right away he signed a contract with Henan Rebecca Hair Products, Inc. located 120 miles away from the labor camp in Xuchang City. Qu also instituted the use of straitjackets in the torture of practitioners. Within several months of his arrival there, three Falun Gong practitioners were tortured to death.

› 1.2.3(b) Terrible Hygiene in Jianxin Forced Labor Camp in Tianjin

Jianxin Forced Labor Camp in Tianjin was expanded specially to handle the persecution of Falun Gong practitioners. Several hundred were detained there after the Sixth Division for female detainees was established. Most of the detained practitioners were over 50, with the oldest being 73.

The labor camp forced practitioners to work for as long as 17-18 hours each day. If they could not finish their assigned workload, they were not allowed to sleep; some of them even had to work through the night without sleep for several days, or at most they were allowed to sleep for only one or two hours a day.

Many of the practitioners, especially the older ones, began practicing Falun Gong in order to heal their illnesses and improve their health. In the labor camp, they were forbidden from studying Falun Gong books and doing the exercises. In addition to the prolonged and exhausting work, they endured intolerable mental and physical stress, causing some to develop health problems.

The authorities also forced Falun Gong practitioners who had scabies and whose hands oozed pus to process food products. Some inmates and prostitutes whose bodies oozed pus and who had sexually transmitted diseases were ordered to pick sunflower seeds, package chocolates and candies, and fold dessert trays and moon cake trays. They did all this work on their beds, a serious violation of food hygiene regulations. They even ordered inmates with contagious diseases to package food containing children's toys.

› 1.2.3(c) Toxic Materials at Jiamusi Forced Labor Camp in Heilongjiang Province

To make money for themselves, guards in the Jiamusi Forced Labor Camp in Heilongjiang Province took on illegal production projects and forced inmates to do the work. They used an inferior grade of rubber with toxicity levels exceeding industry standards to make cell phone cases. The health of the inmates who handled these materials was seriously harmed. Because of the hard labor and toxic materials, Falun Gong practitioners suffered tremendously and were not able to work after a while. Practitioners who refused to do the work were severely beaten.

Practitioners were also subjected to forced labor involving other carcinogenic materials. Starting on March 8, 2003, all of the inmates from the No.9 Brigade of the Jiamusi Labor Camp, totaling more than 80 people, were forced to make cell phone cases. The factory provided the raw materials and the labor camp provided the manpower. The planned annual production was valued at three million yuan, which was tax-exempt, and both parties earned tremendous profits from this deal.

The rubber was of poor quality and gave off irritating gases that brought on a choking sensation. The guards on duty couldn't endure the smell and asked the technical supervision bureau to send their people to investigate. Lab tests revealed that the toxin levels in the raw materials used were well beyond industry standards and could cause cancer. Thus, the guards wore large face masks and never entered the production area while the practitioners were working. After they were sold, these cell phone cases harmed consumers as well.

In July 2002, authorities responsible for the No.7 Brigade forced Falun Gong practitioners to construct paper boxes for moon cakes using toxic and foul-smelling glue. Many practitioners became ill with inflamed and swollen eyes.

› 1.2.3(d) Name-Brand Bedding Produced at No.1 Women's Forced Labor Camp in Shandong Province

The No.1 Women's Forced Labor Camp in Shandong Province worked with several factories to force Falun Gong practitioners to make bedding products, process plastic cement packages, and put name-brand labels on quilts.

Falun Gong practitioners detained in Division Five of the labor camp suffered the most. Their workshop was located in the basement of the labor camp cafeteria, where the sewer pipes ran. The room was low and dark, and foul-smelling water from the pipes constantly leaked into the room. There were a dozen sewing machines, both electric and manual, as well as eight 3-meter-long work tables in the room. The exit to the basement room was blocked off to serve as the restroom, which consisted of a chamber pot. Since no wall separated the restroom from the workshop, the stench was overwhelming. When practitioners worked in the basement room, the noise of the sewing machines and from machines in the kitchen above was deafening.

Female Falun Gong practitioners were forced to work in this basement for 12 to 15 hours every day and were deprived of daylight and fresh air, in addition to having to endure noise of more than 200 decibels. Their health drastically declined, and practitioners fell ill with colds, headaches, upset stomachs, gastrointestinal problems, and impaired hearing. They frequently asked the guards for a ten-minute break at noon or in the evening, but guards Niu Xuelian and Zhao Jie refused to allow them a break.

The guards also extended the practitioners' work time. If the daily production quota was not met, the guards cursed at the practitioners, deducted points from them, and extended their terms. Guard Zhao Jie claimed, "The government cannot feed you for nothing! If you don't do a good job, you'll be punished in other ways! We have more than enough ways to deal with you!"

› 1.2.3(e) Impossible Quotas at Heizuizi Women's Forced Labor Camp in Jilin Province[7]

Overworking practitioners is a tactic used by labor camp officials to break them down physically and mentally. This was the case in Heizuizi Women's Forced Labor Camp in Changchun, Jilin Province. For example, each person was required to finish 500 masks per day when it was only possible to do about 300. Each person processing handicraft products or small articles of clothing was required to finish between 100 and 150 pieces per day. It was impossible to finish. Any practitioner who didn't meet the impossible quota was punished and beaten.

In addition to enduring extreme stress and physical labor, practitioners were not allowed to do the Falun Gong exercises. Many of them developed health problems, such as heart disease, high blood pressure, coughing up blood, and lung problems. Even when they couldn't get up, the guards still forced them to go to work.

§§1.2.4 After Labor Camps Were Abolished, Detainees Were Moved to More Covert Facilities[8]

After the atrocities in "re-education through labor" (RTL) camps came to light over the years and captured attention worldwide, China announced the abolishment of its labor camp system in 2013.

As discussed above, replacing the decades-old labor camps are more covert brainwashing centers (labeled as "legal education centers" or "rehabilitation centers"), which exist outside of China's judicial framework. These black jails have less oversight and more deniability. Having learned from the labor camp experience, the Chinese regime has adopted a policy of not letting a given black jail gain too much notoriety, lest it become the subject of international scrutiny. When such a facility becomes too well-known, it disappears, only to re-emerge somewhere else to continue its role in carrying out the persecution of Falun Gong. These black jails, new and old, are staffed with personnel from the now-closed labor camps.[9]

In March 2014, four human rights lawyers were beaten and tortured by the police for seeking the release of Falun Gong practitioners detained in a black jail in Heilongjiang Province. The incident focused international attention on the Chinese regime's system of extralegal brainwashing facilities. True to form, the "Jiansanjiang Farm Legal Education Center"[10] involved in the lawyers' incident in March was shut down on April 28. However, Falun Gong practitioners detained there continued to be held without due process.[11]

In addition, the personnel in charge of the Jiansanjiang brainwashing center set up a new facility in Qiqihar, another city in the same province. In fact, two of the officials managing the new Qiqihar brainwashing center previously held the roles of division head and deputy director at the now-closed Qiqihar Labor Camp.[12] The new facility, officially named the "Qiqihar Drug Rehabilitation Center," has now replaced Jiansanjiang as Heilongjiang's designated provincial-level brainwashing center.[13]

Temporary brainwashing centers have also appeared in more clandestine locations. In Jilin Province, the Meihekou City 610 Office set up a brainwashing center in Shuangxing Middle School,[14] where around ten practitioners were detained on July 1, 2014. A June 2014 report described a brainwashing center held in a hotel in Jiangsu Province.[15]

In the Jiangjin District of Chongqing, several brainwashing centers have been set up in rental houses, including one located on the ground floor of a building at the Jindudingyuan Condominium Complex since 2010.[16] As is typical of brainwashing centers, each room (cell) holds one practitioner and two "monitors" responsible for watching the practitioner around the clock. These monitors are usually "transformed" practitioners who are made to cooperate with guards in the transformation of other practitioners. In addition to physical and psychological torture in brainwashing centers, reports regularly allege forced injections of nerve-damaging psychiatric drugs, force-feeding of drugged food, and even involvement in organ harvesting from living prisoners. These cases of torture and psychiatric experimentation have been corroborated by the 2014 Annual Report published by the United States Commission on International Religious Freedom.[17]

As long as the regime's core policy of violent repression has not changed, no amount of euphemisms and superficial promises can mask the atrocities that continue to take place.

§1.3 Mental Hospitals

Mental hospitals and psychiatric facilities have been used extensively to pressure practitioners to renounce Falun Gong. For example, "ankang" hospitals—high-security psychiatric hospitals directly administered by the Chinese Ministry of Public Security—have been noted as places of abuse in the U.S. Department of State's (DOS) annual human rights country reports for China for several years.[18]

The 2011 DOS report states:

> *Regulations governing security officials' ability to remand a person to an ankang facility were not clear, and detainees had no*

mechanism for objecting to claims of mental illness by security officials. Patients in these hospitals reportedly were medicated against their will and forcibly subjected to electric shock treatment.

Compared to documented abuses in Chinese psychiatric institutions, ankang facilities—which ironically translate as "peace and health facilities [for the mentally ill]"—are not as widely known. They operate so secretively that many veteran psychiatrists, lawyers specializing in the rights of the mentally ill, and criminal psychology professors have stated that they knew nothing about such facilities. Family visits to Falun Gong practitioners in ankang facilities are forbidden. Many family members don't know the whereabouts of their loved ones who are incarcerated in such hospitals.[19]

§§1.3.1 Similarities to Labor Camps

Ankang hospitals are extralegal entities that operate in a strikingly similar manner to the former labor camp system that was abolished in 2013. The police can arbitrarily send anyone to these hospitals for unlawful incarceration without due process.

In fact, the administrative department for ankang hospitals is the same department that is in charge of detention centers. Therefore, the police frequently rotate Falun Gong practitioners between detention centers, brainwashing centers, and ankang facilities, subjecting them to intensive brainwashing tactics at each facility. Practitioners who refuse to renounce their belief after incarcerations in detention centers, labor camps, and brainwashing centers are often transferred to ankang hospitals for more barbaric psychiatric abuse.

The Chinese Communist Party frequently uses mental health facilities to torture dissidents and political activists. Although abuses have been reported at a wide variety of mental health treatment facilities in China, only ankang hospitals are officially authorized to hold patients against their will and restrict their freedom. These facilities have a long history of "maintaining domestic security" for the communist regime. As early as January 1988, the Ministry of Public Security established standards for forcibly committing patients to ankang facilities.

Among the five populations targeted, two were classed as "seriously interfering with public order" and those who "disrupt social stability." Falun Gong practitioners, political dissidents, and citizens who dare to protest government policies are frequently tagged with these labels to justify confining them in ankang hospitals.

More ankang hospitals were established after the persecution of Falun Gong began in 1999. In September 2004, the Ministry of Public Security issued a public notice requiring provinces, autonomous regions, and municipalities to set up ankang hospitals as soon as possible if they didn't have them already.

§§1.3.2 Loophole in the Mental Health Code Allows Healthy People to Be Confined Against Their Will in Ankang Hospitals

The Mental Health Code was formally implemented in China on May 1, 2013. The code sets out the principle of voluntary hospitalization and states that only those with "severe symptoms" and who present a "danger of harming others" can be forcibly detained in mental health facilities. However, the code leaves loopholes that do not protect citizens from being arbitrarily labelled as mentally ill. In deciding upon whether a person poses a "danger of harming others," there is a huge gray area that police and relevant government agencies have exploited in the persecution of Falun Gong practitioners, political dissidents, and petitioners.

There is no third-party oversight of ankang facilities. Police departments both administer ankang hospitals and decide who to take to these facilities. Whether an individual is diagnosed with mental disorders, what medications he is given and how they are administered, and when he is released are all under police control.

Since the implementation of the Mental Health Code, many Falun Gong practitioners continue to be detained in ankang hospitals or have been newly incarcerated in such facilities.

§§1.3.3 Psychiatric Drugs Abused to Torture Falun Gong Practitioners

Ever since the persecution of Falun Gong began in 1999, many practitioners have been falsely labeled as mentally ill. They are incarcerated in ankang hospitals, injected with drugs that damage the central nervous system, subjected to electric shocks, force-fed, and beaten. All these "treatments" are currently banned by the international medical profession. Many victims have developed true mental illness or have died as a result of the CCP's frequent abuse of drugs in ankang hospitals. Some examples are presented below:

Ms. Liang Zhiqin and other Falun Gong practitioners were taken to Tangshan Ankang Hospital in the fall of 2000 and injected with nerve-damaging drugs. Most of the practitioners later recounted that the injections were painful and produced severe side effects that persisted for a long time. The effects included heart discomfort, a stiff tongue, severely altered gait, nervousness, abnormal thoughts, dull eyes, and memory loss.

Ms. Liang Zhiqin suffered heart failure and went into shock twice after being injected with psychiatric drugs. She could not take care of herself for the three years before she eventually passed away in 2009.

Another practitioner, Ms. Li Fengzhen, had severe memory loss after being given injections of unknown drugs in an ankang hospital. She could not take care of herself and became emaciated.

Practitioner Yang Baochun from Handan, Hebei Province, was tortured in Handan Labor Camp in 2002, resulting in the amputation of his right leg. The labor camp sent him to Handan Ankang Hospital three times, where he was injected with nerve-damaging drugs for five years. By the time his family finally took him home in 2009, he had truly become mentally ill.

§§1.3.4 Psychiatric Abuse Drives Young Woman Insane[20]

On the morning of February 13, 2015, a grisly discovery was made in a village in Laiyang City, Shandong Province. Villagers found the body of a woman in her mid-30s floating in a well. She was later identified as Liu Zhimei.

A bright student with big dreams, Ms. Liu's aspirations were cut short when she was expelled from Tsinghua University (known as China's MIT) at the age of 21 because she refused to give up her belief in Falun Gong. Ms. Liu was arrested and spent six years in prison, where she was repeatedly drugged. Just before her release in 2008, she was injected with a large dose of unknown drugs.

Her family later suspected this to be the cause of long-lasting psychotic episodes she suffered. She would ramble nonsensically and wave her arms in the air as if she were running. At night she would wet her bed and sleep on the urine-soaked mattress. When asked her age, she either remained silent or answered "21." For Ms. Liu, time seemed to have stopped at age 21.

Ms. Liu died within seven years of her release from prison. The young woman was one of many Falun Gong practitioners from Shandong Province subjected to psychiatric abuse while imprisoned for their faith.

› 1.3.4(a) More Deaths Due to Psychiatric Abuse

Three other Falun Gong practitioners from Shandong Province died as a result of psychiatric abuse.

Case 1: Su Gang

Su Gang was from the city of Zibo and worked as a software engineer for the Sinopec Qilu Petrochemical Company. On May 23, 2000, the thirty-two-year-old was picked up and taken to the Weifang Mental Hospital.

Mr. Su was injected daily with unknown drugs and chemicals, causing severe nerve damage. When his family learned of his detainment and abuse, his uncle Su Lianxi went on a hunger strike in protest. Hospital officials released the young man to his father.

Nine days of drug injections had taken their toll, however. Su Gang looked lifeless and numb, his eyes dull. He was extremely weak, his face was pale, and his body had stiffened. By the morning of June 10, Mr. Su was dead.

Case 2: Xu Guiqin

When thirty-eight-year-old Xu Guiqin was released from prison for practicing Falun Gong, a doctor told her family to watch her closely and not let her move around on her own. Her life was in grave danger.

Just before her release, she had been injected with four vials of nerve-damaging drugs. As a result, her face swelled up and her tongue stiffened. As she couldn't eat, she became emaciated. Her body was numb, and she suffered severe memory loss.

At home, Xu Guiqin's physical and mental state worsened with each passing day. She died nine days later, on December 10, 2002.

Case 3: Zhang Dezhen

While Zhang Dezhen, 38, was being held in the Mengyin Detention Center, she was injected with unknown drugs by staff member Wang Chunxiao and a doctor from the Mengyin Hospital. She ended up in critical condition. When doctors injected her again with unknown drugs on January 31, 2003, Ms. Zhang died.

The individuals involved in her death were Lei Yancheng from the Mengyin 610 Office, detention center chief Sun Kehai, and hospital director Guo Xingbao.

§1.4 Rubber-Stamp Judicial System

As discussed earlier, Jiang Zemin gave the 610 Office power over the entire judicial and law enforcement system. He also issued a series of secret directives against Falun Gong practitioners, including to "ruin their reputations, bankrupt them financially, and destroy them physically;" "beat them to death and count the deaths as suicide;" and "cremate them without verifying their identities."

As a result, nothing is deemed excessive when it comes to Falun Gong practitioners. Under pressure and directives from the 610 Office, the judicial system goes all out to put practitioners behind bars despite the complete lack of legal grounds for the verdicts.

The end result is that the police have no reservations when it comes to arresting practitioners, the procuratorates have no qualms in filing fabricated allegations against them, and the courts comply by handing down pre-determined heavy sentences.

§§1.4.1 Arrested for Holding a Press Conference[21]

As news media inside and outside China repeated the slander published by CCP-controlled media, about 30 Falun Gong practitioners successfully hosted a press conference in suburban Beijing on October 28, 1999. They refuted the lies told by Jiang Zemin and provided the first opportunity for international media to gain a direct understanding of Falun Gong practitioners in mainland China.

On October 28, the reports of the Associated Press and Reuters had already spread all over the world. The next day, the *New York Times* published the photos and story about this press conference on its front page. At the time, practitioners in the United States were informing government officials in Washington, D.C. about the situation of Falun Gong in China. When the officials read these reports, they expressed their admiration for the courage of practitioners in China.

The *South China Morning Post* (SCMP), the most influential English paper in Asia, covered the press conference with large photos that filled an entire page. Many major newspapers in Europe also gave prominent coverage to this story. The practitioners who attended the press conference were all eventually arrested. Mr. Jiang Zhaohui, then 36 years old, was sentenced to five years in prison. Ms. Ding Yan, then 31, was sentenced to three years of imprisonment. She died of torture in Chengde Prison on August 18, 2001. Mr. Cai Mingtao, then 27, was sent to a brainwashing center in Hubei Province, where he was frequently beaten and kicked while handcuffed and shackled. He died on October 5, 2000.

§§1.4.2 Imprisoned for Putting Up Posters

Because all legal channels for protesting the persecution have been closed, Falun Gong practitioners have raised awareness of their plight by printing and distributing flyers and pamphlets, as well as putting up banners and posters in public places.

Mr. Wang Baoshan, a Falun Gong practitioner in Tangshan City, Hebei Province, was sentenced to five and a half years and fined 20,000 yuan after he was suspected of hanging a banner that said, "The World Needs Truthfulness-Compassion-Forbearance (真善忍)."[25]

He was arrested at work on July 3, 2017, days after the banner was found in a neighborhood on June 29. The police alleged that the man seen in the surveillance video hanging the banner was Mr. Wang, but the Fengrun District Procuratorate twice returned the case, citing insufficient evidence.

The police tried a third time, and the case was assigned to the Zunhua City Procuratorate, which filed an indictment against Mr. Wang before forwarding the case to the Zunhua City Court.

Mr. Wang appeared in court on May 9, 2018 and was sentenced on July 12. The verdict noted that, while the allegation that Mr. Wang had hung the said banner lacked proof and was inadmissible, the Falun Gong books, informational materials, and printer confiscated from Mr. Wang's home were sufficient evidence to convict him.

Although court officials attempted to block his appeal, his attorney managed to submit the appeal paperwork on July 30. The attorney contacted the Tangshan Intermediate Court numerous times afterward, protesting the trial court's violation of legal procedures and requesting an open hearing in the appeals case.

It was not until October 18 that the attorney discovered that the intermediate court had reached a decision on September 10 to uphold the original verdict without holding a hearing. When the attorney went to the detention center on October 22 to visit his client, an officer said Mr. Wang had been transferred to Jidong Second Prison on October 17.

Mr. Wang's wife went to the prison on November 5, but she wasn't allowed to see her husband until she made repeated requests. An officer surnamed Che videotaped the visit and said future visits would be canceled if Mr. Wang refused to give up his belief. His wife learned that Mr. Wang had been forced to work in a sewing unit for nine hours a day. The pungent smell of the fabrics made him sick.

Mr. Wang filed complaints against those who had arrested and prosecuted him without legal basis. His family also sent the complaint letters to the Supreme People's Procuratorate. They have not received a response.

§§1.4.3 Arrested During the Olympics and at Other "Sensitive" Times[26]

Police in China often carry out mass arrests of Falun Gong practitioners around "sensitive" times, such as the Chinese New Year and key Communist Party conferences. For example, 405 practitioners were confirmed arrested in March 2015, with 123 tried and 81 illegally sentenced. Most of the arrests took place in the first half of the month during the CCP legislative sessions, including the 12th National People's Congress (March 5-15) and the 12th Chinese People's Political Consultative Conference (March 3-13).

In May 2008, police in many parts of China began to secretly arrest Falun Gong practitioners under the pretext of security for the Olympic Games.

On May 21, 2008, Mr. Shao Changpu and Ms. Fu Lihong were arrested in Songyuan City. Afterward, Songyuan City police ransacked Mr. Shao's home and arrested his younger sister.

Mr. Shao and Ms. Fu were held in the detention center in Songyuan City. They were only given two meals a day and forced to work without pay. Ms. Fu was emaciated. Mr. Shao was sentenced to one year of forced labor and transferred to Changchun City Heizuizi Forced Labor Camp.

Practitioners Zhu Decai, Wang Yuanzhang, Yan Xianyu, Liu Qing, and others, as well as Chen Lixin (not a practitioner), were also arrested and taken to Yinmahe Forced Labor Camp in Jiutai City. Practitioners Liu Shuqin, Gao Mian, Xu Hui, Ms. Zhang Hongqin, Ms. Wang Shuqin, Ms. Mou Guiling, and others were held in Heizuizi Labor Camp in Changchun City.

On July 11, 2008, after midnight, Songyuan City and Fuyu County police officers were led by the security directors of the villages to execute another round of arrests and harassment targeting Falun Gong practitioners in Fuyu County. Ms. Wang Jinxia from Zhangbao Village, Caijiagou Town, was arrested and detained in the Fuyu Detention Center. Li Xiaohui from Sanchahe Town was arrested by Daoxi Street Police Station police and taken to Fuyu County Detention Center. Wang Enhui from Yushugou managed to escape. The police also harassed and arrested others in town who had practiced Falun Gong before.

It has been said that the police implemented the arrests according to lists of practitioners they had collected before 1999. Some of the people on the lists had stopped practicing or had passed away, but the police harassed their families and sometimes took them away anyway.

Wang Cuixiang, 48, from Zouping County, Shandong, was persecuted before the Beijing Olympics. She was tortured in Wangcun Forced Labor Camp until her health severely deteriorated and she could no longer take care of herself. She died in November 2010.

§§1.4.4 Woman Beaten Unconscious, Police Arrest Her Instead of Assailant[22]

Ms. Hang Shizhen was ambushed and beaten on the night of May 12, 2019, when she was hanging up banners with messages about Falun Gong. The assailant held Ms. Hang down, sat on her, and punched her in the head. Ms. Hang's head was covered in blood and her face was disfigured. She lost four front teeth and blood gushed from her mouth. Her nose was broken, and she passed out.

During the assault, the assailant made a call. Several police cars came shortly afterward. Instead of questioning or arresting the assailant, they took Ms. Hang to Wanquan Town Police Station.

The police attempted to transfer Ms. Hang to Zhangjiakou Detention Center the next day, on May 13, 2019, but after she failed the health exam with hypertension and severe wounds from the beating, they had no choice but to release her. Ms. Hang suffered a broken nose, loss of teeth, and soft tissue injuries to her face and chest.

§§1.4.5 One Police Station, Several Deaths, Countless Brutalities[23]

Mr. Huang Guodong, a Falun Gong practitioner in Heilongjiang Province, died on October 31, 2017. Several months before his death, he had difficulty eating and going to the restroom because of the physical and mental abuse he endured while he was detained.

Mr. Huang was first held in Nanshan Police Station and then in Mudanjiang Prison. Because of his belief in Falun Gong, he was tortured in both places. In the police station, the guards hung him up by his thumbs and beat him. After he passed out from the pain, they scraped his ribs with coins and stabbed toothpicks into his fingertips to wake him up. As soon as he regained consciousness, the torture began again.

Mr. Huang's plight was not unique. Many other practitioners also suffered tremendously in this police station for practicing Falun Gong, including Ms. Gao Bingrong and Mr. Cui Cunyi, who both lost their lives due to the physical and mental abuse. Other practitioners, such as Mr. Zhao Jun, were left disabled by torture.

› 1.4.5(a) Ms. Gao Bingrong: Tortured to Mental Disorder and Death

Ms. Gao lived in Tielinghe Town, where Nanshan Police Station is located. The practice of Falun Gong improved her health and her family life. In February 2001, Miao Qiang, assistant director of Nanshan Police Station, and several other officers arrested her.

Six male officers beat Ms. Gao from 7 p.m. to 1:30 a.m. the next day, causing severe injury. Miao ordered Ms. Gao to curse the founder of

Falun Gong and to stomp on and tear apart Falun Gong books. Instead of having Ms. Gao's injuries treated, officials took her to the Mudanjiang Detention Center.

By the time she was admitted to the detention center, Ms. Gao was already crippled. Her face and limbs were swollen, her eyes were narrow slits, and there were several egg-sized lumps on her head. She kept crying and cowering as if to avoid being hit. Guards and inmates had to hold her down whenever this happened. She got worse by the day and died about a year after she was released.

› 1.4.5(b) Mr. Cui Cunyi: Five Ribs Broken, Entire Lung Blackened

Because of the persecution of Falun Gong, fifty-four-year-old Mr. Cui Cunyi was forced to stay away from home to avoid arrest. "Tell him to come back and he will be just fine," said one local police officer to his family. Shortly after Mr. Cui returned, the police arrested him on May 13, 2002, and took him to Nanshan Police Station. Two days later, his family was notified of his death. A postmortem exam revealed that Mr. Cui had bruises all over his body, five broken ribs, an entirely blackened lung, swollen eyes, and blackened legs. But the results of the exam were not handed over to his family, nor were they allowed to take pictures or videos, either of the body or the exam results.

When the family planned to appeal to the Heilongjiang provincial government, the police barred them from all public transport to stop them. After constant demands from his family members and their appeals to the provincial government and Beijing, Mudanjiang Police Department paid the family 500,000 yuan. Because of cases like Mr. Cui's, the United Nations human rights organization included the Nanshan Police Station in one of its reports in 2005 and issued a statement requesting co-inspection. No officials have been held responsible, however.

› 1.4.5(c) Mr. Zhao Jun: Toothpicks Stabbed under Fingernails and Tortured to Disability; Son Held Hostage

Officers at Nanshan Police Station often stabbed practitioners' fingertips with toothpicks. Xie Chunsheng, director of the police station, and Miao went to Mr. Zhao Jun's home on February 24, 2001. Xie asked Mr. Zhao to come out for a chat. As soon as Mr. Zhao stepped out of the door while still in sandals, officers forced him into a police van and took him to the police station.

That evening, Mr. Zhao was tied up tightly three times, and he passed out due to the pain three times. Guards then scraped his ribs with coins and stabbed toothpicks under his fingernails to wake him up. His arms were severely injured, and a medical exam confirmed disability caused by nerve damage.

Seeing that was not enough to make Mr. Zhao give in, officers arrested his son Zhao Dan, a medical student who did not practice Falun Gong. They handcuffed Zhao Dan to heating pipes and covered his head with thick blankets, almost suffocating him. They also deprived him of access to water or a toilet. The next morning, two officers took Zhao Dan to Mr. Zhao and yelled, "Hey! Take a look at your son!" They then took Zhao Dan away immediately. Thinking how he himself had already been beaten to disability in just one night, Mr. Zhao was worried his son would also be tortured to disability. In anger and grief, he replied, "Release my son and I will admit to anything you charge me with." The police extorted 5,000 yuan from the family and released Zhao Dan.

› 1.4.5(d) Mr. Huang Guodong: Blood All Over the Room

Mr. Huang worked in a factory, where his hard work and generosity earned him the respect of his coworkers and neighbors. He said the practice of Falun Gong made him more cheerful and healthy. "Falun Gong and the principles of Truthfulness-Compassion-Forbearance (真善忍) are the best. I cannot live without them," he once said.

For distributing information to expose the persecution of Falun Gong, Mr. Huang and his son were arrested in late February 2001 and taken to the Nanshan Police Station.

Miao Qiang and other officers tied his thumbs together, hung him up by his thumbs, and beat him. After he lost consciousness, they scraped his ribs with coins and stabbed toothpicks into his fingertips to wake him up—just like what they did to Mr. Zhao—followed by further torture. Mr. Huang screamed from the pain. But the torture continued for 24 hours. His head was swollen, and he had bruises all over. He also lost control of his bowels. There was blood all over the room.

But that was just the beginning. Handcuffing him and chaining his feet, officers put him in a detention center, where Miao and other officers continued to beat him. Mr. Huang's wife contacted the 610 Office and the police station asking for his release. But the request was denied, and police in turn asked her for money. One inmate who worked in the dining hall said they were told to add unknown drugs to Mr. Huang's food so that he had constant diarrhea. The guards then asked Mr. Huang—who did not know the plot then—why the Falun Gong exercises did not improve his health, in an attempt to make him renounce his belief.

Physical abuse and unknown drugs left him emaciated and in very poor health in about 10 months. His case was included in the 2001 United Nations Human Rights Report. Instead of being released, however, Mr. Huang was tried on December 12, 2001. He was too weak to speak in court and was sentenced to 10 years in prison. He was taken to Mudanjiang Prison, where he was shocked with electric batons on his genitals and anus, exposed to cold, malnourished, and tortured in other ways.

Many other practitioners were similarly abused. Mr. Zhang Yuliang was beaten by Miao in 2001, resulting in internal injuries and blood in his urine for a long time. He was sentenced to five years in prison. After his relatives in Canada raised his case to the Canadian government, Canadian Minister of Foreign Affairs John Baird wrote back, saying he had been working closely with then Prime Minister Stephen Harper to contact the Chinese government to release detained Falun Gong practitioners.

§§1.4.6 Police, Procuratorate, and Court Violate Legal Procedures to Convict Falun Gong Practitioner[24]

A forty-eight-year-old woman in Guiyang City was sentenced to 4.5 years in prison for refusing to renounce Falun Gong.

Ms. Zhang Juhong credits Falun Gong for giving her hope. Her first husband died of a medication error just a few years into their marriage. Their son drowned at the age of 12. She remarried, but her second husband smoked, drank, and beat her.

Her misery took a toll on her health. She came across Falun Gong, which rekindled her will to live. Not only did she become healthy, but she also mended her strained relationship with her husband. She never wavered in her faith when the persecution of Falun Gong began in July 1999.

Ms. Zhang's pursuit of health and happiness landed her in police custody on multiple occasions. Her latest arrest took place on July 24, 2016, and she appeared in court on February 13, 2018. Her lawyer, Mr. Li Guisheng, was informed on March 2 that she had been convicted. He agreed to continue representing her as she fought for her constitutional right to freedom of belief. He has helped her submit an appeal to Guiyang City Intermediate Court.

The local Huaxi District police, procuratorate, and court had all violated legal procedures as they worked to prosecute Ms. Zhang for her faith. Her family is in the process of filing complaints with the Guiyang City Discipline and Monitoring Committee against the responsible parties.

(a) Police Fail to Present Alleged Prosecution Evidence

Prosecutor Zhao Tingsong cited two pieces of evidence against Ms. Zhang. The first one was that she was caught distributing Falun Gong informational materials. Officers Luo Jisong and Chen Donghao were called in to be cross-examined. They alleged that they found 75 copies of a variety of Falun Gong materials on Ms. Zhang when they arrested her on April 17, 2014.

When Ms. Zhang's lawyer asked to see the materials in court, the officers claimed that they had put them away "somewhere." They also failed to explain why they used materials confiscated from Ms. Zhang during her earlier arrest in 2014 but not her latest arrest in 2016.

(b) Lawful Complaint Against Jiang Zemin Becomes Prosecution Evidence

The second piece of prosecution evidence was Ms. Zhang's criminal complaint filed against former Chinese dictator Jiang Zemin on July 22, 2015.

Ms. Zhang's lawyer argued that it was his client's constitutional right to hold Jiang responsible for initiating the persecution of Falun Gong.

He further asked how the police could have had access to the complaints, which were mailed to the Supreme People's Procuratorate and Supreme People's Court. He suspected that police either had intercepted the mail or received the complaints from the two agencies.

Prosecutor Zhao alleged that the provincial anti-cult office had examined Ms. Zhang's criminal complaints and verified that they were Falun Gong materials. The lawyer emphasized that no law in China criminalizes Falun Gong or labels it a cult. He also argued that the anti-cult office did not have any legal authority to verify prosecution evidence.

(c) Missing "81 Days of Detention"

Soon after her arrest, Ms. Zhang was sent to Lannigou Brainwashing Center, where she was held for 81 days before being transferred to Guiyang City First Detention Center. The police and the procuratorate, however, never mentioned the 81 days on the indictment. During the court hearing, Ms. Zhang's lawyer asked whether the police should conduct an investigation before filing cases against someone or if it should be the other way around. Officers Luo and Chen replied that investigation should come first.

The lawyer asked why his client was held for 81 days before any investigation was carried out and why the detention wasn't shown on the indictment. The police had no answer. The lawyer said the 81 days of detention was completely illegal. Judge Zhang Decai warned him not to use the word "illegal." Since the 81 days of detention was missing from the indictment, Ms. Zhang's four-and-a-half-year prison sentence won't take into account the 81 days that she has already served.

(d) Court Officials Tried to Pressure Ms. Zhang into Dismissing Her Lawyer

Clerk Zhang Li (no relation to Ms. Zhang) and deputy president Wu of the Huaxi District Court visited the detention center three times in three days, but they failed to pressure Ms. Zhang into dismissing her lawyer.

Zhang and Wu first showed up on December 23, 2017 and talked to Ms. Zhang for three hours. They warned her that using a lawyer would do her no good and that it would be much better if she testified in her own defense. Ms. Zhang didn't say yes or no to their request. The two men came again at 10 a.m. on December 25, and this time they promised to give her probation and release her in January 2018 if she agreed to drop her lawyer. Ms. Zhang said that she didn't mind dropping her lawyer, but she requested an acquittal. They replied that it was impossible to clear all charges against her.

They returned at 7 that evening and asked if she had made up her mind to drop her lawyer. She told them that she had decided to retain legal representation. They threatened to give her a heavy sentence and left. None of the conversations between the two officials and Ms. Zhang were recorded, as required by law.

(e) Court Clerk Lies about Ms. Zhang's Legal Reprsentation Request

Ms. Zhang's lawyer, Mr. Li Guisheng, received a copy of the indictment, which was dated November 28, 2017, on December 19, 2017.

The court notified him on December 24 that his client would be tried the next day. By law, the court must give defendants and their lawyers at least ten days advance notice. Mr. Li arrived at the courthouse at 1 p.m. on December 25. No one was there. It wasn't until 4 p.m. that clerk Zhang Li showed up.

Zhang waved a piece of paper, saying that it was a written record of what Ms. Zhang had told him. He said that the detention center called him on December 22 to report that Ms. Zhang was very emotional and asked to see a court official. He said he went, and Ms. Zhang told him that her lawyer wasn't doing a good job and she wanted to drop him. He said he promised to give her a lighter sentence if she agreed to admit guilt in court.

Mr. Li didn't believe Zhang, as he knew how much Ms. Zhang wanted to seek justice for herself, as no law in China criminalizes Falun Gong. He wanted to verify her decision with her, but the detention center refused to allow him to visit her twice, on December 28, 2017, and again on January 3, 2018. The guards showed him a document issued by the court that stated the detention center would not grant any meetings with Ms. Zhang.

Mr. Li told the court he planned to file a complaint against them for violating legal procedures. Zhang Li called him on January 4 to say that Ms. Zhang had agreed to use him as a lawyer again.

Mr. Li was then allowed to see Ms. Zhang and learned how Zhang Li and Wu tried to pressure her into dropping him. Ms. Zhang also said Zhang Li never went to the detention center on December 22 as he claimed.

(f) Family Forced to Drop Non-Lawyer Defender

Ms. Zhang also had a non-lawyer defender, Mr. Zhou Jianzhong, a distant uncle. Mr. Zhou practices Falun Gong, too, and understands that the persecution of Falun Gong is illegal.

Mr. Zhou encountered obstacles while trying to defend his niece. He submitted a power of attorney signed by Ms. Zhang to the court in March 2017. Zhang Li demanded that he show proof that he had no criminal record. Mr. Zhou complied, but he wasn't given a chance to sign his name on the required paperwork until December 18.

As a defender, Mr. Zhou got to review Ms. Zhang's case. He noted that her criminal complaint against Jiang Zemin was labeled Falun Gong promotional materials. He called Zhang Li on December 21 to say that he planned to submit a request to dismiss the alleged evidence regarding Ms. Zhang's criminal complaint.

He went to the court the following day but couldn't find Zhang Li. It wasn't until January 22, 2018, that he saw Zhang Li and his assistant again at a pre-trial meeting. They told him that he was no longer allowed to defend his niece. When he asked to see vice president Wu, Zhang Li said there was no need.

While the two court officials were intimidating Ms. Zhang at the detention center on December 25, her nephew was warned that day by a local street committee member to not engage Mr. Zhou to defend Ms. Zhang. The committee member said that Mr. Zhou was a distant relative and that they had better not use him. Intimidated, Ms. Zhang's nephew and other family members wrote to the court on December 27 to drop Mr. Zhou as a defender.

§§1.4.7 Verdict Pre-Determined One Month Before Secret Court Hearing[25]

A Yinan County resident was sentenced to 4.5 years on January 10, 2019, by the Yinan Court for his faith in Falun Gong. He has started to serve time at Jinan Prison. His family has yet to receive any court documents regarding the verdict.

As early as October 2018, Mr. Du Yihe's family had heard rumors from an acquaintance with government connections that the authorities had decided to sentence him to four years in prison. This was one month before his secret hearing inside the makeshift courtroom at the Yinan Detention Center on November 24, 2018. Mr. Du, 56, a father of three sons, was arrested on May 28, 2018, shortly before the Shanghai Cooperation Organization (SCO) summit held in Qingdao City, Shandong Province, June 9-10, 2018. It was reported that the police arrested him to prevent him from leaving home to work in another city.

Mr. Du was denied family visits at the Yinan County Detention Center. When his family went there to request his release, a guard told them, "Mr. Du likes it in there and doesn't want to leave."

§§1.4.8 Sentenced for Tapping into China's State Television to Broadcast Facts[26]

Facing the government's total control of the media in China to spread defamatory propaganda about Falun Gong, practitioners have employed various means to refute the lies and inform the public about the persecution of Falun Gong. In Changchun, Jilin Province, 18 practitioners tapped into the state cable television broadcast network around 8 p.m. on March 5, 2002. They broadcast the programs "Self-immolation or Hoax?" and "Falun Dafa Spreads Worldwide" on eight channels simultaneously for about 45 minutes.

The entire city of Changchun was stunned, and some thought that the ban on Falun Gong had been lifted. Jiang Zemin, the former head of the Chinese communist regime, gave a secret order to "kill all Falun Gong practitioners involved." Within days, more than 5,000 practitioners in the Changchun area were arrested, and seven were beaten to death. Many were forced to leave their homes to avoid persecution. Fifteen were later given heavy sentences, and three of them died as a result of torture.

› 1.4.8(a) Jiang Issues a Secret Order

The Minghui website reported that Jiang Zemin met with Luo Gan, the head of the 610 Office, on the night of March 5, 2002. Then he ordered the Shenyang Military Area Command to second-degree combat readiness. Both the Changchun military sub-command and Jilin Armed Police were ordered to first-degree combat readiness to search for Falun Gong practitioners who had anything to do with intercepting the television signal.

Through Luo Gan, Jiang authorized all police officers to open fire and kill any practitioners suspected of being involved in the interception: "You can simply kill them." They demanded that the Changchun and Jilin Province police solve the case in one week. "Otherwise, police chiefs at all levels in Changchun, as well as the Party secretary of the area, will be removed from their posts," read one of the communications.

Wang Yunkun, the Party secretary of Jilin Province, who was at the 15th National People's Congress in Beijing, was ordered to return to his duty station immediately. Liu Jing, the 610 Office chief and deputy minister of Public Security, was dispatched to Changchun to oversee the case in person.

› 1.4.8(b) Seven Practitioners Die Shortly after Arrest

A total of seven practitioners died within days of their arrest.

Ms. Li Rong, a Jilin University graduate, 35 years old when she died, worked at the Jilin Province Pharmaceutical Research Institute. She was arrested in March and died while in detention around the end of March or the beginning of April. The details of her death are unknown.

Ms. Shen Jianli, a lecturer at the Department of Applied Mathematics of Jilin University, was arrested the day after the incident. She was persecuted to death at the age of 34, around the end of April.

Mr. Liu Haibo was arrested at his home on the evening of March 11, 2002. The police beat him in front of his wife and son and broke one of his ankles. They tortured and interrogated him until 1 a.m. that night, until he had no pulse. Although they rushed him to the hospital, the thirty-four-year-old doctor died during treatment.

A practitioner believed to be in his 30s was beaten to death on March 16, 2002 in Jinchen Police Department in Changchun. According to a witness, he exhibited several visible wounds and showed signs of internal bleeding after the beatings.

Mr. Liu Yi was beaten to death at the age of 34 in the Luyuan District Police Department office.

On March 20, 2002, fifty-four-year-old Ms. Li Shuqin was arrested by Changjiu Road Police Station officers and then tortured to death in the 3rd Detention Center in Changchun.

Mr. Hou Mingkai was beaten to death hours after he was arrested at his home on August 20, 2002. He was 34.

› 1.4.8(c) Fifteen Practitioners Sentenced

Changchun City Intermediate Court sentenced the following 15 practitioners on September 20, 2002:

- Ms. Zhou Ruijun and Mr. Liu Weiming: 20 years
- Mr. Liu Chengjun and Mr. Liang Zhenxing: 19 years
- Mr. Zhang Wen: 18 years
- Mr. Lei Ming, Mr. Sun Changjun and Mr. Li Dehai: 17 years
- Mr. Zhao Jian: 15 years
- Mr. Yun Qingbin and Mr. Liu Dong: 14 years
- Mr. Wei Xiushan: 12 years
- Mr. Zhuang Xiankun and Ms. Chen Yanmei: 11 years
- Mr. Li Xiaojie: 4 years

Mr. Liu Chengjun and Mr. Liang Zhenxing were persecuted to death in prison on December 26, 2003, and May 1, 2010, respectively. Mr. Lei Ming was released on medical parole when he was near death from torture. He passed away on August 6, 2006. Mr. Yun Qingbin was tortured, had a mental breakdown, and was released on medical parole Ms. Zhou Ruijun is still in the Changchun Women's Prison. Mr. Sun Changjun is still in the Jilin Second Prison. Mr. Zhao Jian, Mr. Wei Xiushan, Mr. Zhuang Xiankun, Ms. Chen Yanmei, and Mr. Li Xiaojie have been released.

› 1.4.8(d) Historical Impact

The international media described "tapping into TV systems in Changchun on March 5" as one of the most courageous acts carried out by Falun Gong practitioners. It showed that the brutal persecution in China did not stop practitioners from speaking out about Falun Gong and the persecution. After that, similar incidents occurred across China.

Four years after Mr. Liu Chengjun was persecuted to death, the Asia Pacific Human Rights Foundation in Australia held the 2007 Human Rights Awards Ceremony in the Parliament House of New South Wales on September 5. Mr. Liu was the recipient of the Fidelity Vindicator Award.

The Asia Pacific Human Rights Foundation honored Mr. Liu for broadcasting the true story to millions of TV viewers and setting a great example for non-governmental movements that protect human rights.

The Falun Gong Association received the award on Mr. Liu's behalf. A representitive of the association expressed his wish that the award would enable more people to learn the value of the truth. He called for all to stand together in safeguarding justice and ending the persecution.

§1.5 Imprisoned Practitioners' Rights Violated

The CCP's violating of Falun Gong practitioners' human rights does not end at sentencing them. Imprisoned practitioners are often deprived of the most basic rights granted to non-practitioner inmates, who are often incentivized with term reductions to abuse practitioners. Below are a few illustrative examples.

§§1.5.1 Liaoning Women's Prison and Its "Correction Division"[27]

Falun Gong practitioners have been incarcerated in Liaoning Province Women's Prison since the CCP started persecuting the practice in 1999. They have been tortured physically and mentally in the CCP's attempts to force them to "transform" and give up their belief. Guards never allow practitioners to come into contact with visiting officials.

There are 13 divisions in the prison, and Falun Gong practitioners are incarcerated in almost every one. However, the most severe abuses take place in Division 12, which is called the "Concentration and

Correction Division" or the "Hospital Division." Before 2000, it was called the "Insane Group." It was designated as the Concentration and Correction Division in 2010, and its sole purpose became to "transform" Falun Gong practitioners.

When the notorious Masanjia Forced Labor Camp was shut down, all Falun Gong practitioners who were held there were transferred to the newly established Masanjia Division in Liaoning Province Women's Prison.

› 1.5.1(a) Tactics Used in the Correction Division

(1) Breaking Practitioners' Will

Chen Shuo, the section leader who took the lead in persecuting Falun Gong practitioners in the Correction Division, makes daily life for the practitioners as restrictive, difficult, and awful as possible. Practitioners' personal grooming articles are taken away, and they are not allowed to use the restroom or toilet paper. They are not allowed to wash their face, brush their teeth, or change their underwear.

Practitioners also have to sleep on a wooden board with no mattress or blanket, regardless of the season. The practitioners are allowed very little food, yet they are subjected to strenuous physical punishment every day, including prolonged standing and repetitive squatting. They are frequently beaten, shocked with electric batons, detained in an isolated cell, and forced to watch videos that defame Falun Gong.

Whoever refuses to be "transformed" gets 10 years added to her term, and none of the other prisoners will be released. This incentivizes other prisoners to do their utmost to intimidate and threaten practitioners.

(2) Instigating Inmates to Torture Practitioners

Guards instigated inmates Shan Lili, Xu Yingmei, Li Li, Guan Cui, Yang Fan, Wang Rui, and many others to torture Falun Gong practitioners.

Ms. Guo Hongyan was tortured so badly that she had to be taken to a hospital. Ms. Liu Xiaoya was tortured until she was skin and bones.

Ms. Chen Yazhou was shocked with electric batons. A practitioner in her 60s was forced to do slave labor in the daytime and then squat under a table for the entire night. She was later incarcerated in a small, isolated cell. Another practitioner was not allowed to wash her face, teeth, or clothes for six months, and the inmates cursed at her because of her resulting smell.

The guards take the lead in torturing the practitioners and instigate inmates to beat and verbally abuse them. Inmates who mistreat practitioners have their terms reduced. The worse the inmates treat practitioners, the more they benefit, such as being given more fruit to eat.

Many inmates try to curry favor with the guards and follow them to persecute practitioners. Some behave even worse than the guards. The guards and inmates deceive practitioners by offering term reductions if they "transform." However, if a practitioner agrees to do so, they are told that they have to write statements denouncing Falun Gong in order for the reduction to be approved. When a practitioner signs the statements, the guard says, "You agreed. We didn't force you."

(3) Using Collective Punishment to Incite Hatred

Division 12 of Liaoning Province Women's Prison is further divided into five small groups. If any practitioner in the smaller group refuses to "transform," everyone in the group is punished. They are either not allowed to watch TV or have to write out the prison rules three times. As a result, inmates develop animosity toward practitioners and Falun Gong in general.

Practitioners who refuse to "transform" are not allowed to purchase any food or daily necessities in the prison. They are also denied family visits, phone calls, and mail. They are totally isolated from the outside world.

The guards use the basest words imaginable to verbally abuse practitioners, some of whom are the age of the guards' grandmothers. Many practitioners give in because they can't endure the insults and abuse. Once they "transform," the guards and inmates change their attitude immediately and smile at them. The environment changes, too, and becomes very relaxed. If a practitioner returns to their belief in Falun Gong, however, the guards and inmates go right back to abusing her.

Because non-Falun Gong inmates in the Correction Division are not assigned as much work as those in other divisions, they do whatever they can to be transferred there. Their families bribe whoever they can to help them avoid the forced labor required in other divisions.

§§1.5.2 Inmates Made to Torture Practitioners at Heilongjiang Province Women's Prison[28]

Heilongjiang Women's Prison, located in Harbin, Heilongjiang Province, is responsible for severely torturing Falun Gong practitioners. The guards incite criminal inmates to attack practitioners. Those who do gain favor with prison authorities.

› 1.5.2(a) Term Reductions Used as Incentive for Criminals to Attack Practitioners

Ward No.11 has been used to "transform" practitioners and thus developed a comprehensive system to carry out attacks on practitioners. Ji Na, a division deputy head, offered a point system to reward criminal inmates who were cruel to practitioners.

During late summer 2012, so-called experts hired by the 610 Office scolded inmates who were not "tough" enough in handling practitioners and offered more points for "underperformers" in order to beef up their attacks on practitioners. Determined practitioners were deprived of sleep for several days straight, handcuffed or shackled, and not allowed to use the restroom. All incoming practitioners were met with verbal abuse and beatings upon their arrival in Ward No.11.

Next they were forced to watch videos that slandered Falun Gong every day. Such brainwashing lasted somewhere between one and three months, and the practitioners were kept in complete isolation during this time.

Inmate Cui Xiang, a forty-four-year-old convicted murderer, received a term reduction for directing the secret torture of practitioners, including forcing them to sit still on a small bench for extended periods of time. As a result, some practitioners developed sores on their buttocks that eventually became infected. Cui boasted that she would continue to abuse practitioners upon her release. Inmate Tang Yongxia, 48, was also instrumental in monitoring and abusing practitioners.

Other inmates who wanted term reductions followed the directions of Cui and Tang to beat practitioners, often while the victims were handcuffed or shackled. In March 2012, inmate Ma Guirong gathered a group of inmates to beat Ms. Wang Jianhui.

› 1.5.2(b) Prison Hospital Tortures Healthy Practitioners

Ward No.10 serves as the prison hospital, where non-practitioner detainees are treated for their illnesses or injuries. Healthy Falun Gong practitioners, on the other hand, are taken there to be subjected to brutal mental and physical abuse. Ever since she was promoted to hospital director in 2008, former guard Zhao Huihua has enticed criminal inmates with term reductions in exchange for torturing practitioners.

While force-feeding practitioner Ms. Li Yushu, inmate Wang Xinhua forced food down Ms. Li's throat with chopsticks. The repeated poking and thrusting severely injured Ms. Li's throat and caused a hemorrhage.

Practitioner Ms. Hu Aiyun refused to be force-fed and was grabbed by her hair and brutally beaten by inmates Wang Wei and Li Kun until she passed out. Wang said, "This is the sick inmate division. It is normal if a couple of inmates die."[29]

Ms. Wei Jun, a teacher in her 40s from Daqing City, was often beaten by inmates and lost several teeth as a result. She was also made to sit on a small bench from 6 a.m. to 12 a.m. Ms. Wei was allowed very little sleep and sometimes passed out.

§§1.5.3 Tianjin Man Finally Allowed to Appeal His Case Five Years into a Seven-Year Term[30]

Mr. Huang Liqiao, an engineer from Tianjin, was arrested on April 7, 2012, and sentenced to 7 years in prison months later for refusing to renounce Falun Gong. He immediately filed an appeal, but Binhai Prison withheld the paperwork. He tried a few more times over the next several years, only to find out that none of his appeal letters were sent out.

His wife, Ms. Ge Xiulan, has been working to seek his release since day one. She was detained for 25 days at one point and had been denied visits with her husband since his arrest. Upon her release, she filed a complaint against the prison, which eventually relented and granted her a meeting with her husband. Ms. Ge brought a lawyer with her to see her husband on March 21, 2017. The guards prohibited the lawyer from taking notes or asking Mr. Huang about his imprisonment. She and the lawyer visited Tianjin First Intermediate Court the next day to submit Mr. Huang's appeal to contest the unjust prison sentence.

§§1.5.4 Imprisoned Woman's Letters to Lawyer Withheld by Prison[31]

Ms. Huang Qian, 47, was arrested at her home in Guangzhou City on February 3, 2015, for blogging about the persecution she suffered for refusing to renounce Falun Gong. Entitled "Gulag Memoirs," her posts documented how she had been repeatedly arrested, detained, and tortured since the persecution of Falun Gong began in 1999. She was given three years of forced labor in June 2001 and sentenced to four years in prison in October 2008.

The former employee of Guangzhou Book Center was sentenced to five years in prison on December 30, 2016, following her latest arrest. She was admitted to Guangdong Province Women's Prison in June 2017.

The guards tortured her on a regular basis and withheld her letters to her lawyer asking him to help her file appeals. In addition, her mother passed away not long after her transfer to prison, but she wasn't allowed to attend the funeral.

Ms. Huang's family visited her and noticed that she had lost a significant amount of weight. She pleaded for her family to get her out of the prison. When her family inquired with a guard about her condition, he threatened to revoke their visitation rights.

§§1.5.5 Prison Ignores Criminal's Assault of Falun Gong Practitioner Serving 11 Years for His Faith[32]

Mr. Wang Shouda, an Inner Mongolian man serving 11 years in Hohhot Second Prison for refusing to renounce Falun Gong, was twice abused by an inmate within several months. To this day, prison officials haven't taken action to hold the perpetrator responsible.

› 1.5.5(a) Head Injuries Sustained in Prison

The first incident of abuse took place on October 16, 2018. Inmate Wang Jining slammed Mr. Wang, who is in his 50s, to the ground and hit his head on the concrete floor. At the time, Mr. Wang had not eaten for nearly a month and was very weak. Physical abuse like this could have easily taken his life. Although the prison officials conducted an investigation, they did nothing to hold inmate Wang responsible.

The second incident happened at 10 p.m. on December 19, 2018. Wang Jining beat Mr. Wang again, knocking out one of his teeth and injuring his eyes. Mr. Wang's eyes became so swollen that he could not see. The guards were aware of the beating, but they didn't provide Mr. Wang with immediate medical treatment.

In prison, those who beat others are usually taken to solitary confinement immediately. But Wang Jining has not faced any consequences for his abuse of Mr. Wang, who, on the other hand, has not been allowed to leave his cell for breaks like other prisoners.

› 1.5.5(b) Secretly Sentenced, Abused in Prison

Mr. Wang lives in Ordos City in east Inner Mongolia. He and two other Falun Gong practitioners, Mr. Guo Bingqiang and Ms. Bai Tuoya, were arrested on June 19, 2011. They were taken to the Dongsheng Detention Center. Mr. Wang's family did not hear anything about him until December 2012, when they were notified that he had been sentenced to 11 years and moved to Hohhot Second Prison.

Inside the prison, Mr. Wang was forced to do heavy labor and attend brainwashing sessions. The guards instigated inmates to beat him. Zhou Junqing and Fan Zhiqiang, two officers in the prison, immobilized Mr. Wang on the floor on November 16, 2017. They pulled two front teeth from his mouth and stuffed his mouth with toilet paper. Mr. Wang was then kept in solitary confinement for nearly three months and was not let out until his life was in danger. Mr. Wang filed a formal complaint, but it went nowhere.

§§1.5.6 Stroke Patient Denied Medical Parole, Dies in Prison While Serving Time for His Faith[33]

A Panzhihua City, Sichuan Province, resident died less than nine months after he began serving time for his faith in Falun Gong in a prison in Yunnan Province.

The sixty-five-year-old man suffered several strokes and had dangerously high blood pressure but was repeatedly denied medical parole.

Mr. Liao Jianfu's death was preceded by two prior prison terms totaling 10.5 years between 2002 and 2013.

Mr. Liao was last arrested in October 2016 for putting up informational posters about Falun Gong. Three other practitioners who were with him, Mr. Song Nansu (70), Mr. Fu Wende (70), and Mr. Zhou Fuming (in his 60s), were also arrested.

The four practitioners appeared in the Yuping County Court on March 22, 2018. They were frequently interrupted by the judge as they read their defense statements. The judge then sentenced Mr. Liao to four years in prison, Mr. Song and Mr. Fu to three and a half years, and Mr. Zhou to two years. Mr. Liao, Mr. Fu, and Mr. Zhou were transferred to Yunnan Province No.1 Prison, and Mr. Song to Yunnan Province No.2 Prison on August 21, 2018. While imprisoned, Mr. Liao had cerebral hemorrhages on multiple occasions, but prison authorities refused to release him on medical parole.

§§1.5.7 Imprisoned Woman Denied Family Visits for Four Months for Doing Falun Gong Exercises[34]

Ms. Zhang Wei has been denied family visits for four months because she did the Falun Gong exercises in Liaoning Women's Prison, where she is serving an eight-and-a-half-year term for not renouncing her faith.

Ms. Zhang, a resident of Dandong City, Liaoning Province, has already served three years in Liaoning Women's Prison since the spring of 2016. She has been frequently beaten by guards and inmates for not giving up her faith, causing severe injuries to her back and legs. She did the Falun Gong exercises to recover her health, only to be denied family visits starting in April 2019.

Ms. Zhang's husband went to the prison on June 27, 2019. Two guards told him, "Zhang Wei did the Falun Gong exercises in front of hundreds of people at the prison factory. She broke our rules here. We are denying her all visits!"

One of her family members said to the guards, "We haven't seen her for four months and are very worried about her, especially her eighty-year-old mother. Zhang Wei almost died after she was tortured while serving her first prison term here in 2002. She was beaten again this time. How can we not worry about her?" The guards replied, "If she doesn't follow the prison rules, we will lock her in solitary confinement with her hands cuffed."

Her husband asked the guards, "She still has several years to serve here. Will you keep her hands cuffed all the time if she doesn't stop doing the exercises?"

No matter what the family members said, the guards still refused to allow them to see Ms. Zhang. Ms. Zhang's family next went to the local Procuratorate to complain about the prison. They were directed to the Provincial Prison Administration Office, which referred them to the Provincial Prison Petition Office. A staff member at the Provincial Prison Petition Office asked Ms. Zhang's family to file a complaint with the internal petition office at the prison directly. "If you are still not satisfied with their response, you can come back and talk to us," the staff member said.

Ms. Zhang's family went to the prison's petition office the next day with the complaint, only to be rejected. They returned to the provincial prison petition office and were received by the same person as the day before. That staff member read their complaint and went to another room to call his supervisor. When he returned about four minutes later, he told Ms. Zhang's family that the case couldn't be accepted and that the family had to talk with the prison authorities themselves.

Ms. Zhang's family made another attempt to contact the prison but were told that as long as she does the Falun Gong exercises, they will not be allowed to visit her.

Ms. Zhang's husband planned to hire a lawyer to seek justice for her.

Chapter 2: Denial of Employment, Education, Housing, and Economic Security

Below is the personal account of Mr. He Lifang, whose family faced hatred, discrimination, and humiliation with the onset of the persecution of Falun Gong in July 1999:

I was once beaten by 17 inmates while detained for my faith in 2001. The police released me on bail when I was in critical condition, but they harassed me at home all the time. I managed to escape their surveillance and left home. The Jimo 610 Office received a tip that I might be hiding in a certain area, and they plastered a wanted list with my photo everywhere in that area. They also cancelled my ID card as another way of depriving me of freedom and basic human rights.

Officials also harassed, interrogated, and arrested my parents many times, forcing them to provide my information. Every Chinese New Year, officials dispatched people near my relatives' place attempting to arrest me.

My business was very successful when the persecution started in 1999. But because of the Communist Party's slanderous propaganda, many of my clients were misled and treated me like an enemy. One neighbor who used to be friendly swore at me and my family. Even children sometimes cursed at us because they too had been influenced by the propaganda.

The fallout has extended to many areas of our lives. Because my family practices Falun Gong, my nephew did not pass the political review to join the army. When his father—my elder brother—failed to force my parents to give up their belief, he broke all their windows and planned to work with the village administration to get their house torn down, all the while threatening to kill them. As a result, whenever they heard his voice, my parents would hide in the woods and dare not return home.

Like Mr. He, Falun Gong practitioners in every corner of China had their lives turned upside down overnight. The communist regime effectively turned the entire country against the spiritual group with an extensive propaganda campaign. No matter who they are, wherever they go, as long as they don't give up practicing Falun Gong, they are labeled enemies of the Party and subjected to ruthless persecution.

Falun Gong practitioners are deprived of the most basic rights to survival. Students are expelled from school or denied admission. Employees are fired from their jobs and have their pensions suspended when they retire. For established individuals, the regime can take everything away from them, including their businesses, houses, and bank savings.

The regime has successfully used its system of brainwashing and thought control to turn children against parents, husbands against wives, and students against teachers. Individuals are given incentives or bonuses for reporting a Falun Gong practitioner to the authorities. Police officers are promoted for actively torturing and brainwashing practitioners. The police can knock on the door or break into practitioners' homes in the middle of the night, ransack their residences, and arrest them. A practitioner may be denied an ID or passport, causing great inconvenience in their everyday life. Even when they are able to obtain an ID, it may be flagged for surveillance, and one may be arrested simply for trying to take a train to visit their parents.

With recent advancements and adoption of artificial intelligence, facial recognition, and social platforms like WeChat (the predominant social media app used for nearly everything in daily life, including buying street food and hailing a taxi), the surveillance of Chinese people has never been stricter. The communist regime has effectively turned the entire country into a big prison.

§2.1 The School System's Role in the Persecution

From elementary schools to universities, the entire is strictly controlled by the communist regime. Each school and even grade level is assigned its own Communist Party secretary, who closely monitors whether each student's thoughts are aligned with the Party. Students found to practice Falun Gong face discrimination by their friends, classmates, and teachers. Many have been expelled from school and never allowed to return.

Practitioners aren't the only victims, however. Anti-Falun Gong propaganda has been added to textbooks, and students are forced to defame Falun Gong as part of their exams. If they resist, they are subjected to the same fate as a Falun Gong practitioner.

Over the past two decades, an entire generation has thus been indoctrinated with misinformation that maligns Falun Gong. The members of that generation have also involuntarily become accomplices to the persecution. As students grow up and enter society, they bring the propaganda with them and pass it down to the next generation, causing the targeted group to be marginalized for a long period of time.

§§2.1.1 Denied Educational Opportunities

Case 1: Middle School Student Kicked Out of School and Forced into Homelessness for Practicing Falun Gong[35]

Liu Wenjuan, a middle school student in Fujian Province, was forced by school administrators to write a statement renouncing Falun Gong. When she refused, the principal, Lin Jianfeng, got angry and prevented Liu from attending classes using various excuses.

Liu was later arrested and forced to quit school after she shared her experience of practicing Falun Gong with her teachers. When the authorities kept harassing her at home, she was forced to live away from home to avoid further persecution.

Case 2: High School Student Driven Out of School for Passing Out Falun Gong Information[36]

Li Qun was reported to her teacher when she gave her classmate a Falun Gong informational booklet. The teachers spent hours talking to her and attempted to force her to renounce Falun Gong.

When Li tried to explain Falun Gong to her teachers, they refused to listen and told her parents to take her home. She was eventually expelled from school after she refused to write a statement renouncing Falun Gong.

Case 3: Young Man Not Allowed to Attend College and Taken to a Labor Camp for a Year[37]

Although Mr. Liu Xiaolin did well on his college entrance exam and was admitted to a university, he wasn't allowed to attend college after the authorities found out that he practiced Falun Gong.

The eighteen-year-old was also sent to a forced labor camp when he expressed his discontent with the persecution on the Internet. His parents, Mr. Liu Zonggang and Ms. Sui Qiaohong, were also arrested and taken to a labor camp.

Mr. Liu was placed under constant surveillance and frequently harassed after he was released.

Case 4: PhD Candidate Denied Thesis Defense, Father Pressured by Chinese Academy of Sciences to Report Son[38]

Mr. Yu Ya'ou, a PhD candidate at the Chinese Academy of Sciences, South China Botanical Garden, was deprived of his right to defend his thesis because it included a sentence expressing his gratitude to Falun Gong.

Under instructions from the 610 Office, the leadership of the South

China Botanical Garden threatened Mr. Yu with the school's enrollment regulations and student management provisions. They also made his father report him to the 610 Office and send his son to a brainwashing center.

Case 5: College Freshman Detained in Shanghai for Practicing Falun Gong and Distributing Information[39]

Mr. Zhong Yiming, a nineteen-year-old freshman at Shanghai Jiao Tong University, was detained in early July 2019 for practicing and distributing information about Falun Gong.

School officials said that he had been recorded on surveillance cameras while distributing Falun Gong materials on campus. Their investigation found that Mr. Zhong had bought a printer with the money he had saved from his allowance and printed Falun Gong informational materials with it.

The university reported him to Shanghai police, who ordered him to disclose where he had learned Falun Gong and to write a "regret statement" to give up his belief. When Mr. Zhong refused, the police threatened to terminate his college studies and took him to a detention center in Shanghai on July 5, but they didn't inform his parents of the location. His parents stayed in Shanghai for a few days to look for him, to no avail.

University authorities also sent staff to Mr. Zhong's high school, the No.24 High School of Dalian, to investigate him. It was also reported that the Shanghai police had flown to Dalian on July 22 in an attempt to arrest his grandmother, who is in her 80s.

§§2.1.2 Brainwashing of Students and Teachers

To instigate public hatred and justify the persecution, propaganda attacking Falun Gong, such as the Tiananmen self-immolation hoax and the so-called 1,400 Falun Gong death cases, appeared in textbooks, on TV programs, and in newspapers. Propaganda posters and banners covered school campuses. Students were mandated to watch videos and attend seminars and exhibitions to reinforce the propaganda.

Petition drives defaming Falun Gong were circulated, and every student was forced to sign or otherwise face consequences.

Case 1: "This Is the Communist Regime's School, No Other Belief Is Allowed"[40]

At a high school in Heilongjiang Province, more than 5,000 students and teachers were forced to sign agreements not to talk about Falun Gong or read Falun Gong informational materials. Nearly 100 top students were forced to join the Communist Party as a way to reinforce the thought control. If a student was found to have violated the agreement, their teacher would also be implicated.

An 11th grade student, Cao Rui, who didn't practice Falun Gong, was reported to the school administration when she shared some Falun Gong materials she had received with other students and told them that the Party's campaign against Falun Gong was wrong. She faced further retaliation for "disrupting classroom order" when she openly challenged a teacher of politics when he attacked Falun Gong in class.

Cao was later expelled from the school, and administrators even called police to remove Cao and her mother. "This is the communist regime's school, no other belief is allowed," an administrator told Cao's family.

Case 2: Law School Students Ordered to Express Their Attitude Toward Falun Gong During Enrollment Interview[41]

In an enrollment interview notice from the law school of Shanghai University of Finance and Economics in 2010, students had to answer a question about their understanding of Falun Gong.

Such questions are often used as a touchstone to test whether a student completely follows the Party line or exercises independent thinking. Most students compromise their independence and join the crowd to condemn Falun Gong in order to pursue advancement in their studies and careers.

§2.2 Denial of Employment Opportunities and Seizure of Personal Property

With every corner of Chinese society pulled into the persecution campaign, everyone is targeted in the system. After a student graduates from school and enters society, he faces the constant pressure of losing his job or having his personal property seized if the authorities find out that he practices Falun Gong.

§§2.2.1 Practitioners Terminated by Employers

Case 1: Airplane Engineer Unable to Work and Support Family after ID Cards Confiscated[42]

Mr. Liu Yongsheng, an airplane engineer at Chengdu Airplane Construction, was fired from his job in 2007 following a mass arrest of Falun Gong practitioners. He was forced to live away from home and moved from place to place to avoid further persecution.

The authorities withheld his ID and diploma, which prevented him from finding a job for a long time. Despite his expertise, he had to work part-time as a delivery person to make ends meet.

Case 2: Doctor Fired from Hospital[43]

Dr. Chen Jing was arrested while accompanying a child to a police station to inquire about her arrested mother in mid-December 2005. The police beat, verbally abused, and interrogated her. She was soon fired by her employer, Jiamusi Central Hospital, only one year after she started work there.

Her ordeal deepened fears and misunderstandings of Falun Gong among her family, colleagues, and friends.

Case 3: Family Members Implicated[44]

Mr. Li Hongshu's younger brother quit his job in Dalian City and went back home to Panjin City to take care of his mother after both Mr. Li and his father were imprisoned for their faith. His brother was denied a traffic police position in Panjin after he failed the political review in the application process because their father practiced Falun Gong, even though he made the highest score on the exam and passed the interview and physical. This caused tremendous mental distress to his brother, who also had trouble finding a spouse as a result.

§§2.2.2 Personal Companies Forced to Close

Case 1: Detergent Company Forced to Close[45]

In 2003, several Falun Gong practitioners in Chaoyang City, Liaoning Province, set up a joint venture and purchased a patented technology. They started a company called Tianzheng Detergent Company. From management to production, they hired Falun Gong practitioners who had lost their jobs due to the persecution.

Not long after the company started, they quickly built up sales and opened the market by selling their products to over 20 large and medium-sized machine processing companies. Their revenue increased three years in a row.

After the police learned of the practitioner-owned company, they arrested the company owners, Mr. Li Wensheng and Ms. Wu Jinping, and ransacked the company on February 24, 2008. The police also confiscated the safe containing cash, the company's checkbooks, transaction checkbooks, a public seal, financial seal, legal representative seal, and other business items, all of which could be used to withdraw money from their bank accounts. They also seized a company car and arrested their hired chauffeur.

The company was eventually forced to shut down, resulting in millions in losses. Many employees lost their jobs, and their families were left in dire financial straits.

Case 2: Popular Author's Education Company Forced to Close, Books Confiscated[46]

Mr. Wang Xueming (pen name Yun Xiao), a teacher at Damian Middle School in Chengdu City, was fired from his job in March 2003. He then moved to Wuhan City, Hubei Province, and started his own education company, the "Full Virtue Lecture Hall," to provide training in writing. He also published more than 100 articles, poems, and verses in numerous journals and compiled and published several college textbooks. He was selected as one of the "Eleven Network Prose Writers" in 2008.

With his increasing influence, Wuhan police arrested Mr. Wang on October 27, 2011. His father passed away the day he was arrested. The authorities charged Mr. Wang with "operating an illegal business" and closed his company headquarters in Wuhan, as well as several other locations near Wuhan and in Nanchang City, Jiangxi Province. More than 6,000 copies of his personal publications were confiscated. The direct economic losses totaled more than one million yuan.

§2.3 No Place to Live

Case 1: Piano Teacher's House Confiscated, Pension Suspended[47]

Ms. Xie Xia, a piano teacher from Shuangliu County, Sichuan Province, was fired shortly after the persecution of Falun Gong began in 1999. Her employer, Huayang Vocational Middle School, also confiscated her school-subsidized house for which she had paid her share in full.

In the years that followed, Ms. Xie, a single mother, moved from one place to another to find odd jobs to support herself and her child. The local 610 Office ordered landlords not to rent to her, making it harder for her to find a home.

The authorities suspended her pension beginning in July 2014 after the Shuangliu County Social Security Bureau received a secret document from the Dongsheng Town Neighborhood Committee ordering the bureau to transfer her pension to a government-controlled account. The committee members later admitted that the 610 Office had issued the order.

Case 2: House to Be Demolished, Compensation Shorted by One Million Yuan[48]

Because of she practices Falun Gong, Ms. Zhang Guilan received only 300,000 yuan in compensation when her house in Yichun City, Jilin Province, was scheduled for demolition in 2011, when she should have received at least 1,200,000 yuan.

When she told a reporter about it and the reporter interviewed the Party secretary of the Nancha District government, the official said to the reporter, "Zhang Guilan practices Falun Gong, so her compensation should be less than the others. She shouldn't have practiced Falun Gong!"

The reporter then asked, "The law and ordinance for compensation doesn't mention anything specific regarding Falun Gong, so it seems that what you are doing is wrong." The Party secretary said, "Here in the Nancha District, what we say is the law."

When Ms. Zhang refused to move, the authorities turned off her utilities. Her house was surrounded by water, making it impossible for her to live a normal life. The authorities also threatened to arrest her if she refused to move.

Case 3: Forced to Live Away from Home[49]

Mr. Ma Qinghai from Chifeng City, Inner Mongolia, was forced to live away from home with his wife and newborn daughter to avoid the persecution beginning in February 2003. They moved 16 times within three years to hide from the police. While they moved from place to place, their son stayed with his elderly grandparents.

Even when Mr. Ma and his wife weren't home, the police continued to harass his family. During a home search in the evening, the police even looked under the comforter belonging to Ms. Ma's grandmother, who was in her 90s, terrifying her.

Mr. Ma was later arrested in 2005 and sentenced to nine years in prison. He recalled:

> *After begging the guards for a long time, my father was finally allowed to visit me in prison in 2006, the first time in many years. Maybe because I was suffering from generalized edema and completely out of shape, or maybe my father was just thrilled that I was still alive, he just looked at me for a long time and didn't say a word. Looking at him, his hair all gray, I held back my tears and didn't want to tell him what I'd gone through after I was arrested.*
>
> *Another time, my seventeen-year-old son brought my five-year-old daughter to see me. I said something that the guards didn't want to hear. They beat and kicked me in front of my children. My daughter was scared and cried very hard.*
>
> *During the time I was imprisoned, my wife did all kinds of odd jobs to support our children so that they could go to school. Sometimes she also sent some money to me to buy daily necessities.*
>
> *When my wife brought my daughter to see me a few years later, my heart was filled with joy and bitterness. My daughter was much taller and had grown up, but I wasn't there by her side or taking care of her. The persecution didn't only deprive me of freedom, it also took away my ability to be a son, a husband, and a father.*

§2.4 Homes Ransacked

Case 1: Police Use Teargas and Axe to Break into Home[50]

At midnight on August 8, 2009, the police in Manchuri City, Inner Mongolia, attempted to break into Mr. Zhang Yu's home, where he lived with his wife, teenage daughter, and parents. Mr. Zhang's family refused to open the door and held the police back until daybreak. The police then dispatched a fire truck and several dozen officers from the local police station.

The standoff lasted until noon. The police then smashed a window and threw tear gas into Mr. Zhang's home with no regard for the fact that Mr. Zhang's elderly, sick parents and his teenage daughter were inside. Armed police then entered the home through the broken window.

Because the police had broken the lock on Mr. Zhang's door, it could not be opened, so they used an axe to break down the door and took all five family members away.

Case 2: Police Attempt Nighttime Break-In[51]

At 4 a.m. on September 29, 2009, officers appeared at the front gate of Mr. Hao Yin's residence in Tianjin. They announced to his three daughters inside that they wanted to search their home.

When the girls (Xiaojing, Xiaoyan, and Xiaojiao) refused to open the front gate door, several officers repeatedly knocked on it while other officers climbed the front wall and threatened them. When the girls shouted out to their neighbors for help, the officers climbed down and left.

The girls' mother, Ms. Gao Yan'e, was sentenced to three years in prison for talking to people about Falun Gong. The girls' father, Mr. Hao Yin, was arrested without cause, had his home ransacked, and was later sent to forced labor. He managed to escape from the detention center but was then forced to live away from home to avoid further persecution.

Case 3: Personal Property Seized in Home Ransacking[52]

Ten officers broke into Mr. Yao Tiebin and Ms. Zhang Fenrong's apartment in Mudanjiang City, Heilongjiang Province, on July 14, 2008. The police beat the couple when they tried to stop them from searching their home. Their faces were swollen and black and blue. One of the officers said to them, "The state [Chinese Communist Party] doesn't allow you to practice Falun Gong. If you practice Falun Gong, then you violate the law."

The police ransacked their home and took the family's cash, computer, printer, and other belongings. The total value of the property was over 30,000 yuan.

§2.5 Extortion

Case 1: Police Refuse to Return Nearly 60,000 Yuan Seized from Heilongjiang Woman Jailed for Her Faith[53]

The police seized 58,000 yuan in cash from Ms. Luo Caisen when ransacking her home in August 2018 and refused to return it.

The police initially claimed that the money was part of the prosecution evidence and that they could only return it after Ms. Luo's trial. When the police submitted Ms. Luo's case to the Acheng Procuratorate on October 7, however, the money wasn't included. When the prosecutor indicted Ms. Luo and transferred her case to the Acheng Court, he didn't list the money as prosecution evidence either.

When talking to Ms. Luo's lawyer and her family, the Acheng Court judge made it very clear that the money confiscated by the police had nothing to do with the case. Because Ms. Luo's son needed the money for his family business, he found officer Gao after his mother's hearing on December 7, 2018 and asked for the money again.

This time, Gao said that they would return the money after the judge issued a verdict. It was recently confirmed that Ms. Luo was sentenced to a year and a half in prison for not renouncing her faith, but the police still haven't returned the money to her family.

Case 2: Police Confiscate 100,000 Yuan in Cash When Ransacking Couple's Real Estate Office[54]

Mr. Zuo Hongtao and his wife of Qinhuangdao City, Hebei Province, were arrested on June 9, 2017, along with four Falun Gong practitioners who were visiting them. The police ransacked the couple's real estate office, confiscated 100,000 yuan in cash Mr. Zuo kept on hand for business transactions, as well as 50,000 yuan in cash that another practitioner kept at his office.

The police also seized Mr. Zuo's electric motorcycle and office supplies, the second practitioner's new electric motorcycle, and a car that the third practitioner had borrowed from her friend and that was filled with garments she was selling. The police didn't present a search warrant during the home ransacking or provide a list of confiscated items afterward.

The practitioners were later sentenced to 8 to 13 years in prison for not renouncing their faith. Mr. Zuo's wife, Ms. Cui Qiurong, who doesn't practice but supports Falun Gong, was sentenced to 19 months.

§2.6 Withholding of Pensions

Case 1: Police Falsify Employment Document, Wipe 27 Years of Service from Pension Plan[55]

After working at the Bureau of Urban Utilities and Landscaping in Beijing for 30 years, Mr. Wang Shuxiang was surprised to discover that he had nothing in his pension account and his personnel file indicated that he had only two years and nine months of service.

The Dongcheng District Talent Service Center staff told Mr. Wang's wife that the police had taken the file and altered it. When Mrs. Wang visited the local police station, they admitted that they were responsible for changing her husband's personnel file. They promised to give her 30,000 yuan as compensation but refused to fix his employment record.

Case 2: Guizhou Man's Pension Suspended Since 2001[56]

Mr. Zhang Shougang retired in 2000 from the Zunyi City Bureau of Athletics. His employer suspended his pension when he was first arrested in 2001 because he refused to renounce Falun Gong. He has been in dire financial straits for the past 20 years.

Mr. Zhang's son was not yet ten years old when his father was first arrested. The boy was forced to drop out of school when his father was incarcerated, and for six years he had to borrow from relatives to survive.

When his father was released the second time, the boy was in his teens, and they had to sell their house to pay off his debts.

Case 3: Pension Withheld to Pay Off Funds Received During Imprisonment[57]

In recent years, the communist regime issued a new policy that prohibits Chinese citizens from receiving pension payments while they serve time in prison. Thus, many Falun Gong practitioners released from prison have discovered that their pensions had been suspended by the local social security officer in order to repay the funds they had received during their imprisonment.

Ms. He Zhongli returned home on April 14, 2019, after serving three years in prison for not renouncing her faith in Falun Gong.

The seventy-three-year-old woman's retirement pension had been suspended since late 2018. She was told that the benefits wouldn't be reinstated until she pays back all of the funds disbursed to her during her imprisonment.

§2.7 The Present-Day Orwellian State

In addition to missing out on educational opportunities and having their personal property seized, many Falun Gong practitioners also face constant danger and the pressure of being targeted at anytime and anywhere. Especially with the development of surveillance technology, Chinese citizens are being monitored by the communist regime at an unprecedented level.

§§2.7.1 Denial of Passports and IDs

The authorities have confiscated the ID cards of many Falun Gong practitioners, making travel, banking, lodging, and other everyday transactions difficult. When practitioners are given ID cards, they are often flagged, creating barriers to travel and everyday financial transactions. Practitioners continue to be subjected to strict surveillance in their daily lives.

Case 1: Heilongjiang Man Unable to Withdraw Cash from Bank Account without an ID[58]

Mr. Wang Zhibiao applied for a new ID card at the police station on January 20, 2008. He was told to come back on May 20 to get his new card. When he went back as scheduled, he was told that he couldn't have a new ID card because he practiced Falun Gong. Mr. Wang returned to the police station several times but still couldn't get an ID.

His son was getting married in July 2008. Without the ID, Mr. Wang was unable to withdraw cash from his bank account, which affected his son's wedding plans.

Case 2: Parents of Japanese Resident Denied Passports Five Times[59]

From 2004 to 2009, Mr. Zhang Youliang and Ms. Fu Jinyun, two Jiangxi Province natives now residing in Shanghai, were rejected five times when they applied for their passports in order to visit their son in Japan.

The police told them that they were being denied passports because they practiced Falun Gong. The police also arranged for plainclothes officers to monitor the couple's daily activities.

The police wrote on the couple's passport:

> *The information provided on their applications is accurate, but they are Falun Gong practitioners, one of the five categories of people who are not allowed to travel abroad. Their applications have been submitted to higher-ups for review.*

According to a list of "supplementary documents required for personal travel abroad" by the Port of Entry Authority of Hengshi City in Hebei Province,[60] the applicant's local police station must submit documents showing that the applicant is not a Falun Gong practitioner.

Case 3: Heilongjiang Woman Arrested at Train Station Because of Flagged ID, Sentenced to Seven Years in Prison[61]

Ms. Cai Weihua, a Falun Gong practitioner in Harbin City, Heilongjiang Province, was stopped by police on February 6, 2018, as she was about to board a train to visit her parents for the Chinese New Year holiday. It turned out that the police had discovered that Ms. Cai practices Falun Gong after scanning her ID as she went through the security checkpoint.

The police arrested Ms. Cai and her husband, Mr. Li Bowei, who doesn't practice Falun Gong. Officers then took them to their home and ransacked their residence. Ms. Cai was later sentenced to seven years in prison by the Daowai District Court in November 2018 and fined 30,000 yuan.

§§2.7.2 Constant Surveillance

Falun Gong practitioners are monitored while walking on the street, checking into a hotel, mailing a letter, making a donation, sharing on social media, and performing other routine activities. Some were even set up by children who were lured by the police to become "undercover agents."

Case 1: Stopped by the Police While Walking Down the Street[62]

Mr. Guan Yunzhi was stopped by the police when he was walking down the street on July 30, 2014. Upon finding out that he was a Falun Gong practitioner, the police arrested him and interrogated him overnight at the police station. He was detained for over 50 days and had 5,000 yuan extorted from him because the police found Falun Gong-related information on his cellphone.

Case 2: Heilongjiang Couple Harassed by Police after Checking into Beijing Hotel[63]

Ms. Zhang Yanfen and her husband Mr. Tao Yongjun (who doesn't practice Falun Gong) went to Beijing to visit their daughter Ms. Tao Can on April 11, 2012.

Ms. Zhang checked into the hotel with her daughter's ID. Around 7 p.m., police officers knocked on Ms. Zhang's door and ordered her to tell them her daughter's workplace and address. They also called her daughter using Mr. Tao's phone and asked whether she still practiced Falun Gong. She refused to answer.

Case 3: Shandong Woman Arrested and Taken to Forced Labor Camp after Post Office Staff Found Falun Gong Booklet in Her Mail[64]

A postal worker in Longkou City, Shandong Province, reported Ms. Qu Xianghua to the local 610 Office after finding Falun Gong-related information in a letter she had mailed on August 1, 2008. Police officers descended on Ms. Qu's home the next day and arrested her. They also ransacked her home and confiscated her computer and printer.

Ms. Qu was given a year and a half of forced labor in late August. She was severely tortured and pressured to provide information on other practitioners to the police.

Case 4: Impoverished Farmer Arrested after Donating to Sichuan Earthquake Crisis[65]

When he heard about the 7.9-magnitude earthquake in Sichuan Province in 2008, Mr. Yin Zemin, a Falun Gong practitioner from Hebei Province, consulted with his family and decided to donate 500 yuan they had saved for his father's medical care to relief efforts in the devastated area.

After the local police found out about his donation, they arrested Mr. Yin on June 6, 2008, based on the reasoning that "Falun Gong practitioners do not have money; therefore, someone with the resources to donate 500 yuan must be a 'coordinator.'"

Case 5: Woman Sentenced to Prison for Sharing Falun Gong Audio on Social Media[66]

Ms. Che Guoping of Dezhou City, Shandong Province, was on her way home from work on May 22, 2017, when more than ten officers seized her.

The Huaneng Power Company employee was targeted because she shared an audio file with information about Falun Gong on social media. The officers ransacked her home and confiscated more than ten cell phones, one iPad, and other personal belongings.

Ms. Che appeared in the Decheng District Court on November 9, 2017 and was sentenced to three and a half years in prison with a 5,000-yuan fine in December 2017.

Case 6: Police Lure Children with Money to Act as "Undercover Agents"[67]

Police in Sichuan Province have used money to lure children to be their "undercover agents." They made the children go to Falun Gong practitioners' homes and pretend to ask for information about Falun Gong or to follow and monitor the practitioners, who were later arrested. Each child was given 10 yuan as a reward.

On the morning of November 10, 2006, several students went to Ms. Li Zefen's home and asked whether she still had Falun Gong informational materials. "We really like the Falun Gong bookmarks and we want some more," they said. Ms. Li let the children in. She brought out stools so they could sit in her yard. Before long, two police vehicles arrived. Several officers ransacked Ms. Li's home and took her away. Ms. Li was later given one year and three months of forced labor.

§2.8 Families Turned Against Practitioners

When coercion and torture fail to force practitioners to give up their faith, the authorities resort to arranging emotional pleas from family members to wear down the practitioners' mental defenses. While some practitioners' families still supported them, some turned against them and assisted the authorities in persecuting the practitioners in order to protect their own interests.

Ms. Ding Xiaoxia, a middle school English teacher in Jilin Province, recalled how the leaders at her school used this strategy to force her to give up practicing Falun Gong:[68]

After several rounds of brainwashing I still refused to renounce Falun Gong, so they asked my family to help persuade me. My parents first came to my school. They beat me and scolded me. Then it was my husband. Next it was my son, who had just graduated from middle school. As soon as he saw me, he knelt down in front of me, crying, 'Mom, don't do it anymore. I miss you so much. Let's go home.' My heart was broken, but I remained silent to his plea.

Another time, they asked my older sister to persuade me. She said that my dad was in the hospital and in critical condition. She cried to me that it was because of me that my dad's health began to deteriorate. If I agreed to give up my faith, maybe he still had a chance to recover. But if I insisted on holding on to my faith, they wouldn't forgive me if anything happened to my dad. I believed her. Surrendering to strong family emotions and worried that I would lose my dad, I wrote the statement renouncing Falun Gong.

The school leaders were elated and finally let me go home. When I got there, I realized that I had been deceived. My father was perfectly fine and had never gone to the hospital.

In a political performance review, family members of air force personnel had to fill out a form and answer questions about their attitudes toward Falun Gong and whether they had engaged in "illegal Falun Gong activities."[69]

Case 1: Indoctrinated Daughter Turns In, Assaults Mother[70]

After the persecution of Falun Gong began in 1999, Ms. Hu Lingying's daughter, Li Huaying, strongly opposed her continuing to practice. Li assaulted and abused her mother several times. She also reported Ms. Hu to the police, resulting in her detention.

In July 2003, Ms. Hu was reported again and taken to the police station. After the police ordered Li to take her home, she locked Ms. Hu at home every day, fearing that she would go out.

When Ms. Hu demanded that she unlock the door, Li used a nail to attack her head, back, and upper body. Ms. Hu's head was covered with blood, and her face was swollen. Even though Ms. Hu was severely injured, Li never sought any medical care for her.

Case 2: Ex-Husband Receives Honor Certificate for His Active Role in the Persecution[71]

Liu Jun, the deputy secretary of the Communist Party Committee of Yongyang Town, Hebei Province, and ex-husband of practitioner Ms. Liu Xiufeng, was given an Honor Certificate in 2001 for his active role in the persecution and dissociating himself from Ms. Liu by divorcing her. Ms. Liu recalled:

> *To force me to give up the practice, my ex-husband beat me often, leaving bruises on my face and body. The local 610 Office director once said to him, "If she is still so stubborn, you can beat her until she is disabled. It would be better if you crippled her rather than allow her to go to Beijing or go out to promote Falun Gong again."*

Even though Liu Jun had learned Falun Gong before, he completely gave in to the Party after the persecution began. While Ms. Liu was held in a detention center in 2001, he divorced her and only gave her 200 yuan. He married again even before she received the divorce decree. He also destroyed all of Ms. Liu's Falun Gong books and materials.

Case 3: Mother Beaten to Death by Son for Practicing Falun Gong[72]

Ms. Lu Shurong died due to injuries when her own son, Du Xuedong, beat her because of her faith in Falun Gong on October 21, 2018. She was 77.

Du, in his 50s, twice posted bail to get his mother released after she was arrested for refusing to renounce her belief. A military veteran, Du was trained to follow orders, and he grew increasingly hostile to his mother after she continued practicing Falun Gong following her release.

He was also worried that his mother's faith would affect his son's chance of becoming a government employee.

On September 27, 2018, Du came home intoxicated. As soon as he entered the door, he began to beat his mother. When his father, Du

Zhongsan tried to stop him, the son struck his eighty-three-year-old father, too. The son continued to beat his mother for more than an hour. She suffered ten broken ribs and a broken wrist. She had bruises all over her body and her face was bruised and swollen.

After Ms. Lu was taken to the hospital, the doctor found multiple fractures in one rib, and the broken rib had pierced her lung. Most of her internal organs were also severely injured. The hospital issued several critical condition notices during the 24 days she was hospitalized before she died.

Chapter 3: The Suffering of Falun Gong Practitioners' Children

Ms. Wang Jingqi recounts her family's ordeal in the persecution of Falun Gong:[73]

Our life went from heaven to hell. Father was very troubled. He smoked every day to escape the reality. I was in college and worried about my schoolwork and Mother's safety. I heard that she was beaten and tortured with electric batons in a detention center. I really wanted to shout at the guards to stop, but I kept quiet because it might have brought her more trouble.

At home, I turned my outrage to pounding on the keys on the piano when I played. Father was silent. He smoked with his head down, hiding all his worry, anger, and guilt because he could not protect his wife and prevent her from being hurt.

Mother was frequently arrested and detained and missed many important moments in my life—my college graduation, my first job, and my wedding. Despite the inhuman torture, Mother never gave up her practice. The reason was simple: she would have died many times if she had not practiced Falun Dafa. During her third detention, Mother began a hunger strike to protest the persecution and her weight dropped from 60 kg to 35kg. When the guards force-fed her, they, knocked out her teeth and pulled out most of her hair. She was sent home in critical condition.

Once home, Mom resumed the Falun Dafa exercises, read the teachings, and quickly recovered. A month later, she could walk. Although she had not regained all the weight she had lost, her hair had grown out again. She asked me not to hate the police. "Be compassionate to these poor people," she said to me. Her words were like a breeze to my heart, removing my sadness and hate. I am so grateful to Falun Dafa.

In March 2009, Mother was detained a fourth time. A phone call woke me up at night. While on a business trip, Father passed away from a heart attack. When I saw him at the hospital, his body was already a cold, stiff corpse.

It was the most devastating moment of my life. Relatives helped me arrange for him to be cremated. As I carried his ashes out of the funeral parlor, I could not hear a sound except my own breathing and heartbeat. My mind was clear. I knew who killed my father. He had suffered so much pressure and pain. He would not have died so early if the persecution of Falun Dafa had not happened.

Like Wang Jingqi, many children's lives were turned upside down when the Chinese communist regime suddenly launched its nationwide campaign of persecution of Falun Gong.

While people of all ages have suffered as a result, the pain inflicted on children is the most heartbreaking and detrimental to society. Children in school are brainwashed to make them hate Falun Gong. As the hope of the future, they are trained to be loyal to the CCP instead of being taught to think independently.

In addition to brainwashing, many children also grow up in fear, their families destroyed by the CCP. Some children became homeless orphans when both of their parents were sentenced to long prison terms or were tortured to death, some had to move from place to place to hide from the police, some were humiliated and bullied by their classmates, some were expelled from school and deprived of an education, some were detained and tortured themselves, and some became insane or even died young after being tortured or from tremendous mental trauma that even adults would not be able to endure.

In the 20 years that have passed, an infant would now be a college student, the college students back then are now middle-aged, establishing their own families and starting the next generation. Growing up in fear and witnessing their loved ones being arrested and tortured again and again will have long-lasting impact on these children, their extended families, and their own children.

§3.1 Brainwashing of Children

The CCP not only brainwashes Falun Gong practitioners but also instills hatred of Falun Gong in non-practitioners, especially children. An entire generation of Chinese has now grown up immersed in CCP propaganda defaming Falun Gong in schools and other settings.

A ten-year-old Chinese-American student who visited his family in China in February 2001 wrote:[74]

> *When we talked about Falun Gong, my cousin had only heard the one-sided story promoted by the Chinese government. He had never met a real practitioner. When the Chinese government told people to sign their names saying Falun Gong was not good, every middle school and elementary school student had to sign it, even if it was against their will. My nine-year-old cousin also had to sign it. In the first week of school, they didn't teach anything. They just showed [the students] how to lie. Their textbook said the U.S. was using Falun Gong to destroy China.*

At that time, the Chinese Anti-Cult Association (CACA), a government agency under the China Society and Technology Association, was promoting a "One Million Signatures" campaign on school campuses in which teachers and administrators forced students to sign denunciations against Falun Gong. The CCP then promoted these signatures through state-run media and presented them to the United Nations as evidence of "the people's will" to suppress Falun Gong.[75]

Just 12 days after the campaign was launched in Beijing, China Central Television (CCTV) broadcast the "Tiananmen self-immolation" hoax on January 23, 2001, which went hand in hand with the Communist Party's push to escalate the persecution of Falun Gong. The campaign was then promoted through the education system across the country.

At an elementary school in Liaoning Province in March 2001, over a thousand students were handed a red flyer from the school and told to show it to their parents. The flyer made six points: "Uphold Science, Refuse Flyers [about Falun Gong]," etc.

Three days later, the school halted all classes and started the signature drive. All the students were told to stand in a line. After they were counted, the students were then told to walk to the tables and sign their names. Seven or eight teachers stood by the tables to monitor them.[76]

Qu Mingjun, an eight-year-old girl, wrote this to Minghui: "The other day, our teacher at school told us that we all should sign in support of the Anti-Falun Gong movement. I refused to sign. We were looking for opportunities to escape, but our teacher stood in front of us the whole time. So, I was forced to sign my name. I felt like crying when I got home. I am writing this letter to invalidate my signature."[77]

In addition to the students, school staff (including retirees) were also required to sign under threat of "expulsion from their position and detention in a labor re-education camp."[78]

Two months into the signature campaign, the CACA delegation brought more than 1.5 million signatures to the United Nations' Human Rights Conference in Geneva in March 2001, claiming that China's human rights were "at their best" and that these signatures reflected the "the wish of the Chinese people."[79]

§§3.1.1 CACA Behind Brainwashing Campaigns

CACA was created to motivate people on all social levels to join the movement to criticize Falun Gong and pressure Falun Gong practitioners to renounce their faith.

Wang Yusheng, the deputy director and secretary general of CACA, claimed in 2003, "Since CACA was founded in November 2000, it has held nearly one thousand exhibits and propaganda activities around the country and hosted more than a thousand conferences and forums. It has also established the 'China anti-cult website' and produced more than 20 films and 400,000 books."[80]

The association also compiled textbooks that slander Falun Gong and incorporated them into the "Nine-Year Compulsory Primary School Experimental Textbook" with the Tiananmen self-immolation hoax as the core of the anti-Falun Gong propaganda.

§§3.1.2 Brainwashing Starts in Elementary School

Thoughts and Moral Education (tenth volume) is a textbook for elementary schools printed in November 2003, for the third time, by People's Education House. It highlighted the self-immolation hoax as a case study and promoted hatred of Falun Gong.[81] Below is a translated excerpt of the text:

Read the following story and talk about your thoughts.

She was a beloved, beautiful girl. Many of her classmates called her 'Sweetheart.' But when her mother became obsessed with Falun Gong, her misfortune began.

Although little Siying is no longer with us, her heartbreaking scream, 'Uncle, save me!' still echoes in our ears. This 12-year-old girl paid the price of a disfigured face and burnt hands, and finally realized the truth of the cult. Her words, "Mom lied to me," is her denunciation of blood and tears against Falun Gong. But who deceived her mother? It was Li Hongzhi and the crooked lies of Falun Gong!

§§3.1.3 Other Forms of Brainwashing

To justify the persecution of Falun Gong, many other propaganda and brainwashing activities of unprecedented depth and breadth were designed and implemented.

At the Shengli Oilfield in Shandong Province, the CACA sponsored dramatic performances defaming Falun Gong and broadcast them on TV and forced teachers to compile songs smearing Falun Gong for schoolchildren to sing.

On October 15, 2003, the association offered prizes in a questionnaire contest designed to smear Falun Gong and published the answers in the *Shenli Daily* newspaper.

The association also directed teachers and students to write articles to smear Falun Gong and advocated a student movement to "say no to cults" in 2002. They selected 208 articles out of the 1,775 submitted and held a presentation that was compiled into a collection called "The Sunlight Bud," the first nationally published collection of "anti-cult" works.[82]

In Hebei Province, *Yanzhao Evening Post* published a full page of articles selected from the "Hebei Province Anti-Cult Award Winning Articles," sponsored by the Hebei Province 610 Office on November 17, 2004.

In an article entitled "The Faded and Fallen Leaves in the Rain" by Wang Nan from Handan Technology High School, the author claimed his mother had divorced his father because she practiced Falun Gong. According to the article, the day following the divorce decree, the mother supposedly committed suicide along with several other female practitioners by cutting their stomachs open.

When local Falun Gong practitioners contacted the newspaper and asked whether the article had been investigated and its authenticity verified, the person who answered the phone replied, "These articles are not ours. The provincial 610 Office arranged to have a full page for their own publications."[83]

§3.2 Early Deaths

Some children of Falun Gong practitioners died after they were forcibly separated from their parents and deprived of basic conditions for survival, and some passed away from the abuses they suffered themselves for practicing Falun Gong.

Case 1: Four-Year-Old Girl Traumatized and Dies[84]

When Wang Shujie was only two, she witnessed the police arrest her parents several times in front her. During a police raid on December 3, 2000, the officer yelled at her father and slapped his face with a book. Shujie passed out from the shock and fear.

After she came to, she had a fever and was sweating. She shook her head back and forth due to severe pain in her head. She was restless and uneasy and banged her head against the wall. The police went to Shujie's home over and over again to arrest her family members. When her father was detained, she held a picture of herself with her father and cried bitterly.

The police returned in less than a year, wielding batons, to arrest Shujie's parents again. She was awakened after having fallen asleep minutes before and shouted, "Daddy, Mommy, I won't let you go!"

The repeated mental trauma and chronic fear led to a deterioration in her health, and she had difficulty eating and sleeping. For two years, she simply didn't grow.

When Shujie was four, the doctor found a benign growth in her brain. Shortly after she was operated on, however, she stopped breathing and died in July 2002.

Case 2: Fourteen-Year-Old Honor Student Dies[85]

Zhang Cheng started practicing Falun Dafa in 1994 with her father. After the persecution began, her father went to Beijing to appeal for the right to practice.

The police barged into their home and took away almost everything. Zhang Cheng was constantly harassed, and she soon developed leukemia. She passed away in February 2001.

Case 3: Father Exiled, Mother Persecuted to Death, Son Dies[86]

Sun Feng was in the sixth grade and his parents both practiced Falun Gong. After the persecution started, his dad, Mr. Sun Hongchang, had to leave home in 2000 to avoid arrest. His mother, Ms. Wang Xiuxia, went to Beijing to protest and was arrested numerous times. She died as a result of torture 16 days after she was arrested again on May 19, 2003. Her family wasn't even allowed to see her body, because the police immediately put her in a coffin and buried her.

Sun Feng was only 12 at that time. He couldn't accept the fact that his mother had died. He not only had to endure the pain of losing his mother but also had to worry about his father. He was scared every day, which adversely affected him mentally. He lived with his relatives and rarely spoke.

His sorrow and fear took a toll on his health in late 2004. He frequently fainted and was rushed to Shenyang Medical University for emergency treatment. He seemed to stabilize only after he was given a blood transfusion. Lonely and greatly missing his parents, Sun Feng passed away on March 26, 2006. He was 14 years old.

Case 4: Eighteen-Year-Old Girl Expelled from School, Raped by a Thug, Dies from Tuberculosis after Being Homeless[87]

Ms. Zhang Yichao, a vivacious and cheerful girl deeply loved by her parents, relatives, and friends was expelled from school because both of her parents practiced Falun Gong and she refused to sign an anti-Falun Gong petition.

After her parents' company intervened, the school agreed to let her return. However, the school's Party secretary Meng Xianmin called her in for a conversation every week. They demanded that she write a report each week and distance herself from Falun Gong and her parents. During the time when both of her parents were detained, a group of children who hated Falun Gong due to the propaganda broke the door and several windows in her home. Yichao, who was at home alone, was scared to death.

A few months later, both of her parents were sent to forced labor camps and Yichao was permanently expelled from school. At the age of 15, she was forced to live away from home and moved frequently to avoid the constant harassment by the authorities.

One night, a thug smashed the window, broke into her room, and raped her. Yichao later contracted tuberculosis when she was doing odd jobs. She did not have any money to see a doctor and was unwilling to go home. On the morning of April 6, 2005, she died in a hospital.

She was 18 years old. Eight months after Yichao passed away, on December 17, 2005, her mother Ms. Fu Guiying also died as a result of the persecution.[88]

§3.3 Orphaned

"I am nearly 10 years old. My mother was tortured to death in 2001 because she practiced Falun Gong, and I don't even know what she looked like. Now I have no mother. My father Xiao Sixian is in your prison. I am now an orphan with no one to take care of me. My father has not done anything wrong. Everyone says he is a good man. Please, stop persecuting him.

"My teacher told me that prisons are where bad people are locked up. Why is my father in prison, even though he does not steal, and everyone in school likes him and says he is a good teacher? Did my teacher lie to me, or are you deceiving people?"

– Xiao Sixian's daughter Xiao Xixi, in a letter to officials at Duyun Prison, Guizhou Province

Many children became orphans after their parents were tortured to death or given lengthy sentences, and they had to live with their relatives or be sent to an orphanage.

Case 1: Mr. Wang Kemin's Son Orphaned[89]

Mr. Wang Kemin was a middle school teacher in Daqing City, Heilongjiang Province. His wife died in a car accident soon after he was arrested and sent to a forced labor camp in 2000. Three years later, he was arrested again while relocating frequently to avoid the persecution. He passed away the very day he was arrested. His son, who was nine years old, became an orphan.

Case 2: Young Boy Loses His Mom, Forced to Quit School to Help Make Ends Meet[90]

Wang Defu's mother, Ms. Zhang Haiyan, went to Beijing to appeal for Falun Gong in 2001, when he was nine years old. She was arrested and sent to Masanjia Forced Labor Camp for two years. She was tortured and eventually died in 2004. His mother's death crushed him. He cried, "I'll never see my mommy again!"

Defu lived with his family in a run-down mud brick house with a damaged roof, which they couldn't afford to fix. Ms. Zhang had been the family's main breadwinner, and her death left the family in dire financial straits. Defu had to quit school to work with his father as a shepherd to make ends meet.

Case 3: Mother Tortured to Death, Piao Yonghe's Grandmother Works 11 Hours a Day to Pay for His Education[91]

"I heard the lotus flowers in Beishan Park are now in full bloom. After dinner, I was in a hurry to ask mom to take me to see them..." Piao Yonghe wrote in an essay after his mother, Ms. Cui Zhengshu, passed away after being tortured in Heizuizi Women's Labor Camp.

Ms. Cui was arrested in March 2002 and given three years of forced labor for printing informational materials about Falun Gong. Because Yonghe's father was having trouble finding a job because he also practices Falun Gong, his seventy-three-year-old grandmother worked 11 hours a day to make 400 yuan per month to pay for his schooling.

Case 4: The Plight of Orphan Wu Yingqi[92]

Shortly after Wu Yingqi lost his mother in a car accident, his father Mr. Wu Yueqing was arrested in December 2001 and sentenced to 12 years for making informational materials about Falun Gong.

Mr. Wu was severely tortured and contracted tuberculosis. He was sent home when he was near death and passed away on December 23, 2007.

Yingqi lived with his aunt Ms. Wu Yuexia when his father was imprisoned, but he was then sent to the local orphanage after his aunt was also arrested and sent to the labor camp for her faith in Falun Gong.

Case 5: Family Reunited Only to be Torn Apart Again[93]

From the time he was three years old, Shao Linyao watched the police take his parents away again and again. He was lonely, terrified and sad because he missed his family.

After his mother Ms. Mu Ping was released on bail after nearly three years of torture in the labor camp, Linyao never left her side, fearing he would lose her again. He didn't want to go to bed until his mother came home after having gone out. He just sat there until she came home. He said in tears, "I was so afraid that you'd been arrested again by the bad people. If you don't come back, I can't calm down." But little did Linyao know that his dad, Mr. Shao Hui, had already been persecuted to death in 2002. Ms. Mu was arrested again in 2006 and sentenced to seven years in prison.

After his mother's arrest, Linyao lived with his grandparents, although their health was deteriorating and their lives were difficult.

§3.4 Families Separated

Case 1: Xiaolong's Bitter Childhood[94]

Since he was seven years old, Zhang Xiaolong had to live with his grandparents, because his parents Mr. Zhang Chuanzheng and Ms. Guo Xiuhong were forced to live away from home to avoid persecution. The couple was arrested in 2002 and sentenced to ten years in prison a year later.

Xiaolong became withdrawn and couldn't understand why his parents were being persecuted. He was dealt another heavy blow when his grandfather passed away. Xiaolong didn't eat for two days and couldn't stop crying. He and his grandmother struggled to make ends meet while their home was falling apart with cracks and leaks everywhere.

Case 2: Five-Year-Old: "I Miss My Mommy—I Want My Mommy and Daddy Back!"[95]

Mingyuan went with his grandmother to the detention center many times to seek his mother's release, but they were unsuccessful.

When Sun Mingyuan heard that his mother had been tortured and was in critical condition, the five-year-old went with his grandmother to seek her release. He held up a board that said:

> *My name is Sun Mingyuan and I am five years old. My daddy was illegally sentenced to 12 years in prison because he practices Falun Gong. Officers from the Dehui Police Station arrested my mommy on December 14, 2004. Now she has been on a hunger strike for 48 days and is in critical condition. I am lonely, helpless, and separated from my parents. Please help me. I miss my mommy. I want my mommy back and I want my daddy back.*

Case 3: A Letter from a Mother Imprisoned for Her Faith[96]

Ms. Liu Xinying, a nurse and Falun Gong practitioner in Dalian, is serving five and a half years in prison for her faith in Falun Gong. Her arrest[97] came only a few months after her husband, Mr. Qu Hui, passed away after living as a tetraplegic confined to his bed for 13 years after being tortured in a forced labor camp. He was in constant pain, and Ms. Liu took care of him day and night until he passed away on February 9, 2014, while taking care of their teenage daughter.

With Ms. Liu in prison, her daughter, a minor, was left at home by herself. Below is a letter Ms. Liu wrote to her daughter from prison on her 17th birthday.

> *Xinxin:*
>
> *My most darling baby girl, thank you for coming to our family like an angel, and thank you for all the joy you have brought us! ... On your 17th birthday, I'm sending you best wishes from afar. I hope that your life will be filled with happiness and sunshine. I wish you safety during the time I'm away. I hope that, after this*

period of separation, both of us will shine with a pure glow of being reborn like phoenixes rising from the ashes.

There are so many things I want to tell you that I don't know where to start. ...For 13 years, you witnessed the tremendous sufferings of your dad after he became disabled from torture. You were young and had many questions. You once asked me, "Other kids' daddies can stand. Why does my daddy have to stay in bed?" Your question made me determined to seek justice for your dad because I don't want your innocent mind to be overshadowed by the darkness of our society.

Mom has always thought that education is very important. I wish that after you grow up, you can be a good person—good to other people and good for society.

You cannot change who you are as a person because of your dad's suffering. Because after a person is born, he is given responsibilities to shoulder. This is not something that can be changed or denied.

...

For a society or a nation to prosper, an abundance of materials or wealth are not enough. It needs even more the solid foundation of people's morality and kindness. In that regard, we are still playing a positive role and contributing to society.

It is a traditional value that families are the bedrock of society. The stability of each family ensures the stability of society. But now, our family has fallen apart. The day your dad died, the family that I had spent so much time and effort to bring together fell apart. ...

Thank you for being with me and consoling me during that period, especially when your dad died and I was crying so hard holding his hands. "Don't cry, Mom. You've done your best," you said to me.

Only seven months after your dad left us, I was arrested again and sentenced to five and a half years in prison, leaving you at home alone. ... My heart bleeds whenever I think of this. ... I barely hung on to life by a thread, a thread of hope, faith, and the sense of responsibility. I didn't want you to become an orphan or your grandfather to lose his daughter after losing his companion. I couldn't let my family and friends who love me so much lose me. I didn't want to become the next tragedy myself or add one more sin to the perpetrators. With strong faith, I survived.

Now you are in your last year in high school, and you will take the college entrance exam next year. I hope you can take it seriously and study hard. ...This summer when you came to visit me, I felt very happy to see you, calm and composed. You said to me, "Mom, everything you've taught me is helping me to do well everything in front of me now. Don't worry about me." ...

Thank everyone who has helped you while I'm away. May happiness and good luck be with these good-hearted people always!

Love you, Mom

September 20, 2015

§3.5 Driven Insane

Many children suffered mental collapse when the trauma and pain of the persecution exceeded their limits.

Case 1: Teenage Girl Driven Insane after Being Forced to Watch Parents Tortured by Police[98]

When she was 16, Yuanyuan was forced to watch her parents Mr. Hou Guozhong and Ms. Cheng Xiuhuan being tortured at the police station for practicing Falun Gong. The officers beat the couple; tied them to a "tiger bench" torture device; stretched their arms, legs, and heads at the same time; and suspended them with their hands tied behind their backs.

The police also repeatedly force-fed bottles of mustard oil into their noses and mouths and then covered their heads with several heavy-duty plastic bags. After they passed out, the police poured cold water on them to revive them. Sheng Xiaojiang, the deputy police chief, often shouted while directing the torture, "Beat them to death! It's fine to beat them to death!"

Yuanyuan was traumatized by the experience.

After she was released, the police often forced Yuanyuan to stand at the entrance of their apartment building on hot summer days without moving for hours. They threatened to beat her parents if she dared to move. Fearing that her parents would suffer more torture, Yuanyuan stood still until her feet became swollen and turned purple.

The fear, anxiety, and mental trauma took a toll on the teenage girl. Once an outstanding student, she quit school and began to wander about. With no income, she picked food from garbage bins.

After her parents were released, they were devastated to see that their daughter had gone insane. Now 32, Yuanyuan cannot take care of herself and her parents have to watch her at all times.

Case 2: High School Student Persecuted to Mental Collapse for Practicing Falun Gong[99]

Wang Jinghua had always been an outstanding student from elementary school to high school. He excelled academically and was kind to everyone at school. But because he talked to his classmates about Falun Gong, he was constantly harassed and pressured by his teacher, the local police, and agents from the 610 Office to stop practicing Falun Gong.

One of Jinghua's teachers cooperated with the 610 Office agents to search his desk and school bag to see if he had Falun Gong materials. They also forced his parents to sign a guarantee statement to renounce Falun Gong and ordered one of them to be with him all the time at school. His parents, pressured by the authorities, often criticized him. His friends at school also began to distance themselves from Jinghua.

Because Jinghua refused to renounce his faith, the school authorities expelled him. But his parents appealed, and the principal agreed to only suspend him for a year. But when he went back to school a year later, they refused to re-enroll him.

Jinghua eventually suffered a mental collapse in 2006 at the age of 19.

Case 3: Eighteen-Year-Old Tortured to Mental Collapse[100]

Ms. Zhang Conghui, an eighteen-year-old high school student, was expelled from her school because she wrote "Please remember Falun Dafa is good" to a classmate. Conghui felt she had no choice but to go to Tiananmen Square to appeal for justice, only to be arrested and sent to a brainwashing center.

The guards savagely beat her and didn't allow her to sleep for three days. They also shocked her with electric batons and hired someone to monitor her around the clock. When she was released two months later, her hands were covered with bruises, she had a vacant expression, and she acted oddly and appeared confused.

§3.6 Violence and Brutality

Agents of the 610 Office ransacked Jiajia's home in front of her. "We want to destroy your family," they shouted as they put valuables into their own pockets. Jiajia, 6, stood there petrified, clinging to her mother, not daring to say a word. The agents took her with her family to the Domestic Security Division, where she witnessed the agents brutalize her parents and grandparents.

Jiajia and her grandmother were released at midnight. Jiajia was still shaking with fear, so her grandmother had to lift her into the car. She was deeply traumatized by the whole experience. Whenever she saw a police officer or police car again, she would get very scared and find a place to hide. "The bad people are coming!" she cried out to her parents.[101] Some children were traumatized when their homes were ransacked or their parents tortured. Some became the targets of violence and brutality themselves.

Case 1: Ten-Year-Old Girl Beaten and Locked in a Metal Cage by Police[102]

Cheng Siying, a ten-year-old elementary school student in Sichuan Province, was reported to the local Domestic Security Division on August 7, 2008, for giving her teacher a copy of a Falun Gong pamphlet. Gou Yongqiong, the head of the Domestic Security Division, and two other officers went to her school and arrested her. Gou also gave every student in the school one yuan to encourage them to turn in Falun Gong practitioners.

The officers slapped Siying in the face, chained her hands and feet, and locked her in a metal cage. The police also arrested her parents that evening and ransacked their home, confiscating their printer and other supplies.

When Siying returned to school four days later, her teacher threw her backpack out of the classroom and didn't let her attend classes. Because her parents' whereabouts were unknown, the young girl had to leave her home to avoid being arrested again.

Case 2: Thirteen-Year-Old Force-Fed for Two Weeks[103]

Chen Si, a middle school student in Chongqing, was arrested while passing out informational materials about Falun Gong in the summer of 2001. Despite her age, the police beat and kicked her.

The police later took her to Geleshan Brainwashing Center and interrogated her for the source of the materials. When Si went on a hunger strike to protest the arbitrary detention, she was force-fed for two weeks.

The police also posted Si's photo in the newspaper in order to identify her. They tricked her father into going to the brainwashing center but didn't let him see her. After the new semester began, the local 610 Office didn't let her return to school because she didn't give up practicing Falun Gong.

Case 3: Thirteen-Year-Old Boy Beaten by Police When He Went to the Public Security Bureau to Look for His Mother[104]

Thirteen-year-old Sheng Wei carried his three-year-old sister Yangyang, took a bus, and went to the police station to look for his mother Ms. Yang Zhonghong, who was arrested a month earlier for talking to people about Falun Gong. The police responded by hitting and kicking him and stepping on his face. Wei's face was injured, his ears started to ring, and the sleeve of his sweater was torn. He passed out.

When the police took Wei home in a police car, an officer grabbed Wei by the hair and yanked out a fistful, cursing at the young boy. In great pain, Wei said, "I have no mother now, and I cannot find my father. There is no one to take care of us, and we have no food at home, yet you still hit me. I don't feel like living anymore."

Case 4: Sixth Grader Beaten at School[105]

After the procuratorate twice returned the case against Mr. You Haijun for his faith in Falun Gong, the police harassed his sixth-grade daughter You Qing at school and forced her to report her father's "crime." The thirteen-year-old girl was so terrified by the police that her legs kept shaking and she was unable to speak for several days. After several failed attempts to extract information from Qing, the police ordered her math teacher Chen Xiuling to beat her.

During math class, Chen always told Qing to stand up and answer questions. When she couldn't answer, Chen would hit her with a pointer, slap her in the face, or kick her with her high heels in front of the other students, many of whom were horrified. Qing began to resist going to school. When it was time to go to school, she began to shiver and dared not to go. She almost committed suicide out of fear.

Case 5: Officer Points Gun at Fourteen-Year-Old Girl: "Keep Crying and I'll Execute You!"[106]

Ms. Wang Airong's daughter ran out of their home after the police as they arrested her mother and were about to take her to the police station. The officers shoved the forteen-year-old girl and hit her in the ribs. The girl bit the officer. He then grabbed her collar and threw her into the air. She landed on the ground. Despite the intense pain, the girl stood up and ran to the police. Crying hard, she begged them to let go of her mother. The officer took out a gun, pointed it at her, and said, "Keep crying and I'll execute you!" Then they got into the car and left. For a long time, the girl had a hard time breathing because of the pain in her ribs and chest.

§3.7 Detention

After my parents were arrested, I was left at home with my eleven-year-old sister and our seventy-year-old grandpa who had difficulty walking. There was no one to take care of us, so we stayed with my aunt and asked for her help.

In early 2001, several of my aunts were also arrested and sent to a brainwashing center for practicing Falun Gong. I was four years old that year. Because I was too young and no one could take care of me at home, I was taken to the brainwashing center with my aunts. Every day, I saw the police officers and other thugs beat Falun Gong practitioners after they got drunk. I was so scared. I hid in the arms of one of my aunts and dared not watch. I cried every day, wondering where my parents went.

Above is Mr. Zhao Haijun's daughter's recollection of her family's suffering.[107] Many children, from toddlers to teenagers, were arrested with their parents and kept in detention facilities for days or even weeks. Some were even taken to labor camps.

Case 1: The Eight-Month-Old Prisoner[108]

Eight-month-old Tianci was sound asleep when several officers broke into his home and arrested his mother Ms. Liu Nana for her faith in Falun Gong.

Both mother and son were forced into a police car and taken to an unknown place. That same night, ten people in Tianci's extended family, including two of his toddler-aged cousins, were also arrested and taken to the same location.

Tianci was put in the same room with his mother. Unaware of his family's dire situation, the little boy had a smile on his face and kept trying to get out of the room to play. Three days later, the police released Ms. Liu and Tianci, having failed to get any information from her.

Before leaving, Ms. Liu asked to see her parents-in-law. She couldn't help but cry upon seeing her father-in-law tied to an interrogation chair. She had no idea that her own parents and brother had also been arrested.

Case 2: One-Year-Old Detained for More Than a Year in a Brainwashing Center[109]

When Guo Yuetong was one year old, she was arrested with her mother and held in a brainwashing center for more than a year. Yuetong's mother, Ms. Liu Aihua, was persecuted for not renouncing her faith in Falun Gong.

In the brainwashing center, Yuetong witnessed her mother being tortured, including being beaten, force-fed and shocked with electric batons. Every time the guards tortured her mother, Yuetong was so scared that she hid in the corner and cried. When no guards were around, little Yuetong just stood by the bars of the cell and looked out.

She was already three years old when she was allowed to go home. Yet she was arrested three years later and detained with her mother again.

Case 3: Ten-Year-Old Kept at a Brainwashing Center for Three Weeks Before Being Sent to a Nursing Home[110]

Li Ying was only ten years old when she was arrested with her mother Ms. Chen Shulan in September 2002. While Ying was taken to a brainwashing center, her mother was later sentenced to seven and a half years in prison. The authorities attempted to force Ying to give up practicing Falun Gong through intimidation and brainwashing. When she refused, they didn't let her sleep at night.

To be allowed to go back to school, the young girl gave in and signed her name on a statement prepared by the authorities. However, she still had no freedom. She was taken to school during the day and returned to the brainwashing center after school. She was finally allowed to leave the brainwashing center three weeks later. With her mother still in prison and five of her family members having died as a result of the persecution, including her grandparents, two uncles and an aunt, Ying lived with her teachers for three months before being sent to a nursing home. She was kept there for 25 months and was not given enough food and confined under constant surveillance. After Ying was finally released, she quit school and did odd jobs to survive.

Case 4: Sixteen-Year-Old Imprisoned in a Labor Camp for Two Years[111]

Wang Jing, cousin of the above-mentioned Wang Shujie who died from mental trauma at the age of four, was forced to leave school and banned from applying to college because she and her parents practiced Falun Gong. Jing was arrested and taken to a detention facility when she went to Beijing to appeal for Falun Gong in March 2001. When she turned 16, she was sent to a forced labor camp for two years. She was forced to do sewing work and was deprived of sleep.

§3.8 Rape

While many female Falun Gong practitioners were raped by the police officers or prison guards, some practitioners' daughters were also subjected to sexual assaults or rape during the time their parents were held in custody with no one to look after them.[112]

Case 1: Thirteen-Year-Old Raped While Mother Imprisoned

Lian (alias), a Falun Gong practitioner in Harbin, Heilongjiang Province, was arrested in May 2000 when she went to Beijing to appeal for her faith. While she was detained, her son and daughter were left attended. The forteen-year-old boy drowned. Shortly after Lian was released, she was arrested again in August 2001. When her thirteen-year-old daughter was left at home alone, a thug broke into her room and raped her.

Case 2: Parents Tortured to Death, Nine-Year-Old Raped in Mental Hospital

Ms. Liu from Jilin Province was arrested in the summer of 2002 when she went to Beijing to appeal for Falun Gong. She was taken to Changping Mental Hospital, which was full of police officers and thugs, most holding leather belts to beat Falun Gong practitioners. During the three nights Ms. Liu was held in the mental hospital, three thugs came to her room and gang-raped a nine-year-old girl, whose parents were tortured to death in the mental hospital for practicing Falun Gong. "Her screams were appalling and soul-breaking, but no one in the room dared to say a word."

Chapter 4: Torture Methods

The police brought the mustard oil, which was imported from Japan, in the middle of the night. With a large syringe, they injected the mustard oil into my nose. I immediately felt a very intense, scorching pain in my chest. I felt as if my internal organs were shaking. I couldn't open my eyes. My head was exploding. I was going crazy. Words can't describe how painful it was.

After I lost consciousness, the police poured cold water on me to wake me up. Then they again force-fed me with the mustard oil until I passed out again. They repeated the torture several times. While force-feeding me with mustard oil, one officer said to me, 'Do you know Jiang Pai? This was what we did to her. She was even put in an iron chair that was plugged into electricity while being force-fed mustard oil.'"

Above, Ms. Liu Ying, a nurse from Daqing city, describes her experience of being force-fed with mustard oil in a detention center. The other practitioner, Ms. Jiang Pai, died from the complications of force-feedings on June 28, 2007. She was 34.[113]

Almost every Falun Gong practitioner who has been held in the CCP's detention facilities can describe at least one form of torture they were subjected to. In addition to brainwashing, coercion, and financial devastation, torture is a main tactic used by the communist authorities to try to force Falun Gong practitioners to renounce their faith.

From everyday objects such as toothbrushes to torture instruments such as the tiger bench, from cold temperatures to loud noises, from force-feeding to sexual humiliation, from tying the victim in painful positions to prolonged isolation, over one hundred methods of torture have been described by Falun Gong practitioners released from Chinese police stations, detention centers, or prisons. Such torture not only causes severe physical harm to the practitioners but also induces long-lasting emotional trauma.

§4.1 Beating

"Beating Falun Gong practitioners to death is nothing and will be counted as suicide or death from illnesses. You should show absolutely no pity, especially toward those who refuse to 'reform.' The Party and government are behind you! So, carry out this order without any reservation!"

Above is what the guards at Duyun Prison, Guizhou Province, said to inmates to encourage them to use all types of mental and physical methods to torture Falun Gong practitioners.[114]

§§4.1.1 Beating with Bare Hands

Beating is one of the most common forms of torture used on Falun Gong practitioners. The perpetrator often targets the victim's sensitive parts, such as the nose, eyes, or genitals. Some practitioners were beaten for a long period of time or with excessive force. One practitioner reported being slapped in the face over 500 times.

Case 1: Death After Nine Months of Mistreatment

To deprive Mr. Ding Lihong of sleep, guards at Shijiazhuang Brainwashing Center in Hebei Province hit his head with anything they could find, struck his legs, twisted his ears, and pulled on his eyelids. In particular, guard Zhao Juyong pinched his eyeballs and gouged his eyes. Within nine months, Mr. Ding died due to mistreatment. He was 36.[115]

Case 2: Brutality Against Women

Ms. Wang Xiuyuan from Shenyang City, Liaoning Province, was arrested on April 19, 2002 and taken to Longshan Forced Labor Camp for two years. In July 2002, Ms. Wang was kicked in the chest by a guard and landed four meters away. When she stood up, the guard slapped her, causing blood to ooze from her nose and the corner of her eye. The guard kicked her again, making her fall over and hit a heating pipe, which caused a bleeding head wound.[116]

Ms. Jia Shuying was sentenced to five years in prison in 2002. In Heilongjiang Province, she was subjected to various tortures aimed at forcing her to give up her faith.

"Prison guard Xiao Lin was famous for his cruelty. All the inmates were scared just to see him. One time, he dragged me into a room and began to slap me in the face. When he got tired, he sat down on a chair. He rested his hands and kicked me. The pain was even more intense. He ended up slapping me in the face over one hundred times. When another guard present thought it was too much and wanted to take me out of there, Xiao stomped on me. I couldn't breathe. I fell against the wall and lost consciousness.

"I had excruciating pain on the right side of my chest for over six months. I had to breathe very shallowly and slowly. Sometimes the pain was so intense that it made me sweat. At night, I couldn't sleep because of the pain. It was really killing me. I later realized that Xiao had broken a rib when he kicked me."[117]

§§4.1.2 Beating with Objects

Chinese prisons use everyday items that one would least expect to torture people. For example, a watermelon was used to hit a Falun Gong practitioner on the head, spoons and coins to scrape a practitioner's ribcage, and a hanger to strike someone in the throat.

In other words, if it inflicts harm, any object, such as metal, plastic, leather, rubber, wood, or paper, can be used as an instrument of torture.

In one case, the police put a book on the practitioner's abdomen and then whipped the book with a rubber tube. The beating was more than enough to cause internal injuries, but the book provided enough padding that no external injuries were visible.

Case 1: Chinese Medicine Doctor Tortured in Over a Hundred Ways

Mr. Shao Chengluo, 68, a doctor of Chinese medicine, was sentenced to a seven-year term at Shandong Prison in 2006. He was tortured in over a hundred different ways, such as being stabbed with a needle, having his ribs scraped with toothbrushes or wooden sticks, and a having toothbrush twisted between his fingers.

One time, the guards tied Mr. Shao's hands and legs together and placed him on an upside-down stool. They then kicked the stool out from under him.

The guards also instigated inmates to pull out his eyebrows and whiskers. They put salt on his wounds and burned his knees and ankles with a hot iron. In an attempt to force-feed him, they pried open his mouth with a screwdriver and damaged his teeth.

Mr. Shao had injuries all over his body, including a deformed spine, broken bones in his fingers and toes, and injuries to his neck, ribs, arms, and abdomen. His muscles atrophied, his weight dropped below 100 pounds, and he can no longer straighten the fingers of his left hand.[118]

Case 2: Woman Beaten with a Roll of Newspaper

Ms. Geng Li was arrested and taken to the Xiheying Town Police Station in 2007. At least four police officers hit her mouth, face, head, and arms with rolls of newspaper. When the paper rolls wore out, they made new ones and continued. Her face and her mouth were severely swollen.

They then shocked her with electric batons on her arms and back and tried to force her to kneel down. When she refused to comply, they kicked her legs until she could no longer stand.

At one point, an officer stepped on one of her legs, while another hit her knees with a rubber stick. They then pulled her up and hit her buttocks. One policeman also used a rubber stick to repeatedly hit her legs, feet, arms, and shoulders. The beating left her covered in purple bruises.[119]

Case 3: Woman Whipped with Rubber Hose

Ms. Zhu Xiumin from Daqing City, Heilongjiang Province, once recounted how the police beat her with a rubber hose after she was arrested for intercepting cable TV signals and broadcasting videos about the persecution of Falun Gong:[120]

The two officers who had arrested me started to beat and interrogate me. One of them took off my shoes and socks and made me stand on the cement barefoot. My calves were bound to the legs of the metal chair with chains. My arms were shackled to either side of the chair and I was handcuffed.

The officer held a piece of rubber hose twisted into three sections and whipped the backs of my legs. He whipped and shouted, "I will focus on your legs until the tips of your toes turn blue and black and then fall off." He kept lashing me non-stop. Because my legs were bound, I could not move.

I could not help but cry out. It hurt so much. He laughed at my pain and swore at me, using foul language. From then on, I did not utter a sound. He hit me with all his might for half a day and was astonished to see that I did not have any reaction or even an expression on my face. He loosened the chains a little and then continued to whip me again. No matter how hard he hit me, I still did not make a sound, and there was no expression on my face. I kept watching him as he whipped me, and he gradually stopped.

I nearly fainted from the pain. I could not escape. Words cannot describe the pain. Time crept by. Every second was torment, and I hovered between life and death. Death would have been easier. I had but one thought: "I cannot submit to them. I will not bow to them nor let them take pleasure in my suffering."

§4.2 Force-Feeding

Tube feeding is done by inserting a tube into the nose, up through the nasal cavity, and down the esophagus to the stomach. A liquid nutrient is then forced through the tube. What is normally a life-saving medical treatment has been used by the Chinese Communist Party to persecute Falun Gong practitioners who go on hunger strikes in detention centers, labor camps, and prisons.

Because they aren't medically trained, prison guards and inmates often make mistakes when they force-feed practitioners, such as inserting the tube into the victim's lungs. All it takes is a small mistake using this method to kill someone.

To increase the practitioners' suffering, the perpetrators sometimes force-feed practitioners with concentrated salt water or very spicy water, scalding food, feces, or psychiatric or toxic drugs. Some practitioners held long-term hunger strikes as a last resort to protest the persecution. As a result, they were force-fed for years while they were imprisoned.

In some cases, force-feeding is combined with other forms of torture, such as exposing practitioners to extreme light or heat or forcing them to watch propaganda videos attacking Falun Gong. Some were tied to a bed for months and developed bed sores.

Case 1: Woman Dies from Force-Feeding[121]

Ms. Sun Lianxia from Dalian City, Liaoning Province, was arrested when she went to Beijing to protest the persecution of Falun Gong in the autumn of 2000. At Dalian Forced Labor Camp, she went on a hunger strike and was force-fed by the guards and criminal inmates.

Her nasal cavity and esophageal mucosa were injured, and her nostril bled when the feeding tube was inserted. Because her nostril was blocked, she had to breathe through her mouth. She could not stop coughing up phlegm from her throat and inflamed esophagus. She vomited blood, which made force-feeding difficult.

In the last two hours of her life, with Ms. Sun in critical condition, the force-feeding did not stop. She passed away on January 16, 2001, at the age of 50.

Case 2: Engineer Survives Daily Force-Feeding During Five-Year Imprisonment[122]

Mr. Qu Yanlai, an energy engineer, embarked on a hunger strike the first day he was arrested in September 2002. He was force-fed during the five years he served time at Tilanqiao Prison in Shanghai.

"The first time the doctor inserted the feeding tube into my stomach, it felt like a fiery snake was drilling into my body. It was excruciating," Mr. Qu said.

In their attempt to force him to give up his hunger strike, the guards and doctors used all kinds of ways to torture him, such as using a thick feeding tube, pulling the feeding tube back and forth during force-feeding, or limiting the amount of food to starve him. Without enough nutrients, he felt drowsy and developed a constant pain around his heart and liver.

When he was treated in the prison hospital for gastric hemorrhaging, the inmates tied him tightly to the bed, sometimes with a tire underneath him or after elevating the bed. Many of his blood vessels broke as a result of being tied to the bed in this manner for several months.

The prison doctor added potassium chloride to his infusions, which stimulated his blood vessels and caused him enormous pain.

During his hospitalization, the inmates slowed the rate of the infusion. Three bottles that normally emptied in three hours was extended to 19 hours. His arms usually swelled badly after each infusion.

Recalling the torture, Mr. Qu said, "It was extremely painful to be tied to the bed with five ropes. The torment was beyond words. Every minute and every second was difficult to endure. But I thought to myself, 'Doesn't a day only have 24 hours?! Each hour has 60 minutes, and each minute has 60 seconds.' I asked myself, 'Can you endure one more second? No problem! Then I will just endure it second by second until the persecution ends.'"

§4.3 Stressful Positions

Some practitioners were forced to maintain painful physical positions for long periods of time, such as standing, holding up one's arm or leg, sitting on a small stool, being hung up by the wrists, being tied in a spread-eagle position, or having the hands and feet chained together.

§§4.3.1 Sitting on a Small Stool

Sitting on a small stool is a widely used form of torture in Chinese labor camps and prisons. At first sight, it may appear inconsequential. But when a person is required to sit on it for prolonged periods of time, with the legs forced together and hands on the knees, without looking around, moving or talking, it is a very cruel form of torture. One practitioner who experienced the torture said: "That kind of pain is beyond description. It makes a single day feel like a year and that living is worse than death."

Within an hour of sitting on the stool, one feels discomfort followed by pain. The pain becomes excruciating, like countless arrows piercing through the lower body and worms gnawing on the bones. Some practitioners have been forced to sit on this small stool every day for months, a year, or even two years. Some have developed open, bleeding, festering wounds on their buttocks—some with their bones protruding.

If the practitioner moves at all, the inmates on guard use a copper wire to poke the practitioner's back; some practitioners have wounds all over their backs, like the holes in a sieve.[123]

§§4.3.2 Tying with Ropes at Xuchang Labor Camp

At Xuchang Labor Camp in Henan Province, one of the commonly used tortures was tying people up with ropes.

Practitioners who have been subjected to this torture described it this way: The perpetrators first tie a rope around one's arms a few times, then push the arms behind the back, and finally bring the rope over the shoulders. The more the rope is tightened, the higher the arms are pulled up behind the body. When the ropes are over-tightened, the practitioner can't even stand up. The practitioner is in excruciating pain, and it only takes a few minutes to disable a person in this manner. When the rope is removed, the bones in one's arms feel like they are breaking, and afterwards the arms are numb for a long period of time.

No regular inmate can survive this torture more than twice. However, the guards often used it to torture practitioners, subjecting them to it five to six times. Practitioner Mr. Li Xingcheng from Nanzhao, Nanyang City, underwent the roping torture seven times, leaving his wrists swollen and covered with serious injuries.[124]

§§4.3.3 Woman Dies from the "Straitjacket" Torture

While detained in Shibalihe Forced Labor Camp in Henan Province, Ms. Guan Ge died in a "straitjacket" in 2003. Made of tightly woven canvas, the jacket is put on the victim from the front and tightened behind the back. The sleeves have straps on them and are about 10 inches longer than the victim's arms. The guards cross and tie the victims' arms behind their backs. Then they pull their arms up over their shoulders to the front of their chest, tie up their legs and then hang them up in the air from windows or chairs.

According to Ms. Guan's mother, who saw her body:[125]

> *She had many cuts and bruises. Her eyes were open, and there was blood on her mouth. There was a big bump and deep cuts on her head. Her ears had been hit so hard that they had collapsed. There was a small piece of tissue missing on her left arm, and a large bump on the back of her neck. A three-centimeter-long purple scar was visible on her lower back, and her entire left leg was bruised. Her hands were tightly clenched into fists.*

§§4.3.4 Hands and Feet Chained Together

Another woman, Ms. Wang Kefei, died on December 20, 2001, while in Tiebei Detention Center in Jilin Province.

Because she did the Falun Gong exercises, the guards put heavy shackles on her feet, handcuffed her, and then connected the shackles and cuffs with a short chain, leaving her unable to sit, squat, stand, or lie down. She had to remain curled up at all times. She couldn't eat, drink, or use the toilet by herself. After being restrained this way for a long time, the victim suffers extensive muscle strain, swollen limbs, and insomnia. Most people can only endure the torture for up to 48 hours, but Ms. Wang was restrained this way for 11 days straight.

In order to inflict more pain, the guards ordered her to go up and down the stairs to go to interrogation sessions. She had to toil along a few inches at a time in the long, dark hallway. People could hear the noise of her shackles dragging on the cement floor from far away.[126]

§§4.3.5 Stretching Torture at Notorious Masanjia Labor Camp

In the notorious Masanjia Forced Labor Camp in Liaoning Province, many practitioners were subjected to the following "stretching" torture.

Mr. Cai Chao, 22, had to stand at one end of the bed. His feet were tied to a beam 20 cm above the floor, his thighs were against the headboard, and his upper body was at a 90-degree angle with his hands cuffed and pulled toward the other end of the bed by a rope. If the guards felt that his hands had gone numb, they released him and then repeated the torture 10 minutes later. During that time, the guards also shocked his neck, hands, stomach, and back. They tortured Mr. Cai this way three times over five hours. After he was let down, he could not raise his arms or stand up, and it took him a month and a half to recover.

Mr. Li Hailong was also stretched three times over three and a half hours. Even two months later he could not walk normally.

§§4.3.6 Death Bed

The death bed is a wooden board that the practitioner is tied onto in a spread-eagle position. It gets its name from the fact that the victims aren't released even to sleep, eat, or relieve themselves. This torture is usually combined with force-feeding and other torments.

Ms. Duan Xueqin from Inner Mongolia was restrained on the death bed for such a long period of time that her muscles atrophied and she lost strength. Meanwhile, the guards verbally abused her, spat in her face, poked her arms, hit her breasts and removed her pants to humiliate her. The guards also denied her toilet access.

When Ms. Duan was released from the death bed two weeks later, her body was stiff and she was unable to walk. The inmates had to pinch her to make her walk. Before she recovered her muscle strength, she had to kneel to have a bowel movement (most restrooms in China only have a squat toilet).[127]

§4.4 Sensory Bombardment

When Ms. Zhao Lerong groaned in pain under the baking sun, the guards taped her mouth shut with adhesive and tied her hands. They gloated, "You are a sunflower. You turn whichever way the sun shines."[128]

The authorities came up with forms of torture that targeted practitioners' senses by overloading them with excessive noise, light, heat, or cold.

Some practitioners were force-fed rancid substances, and some had feces smeared on their faces and in their mouths, poured over them, or made to soak in it. Some guards pushed practitioners' heads into latrines or held them in pigsties or other filthy settings.

Other detention facilities use animals and insects, such as ants, wasps, mosquitoes, scorpions, spiders, rats, snakes, and attack dogs to terrorize practitioners. In addition to physiological distress and harm, such sensory bombardment can also inflict extreme mental disorientation and suffering.

§§4.4.1 Extreme Heat

Guards often burn practitioners with open flames, irons, boiling water, and cigarettes. They also force them to stand under the baking sun for long hours or lock them in extremely hot rooms with winter clothes on.

Authorities at the No.3 Detention Center in the Shuangyang District of Changchun City, Jilin Province, tied practitioners to metal chairs and placed 2,000-watt electric heaters below them, which made the chairs unbearably hot. They also put a bright light bulb on each side of the victim's head. This torture went on for a minimum of two hours.[129]

§§4.4.2 Freezing

Exposure to low temperatures for an extended period of time can also lead to serious and permanent injury.

Mr. He Huajiang was tied to a chair in a bathroom and had his mouth sealed tight in December. Guards opened the window to let in the cold as they kept pouring cold water over him, all the while beating him frequently. He died two hours later, at the age of 42.[130]

Ms. Qiu Liying was once left outside in a thin shirt and sandals when it was -20°C (-4°F) for doing the Falun Gong exercises. The guards handcuffed her hands behind her back and hung her up on a tree. Her runny nose formed a meter-long icicle. The flesh on both of her hands cracked open due to the cold, and blood seeped out.[131]

Mr. Yang Baochun was made to stand in the snow barefoot. When he was allowed back in, guards poured hot water over his feet, which soon began to fester. The guards didn't send him to a hospital until it became clear that his life was in danger. Doctors were forced to amputate his right leg.[132]

§§4.4.3 Deafening Noise

Many practitioners have suffered hearing loss after being forced to listen to loud, high-pitched noise for extended periods of time.[133] For example, guards or inmates would place a bucket over a practitioner's head and pound on the bucket, which causes deafening noise and can lead to mental disorientation.

Mr. Liu Peng, a practitioner from Shanghai, was sentenced to five years in prison in 2008. He was held in Tilanqiao Prison in Shanghai. Guard Wang Haocheng ordered inmates to torture him. He was forced to stand facing a wall from 7 a.m. to 9 p.m. They also placed loudspeakers next to his ears in a small room and turned up the volume. He had hearing loss in both ears.

Ms. Mo Qingbo from Nanning City was held in a confinement cell in the Guangxi Women's Forced Labor Camp for refusing to give up Falun Gong. For three months, the guards played wild shrieks and ghostly howls throughout the day and night to deprive her of sleep. When she was let out of the small cell, she appeared mentally disoriented.

§§4.4.4 Assault on the Senses of Smell and Taste

Some guards use human excrement and urine and other foul-smelling and irritating substances to humiliate and torture Falun Gong practitioners. Some stuffed practitioners' mouths with used sanitary pads, rags, unwashed socks, or underwear.

Mr. Liu Ze was deprived of sleep for more than 20 days, beaten, and verbally abused in Zhongba Men's Forced Labor Camp. The perpetrators slammed his head against the wall, resulting in swelling and bruises. They forced him to eat feces. In the end he became mentally disordered and began to eat the feces.[134]

Mr. Liu Quanwang was an employee at the Xiaolinghe Coal Mine in Liaoning Province. When he served a two-year term at Beijing Tuanhe Forced Labor Camp, the guards ordered the inmates to block the toilet drain and had several of them urinate in the bowl. Then the guards forced Mr. Liu's head into the bowl and placed their feet on top, almost suffocating him. When Mr. Liu went on a hunger strike to protest the abuse, the guards force-fed him sewer water with human waste, causing him to vomit uncontrollably.[135]

§§4.4.5 Animal and Insect Bites

During insect and mosquito season, the victim is bound to a chair in a place where mosquitoes and insects are swarming. The victim is subjected to great numbers of bites from these insects while immobilized and unable to scratch the bites or fend off the insects, leaving the victim susceptible to disease carried by the insects.

Because Mr. Xu Yushan refused to give up his belief, a guard at Suihua Forced Labor Camp rubbed sugar water around his genitals and put a large number of ants on the area.

Ms. Jia Haiying from Inner Mongolia was once tied to a tree close to a filthy pigsty on a humid summer evening. She was wearing shorts and a sleeveless shirt, and swarms of mosquitoes and flies soon covered her body. With her hands cuffed, she couldn't move or swat away the bloodthirsty insects. She said the ordeal was simply unbearable.[136]

Other animals used to torture practitioners include snakes, scorpions, wasps, spiders, mice, rabbits, pigs, and attack dogs.[137]

§4.5 Restricting Basic Needs

Some of the torture methods used on Falun Gong practitioners by communist officials are not visible. They include restricting a person's most basic needs, including eating, sleeping, and using the restroom. This torture is usually designed to wear down practitioners' willpower and their capacity for psychological resistance.

§§4.5.1 Food Deprivation

"Mr. Mou Lunhui lost consciousness a total of five times in three days due to brutal beatings by the guards. As if that was not enough, the guards gave him almost nothing to eat during those three days. Ten grains of rice were all he got for three meals each day."

"30 grains of rice for three days" may sound inconceivably cruel, but that is what happened in Xishanping Labor Camp in Chongqing. Many other practitioners detained in the same labor camp as Mr. Mou were also subjected to "hunger therapy." Though they were given a bit more food than Mr. Mou, it was barely enough to subsist on.

When the practitioners became dangerously weak after a period of "hunger therapy,"[138] the guards resumed normal rations to keep them alive. However, before the practitioners were able to fully recover, they were put back on the "hunger therapy."

What happened at Xishanping Labor Camp is not an isolated phenomenon. Many other detention facilities across China have also been known to use food deprivation in their attempts to make practitioners renounce Falun Gong. Many practitioners experienced severe complications as a result of this torture. A practitioner detained in Shanghai Women's Prison lost about 60 pounds in six months. She was so hungry that she ate rotten cabbage leaves that she found in a trash can. Even that was soon taken away when the guards removed the trash can after discovering that she had found a source of food.

Limiting mealtimes is another way to reduce practitioners' food consumption. Practitioners detained in Wumaping Prison in Sichuan Province were given 20 seconds to finish a small bowl of rice per meal and could only watch as the guards snatched their bowls away before they really had a chance to eat.

Mr. Zhang Weijie was made to go through a torture dubbed "three-ones" while detained in Fanjiatai Prison in Hubei Province. He was allowed only one hour of sleep, one trip to the toilet, and one bite of food per meal per day.

§§4.5.2 Sleep Deprivation

Prolonged sleep deprivation is an especially insidious form of torture that affects both mental and physical functions. It can cause serious mental impairment or hallucinations and sometimes even death.

Ms. Li Xiuzhen was deprived of sleep for 28 days in Jinan Prison. When she could no longer keep her eyes open, the perpetrators stuck scotch tape around her eye sockets and pulled it up and down. Sometimes, they even used the end of a broom to prop open her eyelids. She eventually died in October 2009.[139]

Mr. Wang Yonghang, a Falun Gong practitioner and attorney from Dalian City, Liaoning Province, represented and defended several Falun Gong practitioners against charges fabricated by the Chinese regime.

He was arrested by more than 20 police officers in July 2009 and sentenced to seven years in prison.

To force him to renounce Falun Gong, the guards didn't allow him to sleep for 13 days. He recounted his ordeal below:[140]

During the first three days, I wasn't given anything to eat and was taken to the toilet twice. To me, the most difficult part was thirst and sleepiness. The two high-voltage light bulbs shining in front of me made me feel even thirstier. The inmates watching me were ready to punch me to stop me from dozing off. One day, an inmate hit me on my back and ribs when other inmates stepped out. I passed out from the tremendous pain.

Starting on the fourth day, I wasn't even allowed to go to the toilet. I was allowed to urinate once a day in my iron chair. I was given 250 ml of water every day. Since I ate so little, I didn't have any bowel movements for the following ten days.

Because the door and windows were all covered, I couldn't tell day from night. I only had a rough idea of what time it was by hearing the footsteps of inmates going out to work in the morning and coming back to their cells in the evening. But I became so disoriented in a few days that I even lost such judgment.

At first, police came in and questioned me. Then they stopped coming because the air was so foul in the room. One day they set up a video camera about a foot in front of my face. That way, the police could see my face clearly from their office. Of course, the camera did not capture the inmate sitting next to me and hitting me whenever I closed my eyes. I wore a pair of old wool socks. A few days later, the socks became too smelly and were thrown into a corner of the room.

When I felt that I could no longer endure the sleep deprivation, I shouted, 'Falun Dafa is good!' At those times, they would stuff my mouth with a rag. But inmate Zheng Jie who had hit me before always used my own smelly socks to stuff my mouth. The socks shed terribly and left a lot of lint in my mouth. As I wasn't given much water to drink, I had a really dry mouth and couldn't even spit out the lint.

About six days into the sleep deprivation, I started to hallucinate. One day, my mind became blank. I tried very hard to remember, but I couldn't think of anything. I couldn't remember who I was or whether I was alive. I was completely terrified and had a mental breakdown.

According to what people told me later, I stood up, broke the handcuffs, and started shouting and screaming. They tied me up to a bench and stuffed my mouth with a rag. I knew they wanted to drive me insane. I was not afraid of dying, but I was afraid of going crazy. If I became crazy, they would use it to defame Falun Dafa.

After that incident, I wrote a guarantee statement that I would no longer practice Falun Gong, but I also made it clear that deep down in my heart I'd never betray my faith. They said that as long as I signed my name on the statement, they didn't care whether I was still firm in my faith in my heart.

§§4.5.3 Denying Access to a Toilet

Denial of toilet access is another kind of torture that is often used. Some detention centers limited defecation time to two or three minutes. One would be viciously beaten if one did not get up when the time ran out. As a result, one had to push the waste back and leave the restroom.

On top of that, practitioners sometimes were only allowed to use the toilet once a day to urinate or once every three days to defecate. This led to health problems and forced victims to urinate or defecate in their pants.

While Ms. Liu Guihua was detained at Wanjia Forced Labor Camp in Heilongjiang Province, the guards tied her hands and hung her upside down for two days. She was not taken down even when she needed to use the toilet. She had to relieve herself in her pants. Guards then pulled down her pants and covered her mouth with her pants soiled by urine and feces.[141]

Ms. Hu Ruilian, a practitioner in Leshan City, Sichuan Province, was force-fed a large quantity of water and not allowed to use the restroom while detained in Nanmusi Forced Labor Camp in 2001.[142]

§§4.5.4 Not Allowed to Take Showers or Buy Daily Necessities

Ms. He Lianchun from Yunnan Province was sentenced to prison in 2001 and again in 2009 for a total of 17 years. In addition to many physical abuses, the guards also used more subtle ways to torture her, including not allowing her to take showers or buy daily necessities, such as toilet paper, toothpaste, soap, or laundry detergent. She recalled:[143]

After not taking a shower for months, I smelled really bad. All the inmates in my room began to blame me. I told them it wasn't that I didn't want to take a shower, the guards didn't let me. The inmates couldn't endure the smell anymore and appealed to the guards. They finally let me take showers once in a while. Because I wasn't allowed to buy sanitary pads, I had to use newspaper or any other paper I could find when I had my period.

§4.6 Electric Shocks

My arms were then pulled back through the holes on the back of the iron chair and cuffed. Electrodes were attached to my thumbs and connected to a generator to shock me. I was shocked from 9 a.m. until after 5 p.m.

Sometime later, a police officer took the electrodes off my right thumb and clipped it to my genitals. He then turned up the generator and shocked me for five or six more hours. My body kept convulsing and my heart hurt terribly. I felt like dying.

This was what Mr. Yang Licheng, in his 70s, endured in Xingongdi Police Station in 2009.[144]

Shocking practitioners with electric batons can cause severe pain and burns. Guards often target victims' sensitive areas, including the face, eyes, neck, hands, nipples, and genitals. In addition to electric batons, some guards used a hand-cranked device to generate electricity, and some restrained practitioners in metal chairs to increase the pain.

Case 1: Face Disfigured

Ms. Gao Rongrong, an accountant in Shenyang City, Liaoning Province, was disfigured from seven hours of electric shock torture. Her face was covered with blisters, and her hair was matted with pus and blood. She could only open her eyes a crack because of her swollen face, and her mouth was severely swollen and deformed.[145]

Case 2: Shocked with Six 150,000-Volt Electric Batons

Mr. Mu Junkui, 49, a businessman in Changchun City, Jilin Province, was once shocked with six 150,000-volt electric batons all over his body. He was severely burned. The pain was so excruciating that he felt his head was exploding. He was drenched in sweat. Because he'd clenched his teeth so tightly when he was being shocked, all of his teeth loosened, and he couldn't eat solid food for more than two weeks.[146]

Case 3: "I Felt I Was Being Bitten by a Snake"

Ms. Zhao Yuhong of Zhaoyuan City, Shandong Province, was arrested in 2002 for putting up self-adhesive stickers reading "Falun Dafa is good." While held in Mengzhi Police Station, she was restrained to a chair with her hands cuffed. The police connected her to an old-fashioned crank telephone to shock her. As they cranked the handle rapidly, the electricity went through her whole body and she felt that she was being bitten by a snake and her eyeballs were about to pop out.[147]

§4.7 Waterboarding and Suffocation

Waterboarding, also called simulated drowning, is one of the most brutal torture methods known to mankind.

At Masanjia Labor Camp in Liaoning Province, the practitioners' limbs were tied up and their mouths stuffed with socks and sealed with tape. Guards then poured water over their faces. With the mouth covered and limbs restrained, the victim can only breathe through the nose, which is now filled with water. This easily leads to suffocation, resembling death by drowning. The brain becomes totally blank.

Case 1: The Dripping Water Torture

Another tactic is to drip cold water onto the top of the head. The victim feels extremely cold at first and then becomes numb. The victim then feels as if his head has popped open and his brain is being smashed. This type of torture is usually administered over a long period of time, causing more pain than just pouring cold water over the person. This tactic was used in Hailin Detention Center and Mudanjiang Detention Center in Heilongjiang Province.

Mr. Wang Xiaozhong from Mudanjiang City was tortured this way. After being arrested by Yangming police on August 17, 2001, he was beaten and shocked with electric batons. With bruises and wounds all over him, the police kept him at the detention center and continued to torture him with dripping water. He died 12 days after being arrested, at the age of 36.[148]

Case 2: Head Covered with Plastic Bag

The guards sometimes cover the practitioners' heads with plastic bags or a comforter and almost suffocate them.

Mr. Zhang Shunhong and his wife were taken to the Dongji Police Station in Liaoyuan City, Jilin Province, on April 26, 2006, and interrogated with torture for 16 hours. Mr. Zhang had a deep cut on his head that was bleeding profusely. Officer Jiang Yang kept pouring cold water over him and used a fan to blow cold air on him at the same time. Mr. Zhang was shivering with cold. Officer Jiang lit a bundle of cigarettes and tied them to Mr. Zhang's hair so that the cigarettes were dangling in front of his nose. They then put a plastic bag over his head and tied it at his neck. Mr. Zhang died later that day.[149]

§4.8 Solitary Confinement

Below is one example of a practitioner being put in solitary confinement:[150]

> *There are six solitary confinement cells in the Zonghe Building at Mansanjia Labor Camp. Each cell contains a metal bench and is only large enough to fit one person. Practitioners who were confined to the cell had their arms and legs shackled together and were forced to sit on the bench 24 hours a day, with only two opportunities to use the restroom. There is no heat in the cells, and it was extremely cold in the winter, yet the prison guards would not accept any extra clothing from the practitioners' families.*
>
> *Practitioner Wang Xueli, detained in Group 2, Team 3, was confined for 10 days. He developed generalized edema and had great difficulty walking; even now he has not fully recovered. Many practitioners suffered a mental collapse. Some even became comatose.*

Those who are kept in solitary confinement face prolonged isolation and are denied any communication with the outside world, sometimes for years. Most practitioners are restrained in stressful positions most of the time and given very little to eat.

Case 1: Freezing and Starvation in Solitary Confinement

Mr. Xu Wenlong, a thirty-three-year-old artist from Heilongjiang Province, was held in a small cell alone for more than a month in Tailai Prison, where he was required to write daily "thought reports."

When Mr. Xu wrote "I am innocent" in his thought report on January 16, 2013, guard Gao Bin beat and threatened to "keep him in the cell forever."

In the city of Qiqihar, in the northern extremes of China, temperatures often drop to -10°F in January. There was no bed, blanket, or pillow in the small cell, and Mr. Xu had to sleep on the icy cement floor. Dressed in only a thin layer of clothes, with his hands cuffed and feet shackled, he could only sleep for very short periods at a time due to the cold and discomfort.

The guards gave Mr. Xu only two ladles of thin noodle soup each day. Starvation soon led to severe constipation. His weight dropped rapidly, and he was emaciated by the time he was let out of the small cell. His gums were infected because he was not allowed to brush his teeth.[151]

Case 2: Like a Living Hell

Ms. Hu Aiyun, a practitioner from Harbin City, Heilongjiang Province, was once tied to a metal chair and kept in solitary confinement for more than two months:[152]

They locked me in the metal chair. Both my ankles and hands were tied to it and I was unable to move. After a while, I felt very weak. I was losing my strength. My arms, hands, and legs became severely swollen. My feet were like steamed buns that wouldn't even fit into a size 10 shoe. The metal ring around my ankle stuck into the flesh. What scared me the most was my fear and distress. The complete physical restraint drove me crazy. I was depressed. I felt my chest was very tight and I was on the verge of collapsing.

To increase my suffering, the guards played very loud rock music. To avoid hearing the noise themselves, they fled as soon as they hit the play button. The ear-piercing music made the ceiling and the floor in the room vibrate. My head was shaking and my ears were ringing. My heart was beating very fast. It was so overwhelming that my mind went empty and numb. I felt suffocated.

During the several months I was kept in solitary confinement, they didn't let me wash myself or change clothes. The guards left a chamber pot in the room for me to relieve myself. After a few days, the smell in the room was terrible. Insects, mosquitoes, flies, and rats were running everywhere. There was no window in the room, no sight of the blue sky or breath of fresh air.

In the evening, when everyone went to sleep, the quiet around me was even more frightening. I endured second by second, shivering with chills. The nights were unbelievably long.

I had scabies all over my body. The guards then used a blunt steel spoon to scoop out the scabies. I almost fainted because of the pain. My legs kept bleeding.

§4.9 Rape, Sexual Assault, and Sexual Humiliation

Another form of torture consistently used on Falun Gong practitioners is sexual humiliation or assault. It is especially effective in crushing the victims' souls and breaking down their will.

§§4.9.1 Sexual Torture of Women

The abuses include rape, stripping them naked in front of male prison guards, inserting broomsticks or toothbrushes into the vagina, as well as shocking the vagina and breasts with electric batons. Many survivors of such abuse were traumatized and suffered shame, grief, and fear.

Case 1: Eighteen Practitioners Gang-Raped by Prisoners

In one infamous case at the notorious Masanjia Forced Labor Camp, on April 19, 2001, guards put 18 female practitioners into men's cells and allowed the male prisoners to gang-rape them, which led to deaths, disability, or mental instability of the victims.[153]

One of the 18 victims, Ms. Yin Liping, said that her distress and humiliation were exacerbated when she realized the assault had been videotaped.[154]

Case 2: Elderly Woman Raped and Electrically Shocked in Her Vagina

Ms. Zou Jin, then in her late 60s, was raped by two officers shortly after she was arrested in February 2001. The officers then shoved an electric baton into her vagina and shocked her. She cried in pain. The guards took it out only after she lost consciousness. Her vagina was bleeding and swollen, leaving her in intense pain. Ms. Zou couldn't sit or walk for more than a month.[155]

Case 3: Guards Hose Ms. Wang Jinping's Genitals

Guards at Liaoning Province Women's Prison instructed inmates to pull Ms. Wang Jinping's legs wide apart and another inmate to hose her genitals. As a result, Ms. Wang was unable to urinate and became incontinent. Both her legs became swollen and turned black and purple.[156]

Case 4: Prisoners Stuff Hot Peppers into Ms. Zhang Shuxia's Vagina

Ms. Zhang Shuxia was 60 when she was taken to Liaoning Women's Prison in 2005. The police instructed two prisoners to put hot peppers into her vagina. They also forced her to drink salty boiling water that hot peppers had been soaked in. They poured the peppery water over her buttocks and then forced her to drink the soiled water.[157]

Case 5: Sharp Wooden Stick Stabbed into Ms. Wang Lijun's Vagina

Ms. Wang Lijun was tortured at Dalian Forced Labor Camp by having a thick rope rubbed back and forth against her genitals on three occasions. The perpetrators also used a broken wooden stick with sharp ends to stab her vagina, causing her abdomen and genital area to hemorrhage and swell. She couldn't pull up her pants or squat down. She also had trouble urinating.[158]

§§4.9.2 Sexual Torture of Men

Many male Falun Gong practitioners also reported being sexually tortured while they were detained. The assaults against male practitioners often include electric shocks, attacks on their genitals, and having their pubic hair ripped out.

A guard at Benxi Prison shocked Mr. Meng Xianguang's penis and said, "I'm going to make you unable to have any kids." Mr. Meng convulsed from the electric shocks, only for the guards to laugh at him.[159]

Guards at Hegang Forced Labor Camp pinched and pulled Mr. Sun Fengli's penis, which became badly swollen and very painful. He had difficulty urinating and walking. He was humiliated by the inmates.[160]

Guard Zhao Shuang, in Changlinzi Forced Labor Camp, grabbed Mr. Zang Dianyong's testicles. His groin was still painful even a year later.[161]

When Mr. Chen Shaomin served time in Henan Province No.3 Forced Labor Camp in 2004, guard Nie Yong forced his penis into Mr. Chen's mouth and threatened to urinate into his mouth if he didn't give up practicing Falun Gong.[162]

Chapter 5: Persecution Deaths

As of September 10, 2019, a total of 4,343 Falun Gong practitioners have been confirmed to have died as a result of the persecution. The actual death toll is likely higher, as not all cases can be reported in a timely manner due to the information blockade in China.

Below is a small, representative selection of death cases published by Minghui.org.

§5.1 Authorities Remove Imprisoned Woman from Life Support Without Family's Consent[163]

Ms. Li Changfang from Linyi City, Shandong Province, was imprisoned for refusing to give up her faith in Falun Gong. She was hospitalized on July 5, 2019 and operated on the following day without her family's consent. When her family refused to sign a waiver to take her home, the police detained them, including a six-year-old child, for one day.

On July 12, authorities took Ms. Li off oxygen when her family was not around, and she died. They then demanded that her family negotiate compensation terms before revealing where her body was being stored.

§§5.1.1 Key Events Leading Up to Ms. Li's Death

Ms. Li was arrested on October 23, 2018, for refusing to renounce Falun Gong. She was sentenced to two and a half years and fined 10,000 yuan on March 27, 2019. On July 5, 2019, her family rushed to a local hospital after being notified that her condition was life-threatening. Ms. Li was alert and said she had been suffering from abdominal pain for 15 days. She had bruises on her thighs, and her teeth were loose.

The guards at Linyi City Detention Center where Ms. Li had been detained refused to explain what had happened to her that may have resulted in her medical condition and injuries. The doctors at first claimed she had appendicitis and then said she had a gastric perforation.

With so many questions unanswered, Ms. Li's family refused to sign a consent form to agree to surgery.

Directed by the detention center and the police, the doctors still operated on Ms. Li, cutting her open from her chest down to her abdomen on July 6. She never regained consciousness and remained connected to a ventilator after the surgery. On the morning of July 10, more than two dozen officers descended on the hospital. When her family refused to sign a waiver to have her discharged from the hospital, the police arrested her husband, son, daughter, and six-year-old grandson. They weren't released until the following day.

At around 6 p.m. on July 12, when her family was not present, agents from the Linyin City Detention Center and Dongguan Police Station in Linyi City showed up in Ms. Li's ward and removed her oxygen supply. She died shortly afterward.

§5.2 Liaoning Woman Dies 13 Days after Prison Admission[164]

While many families reunited and celebrated the Chinese New Year in February 2019, Ms. Li Yanqiu was sentenced to five years for not renouncing her faith in Falun Gong.

Ms. Li was admitted to Liaoning Women's Prison on February 19, 2019 and died there 13 days later.

Ms. Li was assigned to the "Correction Ward," which was set up specifically to persecute Falun Gong practitioners and try to force them to renounce their faith. She was extremely weak the day she arrived.

She had been on a hunger strike and force-fed since her arrest on December 14, 2018, for distributing calendars with information about Falun Gong.

She continued her hunger strike in prison, so the guards took her to the prison hospital, where she was force-fed. They allowed her family to see her for the first time since her arrest. She used a rollator when she came out to meet them.

Her family applied for medical parole for Ms. Li after the visit, but their request was turned down and they were never allowed to visit her again.

According to inmates who were familiar with her, the guards moved Ms. Li back to the 12th ward after she was force-fed and kept her in solitary confinement in her final days, despite her condition.

The guards stripped off her clothes and made her sit on the cold concrete floor. The temperature was between 25°F and 37°F, and there was no heat in the room. A few days later, she began to pass blood in her urine and was unable to stand on her own, yet the prison officials sought no medical care for her. She died just days later, on March 4, 2019. She was 52.

Ms. Li's sudden death devastated her family. Her elderly father, who used to live with her, had to move in with her older brother after her arrest. In his 80s, the usually very outgoing man became withdrawn and had trouble sleeping after Ms. Li was arrested. He also suffered from frequent nosebleeds, heart discomfort, and dizziness caused by high blood pressure. Fearing that the news might be too much for him, Ms. Li's family hasn't told him about her death.

§5.3 Hebei Woman Falls to Her Death Trying to Escape Arrest[165]

Only a few months before her daughter's wedding, a woman from Wen'an County, Hebei Province, fell to her death as she tried to escape police by climbing down from the balcony of her third-floor apartment. She was 55. The police targeted Ms. Yang Xiaohui for refusing to renounce her faith in Falun Gong. Eight officers knocked on Ms. Yang's door around 11 p.m. on April 8, 2019. When she refused to let them in, they used tools to pry open the door. Ms. Yang's husband and daughter, who were present at the time, were terrified and didn't know what to do.

As the police were about to break in, Ms. Yang rushed to the balcony and tried to escape from there. She tumbled to the ground. Unresponsive, she was taken to the hospital, where she was pronounced dead around 2 a.m. The police closely monitored and videotaped Ms. Yang's family during the attempts to resuscitate her.

Li Zhongjie, the head of the Domestic Security Division, denied any responsibility for Ms. Yang's death and said that they were only following orders from above.

Ms. Yang's family was outraged when the police, who claimed they had to obtain approval from higher-ups before allowing her to be cremated and buried, refused to let them make arrangements for her funeral.

Since 1999, Ms. Yang was repeatedly targeted for not renouncing her faith. Her repeated arrests, harassment, and home-ransacking left her family living in fear for the past two decades, resulting in her husband's poor health. Ms. Yang was taken to brainwashing sessions twice between November 2003 and June 2004. She was kicked in the back and slapped in the face. The brainwashing center staff tied her to a bed and force-fed her, severely injuring her esophagus. They also injected her with unknown drugs that made her unable to fall asleep and, subsequently, hard to wake up.

Ms. Yang's latest ordeal dates back to January 2, 2017, when she and eight other Falun Gong practitioners (two men and six women) traveled to the farmers' market in Daliu Town, Wen'an County, to distribute calendars with information about Falun Gong. They were reported to the police and arrested nine days later. The police ransacked the practitioners' homes and took away their Falun Gong materials.

§5.4 Death of Jin Shunnu

Ms. Jin Shunnu slipped into a coma on October 6, 2018, while being detained for her faith in Falun Gong. After her family rushed to the hospital, the police forced them to sign a liability waiver by threatening to give Ms. Jin a heavy prison sentence if they refused to comply.

Ms. Jin's husband and daughter stayed at the hospital for four days, but she never regained consciousness. She passed away around 4 a.m. on October 10. Her body was cremated on the same day without an autopsy, and the death certificate issued by the hospital said she died from a stroke. She was 66. Ms. Jin was arrested on September 19, 2018, at her local residential committee office. She went there to request documents required to reinstate her pension, which had been suspended because she had previously been imprisoned for 13 years for refusing to renounce Falun Gong.

She explained to the office staff that her imprisonment for her faith was illegal and that her pension should not have been suspended. Instead of issuing her the documents, one staff member called the police. Officers from Xinhua Police Station came and took her to the Nangou Detention Center.

It wasn't clear what happened to Ms. Jin during her brief detention that caused her to fall into a coma and die days later.

While Ms. Jin was imprisoned between 2002 and 2015, her husband Mr. Shen Shan was serving an 11-year term for their shared faith. Their daughter Ms. Shen Chunting was also given three years of forced labor for practicing Falun Gong. The family was finally reunited in 2015, only to lose Ms. Jin three years later.[166]

§5.5 Other Death Cases

Ms. Peng Guangzhen, 70, is seeking justice in the death of her son Mr. Xu Langzhou. Mr. Xu died in suspicious circumstances while incarcerated for his belief in Falun Gong:

> *My husband passed away when our son was five years old. It was not easy to raise two children as a single mother. I survived only because of my son. He was so kind and loved me very much. He told me once: "I will take care of you, Mom, even if I end up a beggar." I worked so hard to raise him. He was strong and healthy, but he died*

when he was only 39. They (Wumaping Prison authorities) said they were not responsible...

Case 1: Mr. Xu Langzhou—Outstanding Police Officer Dies in Prison Under Suspicious Circumstances

While Mr. Xu Langzhou was imprisoned in Guangyuan Prison for six years, he was not allowed to call his family even once. On seven separate occasions, his elderly mother traveled from Panzhihua City to see him, only to be turned away by the guards.

In the winter of 2010, Mr. Xu was transferred to Wumaping Prison in Muchuan County. Because he refused to wear the prison uniform, the prison guards ordered inmates to cut off his clothes. He was allowed to wear only a pair of underpants. Mr. Xu went on a hunger strike to protest the persecution. Finally, in December 2011, the prison authorities allowed his family to send him clothing and 1,000 yuan in cash.

On March 7, 2012, the prison notified Mr. Xu's family that they would be allowed to visit him, claiming that he had to have an operation for a duodenal ulcer. The next day, his mother Ms. Peng Guangzhen was forced to sign documents agreeing to the operation while Mr. Xu was unconscious. Three days after the operation, Mr. Xu was able to eat porridge. The hospital refused to allow his mother to take care of him, so she had to stay in a hotel outside the hospital. On the night of March 18, the hospital informed the family that Mr. Xu had passed away.[167]

Case 2: Ms. Cheng Fuhua—Liaoning Woman Dies Seven Months after Release on Medical Parole

Ms. Cheng Fuhua was abused in the local detention center following her arrest on June 1, 2015, for talking to people about Falun Gong. She went on a hunger strike to protest the mistreatment, only to be retaliated against.

Ms. Cheng developed edema and had frequent fainting episodes. She also lost mobility. The local detention center notified her family in late January 2016 to come pick her up. She was never able to recover from her abuse-induced symptoms. She died on August 6, 2016, at the age of 69.[168]

Case 3: Mr. Hu Guojian—Liaoning Man Dies after Being Comatose for Two Years

Mr. Hu Guojian from Fushun City, Liaoning Province, died on May 15, 2018, after being in a coma for nearly two years. Mr. Hu was arrested on July 7, 2015 and sentenced to four years in prison five months later. He suffered a severe brain hemorrhage from beatings by the guards and fell into a coma. He was operated on but never regained consciousness.

Case 4: Ms. Liu Fengmei—Woman Dies after Endless Torment and Harassment

Shortly after Ms. Liu Fengmei was arrested before the Beijing Olympics in 2008, she was sentenced to 13 years in prison. The prison accepted her even though she failed the physical exam.

After three years of torture, including force-feeding, hard labor, brainwashing, and sitting on a small stool for long hours, Ms. Liu's health deteriorated and she was diagnosed with late-stage breast cancer and ovarian tumors in July 2012. She was released in August 2012, but the local authorities continued to harass her. After two years and four months of agony, Ms. Liu passed away on December 18, 2014. She was 48.

Case 5: Mr. Gao Yixi—Healthy Man Dies Two Days after Hospitalization for Hunger Strike

Mr. Gao Yixi died two days after he was taken to the hospital for being on a hunger strike to protest his and his wife's unlawful arrest and detention for their faith. His death occurred only ten days after he was arrested on April 19, 2016. He was 45. Mr. Gao was in good health when he entered the hospital, despite the hunger strike. In the hospital, he was subjected to continuous infusions. He gradually lost the ability to speak or move and died just 43 hours later. His family noticed handcuff marks on his wrists, severe swelling on his chest, and a sunken abdomen. The police had an autopsy performed the next day but refused to show the report to the family.[169]

Case 6: Ms. Fu Guichun—Forced to Have Abortion, Dies after Eight Years of Persecution in Prison

Ms. Fu Guichun was sentenced to eight years in prison in September 2002, two months after she was forced to have an abortion following her arrest in May 2002. In Harbin Women's Prison, Ms. Fu was held in solitary confinement, hung up by her wrists, frozen, and deprived of sleep in the authorities' attempts to force her to renounce her faith. She developed diabetes and other health issues. When she was released in 2009, she was traumatized and injured both mentally and physically. Ms. Fu died on May 1, 2012, only in her 40s.[170]

Case 7: Mr. Li Kunlian and Ms. Wang Fuqin—Husband and Wife Die Five Years Apart after Three Daughters Arrested for Refusing to Renounce Falun Gong

Ms. Wang Fuqin's three daughters were arrested one after the other around 2004 for refusing to renounce Falun Gong. The youngest one was sentenced to four years in prison. Ms. Wang tried seven times but was never allowed to visit her youngest daughter. She was so traumatized by her daughters' arrests that she had a stroke and died in March 2004 at the age of 69.

Her husband Mr. Li Kunlian suffered a mental breakdown following his wife's death. Every day after dusk, he would grab a knife or stick to scare away "imaginary bad guys" who he thought were coming to take away his loved ones. He died five years later in November 2009, at the age of 71.

Case 8: Mr. Ren Dongsheng—Middle-Aged Man Dies Seven Years after Being Driven Insane While in Custody

Mr. Ren Dongsheng was arrested on March 8, 2006 and sentenced to five years. He suffered unimaginable torture in Gangbei Prison in Tianjin City, such as having his hands burned with a lighter, his face slapped, and his toes stomped on until his toenails fell off. He was forced to eat food dumped on the ground, and, while handcuffed and shackled, meals were intentionally placed out of his reach. When his five-year term expired, he was sent straight to a brainwashing center, where he was tricked into taking an unknown white powder. By the time he was released a week later, his son was shocked to see that his father was no longer the strong, loving man he remembered. Mr. Ren kept mumbling and exhibited strange behaviors. His mother, in her 80s, was so heartbroken to see what had happened to her son after five long years that she collapsed.

Mr. Ren's wife, Ms. Zhang Liqin, also practices Falun Gong. She was fired from her job one month after her husband's arrest. She herself was arrested on February 12, 2009 and sentenced to seven years in prison. When she was released on February 11, 2016, what greeted her at home was a psychotic husband and smashed furniture and windows.

Mr. Ren remained in a psychotic state most of the time after he returned home. He refused to have his hair cut and smashed everything in his sight. He ran out screaming on rainy days. Occasionally, he left home in the middle of the night and returned days later covered in dirt. Whenever someone mentioned the police, Mr. Ren would murmur that he had to run or the police would catch him. He would dash outside and later sleep by the side of the road.

Sometimes he would suddenly wake up in the middle of the night, screaming, "I am not afraid of you." He often mistreated his mother and beat his son. One time, he drove his mother out of the house on New Year's Eve, leaving her standing alone on the street. Another time, he beat his son, who ran crying to his grandmother.

After filing a complaint against the guards who tortured Mr. Ren, his wife Ms. Zhang Liqin was repeatedly harassed and detained by the authorities. She had to live away from home to avoid arrest. She sometimes skipped meals to save money to travel to different places to seek justice for her husband.

Eight days after Ms. Zhang agreed to be questioned by the Tianjin City Superior Court on September 4, 2018, she was heartbroken to lose her husband, who died after seven years of suffering.[171]

Case 9: Mr. Xu Dawei—Cheerful and Amiable Chef Dies after Eight Years of Imprisonment

Mr. Xu Dawei was arrested in January 2001 and later sentenced to eight years in prison. A formerly healthy young man, Mr. Xu was reduced to skin and bones when he was released in February 2009. His body was covered with injuries and bruises resulting from electric shock torture and beatings. His face was expressionless, his eyes moved slowly, and he was unable to recognize his family. He died only 13 days after his release. He was 36. After his death, his wife worked tirelessly to seek justice for him. In an open letter to the authorities, Mr. Xu's wife Ms. Chi Lihua wrote the following:[172]

> *I don't want to think about how I spent those eight years waiting anxiously. It is hard for someone who has not experienced it personally to understand. I took care of our young daughter and my elderly parents. The hardships, the misery, the concern, and worries were beyond description. I don't know how many times I wept. I ran out of tears. Only blood dripped from my heart.*
>
> *I had thought that finally the wait was over after eight long years, but what came was a fatal blow. My mother could not take it and fainted when she heard. Both my parents are now no longer alive. I have lost them, and I have no home and no income.*
>
> *Dawei's parents have asked me to come live with them, but I am reluctant to go. To a certain extent, I am not facing reality.*

It is not because they live in a small village in the mountains. And it is not because I do not get along with them. Dawei's parents have not treated me as a daughter-in-law – they have treated me as their own daughter. And I, too, have treated them as my own parents. I don't want to go live with them only because I don't want my presence to remind them of their son. I am even more afraid of what to say when Dawei's ninety-nine-year-old grandmother asks me why Dawei still has not returned home.

Chapter 6: Physical Injuries and Mental Trauma

The persecution of Falun Gong is responsible for untold numbers of tragedies for both practitioners and their families. Even children, the elderly, and the disabled are not spared.

Ms. Wang Bo, a musical prodigy, was sentenced to three years of forced labor when she was only 19 years old when she spoke out against the persecution. After being released in 2005, she was arrested again in 2006 and sentenced to another five years.[173]

Ms. Zhang Chunyu, a former businesswoman, is being abused in Heilongjiang Province Women's Prison while serving a four-and-a-half-year term. She has gone blind in her left eye after being struck by a male guard during an earlier labor camp term.[174]

Ms. Tan Meili, whose legs were disabled after she contracted polio as a child, was repeatedly arrested and sentenced for a total of seven and a half years. She is currently serving four and a half years in prison.[175]

Mr. Liu Dianyuan was sentenced to 11.5 years when he was 79. He previously served seven years in prison.[176]

Simply for upholding their belief in Falun Gong, a family of six in Tongliao, Inner Mongolia, has been repeatedly arrested and detained for a combined total of 41 years. The father, Mr. Tian Fujin, was imprisoned twice and spent about nine years in prison before he was tortured to death. The mother, Ms. Liu Xiurong, was incarcerated for ten years. Most recently, the middle daughter, Ms. Tian Xin, was sentenced to three years in prison in 2015. Her husband divorced her, and her teenage son has been cared for by relatives since her most recent arrest.[177]

Despite brutal torture and lengthy prison terms, the physical suffering is still no match compared to the mental distress that the persecution has inflicted upon practitioners and their family members.

Nothing can erase the pain young Xu Xinyang felt when she saw her imprisoned father, Mr. Xu Dawei, for the first time when she was seven. And then he died only 13 days after being released from prison, full of injuries.[178]

What Ms. Jiang Zixiang, 88, had to endure is beyond description. Ms. Jiang's husband was so distressed by the persecution that he died in the early 2000s. Then her forty-five-year-old son, Mr. Gao Yixi, was tortured to death ten days following his arrest. Her daughter was still serving time in prison for her faith at the time of Mr. Gao's death. It took such a toll on the elderly woman's health that she passed away 20 months later.[179]

Only in her 30s, Ms. Zhao Yuhua lost all of her teeth after her young daughter died from a heart attack, due to the anxiety and fear she felt for her parents, who were forced to live away from home to avoid the persecution. Hearing of the young girl's death, the police took it as an opportunity to arrest Ms. Zhao and waited near her house around the clock.[180]

Mr. Ma Zhanguo's grief-stricken father suffered from high blood pressure and had a stroke when he was not allowed to visit his son following his arrest in October 2016. With Mr. Ma being the only breadwinner for the family, his arrest left the family in great distress. Wanting to help out, his ailing, elderly father Ma Dengke sometimes picked up water bottles, beverage cans, or waste paper to sell to recycling companies to make a little money. He was found dead in a garbage heap.[181]

Ms. Bi Jianhong's mother, Ms. Wang Yanqin, was once forced to watch her daughter being tortured and hear her screams again and again when both of them were imprisoned together for their faith. The mother almost suffered a mental breakdown.[182]

Despite her age, Ms. Liang Yuzhen's ninety-eight-year-old grandmother had her hands pried open by the police as she watched her granddaughter, her only caregiver, being taken away by the police. After learning that the two lawyers were denied visitation rights, the grandmother was outraged. With help, she walked to Heshan Detention Center. The guards there all tried to avoid talking to her and refused to provide any assistance.[183]

Mr. Jin Fuzhang's mother, 84, struggled to take care of herself after her only son was given five years for practicing Falun Gong. She had to do grocery shopping, find a plumber to fix her burst pipe, and install a piece of glass in her kitchen cabinet all by herself.[184]

In Ms. Chen Shulan's case, both of her parents, two brothers, and a younger sister all died as a result of the persecution. As the only survivor, Ms. Chen was sentenced twice for a total of 11.5 years. After years of torture, Ms. Chen now has severe back pain and has to rely on her daughter to take care of her.[185]

Ms. Feng Xiaomei, her sister Ms. Feng Xiaomin, and their parents were once happy. But because of the persecution, Xiaomei lost her father, husband, and sister. Her brother-in-law was imprisoned shortly after eight years of wandering about to avoid the persecution. Xiaomin and her elderly mother were the only two left to take care of her son, Wang Boru, who lost his father at 13, and her nephew, Wang Tianxing, who lost his mother when he was less than two. When Xiaomei was arrested again in 2009, her mother lost all her hair in one night. Boru had to quit school and do odd jobs to support the family. Tianxing was almost sent to an orphanage.[186]

§6.1 Outcomes of Physical Torture and Abuse

Many practitioners became seriously injured, disabled, paralyzed, or driven insane as a result of torture in detention facilities. Below are a few such cases.

Case 1: Former Economist Disabled from Leg Fracture

Ms. Gong Xingcan, a former economist, fell down the stairs when she was trying to escape being tortured in a labor camp. She broke her right leg, with the bones poking out. After she was taken to the hospital, the doctor put a plaster cast on without aligning the bones. This eventually led her right leg to become deformed and one inch shorter than her left leg.[187]

Case 2: Man in His 30s Loses Most of His Teeth After Force Feeding

Mr. Tang Maoting lost most of his teeth after detention center guards used needle-nose pliers to open his mouth and then uterine dilator forceps to force-feed him. He has had to wear dentures since his 30s. The guards also stomped on his back. Without timely medical treatment, his lumbar spine became deformed.[188]

Case 3: Woman's Hands Disabled by Torture at Wanjia Labor Camp

Ms. Fu Li's hands were disabled and her body covered in sores when she was 41 as a result of being tortured in the Wanjia Forced Labor Camp in Heilongjiang Province in 2000.

The police tied a rope around Ms. Fu's thumbs and then hung her up by the rope so that her thumbs sustained the weight of her whole body. After being suspended this way for a long time, her hands became disabled.[189]

Case 4: Disabled Practitioner's Compensation Claim Ignored

Mr. Fan Zhongzhuang from Zhejiang Province was once interrogated for five days in a row, during which time he was not allowed to sleep. The police also shackled his hands and feet and tortured him. On August 27, 2005, the police beat Mr. Fan so severely that vertebrae in his neck were fractured and he became permanently disabled.[190]

Mr. Fan filed a claim with the police for 1.37 million yuan to cover his medical costs and lost wages. Deputy Chief Yang Changchun responded, "The compensation claim is way out of line. If you want compensation, we will agree to 10,000 yuan, but you first have to pay 20 years of interest on it."

Case 5: Woman Blinded While in Custody

Ms. Wu Yangzhen, 73, was retired from the Guangdong Province Institute of Metrology. She became blind in her right eye after just 19 days of detention at a local brainwashing center. The staff first forced Ms. Wu to stand for long hours and then tied her up with her legs crossed for four hours. Occasionally they would release her legs before tying her up in the same position again. The pain was intense, and her vision became blurry as a result of decreased blood flow.

By the time she was taken to the hospital about two weeks later, she was totally blind in her right eye and the vision in her left eye was severely impaired.[191]

Case 6: Woman Remains Hospitalized for Years after Being Beaten Unconscious by Police

Ms. Shi Yunlan had to have a craniotomy after she was beaten unconscious by police on October 9, 2014. She has slurred speech and is paralyzed from the waist down. The local government refused to cover her full medical expenses. A scheduled surgery to repair her skull has been postponed indefinitely for lack of funds.[192]

Case 7: Imprisoned and Tortured for Five Years, Heilongjiang Man Unable to Walk or Speak Upon Release

Mr. Zhang Jinku was arrested on March 29, 2013, after banners reading "Falun Dafa is Good" were found hanging in his town. By the time Mr. Zhang was transferred to Hulan Prison on October 1, 2013, he was already unable to walk due to torture by guards and inmates.

Mr. Zhang was released at the end of his sentence, emaciated and unrecognizable, on June 2, 2018, to find that his wife, Ms. Li Yali had died from the distress his ordeal caused her. She was 47.

When Mr. Zhang's mother asked him why he was so emaciated, he slowly wrote with his non-dominant left hand (his right arm had been broken due to torture in prison), "I was on hunger strikes on and off for about five years. They put drugs in the food." His daughter became distant and withdrawn and was unwilling to visit her paternal grandparents who share the same home as her parents. The young woman wasn't there to welcome her father when he was released.[193]

Case 8: Woman Became Insane, Previously Fed Urine and Feces by Police

Ms. Zhang Juxian was carried out of the hospital at Liaoning Women's Prison covered with a white sheet. Many people thought she had died. In fact, she survived after returning home but was mentally disoriented from then on. Ms. Zhang was previously arrested multiple times, sent to the labor camp twice for a total of five years, and sentenced to prison for three years. She was once fed urine and feces when she went on a hunger strike to protest the persecution.[194]

§6.2 Families' Plights—In Their Own Words

Case 1: Appeal Letter Written by Mr. Mo Zhikui's Mother, Seeking Release of Her Son, Who Is in Serious Condition after Being Tortured in Prison[195]

I am Mo Zhikui's mother and I am 89 years old. It's been over a year since my son was taken away. I am extremely worried about his safety. I keep asking the question: 'My son did not do anything illegal, so why did the police arrest him just for practicing Falun Gong and trying to be a good person?' He's been sentenced to 12 years and suffering ill treatment at Hulan Prison.

Ever since my son was arrested, our family of four generations, otherwise happy, have not enjoyed a single day of comfort and peace. The police ransacked our home and kept asking, 'Who owns the house? Whose name is on the deed?' The local neighborhood committee personnel keep calling to threaten my daughter-in-law. They also went to the kindergarten to question my great granddaughter about where she lived. Whenever I hear a knock on the door, my heart palpitates and I tremble with fear.

My son has been arrested a total of eight times and has suffered so much abuse. You beat him savagely and cursed him. Now he has tuberculosis and is coughing up blood and experiencing numbness in both legs all the way up to his groin. This is a direct result of being ill-treated in prison. My daughter-in-law, grandson, granddaughter, and son-in-law have been denied visits five times after traveling to the prison to see him. One of my grandsons has a congenital disability and my great-granddaughter suffers from a skin disease. Their treatment is costly. Without my son to support us, my family struggles to get by. I am longing every day for my son's return."

Case 2: Account of Ms. Li Songrong, Daughter of Mr. Li Kun and Ms. Liang Guifen, Who Were Repeatedly Arrested and Sentenced for Their Faith[196]

Every time I went to visit my dad in prison, I was very nervous. I didn't know whether I would be able to see him. I wondered how he was doing and if he was being tortured. I reminded myself that I must not cry when I saw him and not make him worry about me. Although we were only allowed to see him for 20 minutes each time, it was so precious for us. Other relatives always said to me, 'Don't worry. Your dad will come back soon.' When I heard other kids talking about the fun times they spent with their dads, I just sat there and listened. I kept telling myself, 'Dad is coming back, very soon.' I repeated the same thing to myself from the time I was 9 years old to when I was 23. When I was 10, I didn't dare to sleep at night. I was afraid that someone might come and ransack our home at any time. It was very cold that winter. Mom took out Dad's winter jacket and put it on me. Mom told stories to help me fall asleep. But in the middle of night, I still woke up.

Outside our home, someone yelled my mom's name and told her to open the door. Mom didn't respond and kept comforting me. After a while, the shouting stopped. We thought they had left. But in no time, we heard people pounding on our door. Every time they hit the door, they also hit my heart. Just as we thought the door was almost broken and my heart had almost stopped beating, Mom went downstairs. I was so scared that I didn't follow her.

After a short conversation, the officers took her away. I cried and begged her not to leave. She said to me, 'It's fine. Just go back to sleep. I will be back shortly.' I had no idea that ' shortly' could be so long. When Mom returned, it was already summer of the following year. In all these years, when I was almost ready to give up and lose hope because of all the pain and suffering, Mom never gave up. She worked very hard and was very frugal in order to support me so that I could go to college. Whenever I complained to her about my frustrations, she always said to me, 'Don't always point fingers at others. You should look at yourself first and think where you didn't do well in the conflict.'

After I graduated and went to another city to work and live by myself, I began to understand how much she has done for me for so many years. She is such a great mom. Her love for me is like the mountains and the ocean, rock steady but gentle.

Just as Dad's release date got closer, Mom, almost 60, was arrested and sentenced again. I just want to live my life with my family. Why is such simple happiness so difficult?

Ever since Mom was arrested, I have been worrying about her all the time and I can't sleep or eat. While I was writing this letter, all the memories of what we suffered and endured, that I had tried so hard to forget, all came back to me so vividly that I burst into tears. I finally understood what it means to cry one's heart out. In the end, I even coughed up blood. I felt very weak all over and the tears wouldn't stop.

Case 3: Poet Ms. Fu Ying Recounts Family's Devastation from Years of Persecution[197]

After surviving more than 3,000 days in prison and enduring countless sufferings, I thought my spring had finally come and my suffering would end, as my release date was drawing near. But the reality was nothing like what I had imagined.

On July 11, 2010, I finally left the prison. Only in my early 40s, my hair had turned gray a long time before. I was glad to see the sun again. Every day in prison, I began to work before the sun came out and didn't return until late at night. It had been a long time since I'd last seen the sun.

Upon returning home, my sisters told me that in the past nine years, many tragedies had taken place in our family. My father Fu Chengyong and third brother-in-law all passed away in 2008 from the distress of the persecution. My uncle also died. My older sister, Fu Wen, suffered brain bleeding three months before I was released. She was operated on and had been bedridden ever since.

In fact, when my father visited me in 2008 for the last time, he said to me, "I can't wait for you any longer." I didn't understand what he meant at that time. I learned later on that he had a surgery after that visit and died a few months later.

Nine months after that, my mother Tong Shuping also left us. I wasn't given any opportunities to fulfill my responsibilities as a daughter. After both of my parents passed away, their house was also forcibly demolished by the authorities.

With my younger sister Fu Yan still serving a 13-year term for practicing Falun Gong, the responsibility of taking care of her daughter fell on my shoulders. When I was imprisoned, it was my mom who cared for the little girl, Qingquan, since my sister's arrest in 2001.

Yan used to have a happy family. But after she was given the lengthy sentence, her husband couldn't stand the pressure and divorced her. He also refused to care for their daughter, nor did he pay any child support to our family.

The poor little girl was deprived of her mother's love and lived with her grandmother since she was 3. I told myself that, no matter how hard it is, I have to take good care of her. I couldn't imagine how she endured all that she had all these years.

To get her a better education, we moved to Shenyang City in 2012. I found a job as a babysitter. Life was difficult, but it was simple and peaceful. Unfortunately, it didn't last long before the police ransacked our home, held me in detention for over 30 days, and closed the Falun Gong practitioner-run school Qingquan was attending. We were left homeless again.

Shortly after that, I met my husband, Ouyang Hongbo. We got married on May 16, 2014. At 46, I finally had a family again.

This time, only 40 days after our wedding, my husband was arrested and later sentenced to six years, leaving me and his eighty-three-year-old father at home alone. Everything was so unreal, just like a dream.

In the persecution of Falun Gong, there are too many such family tragedies and forced separations like ours. The persecution must end. I'm longing for the day the perpetrators are brought to justice.

Chapter 7: Organ Harvesting: An Unprecedented Crime

The killing of Falun Gong practitioners to supply organs for transplantation was first brought to light in 2006.

One witness who came forward was Peter (pseudonym), a journalist who spent six years investigating a hidden facility in Sujiatun, Shenyang Province, that held large numbers of Falun Gong practitioners. Another was Annie (pseudonym), the ex-wife of a surgeon who participated in the removal of corneas from Falun Gong practitioners. Both witnesses said that the victims' organs and tissues were removed while they were still alive and then their bodies were cremated.[198]

Shortly thereafter, a Chinese military doctor corroborated Annie's account and said that Sujiatun was only one component of a network of 36 concentration camps in China.[199]

A number of international investigators, journalists, and non-governmental organizations have since investigated and corroborated these allegations. Minghui released an in-depth report on the issue in 2016: *Minghui Human Rights Report: Falun Gong Practitioners Systematically Murdered in China for Their Organs.*[200]

§7.1 Abundant Organ Availability with Short Wait Times Despite Shortage of Legal Sources

Organ transplantation in China grew rapidly in the early 2000s, and more than 600 hospitals were performing organ transplants by 2007.

While wait times for kidney and liver transplants in the U.S. averaged two to three years, Chinese hospitals could provide organs in one or two weeks. Furthermore, transplants could be scheduled ahead of time, which would require the death of a donor to be planned in advance.

This rapid growth in organ transplants took place in the absence of donations. China only started to establish a national organ donation and allocation system in 2010. The only other organ source identified by the government came from death-row prisoners, but the number of legal executions each year could in no way supply enough organs for the number of transplants performed.[201] Therefore, the sources of most organs used in transplants in China could not be accounted for.

This gap between donations and transplants persists today. While the government announced in 2015 that it stopped sourcing organs from death-row prisoners and began to rely entirely on voluntary donations, its organ donation statistics were found to have been manipulated. Wait times for organs remain in the days to weeks, and transplant tourism to China continues on a large scale despite official statements that the practice has ceased.[202]

§7.2 Missing Falun Gong Practitioners

After the Communist Party launched its nationwide persecution of Falun Gong on July 20, 1999, practitioners from all over China traveled to Beijing to petition the central government to stop the suppression. At its peak in 2000 and 2001, the Beijing Public Security Bureau estimated that more than one million Falun Gong practitioners were petitioning in Beijing.[203] Internal police records indicated that there were more than 830,000 arrests of practitioners for petitioning in Beijing as of April 2001.[204]

§§7.2.1 Unidentified Practitioners

The above figure does not include practitioners who refused to disclose their identities to the police. Many did so to protect their families, colleagues, and friends from retaliation. Under the Communist Party's policy of collective punishment, Falun Gong practitioners' family members can be terminated from their jobs, their colleagues and superiors in the workplace can be denied bonuses, and even their local government officials can be removed from their posts.

This policy effectively turns everyone associated with a Falun Gong practitioner against him. In order to protect their careers, formerly passive local officials did whatever was necessary to stop practitioners from going to Beijing. They also dispatched local police to the National Appeals Office in Beijing to arrest practitioners en masse and transport them back to their hometowns.

As a result, starting in 2000, many practitioners who were arrested refused to give their names and home addresses. This practice was widely seen in Minghui reports of the era as a means of countering collective punishment. As one practitioner recalled telling other detainees,

> *If we don't tell them our names and addresses, even though we may be persecuted more severely, we'll be released after being detained for another week. But if we give our names and addresses, we'll be taken back to a detention center or labor camp in our hometown, and our families and workplaces will be affected.*[205]

§§7.2.2 Transfers to Other Regions

Minghui reported in August 2000 that a large number of practitioners who were arrested in Beijing and refused to disclose their identities were transferred to various detention centers in Tianjin on July 19, 2000. White prisoner transport vehicles formed such a long convoy on the highway that one "could not see the end of it."[206]

One practitioner who was arrested after protesting on Tiananmen Square on December 29, 2000 recalled,

> *Those who didn't give their names were taken away... each person was given a number and had their photo taken. On the night of December 31, the police called out our numbers and put us in police vehicles that each held 12-13 people... The convoy stopped in Jinzhou, where we were distributed to buses to various detention centers. There were 50 of us on my bus, and we were taken to*

Anshan First Detention Center... The police deceived us by offering to let us call our families and promising to protect our privacy, only to see police officers from our hometowns show up. When the deputy head of the Beijing Chongwen District Donghuashi Police Station came to pick people up on January 11, 2001, he identified people using photos and took us back [to Beijing]. When we left Anshan First Detention Center, a police officer there said, "Hurry up and go back. [We] can't release anyone who doesn't give their name or is unclaimed [by their local police force]. There are orders from above. We're not responsible if anyone dies, and no one would even know."[207]

Another practitioner witnessed how unidentified practitioners in Beijing detention centers were moved to northeastern China in 2001:

After December 20, 2000, the number of practitioners sent to detention centers suddenly increased to dozens or even over a hundred each day... All practitioners were assigned a number... Within a few days the cells were full. The guards interrogated them each day and asked for their names. They used electric batons and other forms of torture on the practitioners and also encouraged the inmates to beat the practitioners. Most of the practitioners still refused to tell their names. The guards finally stopped asking and said, "Ok, if you refuse to tell me, I'll send you to a place where you will tell."

In early 2001, groups of practitioners were sent away in big buses in the early morning every other day. An eighteen-year-old girl from Shandong Province shared the same cell with me. Her number was K28. One morning her number was called by mistake. She got on the bus but later returned. She said all of the practitioners were being taken to northeastern China. Later, the guards openly told us that they were sending practitioners to northeastern China.[208]

§7.3 Involvement of the Military

Because the judicial system cannot detain inmates without names or addresses for long, many unidentified practitioners have been transferred to military detention facilities, including the concentration camps referred to by the military doctor at the beginning of this chapter.

China has an extensive military medical system, including general hospitals of the People's Liberation Army (PLA) and each PLA branch, as well as hospitals associated with military medical universities. *Life Week* magazine reported in April 2006 that "98 percent of China's supply of organs is controlled by systems outside the Ministry of Health."[209] Military hospitals and armed police hospitals control a large portion of organ sources, and most civilian hospitals that carry out large numbers of organ transplants have close ties to military hospitals. Many of their transplant surgeons serve in military hospitals concurrently.

In their investigative report *Bloody Harvest*, David Matas and David Kilgour interviewed several patients who went to China for organ transplants. The surgeons who operated on these patients all had military backgrounds. One of the patients was admitted at the Shanghai No.1 People's Hospital. His surgeon was Dr. Tan Jianming, who is the chief surgeon of the Fuzhou General Hospital of the Nanjing Military Region (formerly known as the 93rd Hospital). Tan also performs surgeries at the PLA's 85th Hospital of the Nanjing Military Region in Shanghai.

Another patient went first to Huashan Hospital in Shanghai (affiliated with Fudan University) for a liver transplant. He was placed under the care of Qian Jianmin, deputy director of the liver center at Huashan Hospital. When no matching organ could be found after several days, Qian suggested that he be transferred to Changzheng Hospital in Shanghai, which is affiliated with Second Military Medical University, saying that it was easier to get organs there. A matching liver was found for the patient on the day he transferred to Changzheng Hospital.

Other examples of close ties between civilian and military transplant facilities and personnel can be found in the 2016 *Minghui Human Rights Report: Falun Gong Practitioners Systematically Murdered in China for Their Organs.*

§7.4 Forced Blood Testing

Blood testing is a necessary step for matching potential donors and recipients for organ transplants. Falun Gong practitioners have been subjected to forced blood tests and other organ examinations from before 2006 through to the present day. These tests specifically target Falun Gong practitioners, not other prisoners.

Involuntary blood testing of Falun Gong practitioners takes place routinely in labor camps, detention centers, prisons, and brainwashing centers. Similar accounts were given in interviews by David Matas and David Kilgour in *Bloody Harvest.* Because practitioners are routinely tortured in these facilities, not given medical treatment if adverse conditions are discovered, and not given the test results themselves, investigators have concluded that these tests are not done for the practitioners' health; rather, they are used to locate healthy practitioners for organ matching purposes.

Authorities have also carried out forced blood sampling outside of state detention facilities, either by apprehending practitioners for this purpose or by collecting blood directly in their homes and workplaces. Police in some regions have claimed that the collection of blood samples was for the purpose of building a DNA database of Falun Gong practitioners.[210] [211]

§7.5 Witness Accounts

In addition to the testimonies of Peter, Annie, and the Chinese military doctor at the beginning of this chapter, admissions by individuals involved in the illegal transplant system in various roles have shed light on the Chinese regime's killing for organs.

On November 17, 2006, Israel's largest newspaper reported the arrests of four men accused of pocketing millions of dollars that patients had paid for organ transplants. Yaron Izhak Yodukin, CEO of Medikt Ltd., and his associates faced charges of not reporting income earned by mediating organ transplants for Israelis in China and the Philippines.

The main suspect admitted to an Israeli newspaper that the organs came from Chinese death-row inmates and prisoners of conscience, including Falun Gong practitioners.

Volunteer groups working to stop the persecution of Falun Gong in China received a report from a police officer in 2009 who witnessed doctors removing organs from a female Falun Gong practitioner while she was still alive. The event took place in an operating room on the 15th floor of the General Hospital of the Shenyang Military Region on April 9, 2002. The victim was in her 30s and was a teacher from a middle school. She died with full awareness that her organs were being extracted. The officer also saw the victim being beaten and repeatedly raped in the month before the organ harvesting took place.

§7.6 Admissions in Telephone Investigations

International investigators have made phone calls to Chinese hospitals under the guise of inquiring about the availability of organ transplants on behalf of prospective recipients. Medical staff and other individuals involved in illicit transplants have admitted in these conversations that organs were taken from Falun Gong practitioners.

Below are a few examples; more have been published by people who have volunteered to investigate the persecution of Falun Gong in China over the years.[212]

Case 1: Lu Guoping of Nanning City Minzu Hospital, Guangxi Autonomous Region

Lu Guoping, a surgeon at the Nanning City Minzu Hospital in Guangxi Autonomous Region, acknowledged several times in a phone conversation that Falun Gong practitioners were the source of organ supplies. He said, "Some are from Falun Gong. Some from families of patients." The following is an excerpt of the conversation between Lu and an investigator:

Investigator: Then did your classmate tell you that the [organ transplantation] operations they performed were all [with organ sources from] Falun Gong, is that right?

Doctor Lu: Some are from Falun Gong. Some from families of patients.

Investigator: Oh. Then if I want to find this type for my child, this type [of organ] from Falun Gong, do you think he can help me find any?

Doctor Lu: He definitely can find it for you.

Investigator: What you used before [organs from Falun Gong practitioners], was it from detention center[s] or prison[s]?"

Doctor Lu: From prisons.

Investigator: From prisons? And it was from healthy Falun Gong practitioners...?

Doctor Lu: Correct. We could choose the good ones because we assure the quality in our operations.

Case 2: Representative of the PLA No.307 Hospital Brokered Kidneys from Falun Gong Practitioners

Investigators contacted a broker representative of the People's Liberation Army No.307 Hospital in Beijing under the guise of helping family members and friends to find suitable kidneys for their transplant requests. The contact spanned several weeks.

Excerpt of conversations:

Investigator: then you go ahead and help me check it out, whether...

PLA No.307 Hospital Representative: I told you before, didn't I? I told you before that we told you the real story, we have done two cases. You know, we did two cases.

Investigator: You mean two operations involving Falun Gong practitioners as source?

PLA No.307 Hospital Representative: That's right, we did two cases. The prison told us they did that with Falun Gong. I also told that lady that we indeed performed such operations. Now, however, it is getting more difficult than before.

Investigator: Where did you find the kidney sources before?

PLA No.307 Hospital Representative: From Xicheng District [in Beijing].

Investigator: Alright, besides it, how could you be so sure he (the source) was a Falun Gong practitioner, did you find out for sure?

PLA No.307 Hospital Representative: How to positively identify as Falun Gong practitioner, well, when the time comes --- when the time comes our side, our Boss will have people showing you information, you know, he will show you the information and data, you can be sure.

Investigator: Oh, that's fine.

Case 3: Li Honghui, Director of Yuquan Hospital (No.2 Affiliated Hospital of Tsinghua University)

On April 28, 2006, a Sound of Hope journalist made contact with Li Honghui, director of the Kidney Transplant Department at Yuquan Hospital, also known as No.2 Affiliated Hospital of Tsinghua University. Li admitted that organs were taken from Falun Gong practitioners.

Excerpt of conversation:

Li Honghui: It happened that for the past several years that donor organs were from Falun Gong practitioners.

Investigator: Do you mean that this type of donor was quite easy to get several years ago?

Li Honghui: That's true.

Investigator: Can you supply young and healthy donors, such as people who practice Falun Gong?

Li Honghui: This request can be considered, I will tell you when the time comes.

Chapter 8: Persecution Extended Outside Mainland China

The CCP has extended its persecution of Falun Gong to other countries through its network of 610 Offices and its embassies and consulates, which in turn direct Chinese community, business, and student associations to interfere with Falun Gong activities, collect information about practitioners, and attempt to turn foreign officials, legislators, and civic organizations against Falun Gong. In addition, the CCP pressures media outlets outside of China not to cover Falun Gong events or report on the persecution in China. It also uses Chinese news media in other countries to spread anti-Falun Gong propaganda.

A former diplomat from the Chinese Consulate in Sydney revealed that Chinese embassies and consulates have set up political sections dedicated to monitoring and suppressing overseas dissidents. In Sydney, for example, the consulate's "Special Group Against Falun Gong" consisted of the head of each department, including those responsible for political investigation, culture, visas, education, and Chinese nationals in the foreign country. These special task forces were headed by the ambassador or consul general.[213]

§8.1 Violence and Threats Against Practitioners Abroad

Chinese consulates have recruited members of local Chinese communities to defame and harass Falun Gong practitioners who regularly set up information booths to raise awareness of the persecution in China. For example, mob attacks on Falun Gong practitioners have been linked to the Chinese consul general in New York, Peng Keyu, who was recorded in a phone interview admitting involvement in encouraging the mob participants to attack practitioners.[214] In Hong Kong, such attacks are carried out by other organizations that serve as extensions of the CCP.

§§8.1.1 Australian Falun Gong Practitioners Shot During Chinese Official's Visit to South Africa[215]

Zeng Qinghong, a major player in Jiang Zemin's persecution of Falun Gong, visited South Africa in June 2004. After learning that Zeng Qinghong and other Chinese officials were visiting South Africa, nine Australian Falun Gong practitioners arrived at the Johannesburg International Airport on June 28, seeking to put a stop to the persecution of Falun Gong by filing lawsuits against Chinese officials directing the persecution (practitioners in other countries had filed lawsuits against Jiang Zemin for genocide and torture). Because there were no Falun Gong practitioners in Johannesburg, a practitioner from another city in South Africa picked them up. The nine Australian practitioners left the airport in two cars, heading to the Presidential Guest House in Pretoria.

On the way there, someone in a white car opened fire slightly behind the second vehicle driven by the practitioners, targeting the tires and the driver. The car was hit at least five times. The driver, David Liang, was hit in both feet. The car was severely damaged and came to a stop. The gunmen fled. David Liang was rushed to the nearby Chris Hani-Baragwanath Hospital with crushing fractures in one foot.

§§8.1.2 CCP Agents Break into Practitioners' Homes to Steal Information

On February 8, 2006, CCP agents armed with guns broke into the home of Falun Gong practitioner Dr. Li Yuan in Atlanta, Georgia. Dr. Li was the Chief Technical Officer of *The Epoch Times*. The agents covered him with a heavy comforter until he almost suffocated. Then they took off the comforter and started hitting him, especially in the temples. They taped his mouth, eyes, and ears; tied his arms behind his back, and tied up his legs. He couldn't move, see, or shout.

One of the men asked Dr. Li in Mandarin, "Where is your safe?" They searched upstairs and downstairs for about half an hour and pried open his file cabinets. The agents stole two laptops but left other valuables untouched. Dr. Li's neighbor called the police after the intruders left. Dr. Li was taken to a hospital by ambulance and needed 15 stitches on his face.[216]

On March 10 of the same year, burglars broke into another practitioner's home in Osaka, Japan, and stole two desktop computers, a laptop, and a digital camera but did not touch any cash or other valuables. A police investigation at the scene concluded that the burglary was aimed at stealing information. The home served as an administrative office for *The Epoch Times*, and the break-in took place a day after the newspaper published an article exposing the Chinese regime's killing of Falun Gong practitioners for organs.

The day before the break-in, a Chinese journalist sent to Japan warned *The Epoch Times* staff during an interview, "Recently, Falun Gong practitioners were beaten in Hong Kong, and *The Epoch Times* print office in Hong Kong was smashed. I would like to remind Falun Gong practitioners and groups in Japan to be extremely cautious about their safety." The owner of the home, Mr. Cai, said that he had received harassing phone calls.[217]

§§8.1.3 Chinese Consulates Instigate Attacks and Other Hate Crimes on U.S. Soil

Thirteen practitioners in Flushing, New York, filed a lawsuit in 2015 describing nearly 40 incidents in which Falun Gong practitioners were beaten, harassed, or given death threats in a well-coordinated campaign of violence and intimidation. These threats were accompanied by Chinese-language posters displayed prominently in Flushing urging residents and visitors to "beat Falun Gong believers as they would rats."

In one incident, practitioners Li Xiurong and Cao Lijun were walking in Flushing when they were attacked by Li Huahong, who summoned a mob of almost 30 people. While Cao managed to escape and seek help, the mob held onto Li and yelled, "Kill her!" and "Beat her to death!"

The lawsuit described a similar incident in which three Falun Gong practitioners were walking in Flushing on July 14, 2014, when one of the defendants told them, "You are even worse than dogs. I am going to round you all up and exterminate all of you within three months. I will strangle all of you to death... I'll finish you. I'll dig out your hearts, livers, and lungs. Someone will kill you."

In 2008, mob attacks on Falun Gong practitioners in Flushing were linked to the Chinese Consulate in New York. Consul General Peng Keyu admitted in an audio recording that he had "secretly encouraged" the mob's participants, thanked the mob members personally, and "ran other things on the scene." Several sources reported to *Epoch Times* that Peng paid the mob members between $50 and $100 a day to participate in the disruptive activities.[218]

Similar hate crimes have occurred in other cities, either directly instigated by organizations connected to the CCP or as a result of anti-Falun Gong propaganda spread through CCP-controlled media and associations. After a string of physical attacks on practitioners in San Francisco, U.S. Congressman Ed Royce wrote to the Department of State to express his concern about the "deeply troubling" prospect of official Chinese representatives spreading the persecution of Falun Gong to the U.S.[219] In one such attack, the perpetrator punched an elderly man in the face before issuing a series of profanities at Falun Gong and adding, "If [we] were in mainland China, I would break your leg."

§§8.1.4 Chinese Diplomats Responsible for Violence and Disruptions During State Visits

When Chinese officials visit other countries, local Chinese consulates hire "welcome groups" to wave Chinese flags and prevent Chinese delegations from seeing the banners of Falun Gong practitioners who stage peaceful protests to call for an end to the persecution in China.

In 2014, when welcome groups hired by the CCP in Australia tried to block and even attack practitioners in Brisbane and Canberra during Chinese president Xi Jinping's G20 visit in 2014, the local police moved them away, threw away their flags, and banned them from getting near the Falun Gong protestors. Police officers also helped practitioners to hang their banners up high so that Xi's motorcade could see them.

Two Chinese diplomats were arrested in Argentina and the Czech Republic for using force to disrupt peaceful protests by local Falun Gong practitioners during Chinese delegation visits in the summer of 2014.

In Auckland and Wellington, New Zealand, the police helped the practitioners find the best place to display their banners. When the welcome groups came, the police directed them to stay on the other side of the street. Seven officers were stationed to protect the practitioners.

§§8.1.5 Intimidation and Attacks on Practitioners and Tourists in Hong Kong

Since 2012, the Hong Kong Youth Care Association, which acts as an extension of China's 610 Office, has regularly harassed Falun Gong practitioners and disrupted their events in Hong Kong.[220] Members of the Youth Care Association wear green shirts and routinely surround practitioners at event sites, use megaphones at close range to shout insults and threats, spit on practitioners, and even physically assault them. In one incident, an individual affiliated with the Youth Care Association brandished a large knife to threaten a Falun Gong practitioner. In addition to covering up practitioners' banners, Youth Care Association members have displayed their own banners defaming Falun Gong.

A visitor to Hong Kong recalled an incident from January 2019:[221]

As soon as a practitioner began talking about the CCP's persecution, members of the Youth Care Association stepped in and interrupted. The Youth Care Association members' clothes were covered with words defaming Falun Gong. They also carried loudspeakers and broadcast similar messages.

They did not let tourists read the practitioners' posters and intimidated them by recording them and threatening to post the videos online. Every member of the Youth Care Association had a camcorder under his neck so they could easily record anyone who interacted with practitioners. They were very aggressive. In contrast, the practitioners held banners and poster boards peacefully.

On September 24, 2019, Falun Gong practitioner Ms. Liao Qiulan was attacked by two mobsters in the Lai Chi Kok neighborhood of Hong Kong. After being hit numerous times with expandable batons, her head bled profusely. The attack took place after Ms. Liao left the Cheung Sha Wan Police Station after a meeting to discuss the issuance of a permit for Falun Gong activities on October 1, the CCP's National Day celebration.[222]

§8.2 Persecution in Other Countries and Repatriation of Practitioners to China

Several national governments with ideological ties to the Chinese regime or under direct pressure from Beijing have chosen to cooperate with the CCP's persecution policy at different times by arresting Falun Gong practitioners and/or repatriating them to China, where they face torture or even death.

Case 1: Cambodian Couple Deported, Taken to Forced Labor Camp in China[223]

An elderly Chinese couple were working in Cambodia when their employer discovered that they practiced Falun Gong by illegally inspecting their mail. After their employer reported them to the Chinese Embassy, officials from the embassy and Cambodian police arrested the couple and sent them back to China in August 2002, despite their United Nations refugee status. The couple were subsequently taken to a forced labor camp.

Chinese embassy officials in Cambodia also tried to apprehend two other elderly practitioners, who managed to evade arrest by going into hiding. A high-ranking official from the UN refugee office intervened, and these two practitioners were eventually given refuge in another country.

Case 2: Russia Deports Falun Gong Practitioners Despite UN Refugee Status

Despite having been granted UN refugee status, Ms. Ma Hui and her eight-year-old daughter Ma Jingjing were taken away from their home by six officers from the Deportation Department of the Immigration Bureau in St. Petersburg on March 28, 2007. That night, a Russian policewoman and several Chinese government officers forced the mother and daughter to board a flight to Beijing. However, her family did not see either Ms. Ma or her daughter at the airport in Beijing. They later received a phone call from a man who told them that Ma Jingjing had arrived at Ms. Ma's sister's home, but it was unclear whether Ms. Ma could go home. Her family suspected that she was being held by state security personnel.[224]

On May 12 of the same year, several Russian immigration officers took Mr. Gao Chunman, 73, away from his home without any explanation or documentation. That evening, police informed his Russian wife, Mira, that the authorities had flown Mr. Gao to Moscow to await the earliest flight to Beijing. Mr. Gao, a former professor at Tsinghua University, had fled China due to the persecution of Falun Gong. He was granted UN refugee status in 2003.[225]

Case 3: Vietnam Sentences Two Practitioners for Broadcasting Uncensored News to China via Radio[226]

In November 2011 in Hanoi, Mr. Vu Duc Trung, a thirty-one-year-old CEO of a high-tech company, and his thirty-six-year-old brother-in-law Mr. Le Van Thanh were sentenced to prison, for three and two years respectively. They were charged with "transmitting information illegally onto the telecommunications network" for having broadcast Sound of Hope radio news programs via short-wave radio into China. Sound of Hope's programs typically report on human rights abuses, corruption, and repression of Falun Gong practitioners and other persecuted groups. Trung initiated the broadcasts in April 2009, and the two men were arrested on June 11, 2010.

Their sentence came amid a broader intensification of Vietnamese harassment of the local Falun Gong community following direct pressure from the Chinese Communist Party. According to the indictment, the Vietnamese government arrested the men after a diplomatic memo was sent on May 30, 2010 from the Chinese Embassy to Vietnam's Ministry of Investigation and Security. "The memo stated that the Police Department in China discovered radio signals coming from Vietnamese territory containing the same content about Falun Gong as heard on the Sound of Hope radio station," the indictment reads. "It was recommended that all ... activities of Falun Gong individuals in Vietnamese territory must be attacked and stopped."

The trial was originally scheduled for October. On the morning of the original trial date, at least 30 other Falun Gong practitioners who had been holding a quiet sit-in in front of the Chinese Consulate were taken into custody by Vietnamese authorities. According to eyewitnesses, the individuals were forced onto a bus, some violently, and then separated into smaller groups and taken to separate locations. Several practitioners who had been meditating at Le Van Tam Park were also detained.[227]

Case 4: South Korea Deports Practitioners, Denies Asylum Under CCP Pressure

Between 2009 and 2011, the South Korean government deported at least 10 Falun Gong practitioners back to China and denied asylum to an additional 56 practitioners. An official in the South Korean government told reporters that Li Changchun, a member of the CCP Politburo Standing Committee, pressured the South Korean government to "drive Falun Gong practitioners out of South Korea." This occurred shortly before the South Korean Ministry of Justice started denying asylum applications from Falun Gong practitioners. Repatriations began soon after.[228]

Yin Xiangzi, a practitioner who was deported from South Korea back to China on January 30, 2010, later managed to escape China. Below are excerpts of what she went through after being taken back to China:[229]

State Security agents illegally searched my home, placed me under surveillance, and harassed me.

The police brought in a former practitioner who had been deceived by the CCP to try to brainwash me. This person was cold and calculating. He kept pouring his devious interpretation of Falun Gong into my mind. By then, I had had almost no sleep for 72 hours and wasn't thinking clearly. I signed a guarantee statement promising that I would no longer practice Falun Gong. Then I was released. They demanded that I report to them before I went anywhere. They also started monitoring my phone.

During the interrogations, I found out that the CCP police system had extensive knowledge about Falun Gong practitioners in South Korea. They mentioned on various occasions the names of numerous coordinators in South Korea as well as names of several practitioners who went to South Korea from Yanji City. They asked me if I knew them. They showed me a photograph of the South Korean Tian Guo Marching Band taken in a parade. I noticed that I was in the picture. They asked me to identify Falun Gong practitioners in the photo. They also showed me a list of Falun Gong practitioners who had helped other practitioners apply for refugee status. CCP special agents even visited my Falun Gong practice site in South Korea.

After I was released, although I was not imprisoned, I was in extreme misery. Falun Gong not only restored my health but also gave me a healthy mind. Yet I betrayed Falun Gong against my own conscience. I felt despair, humiliation, and regret.

Ms. Yin decided to start practicing Falun Gong again a month later. She kept a low profile, however, as she was under surveillance and frequently stalked by suspicious individuals. As she recollected:

In mid-March 2011, members of the Yanji 610 Office called and asked to meet with me at a tea house. The meeting lasted about 30 minutes. They told me I could go to South Korea again, with one condition: that I help them to gather information on Falun Gong practitioners in South Korea.

They wanted to recruit me as a CCP special agent and planned to teach me computer skills so I could send Falun Gong intelligence back to them over the Internet. I turned down their offer on the spot. They then said that if I refused to cooperate, there was no chance that I could leave China. My name was on the blacklist at customs, and anyone on that list was restricted from leaving China.

In the several months that followed, I did not hear from them. I lived in constant fear. I moved from place to place several times, yet my fear followed me. I made up my mind to escape from China.

§8.3 Intimidation of Foreign Officials and Civic Organizations

Chinese consulates around the world routinely contact their host countries' organizations and officials, ranging from national politicians to city councilors, for the purposes of defaming Falun Gong and interfering with practitioners' activities. The consulates' strategies include both disinformation campaigns and direct threats.

§§8.3.1 Interference with Peaceful Protests

In addition to blocking, threatening, and assaulting Falun Gong practitioners who hold peaceful protests to raise awareness of the persecution in China, the CCP has also pressured foreign governments to deny practitioners their rights to lawful assembly and free speech during visits by Chinese officials. Some governments have violated their own laws by agreeing to the Chinese regime's demands.

Case 1: Iceland Bows to CCP Pressure and Bars Practitioners from Entry

When then CCP leader Jiang Zemin visited Iceland in June 2002, the Icelandic government barred Falun Gong practitioners from entering the country after being pressured by Chinese officials. This triggered a strong reaction from Icelandic citizens, who rallied to support Falun Gong practitioners.[230] "It's the talk of the town...the whole country is behind Falun Gong," said Joel Chipkar, a Falun Gong practitioner from Canada who was in Iceland for several days. "Every media outlet, every TV station, every radio station, every newspaper... it's been the top story here."

On June 9, 2002, a large group of Icelanders joined Falun Gong practitioners in the park to learn the Falun Gong exercises and express their concern regarding the situation. "I stand with you," offered one man, who added, "If the Chinese delegates try to shoot you, they have to shoot me first."

"We've been getting a steady stream of supportive e-mails and phone calls from the Icelandic people," said Falun Dafa Information Centre spokesperson Peter Jauhal. "We are all touched and encouraged by the outpouring of support."

Most of the letters expressed outrage at the Icelandic government's banning of Falun Gong practitioners during Jiang's visit. Many offered to hold peaceful appeals against the persecution of Falun Gong in the place of those who had been denied entry.

Case 2: Serbia Denies Entry to Falun Gong Practitioners During China Summit

Eleven European Falun Gong practitioners were forcibly removed from Belgrade, Serbia, prior to the CEE-China (Central and Eastern Europe) summit on December 16-17, 2014. They were detained outside of Belgrade during the event and deported to Bulgaria, Slovakia, and Finland after the summit was over. The local authorities denied the practitioners' protest permit application without giving a reason.[231]

Case 3: Practitioners Denied Entry to Hong Kong to Attend Peaceful Protest[232]

About 70 Falun Gong practitioners from Taiwan were deported from Hong Kong on April 26 and 27, 2019 on their way to take part in the "March in Commemoration of the 20th Anniversary of the April 25 Appeal." All of them had legal travel documents to enter Hong Kong.

Ms. Ding, one of the Taiwanese practitioners deported from Hong Kong, recalled:

> *The customs officer in Hong Kong had a strained expression when he saw my name. He asked me to fill out a form and took me into a small room. He told me that even though I had a valid visa, the policy was not to allow me to enter Hong Kong.*

Taiwan's Mainland Affairs Council (MAC) issued a statement condemning the Hong Kong government's mistreatment of Taiwanese citizens. "We regard freedom of speech and freedom of religion as basic human rights. We hope that the Hong Kong government can react rationally to and respect legal and peaceful expressions from citizens of Taiwan," stated Mr. Chiu Chui-cheng, Deputy Minister and spokesperson of the MAC. He went on to question how the Hong Kong government obtained information about Taiwan citizens' travel plans and selectively blocked the entrance of all Falun Gong practitioners on the flight, adding that the next step would be to investigate the invasion of Taiwanese citizens' privacy.

§§8.3.2 Interference with Community Activities

When practitioners apply to participate in parades and other community events, Chinese consulates often contact hosting organizations to demand that they exclude Falun Gong practitioners and withdraw support for their activities.

In San Francisco, practitioners were repeatedly barred from participating in the Chinese New Year Parade by the Chinese Chamber of Commerce at the direction of Rose Pak, a personal friend of Jiang

Zemin who had close ties to the Chinese Consulate and actively supported the persecution of Falun Gong in the San Francisco Bay Area.[233]

In Denmark, Falun Gong practitioners' invitation to participate in an Asian cultural festival in 2002 was suddenly revoked after other Chinese organizations threatened to withdraw from the event after being pressured by the Chinese government. According to the Danish newspaper Politiken, "The Chinese Embassy in Copenhagen was unhappy that [Falun Gong] originally was in the picture at the festival, even though they only planned to perform a [traditional] Chinese dance." The festival organizer later gave practitioners a permit to perform on the last day of the three-day event.[234]

For the 2018 Perth Christmas Parade in Australia, Falun Gong practitioners were told on the morning of the parade that they could not display Falun Gong banners or wear T-shirts bearing the name, nor was the TV station covering the event allowed to mention Falun Gong. No other groups in the parade were given such restrictions. National newspaper *The Australian* reported that a man claiming to work for the General Consulate of China in Perth had called the parade organizer the day before and told them to ban the practitioners from participating.[235]

In Scotland, the Chinese Consulate wrote to the organizer of the Edinburgh One World Festival in 2003, demanding that the festival remove a workshop by practitioners from its program. The organizer ignored the complaint and said, "We can invite whoever we'd like!"[236]

§§8.3.3 Interference with Shen Yun Performances

Shen Yun Performing Arts is a classical Chinese dance and music company founded by Falun Gong practitioners. Its mission is to revive the essence of traditional Chinese culture through performing arts. Because some of Shen Yun's programs depict the persecution of Falun Gong in China on stage, the CCP has systematically attempted to sabotage the show since its inception in 2006.

One of the CCP's strategies is to order its embassies and consulates around the world to pressure theaters not to sign contracts with Shen Yun or to nullify existing agreements, threatening theater managers that their countries' political and economic relations with China would be harmed if they did not comply.[237] This strategy has achieved little success, however, as very few theaters cancelled their contracts with Shen Yun. For example, two German corporations that partnered with Shen Yun received phone calls from the Chinese consulate in Frankfurt, but they refused to cancel the partnership. One company responded by saying, "We have freedom of speech in Germany. We decide what we want to do." [238]

Nevertheless, a small number of venues have bowed to CCP pressure. For example, the Royal Danish Theater suddenly withdrew from a nearly finalized agreement after the Chinese Embassy brought up its issue with Shen Yun in a meeting with the Danish Ministry of Foreign Affairs in 2007. After more rejections in subsequent years, it was revealed in 2018 that the Chinese Embassy had asked the Royal Theater to refuse Shen Yun access to the national stage.[239]

In South Korea, the Chinese regime threatened the Korean Broadcasting Service (KBS) with the loss of $8 billion in revenue from its business deals with China if it allowed Shen Yun to perform in KBS Hall. KBS subsequently canceled its contract with Shen Yun. The cancellation was declared void by the Seoul Southern District Court, but the same court later announced a reversal of its decision half an hour before all administrative offices, courts, embassies, and theaters went on a national holiday, leaving no time to appeal the decision until after the scheduled performances were over.[240]

In addition to threats, the CCP has adopted more underhanded tactics, such as tampering with Shen Yun's tour vehicles. In one case, a cut was made in the front tire of a bus such that it would not instantly deflate but would explode under high pressure on the freeway. The damage was discovered during inspections and did not cause any casualties, however.[241]

In 2010, seven sold-out Shen Yun performances in Hong Kong had to be cancelled after six key production staff members were denied entry visas into the Chinese autonomous region. Although the show's presenters applied for the visas in October 2009, the denials came only a week before the opening show on January 27. Given the late decision, there was no time for the presenters to respond with legal action.[242]

Chinese consulates have also attempted to intimidate audience members to prevent them from attending the show. In some North American cities, these threats were facilitated by Chinese business associations and student associations. Some consulates also told Chinese students that they would not be allowed back into China if they were found in photographic or video footage of the show.[243]

Despite its intentions, the CCP's efforts to prevent politicians and other audience members from watching Shen Yun have instead served to promote the show. In response to receiving defamatory information from Chinese embassies, a German legislator promptly decided to go see the show instead, and the President and a Vice President of the European Parliament jointly sent a congratulatory letter to extend their best wishes for Shen Yun's success in Germany.[244]

§§8.3.4 Interference with Legislation

A resolution condemning the persecution of Falun Gong in China (SJR-10) was passed by the California State Senate's judiciary committee on August 31, 2017. However, the senate unexpectedly voted to refer the bill back to the rules committee, essentially blocking it from coming to a vote in the senate on September 1 as originally planned.

The reason given for the surprise vote was that senators had received emails from the Chinese Consulate in San Francisco suggesting that passage of the resolution might "sabotage the friendship and sustainable development of relationship(s) between California and China."[245]

The decision prompted Falun Gong practitioners to hold rallies in in San Francisco, Sacramento, Los Angeles, and San Diego. State Senator Joel Anderson, the initiator of the bill, expressed outrage at the Chinese regime's extension of its suppression of freedom of speech to the California state senate and its interference as a foreign power in the state's legislative procedure.

It is worth noting that Assemblyman Randy Voepel, a co-signer of the resolution, had previously received a threatening letter from the Chinese Consulate in Los Angeles when he was the mayor of Santee, California. The letter defamed Falun Gong and listed a number of demands: "We hope the City will, from the perspective of China-U.S. relations and the interest of its citizens, consider our requests carefully and not give the Falun Gong [organization] any awards or support, including naming a certain day or week after Falun Gong, Falun Dafa, or its founder. We also ask that the City not allow Falun Gong to register ..." and so on.[246]

In Minnesota, shortly after two bills (SF2090, HF2166) condemning the Chinese regime's harvesting of organs from Falun Gong practitioners were submitted to the house and senate in 2015, the Chinese Consulate in Chicago pressured state legislators, attempting to block the bills before they passed the subcommittees. The consulate sent letters slandering Falun Gong to the legislators, and the Deputy Consul General met with State Senator Dan D. Hall, who authored SF2090. Senator Hall later made a post on his website about the meeting and reaffirmed the importance of religious freedom and free speech.[247]

§§8.3.5 Fraudulent Email Campaigns Aimed to Discredit Falun Gong Practitioners

The Chinese regime has carried out multiple fraudulent email campaigns in its attempts to defame Falun Gong in the eyes of foreign officials. These emails are sent in the name of Falun Gong practitioners abroad, but they are filled with threatening and derogatory language and can typically be traced back to mainland China.

Around World Falun Dafa Day on May 13, 2015, some Canadian Members of Parliament began to receive emails from two different sources. A sender by the name of "Andrew Tang" called the recipient "stupid" for not attending Falun Dafa Day celebrations and losing "the last chance for you to be saved." The other sender told the recipient, "Waiting for you will be a THOROUGH ELIMINATION!" Deputy Green Party Leader Bruce Hyer told practitioners, "It didn't make sense to me, and right away I assumed that it was probably true that those emails came from someplace else."[248]

Similar emails have been received by officials in the U.S., France, Norway, Australia, and New Zealand. After the Christchurch earthquake in 2011, CCP agents sent emails to Auckland city councilors, posing as Falun Gong practitioners and claiming that the earthquake occurred because people there did not believe in Falun Gong. Councilor Dr. Cathy Casey said she believed the emails originated from the Chinese regime because all the Auckland councilors had previously received official emails from the Chinese Consul General defaming Falun Gong and urging people not to attend the Shen Yun show scheduled in Auckland that February.[249]

§§8.3.6 Buying Political Influence with Lavish Entertainment and Blackmail

The Chinese regime routinely invites foreign politicians, professors, professionals, and other influential figures to visit China, where they are given royal treatment in exchange for supporting the CCP's position and praising the regime after they return. Many who have enjoyed these benefits then turn a blind eye to the human rights abuses committed by the CCP or actively help the regime cover up its crimes.

Case 1: Vancouver Mayor Has Falun Gong Protest Site Dismantled after Returning from China

Practitioners in Vancouver, Canada started around-the-clock peaceful protests in front of the Chinese Consulate in August 2001, helping many locals to learn about the persecution of Falun Gong in China. Consul General Yang Qiang asked Mayor Li Jianbao to remove the practitioners' protest structures, but Li refused, citing Canadian values of freedom of speech and freedom of belief. Yang later admitted publicly that he had asked the City of Vancouver many times to remove Falun Gong practitioners' protests but to no avail.

After Sam Sullivan was elected mayor of Vancouver in 2005 and went on a visit to China, however, he applied for an injunction from the Supreme Court of British Columbia in 2006 to remove Falun Gong practitioners' protest boards and small blue hut that had stood in front of the consulate for more than five years. The injunction was granted in 2009, but practitioners later won the case in the British Columbia Court of Appeal the next year.

Sullivan initially denied having any contact with the Chinese Consulate before he made the decision to dismantle the protest site. When he was asked about it again later, he said that he was invited by Yang Qiang to a private dinner held at the former Consul General's residence, where Sullivan told Yang that he had submitted the application to the B.C. Supreme Court and that a decision would be forthcoming.

CCP-controlled newspapers published several articles speaking highly of Sullivan. The *Vancouver Sun* published an interview with Sullivan in which he said, "During my visit in China, they welcomed me with a red carpet and treated me like an emperor. It's a pity that Vancouver doesn't have such a large budget so that I could pay them back."[250]

Case 2: Former Canadian Member of Parliament

Recalls Own Trips to China

Former Canadian MP Rob Anders recalled how the Chinese regime systematically tried to win his favor and that of other Canadian politicians: "The first bait they cast was a business deal. If you don't go for it, they'll move to the second one: young, pretty girls. If you still don't fall into the trap, they'll try alcohol or other things."

He noted that the CCP treated officials' staff and family members the same way: "I know when ministers' staff members went to China, without exception, a girl would come up and ask if they wanted to have some fun, go have dinner together, or go sing karaoke. So, they would drink and have fun. And then it's like a chain reaction ... They'll show you a video recording of you in China. [They'll say], 'you know, we're friends, right? We don't want this kind of video to affect your career, so we'll return the video to you, but we can't guarantee there are no copies. You understand we're friends, so now that we've given you so much help, shouldn't you show some appreciation?'"

Anders described another case in which he went to China with another MP, who brought his forteen-year-old son along. Five minutes after they moved into their hotel, a Chinese girl knocked on his son's door, made flattering comments, and invited him to eat, sing karaoke, and dance. His son left with the girl and was not seen again for the entire week of their stay.[251]

Other Examples of Influence Through Favors and Blackmail

Ottawa Mayor Larry O'Brien used to issue a proclamation for World Falun Dafa Day each year. After taking a business trip to China, however, he refused to do so in May 2010, explaining that he had "made a commitment" in China.[252]

Former Chinese diplomat Chen Yonglin described the case of an Australian Member of Parliament (MP) who had sex with a girl under 16 in China. He was detained, recorded and released without any publicity. Later, he spoke on TV in favor of the Chinese government. Chen explained, "When important delegations go to China, they are under strict surveillance, and if necessary, the CCP will set some traps. It doesn't matter if the delegations are from Australia or Canada."[253]

§8.4 Censorship of International Media Outlets

The CCP has also used Chinese embassies and consulates to censor Chinese language media outlets abroad. For example, the Chinese Consul General in Melbourne, Australia, instructed the heads of local Chinese newspapers not to publish any articles related to Falun Gong before faxing them to the Chinese Consulate for approval. As a result, Chinese newspapers in Melbourne have declined to publish Falun Gong articles ever since, with some outlets telling practitioners that the pressure on them was too great.

In 2008, Reporters Without Borders in Paris published an audio file showing that EutelSat, a French satellite operator, stopped broadcasting NTDTV, an independent television station founded by Falun Gong practitioners, to China because the CCP exerted pressure on EutelSat. Sun Yuxi, the Chinese ambassador to Italy, said in a phone interview, "I have contacted the president and the vice president of EutelSat. I asked them why they help Falun Gong to broadcast to China. They explained to me that they didn't mean to, and they were tricked by others, blah blah blah. Anyway, that was their explanation."

EutelSat informed Sun right after they stopped the broadcast. Sun added, "They also promised us that they would not get involved in any Falun Gong business ... I praised them for stopping the broadcast. I also told them not to get involved anymore. I told them that they need to collaborate with us and promote the positive image of China. They kept apologizing and promised it will not happen again."

When asked what EutelSat would get in return, Sun explained, "They want to collaborate with Chinese Central TV. Also, EutelSat has communication and meteorological satellites, so they want to collaborate with the Chinese aerospace industry. They want to rent our equipment to launch their satellites."[254]

Not all news organizations comply with the CCP's demands, however. In early March 2001, the Chinese Consul General in San Francisco wrote to the World Journal, telling the publication to stop printing ads for Falun Gong, adding that running such ads would damage the Journal's reputation. An executive of the newspaper said that Falun Gong was free to hold its own views.

§8.5 Pressure on Businesses Outside China

Just as the CCP strong-arms foreign firms operating in China to censor information about Falun Gong and engage in discrimination against its practitioners, some companies operating outside China have also bowed to the regime's pressure to protect their access to the Chinese market.

Case 1: Bangkok Marriott Cancels Falun Gong Exercise Class[255]

During a national health conference in Bangkok in 2003, the fitness center manager at the Bangkok Marriott Resort & Spa at Royal Gardens Riverside invited Dr. Paitoon to teach the Falun Gong exercises at the hotel. Three weeks into the agreed-upon classes, Dr. Paitoon received a phone call from a hotel manager, who informed him that the classes could not continue. The manager acknowledged that the hotel had been pressured by the Chinese Embassy to cancel the class.

A fitness center employee later told a journalist that a Chinese guest complained about the Falun Gong class and that some Thais also held negative views of Falun Gong after being influenced by Chinese media in Thailand.

Case 2: UK Acupuncturist Forced to Leave Job After Chinese Consulate Pressures Clinic[256]

Zhao Liping, a doctor of traditional Chinese medicine and a Falun Gong practitioner, was hired as an acupuncturist at a Chinese medical clinic in Edinburgh in November 2002. The next September, she received a letter from the clinic manager asking her not to talk about Falun Gong at the clinic. A week later, in a dialogue with the head of the clinic, Ms. Zhao found out that the clinic had received a warning letter from the Chinese Consulate in Edinburgh.

Ms. Zhao said, "I have done nothing wrong. I am a doctor of Chinese medicine. It is natural for me to introduce Falun Gong to my patients. Falun Gong effectively helps people to gain physical and mental health, which is a well-known fact. I have practiced Falun Gong for many years and have benefited a lot from my cultivation. I would undoubtedly be forced out of my job if I mentioned Falun Gong at my office in China. But to my great surprise, this kind of thing is happening in the UK."

§8.6 Infiltration of Academic Institutions

The CCP has established a presence in Western universities and schools in order to export its ideology and extend its monitoring of and "battle" against Falun Gong practitioners and other targeted groups all over the world. The regime has thus been able to carry out the persecution of Falun Gong through its control over Confucius Institutes and Chinese student associations, as well as by pressuring universities to comply with its censorship demands using economic threats.

§§8.6.1 Confucius Institutes

For most of its reign, the CCP denounced Confucianism, one of the cornerstones of traditional Chinese culture, especially during the Cultural Revolution. In recent years, however, the regime has established "Confucius Institutes" on university campuses around the world. By 2013, 440 Confucius Institutes had opened in 120 countries, and 646 Confucius classrooms were operating in middle and elementary schools.

Rather than teaching traditional Chinese culture and Confucian values, however, these institutes are used by the CCP to export its communist ideology in the name of cultural and language education as part of its "united front" campaign to infiltrate Western society.[257] Instructors at Confucius Institutes are closely vetted by Chinese authorities and required to direct classroom discussion to promote the CCP's views on topics such as human rights and Falun Gong.

A student at the Sofia Confucius Institute in Bulgaria recalled, "By no means did I understand anything about the teachings of the Chinese philosopher Confucius, nor did I get a sense of Eastern philosophy, but rather felt...the [Communist] Party spirit."[258]

An increasing number of universities and school districts have decided to shut down their Confucius Institutes upon learning of its hidden agenda. For example, the Toronto District School Board (TDSB), Canada's largest school board, decided to terminate its agreement with the Confucius Institute in 2014. Michel Juneau-Katsuya, former chief of Asia-Pacific for the Canadian Security Intelligence Service, told TDSB, "There is publicly available information stating clearly that Western counter-intelligence agencies have identified Confucius Institutes as forms of spy agencies used by the [Chinese] government and employed by the [Chinese] government." TDSB trustee Pamela Gough cited "direct connections between the Confucius Institutes and the Communist Party of China" for the trustees' decision, adding, "They were very uncomfortable with the lack of freedom of speech on the part of the teachers hired in China to come over."[259]

In the same year, over 100 faculty members at the University of Chicago co-signed a letter urging university officials to revoke the university's contract with Hanban, the head office of the Confucius Institute. The letter says, in part, "The substantive issue is this is really an anomalous sort of arrangement where an entity outside the university, and a powerful entity, and an entity that has strong interest in what's taught, is in effect seriously influencing who's teaching and what's taught under our name and inside our curriculum."

The Canadian Association of University Teachers (CAUT) passed a resolution in December 2013 to end all ties with Confucius Institutes due to the strong influence exerted on the Institutes by the CCP. James Turk, Executive Director of CAUT, said, "In agreeing to host Confucius Institutes, Canadian universities and colleges are compromising their own integrity by allowing the Chinese Language Council International to have a voice in a number of academic matters, such as curriculum, texts, and topics of class discussion. Such interference is a fundamental violation of academic freedom."[260]

§§8.6.2 Chinese Students and Scholars Associations (CSSAs)

Many Chinese student associations on university campuses are funded and controlled by a Chinese embassy or consulate, which directs the associations to disrupt events held by Falun Gong practitioners and recruit Chinese students to threaten and spy on practitioners. At the Chinese Consulate in Sydney, for example, the education section was tasked with encouraging Chinese students to defame Falun Gong at their universities, provide anti-Falun Gong propaganda materials to Chinese student associations, "deploy international students to engage in targeted battles" against Falun Gong practitioners when they hold events on special occasions, and recruit "reliable" students to "help [the consulate] understand the situation."[261]

› 8.6.2(a) Manipulating Elections to Install Pro-CCP Association Presidents

Chinese consulates commonly win over leaders of Chinese student associations by giving them personal benefits, such as inviting them to gatherings at the consulate, asking them to organize welcome committees when Chinese officials visit their area, and introducing them to political and business leaders in China and in Chinese communities abroad.[262] Consular officials have also been known to manipulate elections of these associations by mobilizing students to support pro-CCP candidates it favors and attack opposing candidates.

Before the 2004 election for CSSA President at the University of Minnesota, two members of the education group at the Chinese Consulate in Chicago invited more than ten CSSA standing committee members to dinner, including two Falun Gong practitioners, Wang Xiaodan and Chi Xuedong. One of the embassy officials recorded everyone's Chinese names and background, which Chinese university they had graduated from, their home address in China, details about their parents, and whether they planned to go back to China in the future. After Wang and Chi left, the other official told the students, "If Falun Gong holds any activities at your university, you should protest and demonstrate against it. While in the U.S., you can only rely on the Chinese consulate. If something happens to you in the U.S., only the consulate can represent you."

Wang Xiaodan was running for president against a student named Li Ming. On the day of the election, more than a hundred students turned up, an unprecedented turnout. When Li Ming gave his speech, he said, "Falun Gong is trying to control the CSSA." When it was Wang

Xiaodan's turn to speak, some students created a disturbance and used profane language. When a student who did not practice Falun Gong voted for Wang Xiaodan, she was attacked on the spot and accused of being "the most deeply hidden Falun Gong element in the CSSA." Li Ming was eventually elected president. Prior to the election, Li once said that the reason he had stepped forward was to prevent Wang Xiaodan from being elected because Wang practiced Falun Gong.

You Youqing, CSSA president from 2002 and 2003 and a standing committee member in 2004, said, "All this was arranged by the Chinese Consulate. The night before the election, the Chinese Consulate called each of the committee members of the CSSA." He recalled many student leaders telling him that they still had families in China and didn't want them to be implicated.[263]

› 8.6.2(b) Disrupting Falun Gong and Other Human Rights Events

Minghui has reported on multiple incidents in which CSSAs were directed to disrupt symposiums and community events held by Falun Gong practitioners.

At Columbia University, CSSA leaders attempted to disrupt a forum on the Chinese regime's killing of Falun Gong practitioners for organs and later posted anti-Falun Gong propaganda on its student club website. After practitioners reached out to university administrators, faculty, and other students to make them aware of the persecution and the Chinese student association's role in defaming Falun Gong on behalf of the CCP, the CSSA was forced to remove the slander from its website, and its leaders were told not to interfere with Falun Gong activities again as their actions were not welcome in the U.S.[264]

In Germany, the CSSA at the Otto von Guericke University Magdeburg posted on its website, "With the support of the education department at the [Chinese] Embassy, a new session of the Chinese students' association was formed with Song Zheyang elected as president." After Falun Gong practitioners participated in a student festival, Song asked a practitioner to give him details about his personal life. The next year, practitioners were not allowed to participate in the festival because the CSSA president had given the host slanderous CCP propaganda and warned the host that conflict would break out among Chinese students if practitioners were allowed to demonstrate the Falun Gong exercises.

Chinese student associations at different universities within the same region have been known to copy verbatim each other's online propaganda attacking Falun Gong and use similar strategies to interfere with the same event,[265] suggesting that the associations are centrally coordinated.

› 8.6.2(c) Recruiting and Coercing Students to Spy on Falun Gong Practitioners

In 2006, Chinese diplomat Wang Pengfei was forced to leave Canada after he was found to be paying Chinese Student Association members at the University of Ottawa to collect information on local Falun Gong practitioners. Zhang Lingdi, who studied at the university, received an email from someone claiming to be Vice President Xu of the university's Chinese Student Association.

The email said, "The Chinese Student Association is directly led by the Education Office of the Chinese Embassy in Canada, and we are watching every move you make." In the email, Xu referred to press conferences and other activities that Zhang had participated in to seek help to rescue her father, Zhang Kunlun, who had been illegally arrested for practicing Falun Gong in China. The email also said, "According to reports from students and an investigation by the Student Association leaders, you are still a Falun Gong practitioner." Presumably as an intimidation tactic, Xu went on to give detailed personal and family information of a Falun Gong practitioner in Ottawa.[266]

Mr. Xu (of no relationship to the Xu above), a Falun Gong practitioner and former deputy president of the CSSA at Florida Atlantic University (FAU), recalled his experience after the persecution of Falun Gong started in 1999:[267]

The president of the CSSA came to see me and tried to persuade me to give up practicing Falun Gong. Of course I refused, and I told him the facts about Falun Gong. In the end, he said awkwardly, "If you don't want to give it up, then I have to report you to the Chinese Consulate in Houston. They are asking me for names."

From then on, even though we used to be good friends, he always looked awkward when he met me. After Falun Gong practitioners applied to participate in the International Students' Festival and were permitted to demonstrate the Falun Gong exercises on stage, he acted as if he were facing a formidable enemy. He went to see the university [administrators] and event organizers several times to create discord, trying to prevent us from participating. He even said, "You are doing this because you don't want to go back to China anymore, but I still have loved ones in China and I still want to go back. They said if I don't do things this way, I would be implicated as well. I can only free myself from trouble by reporting you."

§§8.6.3 Censorship of Foreign Universities by Threatening Revenue from International Students

One of the University of Technology Sydney's (UTS) student organizations was the Falun Dafa Meditation Club, which hosted the Truth-Compassion-Forbearance International Art Exhibition in April 2005 to raise awareness of the persecution of Falun Gong in China.

Following this event, UTS was pressured by the Chinese regime, which threatened the university's investments in Shanghai and Hong Kong. Because UTS recruited many international students from China each year, university administrators initially complied with the CCP's demand and removed information about the Falun Dafa club from the UTS website for a few days.

The UTS Students' Association passed a resolution in June 2005 and wrote to the university leadership, Australian ministers for foreign affairs and education, and other officials in protest of the unfair treatment of the Falun Dafa group. Students' Association President Michelle Sparks wrote in the association's letter to the Minister for Foreign Affairs that, given how long the persecution of Falun Gong had gone on, if the university remained silent amid the persecution, it would be tantamount to being complicit in the crime.

Because UTS later took a principled stand and refused to remove the Falun Dafa club from its website, the Chinese regime blocked access to the university's English website in China. It was allegedly announced at a university council meeting in June that a major reason the university had to increase the number of students paying full tuition was the inaccessibility of its website in China, which resulted in a loss of income from international students.[268]

§8.7 Restricting Practitioners' Ability to Travel

Case 1: Consulates Refuse to Renew Practitioners' Chinese Passports Unless They Renounce Falun Gong

Even when Falun Gong practitioners live abroad as permanent residents or students, the CCP routinely denies their basic rights by denying the renewal of their Chinese passports, effectively rendering them stateless. In these cases, consular officials often refuse to provide a reason for the denial. When pressed, they demand that the practitioner sign a statement denouncing Falun Gong before their passport can be renewed.

Li Qing, a PhD student at Stanford University in 2004, tried to obtain a passport extension from the Chinese consulate in preparation for an academic trip to Germany.[269] After asking why her passport extension had been refused, the director of the Passport Section said, "You go in for activities that defy the government..." He hung up without finishing his explanation.

After Li's supervisor and the university's international student director wrote letters to the consulate, she was given an appointment with the consul. However, the consul required that she sign a guarantee statement not to practice Falun Gong before he would extend her passport. Li refused.

Li's department secretary considered preparing alternative documents to allow her to travel to Germany and re-enter the U.S., but the international student director considered the approach too risky. Li explained the director's concern:

I might not have a problem leaving the States, but once I got stopped at German customs, I might be deported back to China. Since I was on the Chinese government's blacklist as a Falun Gong practitioner, it would be horrible if I were deported back to China ... Both the director and the secretary asked my supervisor to make sure that I would not go to Germany. I was deeply touched. For those people, I was simply a foreign student they had met only once. Their sincere concern for my personal safety was in sharp contrast to my cruel fellow countrymen who made me a refugee unable to go back home again.

Li then recalled:

Several months later, people from the National Security Bureau told my relatives in China, "The nation attaches much importance to your talented daughter. We hope that she will come back to serve the country after she finishes her schooling." My mother replied angrily, "You won't even extend her passport. She doesn't have citizenship anymore. What's the point of talking about serving the country?" People from the National Security Bureau also asked my relatives to persuade me to give up the cultivation practice of Falun Gong.

Case 2: Miss World Canada Denied Entry to China

One instance that drew mass media attention was that of Miss World Canada, Anastasia Lin, who was denied an invitation letter and a visa to enter China for the final round of the Miss World pageant in December 2015. Lin was barred because she is a Falun Gong practitioner and has spoken out to raise awareness of the persecution and other human rights abuses in China.

Outside China, however, Lin gained a large number of supporters. Canadian Foreign Affairs spokesperson Amy Mills said, "Canada commends Ms. Lin for her efforts to raise awareness regarding these issues." She also expressed concern on behalf of the Canadian government that the Chinese government has harassed Ms. Lin's family in China.

The *New York Times* commented, "Her David-and-Goliath clash with the Chinese government has drawn sympathetic media attention and legions of supporters around the world, providing her an even bigger platform to speak out about the imprisonment and torture Falun Gong adherents face in China."

§8.8 Coercing Practitioners to Spy for the CCP

Numerous Falun Gong practitioners who traveled to China have been abducted, interrogated, and blackmailed into spying on other practitioners after returning abroad.

Case 1: Returning to China to Get Married, Students Studying in the U.S. Arrested at Beijing Airport

While going through customs at Beijing Capital International Airport on May 21, 2013, Li Yue, a Chinese student studying in the U.S., was arrested along with her then-fiancé by agents from Beijing Domestic Security Office. The couple had planned to go to her hometown to get married but instead spent the first few weeks of their vacation apart, being interrogated by the police. Under pressure and intimidation, Li Yue agreed to spy on her fellow practitioners and provide intelligence on Falun Gong activities upon her return to the U.S. After returning to America, she decided to expose the plot and her ordeal while in China.

Following her arrest, Li was blindfolded and driven to an apartment that was used for interrogations. Over the course of several days, agents asked her for every detail about Falun Gong activities she had participated in in the U.S, experience-sharing conferences she'd attended, who she went with, and where she stood in the Falun Gong parade. They asked in which theater Shen Yun would be performing in her area and at what hotel the performers would stay. Agents also searched her electronic devices and demanded that she provide the passwords for her Skype, QQ, email, and Renren accounts (a Chinese social media network), through which they could identify and monitor other Falun Gong practitioners.

Before letting her go, the agents told her to return to the U.S. and attend Falun Gong activities as usual, but they required her to report to them regularly using a special email account and a provided cell phone. They told her they would continue to log in to her social media accounts to monitor other practitioners. They instructed her on how to respond to others' inquiries about what had happened to her in China, as her arrest had been reported on Minghui.org. Finally, the agents swore her to secrecy, including her immediate family, threatening to fire her parents from their jobs if she revealed her role as an informant. After Li returned to the U.S., an agent and a police officer contacted her over Skype and gave her seven specific assignments to collect information about other practitioners.

Li's husband was detained in Beijing for three days, taken back to his hometown in Langfang for one week, and transferred to a brainwashing center.[270]

Case 2: British Practitioner Harassed by Beijing State Security Agents

Liang Yunxiang, a Chinese practitioner living in England, went to visit his parents in Beijing in 2010. He was arrested and interrogated for seven hours. In the end, the agents forced him to write a guarantee statement swearing never to attend Falun Gong activities abroad. After returning to England, he received mail from the agents ordering him to stay in contact. Below are excerpts of his experience in China:[271]

> *A customs officer became visibly nervous as he read information on the computer after keying in my passport information. He spoke to another officer, who made a phone call. A minute later, I was "allowed" into Beijing.*
>
> *A man and a woman, both wearing black shirts, started following me.*

The state security officers took me to a six-story residential building named Tianzhulu near Beijing Capital International Airport. Two of them took turns interrogating me. "What activities have you attended overseas?" "Where are the practice sites?" "Where do people study together?" "Do you know members of the Tian Guo Marching Band?" "Have you gone to other countries to attend Falun Gong activities?" They also wanted to know the names of members of the Falun Dafa Association overseas and the telephone numbers of overseas practitioners.

They mentioned the names of several practitioners overseas who were from Beijing and asked me if I knew them. They asked me how I knew where and when activities would be held, whether I knew practitioners in China and had I met them since I returned, whether I had reported my current situation to practitioners overseas, and whether I was a British citizen.

Li, a State Security Bureau chief, yelled at me before I said anything, saying that they knew everything I did outside of China and that I had better come clean about what I did. He told me that if I didn't tell them what activities I had attended and they had to spell them out for me, there would be consequences. My father warned me earlier that if I didn't cooperate, they would turn me over to the police department and put me in a forced labor camp. I was terrified.

The agents took me to an office building near Guanyuan Bridge in the Xicheng District of Beijing. This time, I revealed the names of several practitioners. I also told them the cell phone number of my relative overseas and my email address.

I got back to England on August 28. A few days later, a friend of mine in Australia called me and said that he had received harassing text messages on his cell phone. Later, a coworker of mine, who was also a practitioner, went back to China on business. State Security agents found him and forced him to write a guarantee statement. I then realized that the agents could hack into my email without my password.

On October 8, 2010, I received a threatening email from an agent. He said that if I kept my promise never to attend Falun Dafa activities, they would keep theirs, and China would always welcome me home. Also, they wanted to stay in touch with me.

The agent called my father in January 2011 and harassed him. When my relative overseas went back to China to visit, the State Security agents talked to him and forced him to reveal my address in England.

Part 2: Key Perpetrators of the Persecution

Part 2: Key Perpetrators of the Persecution

世界需要真善忍

Like previous campaigns throughout the Communist Party's history, the anti-Falun Gong campaign was framed and implemented in largely extralegal terms, e.g., "as a violent suppression" (*douzheng*) rather than as an ordinary activity of the criminal justice system. Therefore, Party officials, judges, and police officers are made to operate outside of the law.

Like the targets of earlier "douzheng" campaigns in China, persons identified as Falun Gong practitioners are demonized as "enemies of the state," "hostile elements," "anti-humanity," "anti-society" viruses and other dehumanizing imagery to instigate and legitimize their regular subjection to human rights abuses.

In short, the persecution has no legal basis.

Key Highlights

Former CCP leader Jiang Zemin personally planned and directed the "douzheng" campaign against Falun Gong. Jiang imposed his own will on the top Party leadership to frame Falun Gong as a threat supported by foreign forces, directed the creation of the 610 Office to carry out the campaign, and prepared a framework for the wave of demonizing propaganda that would be used to justify the suppression.

The persecution campaign is carried out through the 610 Office, which is tightly integrated with the Political and Legal Affairs

Committee (PLAC) and extends from the CCP Central Committee all the way down to the neighborhood and village level. The 610 Office coordinates state personnel to carry out the "transformation" of Falun Gong practitioners. As part of this function, it compels judicial and law enforcement personnel to arrest and sentence practitioners who uphold their faith. Local branches of the 610 Office also directly participate in the arrest, detention, torture, and brainwashing of practitioners.

While Jiang Zemin was the architect and driver of the campaign, other high-ranking officials played key roles in launching and materializing the persecution. They include:

- Luo Gan (罗干), member of the Politburo Standing Committee, Secretary of the Central PLAC, head of the Central 610 Office
- Zeng Qinghong (曾庆红), Secretary of the Secretariat of the CCP Central Committee and head of the CCP Organization Department
- Liu Jing (刘京), Deputy Minister of Public Security and head of the 610 Office
- Zhou Yongkang (周永康), Minister of Public Security
- Li Lanqing (李岚清), first head of the Central 610 Office

In directing the persecution of Falun Gong, Jiang Zemin has violated the Chinese Constitution, Chinese Criminal Law, and international law against genocide and crimes against humanity. Since 2015, more than 200,000 Falun Gong practitioners have filed legal complaints against Jiang with China's highest court for the injuries, human rights violations, and economic damages they have suffered as a result of his order.

Chapter 9: Key Perpetrators

In the seven years between Falun Gong's introduction to the public in 1992 and the start of the persecution in 1999, the practice spread quickly by word of mouth as people experienced its effect on health and morality. By the end of the decade, 100 million people were practicing Falun Gong. Spurred by paranoia and jealousy of Falun Gong's surging popularity, CCP leader Jiang Zemin planned, launched, and expanded the persecution, vowing to "annihilate Falun Gong in three months."

§9.1 Role of Jiang Zemin

At the time, Jiang occupied three primary positions: he served as General Secretary of the CCP (1989-2002), President of China (1989-2003), and Chairman of the Central Military Commission (1989-2005). In other words, he had absolute power through control of the Party, government, and military.

After Falun Gong practitioners appealed peacefully at the national appeals office in Beijing on April 25, 1999 to secure the release of practitioners who had been wrongfully arrested in Tianjin (see Appendix 1), Jiang directed the Politburo to take immediate action to attack Falun Gong. When the Politburo opposed his instruction, Jiang pushed forward with his campaign by writing letters and giving speeches to top leaders. He subsequently ordered the formation of the "Central Leading Group for Handling the Falun Gong Issue" and its operational arm, the "610 Office" (named after the date of its founding), to carry out the persecution. Jiang continued to meet resistance and eventually resorted to announcing the campaign against Falun Gong through the Ministry of Civil Affairs.

Jiang continued to oversee the persecution after he retired from his roles as General Secretary and President by using his extended time as Chairman of the Central Military Commission and installing loyal followers in key leadership positions. He expanded the Politburo Standing Committee from seven to nine members, adding Luo Gan (in charge of security forces as the head of the Political and Legal Affairs Committee) and Li Changchun (in charge of propaganda). Jiang also identified other allies to advance his persecution policy, including Zeng Qinghong (member of the Politburo Standing Committee and Secretary of the Secretariat of the CCP Central Committee) and Zhou Yongkang (Minister of Public Security).

§§9.1.1 Persecution Policy

At the outset of the persecution, Jiang issued an order to "ruin their reputation, cut them off financially, and destroy them physically." He also declared that "beating them to death is nothing; beating them to death counts as suicide" and "not to check their identities [after death in police custody] and to directly cremate them."

› 9.1.1(a) Defamation

To justify such a violent, widespread persecution, Jiang initiated a series of propaganda campaigns to portray Falun Gong as an "evil cult" and its practitioners as mentally ill individuals who posed a danger to society. The most notorious campaigns include a staged self-immolation incident on Tiananmen Square in which actors claiming to be Falun Gong practitioners set themselves on fire (see Appendix 2) and a collection of 1,400 deaths allegedly caused by Falun Gong (see Appendix 3). Jiang also vilified Falun Gong as posing a threat to the CCP's rule by mischaracterizing a peaceful appeal by practitioners at the national appeals office as a "siege" of the central government compound (see Appendix 1) and claiming that Falun Gong was a plot by Western governments to destabilize the Chinese regime.

The entire Chinese population has since been inundated with this propaganda through state-controlled TV stations, newspapers, and other media outlets. An entire generation of children has been instilled with hatred toward Falun Gong as a result of the propaganda being added to textbooks, academic exams, and mandatory denunciation activities. The CCP has also extended its defamation of Falun Gong outside of China through international media outlets controlled by the Party and through Chinese embassies and consulates.

› 9.1.1(b) Financial Ruin

As shown in Chapter 2, Falun Gong practitioners have been forced out of their jobs and denied pensions and educational opportunities. The authorities have also taken large sums from practitioners by kidnapping them and demanding money from their families in exchange for their release (an extralegal process) and by confiscating money and personal possessions in home raids.

› 9.1.1(c) Physical Destruction

The directive to "destroy them physically" has been carried out through torture in forced labor camps, prisons, and other detention facilities, as well as the killing of practitioners for organ transplants in state and military hospitals.

§§9.1.2 Retaliation Against Practitioners for Exposing the Persecution Online

While the Chinese regime could effectively censor information about the persecution through its full control over traditional media outlets, increased access to the internet posed a challenge for communist authorities, who rolled out waves of increasingly burdensome content restrictions and monitoring requirements targeting website operators and cybercafes.

In the days surrounding the start of the persecution on July 20, 1999, email communications throughout China went down, and popular Chinese email services like 163.com were inaccessible. The police also monitored online activity for content related to Falun Gong. As of 2002, 20 provinces had special police personnel trained to pursue "subversive" internet users.

Since the beginning of the persecution, practitioners have uploaded information about their local persecution cases to Minghui.org, which then distributes the information to all practitioners in China and elsewhere. Therefore, Chinese authorities saw all usage of Minghui.org as a "major case" to be targeted, no matter which way the information flowed, and it made the website its top censorship priority. Between July 1999 and April 2004, there were at least 97 documented cases of Falun Gong practitioners being detained, imprisoned, taken to forced labor camps, and/or tortured for uploading information to or downloading from Minghui.org. Some practitioners were tortured to death, and others were sentenced to as many as 15 years in prison. Below are a few examples.

Case 1: Yuan Jiang Escapes after Torture, Dies of Injuries[272]

Yuan Jiang began to practice Falun Gong in 1993. After he graduated from Tsinghua University in 1995, he returned to his hometown in Gansu Province and volunteered to run a Falun Gong instruction site. He also worked as a deputy general manager of an IT engineering company under the Lanzhou City Telecommunications Bureau.

After the persecution of Falun Gong began in 1999, Mr. Yuan became the main contact person with Minghui.org in Gansu Province, coordinating the collection and distribution of information between local practitioners and the website.

Mr. Yuan was later demoted from his general manager position because he refused to renounce his faith. He was forced to leave home in January 2001 to avoid further persecution but was arrested on a bus on September 30, 2001 for not carrying identification.

After his arrest, agents from the Gansu Province Public Security Bureau tortured Yuan for nearly a month. Yuan managed to escape around October 26. Severely injured as a result of torture and having held a long-term hunger strike, Mr. Yuan was extremely weak. He had difficulty walking and went into a cave, where he fell unconscious for four days. Meanwhile, two to three thousand military police officers were deployed all over Lanzhou to search for him. They searched virtually all Falun Gong practitioners' homes and even in other counties and cities.

Mr. Yuan later crawled out of the cave and went to a practitioner's home, where he succumbed to internal injuries and passed away on November 9. A practitioner who saw him after he left the cave recalled that he was emaciated beyond recognition, bleeding from his nose and mouth, and barely able to move. His right shin was black and missing chunks of flesh.

After Mr. Yuan passed away, the police launched a massive sweep and arrested many practitioners who had assisted him. His parents' family was also closely monitored. Yu Jinfang, a practitioner in Lanzhou who had helped Mr. Yuan, was arrested and later tortured to death.

Case 2: Wang Chan Tortured to Death after 28 Days in Detention, Mother Unknowingly Hears Him Being Beaten[273]

Mr. Wang Chan worked at the headquarters of the People's Bank of China. After the persecution began, he sent information about Falun Gong to government departments all over China and wrote a letter to Jiang Zemin to urge him to stop the persecution. With Jiang's personal approval, Beijing police detained Wang for three months at the end of 1999 without giving a reason.

After his release, Mr. Wang was forced to leave his home to avoid arrest. Over the next three years, he traveled to more than ten provinces and established communication channels between practitioners in those areas and Minghui.org, allowing people inside and outside of China to receive real-time updates of the persecution. The authorities offered a 100,000-yuan reward for his capture.

Mr. Wang was arrested at a bus stop in Liangshan County, Shandong Province, on the afternoon of August 21, 2002. In the detention center, he was beaten and clubbed by officers, had his hands cuffed behind his back in an excruciating position, and was deprived of sleep for many nights. He was tortured to death in 28 days. An eyewitness saw that Mr. Wang had heavy injuries and a lot of blood on the back of his head.

After Mr. Wang's death, the Jining City 610 Office and police warned his two brothers not to tell their mother that he had been tortured to death. They also threatened the brothers, saying they would lose their jobs if they took Wang's case to higher authorities. Mr. Wang's mother did not find out about his death until she received a letter on September 16 from a person familiar with the matter.

Mr. Wang's mother, Ms. Han Yuhua, was arrested shortly after his arrest. The mother and son were held at the same detention center without them knowing it themselves. Ms. Han recalled:

> *Those few days, every morning at five or six o'clock, I could hear the police beating someone. I couldn't imagine that the person being beaten was my son. I also couldn't imagine that these few days were the closest we'd be to each other before he passed away. Even less could I imagine that my son would be beaten to death almost right next to me while I had no idea it was happening.*
>
> *The night he died, I heard a commotion. I learned after my release that that was when my son was on the verge of death. The perpetrators were afraid of being exposed and didn't tell me anything; instead, they transferred me to Yanzhou City Detention Center. They cremated his body and didn't notify me or allow me to see my son one last time.*

Case 3: More than 40 Arrested, 10 Sentenced for "Leaking State Secrets" by Exposing the Rape of a Practitioner[274]

Ms. Wei Xingyan was a twenty-eight-year-old graduate student at Chongqing University. Two days after she was arrested on May 11, 2003, a police officer raped her in front of two female inmates in Baihelin Detention Center. Ms. Wei went on a hunger strike in protest and was injured while being force-fed, leaving her unable to speak.

After other practitioners in Chongqing sent information about Ms. Wei's case to Minghui.org, the 610 Office ordered Chongqing University to deny that Ms. Wei was a student and even the existence of her major, High Voltage Continuous Current Transmission.

When Zhang Siping, a vice president of the university, was asked a question about this incident at a symposium at Wharton Business School in the U.S., he replied, "Our university will not expel a student for their religious belief... except for Falun Gong." A few days later, Chongqing University published a notice stating that Ms. Wei was a "bargirl" rather than a student.

Meanwhile, the Chongqing 610 Office arrested more than 40 Falun Gong practitioners in its attempt to apprehend the person who publicized the incident. At least 10 were sentenced to between 5 and 14 years in prison for "leaking state secrets." The alleged author and submitter of the Minghui article were each sentenced to 10 years in prison.

§§9.1.3 Crimes Committed by Jiang

In the persecution of Falun Gong, Jiang Zemin has violated both Chinese and international laws, including committing torture, genocide, and crimes against humanity.

› 9.1.3(a) Chinese Constitution

In July 1999, Jiang declared Falun Gong an illegal organization through the Ministry of Civil Affairs. Although the Ministry did not have this authority, it was nonetheless used as a legal basis for the persecution.

Since then, a large number of practitioners have been threatened, arrested, detained, and tortured for their belief. The following articles of the Chinese Constitution have been violated:[275]

> *Article 35: Citizens of the People's Republic of China have the freedom of speech, of the press, of assembly, of association, of procession, and of demonstration.*

> *Article 36: Citizens of the People's Republic of China have the freedom of religious belief.*

No State organ, social group, or individual may compel citizens to believe in, or to not believe in, any religion, or discriminate against citizens who believe in, or do not believe in, any religion.

The State protects normal religious activities.

Article 37: The freedom of the person of citizens of the People's Republic of China is inviolable.

No citizen may be arrested except with the approval or by decision of a people's procuratorate or by decision of a people's court, and arrests must be made by a public security organ.

Unlawful detention or deprivation or restriction of citizens' freedom of the person by other means is prohibited, and unlawful search of the person of citizens is prohibited.

Article 38: The personal dignity of citizens of the People's Republic of China is inviolable. Insult, libel, false accusation, or false incrimination directed against citizens by any means is prohibited.

Article 39: The residences of citizens of the People's Republic of China are inviolable. Unlawful search of, or intrusion into, a citizen's residence is prohibited.

Article 40: The freedom and privacy of correspondence of citizens of the People's Republic of China are protected by law. No organization or individual may, on any ground, infringe upon citizens' freedom and privacy of correspondence, except in cases where, to meet the needs of State security or of a criminal investigation, public security or procuratorial organs are permitted to examine correspondence in accordance with the procedures prescribed by law.

Article 41: Citizens of the People's Republic of China have the right to criticize and make suggestions regarding any State organ or functionary and have the right to make to relevant State organs complaints or charges against, or exposures of, any State organ or functionary for violation of law or dereliction of duty, but must not fabricate or distort facts for purposes of libel or false incrimination.

› 9.1.3(b) Chinese Criminal Law

Jiang has violated articles 247, 232, 248, 254, 234(a), 236, 237, 37, 238, 397, 399, 263, 267, 270, 275, 245, 244, 251, 234, and 246 of Chinese Criminal Law:

> *Article 247 of the Criminal Law of the People's Republic of China (hereinafter "Chinese Criminal Law") prohibits "extort[ing] a confession from criminal suspects or defendants by torture" or "us[ing] force to extract testimony from witnesses."*
>
> *Article 232 of Chinese Criminal Law prohibits "intentionally kill[ing] another."*
>
> *Article 248 of Chinese Criminal Law prohibits "beat[ing] or physically abus[ing]" inmates in the custody of prisons, detention centers, and other guardhouses.*
>
> *Article 254 of Chinese Criminal Law prohibits government employees from "abus[ing] their authority by retaliating against or framing accusers, petitioners, criticizers, or informants, in the name of conducting official business."*
>
> *Article 234(a) of Chinese Criminal Law prohibits "organiz[ing] others to sell human organs," "remov[ing] the organs of a person without the consent thereof," "remov[ing] the organs of a minor," "compel[ling] or cheat[ing] another person to donate organs," and "remov[ing] the body organs of a deceased person against his/her wishes made when he/she was alive" or "where the person has never consented to the removal when he was alive" or "against the wish of the deceased persons' immediate relatives."*
>
> *Article 236 of Chinese Criminal Law prohibits any person from "by violence, coercion or other means, rap[ing] a woman."*
>
> *Article 237 of Chinese Criminal Law prohibits any person from "by violence, coercion, or other means, forc[ing], molest[ing], or humiliat[ing] a woman" or "assembl[ing] a crowd to commit" this crime.*
>
> *Article 37 of the Constitution of the People's Republic of China prohibits the unlawful restriction of a citizen's freedom of the person by detention or other means.*

Article 238 of Chinese Criminal Law prohibits "unlawfully detain[ing] another or depriv[ing] him of his freedom" and requires heavier punishment for "an employee of a state organ [who] abuses his authority" to commit this crime.

Article 397 of Chinese Criminal Law prohibits any state personnel from "abus[ing] their power or neglect[ing] their duties, causing great losses to public property and the state's and people's interests."

Article 399 of Chinese Criminal Law prohibits any judicial personnel from "act[ing] with partiality and defeat[ing] the ends of justice," including "subjecting to prosecution persons they clearly know to be innocent" and "intentionally go[ing] against facts and laws in criminal trials to render judgments that misuse the law."

Article 263 of Chinese Criminal Law prohibits "robbing public or private property using force, coercion, or other methods," including "intruding into others' homes to rob," "causing serious injuries to or death while robbing," and "committing robbery using guns."

Article 267 of Chinese Criminal Law prohibits "seiz[ing] public and private property."

Article 270 of Chinese Criminal Law prohibits "illegally tak[ing] over another person's property in the latter's custody."

Article 275 of Chinese Criminal Law prohibits "intentionally destroy[ing] public or private property."

Article 245 of Chinese Criminal Law prohibits "illegally physically searching others or illegally searching others' residences" or "illegally intruding into others' residences," and requires more severe punishment for judicial workers committing such a crime.

Article 244 of Chinese Criminal Law prohibits "compel[ling] other persons to work by violence, intimidation, or by means of restricting their personal freedom" or "recruit[ing] or transport[ing] personnel therefore or otherwise render[ing] assistance."

Article 251 of Chinese Criminal Law prohibits robbing citizens of the right to religious belief and encroaching on minorities' habits or customs.

Article 234 of Chinese Criminal Law prohibits intentionally injuring the person of another.

Article 246 of Chinese Criminal Law prohibits the fabrication of stories to insult others or insulting others through physical force.

› 9.1.3(c) Crimes Against Humanity

Jurisdiction is appropriate for Counts 15 and 16 under the Convention on the Prevention and Punishment of the Crime of Genocide, signed by the People's Republic of China on April 18, 1983, and ratified on July 17, 1983; and the United Nations Convention against Torture and Other Cruel, Inhuman or Degrading Treatment or Punishment, signed by the People's Republic of China on December 12, 1986, and ratified on October 4, 1988.

Article 1.1 of the Convention Against Torture prohibits "any act by which severe pain or suffering, whether physical or mental, is intentionally inflicted on a person for such purposes as obtaining from him, or a third person, information or a confession, punishing him for an act he or a third person has committed or is suspected of having committed, or intimidating or coercing him or a third person, or for any reason based on discrimination of any kind, when such pain or suffering is inflicted by or at the instigation of or with the consent or acquiescence of a public official or other person acting in an official capacity."

Article 2 of the Convention Against Genocide prohibits a range of acts committed with the "intent to destroy, in whole or in part, a national, ethnical, racial or religious group," including "killing members of the group," "causing serious bodily or mental harm to members of the group," and "deliberately inflicting on the group conditions of life calculated to bring about its physical destruction in whole or in part."

Jurisdiction is appropriate for Counts 17 and 18 under customary international law, the general practice of states, which is accepted and observed as law, as defined by the Statute of the International Court of Justice, art. 38(1)(b), to which the People's Republic of China is a party by virtue of its ratification of the Charter of the United Nations. Customary international law obligates countries to provide universal jurisdiction for the following violations of jus cogens norms: persecution, forced exile, disappearance as a crime against humanity, and prolonged arbitrary detention.

Customary international law (CIL) defines crimes against humanity as a specified set of acts when committed as part of a widespread or systematic attack directed against any civilian population, with knowledge of the attack, including persecution, forced exile, disappearance, and other inhumane acts.

Enforced disappearance is defined as the arrest, detention or abduction of persons by, or with the authorization, support or acquiescence of, a State or a political organization, followed by a refusal to acknowledge that deprivation of freedom or to give information on the fate or whereabouts of those persons, with the intention of removing them from the protection of the law for a prolonged period of time.

Forced exile is defined as the movement of one or more persons to another location by expulsion or other coercive acts.

Persecution is defined as an act carried out against any identifiable group or collectivity on political, racial, national, ethnic, cultural, religious, gender grounds involving the intentional and severe deprivation of fundamental rights contrary to international law by reason of the identity of the group or collectivity.

Jus cogens norms of customary international law prohibit the prolonged arbitrary detention of persons.

› 9.1.3(d) Genocide

The persecution of Falun Gong was launched by former Communist Party leader Jiang Zemin on July 20, 1999. By abusing government agencies, laws, policies, and the entire state apparatus, he suppressed tens of millions of practitioners both physically and spiritually.

According to Articles 6 and 7 of the Rome Statute of the International Criminal Court published by the United Nations on July 17, 1998, Jiang's persecution of Falun Gong practitioners over the past 20 years has amounted to Genocide and Crimes against Humanity.[276]

In Article 6 of the Rome Statute of the International Criminal Court,[277] "genocide" is defined as:

Any of the following acts committed with intent to destroy, in whole or in part, a national, ethnical, racial or religious group, as such:

(a) Killing members of the group;

(b) Causing serious bodily or mental harm to members of the group;

(c) Deliberately inflicting on the group conditions of life calculated to bring about its physical destruction in whole or in part;

(d) Imposing measures intended to prevent births within the group;

(e) Forcibly transferring children of the group to another group.

In Article 7 of the statute, "crime against humanity" is defined as:

Any of the following acts when committed as part of a widespread or systematic attack directed against any civilian population, with knowledge of the attack:

(a) Murder;

(b) Extermination;

(c) Enslavement;

(d) Deportation or forcible transfer of population;

(e) Imprisonment or other severe deprivation of physical liberty in violation of fundamental rules of international law;

(f) Torture;

(g) Rape, sexual slavery, enforced prostitution, forced pregnancy, enforced sterilization, or any other form of sexual violence of comparable gravity;

(h) Persecution against any identifiable group or collectivity on political, racial, national, ethnic, cultural, religious, gender as defined in paragraph 3, or other grounds that are universally

recognized as impermissible under international law, in connection with any act referred to in this paragraph or any crime within the jurisdiction of the Court;

(i) Enforced disappearance of persons;

(j) The crime of apartheid;

(k) Other inhumane acts of a similar character intentionally causing great suffering or serious injury to body or to mental or physical health.

§9.2 Other Key Perpetrators

§§9.2.1 Luo Gan

Between 2002 and 2007, Luo Gan was one of China's top leaders, serving as a member of the nine-person Politburo Standing Committee and as the secretary of the Central PLAC, which became one of China's most powerful political offices and well-funded bureaucracies during his term. He also served as the head of the Central Leading Group for Handling the Falun Gong Issue from 2003 to 2007.

Between 2001 and 2003, when the persecution was most severe, Luo Gan gave at least eight public speeches seeking to force China's political and judicial system to list Falun Gong as the most important "target of attack." The genocide of Falun Gong practitioners was then, and is still today, carried out openly and systematically.

Whenever Luo Gan gave a speech or went somewhere to personally oversee local "progress," the persecution of Falun Gong practitioners in that area or all of China would intensify. For instance, on August 29, 2000, two days after Luo Gan spoke at the "Experience Exchanging and Reward Meeting of Education and Transformation Work of the Ministry of Justice" (also known as the "Transformation Speech"), Boxun News Net reported, "Beijing plans to increase the effort to persecute Falun Gong and to eradicate it within three months."

Even after the international community learned that the CCP's rhetoric against Falun Gong was defamation, and despite increasing internal opposition to the persecution, Luo Gan still gave public speeches encouraging the intensification of efforts to persecute Falun Gong. These include his speech at the "National Political and Judicial Working Meeting" on December 7, 2004; an article published in Qiu Shi magazine in February 2005; and another speech at the "Hero and Models with Meritorious Service in National Public Security Area Assembly Meeting" on August 25, 2005.

In September 2005, several days after Luo gave a public speech, the CCP started to round up and detain large numbers of Falun Gong practitioners everywhere in China. Many were severely tortured.

Luo repeatedly spoke about the so-called "long-term, complicated, and difficult [situation]," indicating that the campaign against Falun Gong was to be long-term and brutal. For example, he said that forced labor camps "must do thorough and complete work on people's thoughts," referring to forced brainwashing.

To prevent people who were "transformed" against their will from practicing Falun Gong again, Luo said, "The forced labor camps need to build up a regular communication and feedback system with the workplaces that have Falun Gong practitioners. When they [Falun Gong practitioners] are released, the communities and residential offices should keep on doing 'thought' work on them. The forced labor camps should set up a communication system with the workplaces of those 'transformed' practitioners to get regular feedback about whether they are practicing again."

According to Luo's speeches, the detailed persecution methods include using "transformed" Falun Gong practitioners to work with the CCP to "transform" other practitioners, as well as developing methods and collecting and spreading persecution experience to the whole country.

§§9.2.2 Zeng Qinghong

As an alternate member of the Politburo, Secretary of the Secretariat of the CCP Central Committee, and head of the CCP Organization

Department, Zeng Qinghong was among the first high-level officials to support Jiang Zemin in persecuting Falun Gong. In the early stage of the persecution, Zeng framed the "struggle" against Falun Gong as an important test for the Communist Party. He used his authority as the head of the Organization Department, which controls staffing within the CCP, to pressure other officials to participate in the persecution.

Zeng was one of the planners of the self-immolation hoax on Tiananmen Square on January 23, 2001 (see Appendix 2). Between January 27 and February 1, Zeng toured Jiangsu, Hunan, and other provinces to defame Falun Gong based on the hoax. He directed that the suppression of Falun Gong be "made an important task to be done quickly and done well with absolutely no hesitation or softness."

On April 20, 2001, at a national conference in Beijing on "thought-study education" for village officials in rural areas, Zeng flattered Jiang Zemin's "Three Represents" political theory and again called on people in the countryside to suppress Falun Gong.

Before October 1, 2001 (National Day in China), Zeng Qinghong and Luo Gan personally organized the "No.3 Storm Operation" that led to the arrest of many Falun Gong practitioners. As part of this operation, the central government dispatched computer networking specialists to each province to monitor and obstruct access to Minghui.org. Police temporarily employed young men monitored public and residential areas and streets in major cities around the clock. A number of practitioners were detained as a result.

Zeng personally directed the persecution in some regions. For example, between January 17 and 23, 2001, he and Luo Gan went to Hunan Province. Luo went to Hengyang City, and Zeng went to Changsha City (the capital of Hunan Province). In six days, over 1,600 Falun Gong practitioners were arrested and taken to forced labor camps in Hengyang, and an unknown number were arrested in Changsha.

Three months later, in late April 2001, Zeng Qinghong went to Hefei City, Anhui Province, where a large number of practitioners were arrested on April 29 and 30 at his direction.

§§9.2.3 Liu Jing

As a former Deputy Minister of Public Security and former director of the Central 610 Office, Liu Jing was one of the main perpetrators of the persecution under Jiang Zemin. Liu devised methods to force Falun Gong practitioners to renounce their faith, gave orders for police to shoot and kill practitioners on sight, coordinated mass arrests of practitioners, and helped orchestrate the self-immolation hoax on Tiananmen Square (see Appendix 2) to defame Falun Gong.

In one example of developing and promoting methods to "transform" practitioners, Liu Jing personally directed six individuals to act as Falun Gong practitioners, infiltrate the Masanjia Forced Labor Camp, and manipulate real practitioners into renouncing Falun Gong by fabricating and misinterpreting Falun Gong teachings. Liu Jing and Luo Gan then gave lectures around the province to have other labor camps, detention centers, and prisons adopt the same "transformation" methods used at Masanjia.

Before the Chinese New Year in February 2002, Liu held a meeting at Nanhu Hotel in Changchun, Jilin Province, where he criticized the province's lack of effectiveness in suppressing practitioners and gave an order to "completely eliminate" Falun Gong. The Changchun Public Security Bureau subsequently conducted large-scale arrests of practitioners several nights in a row. Officers were authorized to shoot to kill practitioners discovered in the act of putting up posters or hanging banners about Falun Gong.

After practitioners broadcast information about the persecution by tapping into TV signals in Changchun on March 5, 2002, Jiang Zemin ordered that the participants be "killed without pardon." He sent Luo Gan, Liu Jing, and other officials to Jilin Province on several occasions to direct the suppression effort there. In a province-wide mass arrest that same month, the authorities in Changchun dispatched more than 6,000 police officers and arrested more than 5,000 Falun Gong practitioners. After being tortured in Changchun, they were moved to jails across Jilin Province and continued to be abused. At least 6 practitioners were killed, and another 15 were sentenced to 4 to 20 years in prison.

When Liu represented China at the 2000 and 2001 meetings of the UN Commission on Human Rights, he defamed Falun Gong and denied that practitioners in China were being arrested and tortured.

§§9.2.4 Zhou Yongkang

Zhou Yongkang was selected to replace Jia Chunwang as Minister of Public Security on December 9, 2002. During the transition, Zhou's role as the new administrator of the "Strike-Hard Campaign" against Falun Gong was emphasized in an APA and Reuters report. For example, in its December 9, 2002, "China Gets a New Public Security Minister," APA (Beijing edition) republished the People's Daily announcement of the appointment of Zhou to the post, which emphasized the "Strike-Hard Campaign" against Falun Gong as one of the key achievements of the former police chief before Zhou.

On December 26, 2002, in "China's Public Security Chief Urges Better Standards of Law Enforcement Work," the British Broadcasting Corporation (BBC) reported the remarks made by Zhou at a video-linked teleconference. Among other things, Zhou urged all public security organizations across China to, "[i]n particular, strictly guard against and 'Strike-Hard' at the trouble-making and undermining activities carried out by hostile forces in and outside this country, [including] the cult organization of Falun Gong."

On May 28, 2004, China News Service reported Zhou's remarks to the ministerial affairs meeting convened by the Ministry of Public Security. Among other topics, "he stressed that they must take effective steps further; strike hard at the unlawful and criminal activities ... and pay close attention to the operational trends in the internal and external hostile forces, the violent terrorist forces, the ethnic splittist forces, the religious extremist forces, and cult organizations like Falun Gong; take tight precautions; and 'Strike-Hard' at their disturbing and destructive activities."

Zhou's direct participation in the persecution was conducted primarily through his management of the 610 Office. Police and security forces (including those from the 610 Office) who arrested, detained, brainwashed, and tortured Falun Gong practitioners took orders from the Public Security Bureau at provincial and/or municipal levels, which are under the Ministry of Public Security that Zhou Yongkang was in charge of.

§§9.2.5 Li Lanqing

As the first head of the Central 610 Office, Li Lanqing used Jiang Zemin's persecutory language in addition to his own ideological influence and stature to implement Jiang's "douzheng" campaign. For example, in February 2001, at a National Award Meeting, Li Lanqing praised members of Chinese security forces for subjecting Falun Gong to "douzheng" and "transformation." He further instructed Party and government leaders at all levels to continue to carry out the "douzheng" campaign against Falun Gong in order to strengthen the confidence and objectives of the Party. Li served as head of the 610 Office from June 1999 to November 2002, when he retired.

Chapter 10: Organizations Leading the Persecution

Since it came to power, the Chinese Communist Party has established a system of rule by the Party rather than rule of law. The Party's decisions are above the judiciary and penal system, turning law enforcement and judicial agencies into mere rubber stamps for the Party. Jiang Hua, former head of the Supreme People's Court, once said, "During wartime, it was up to the Party committee to decide who should be arrested or even killed, whether it was in the people's army or in the revolutionary base. People have followed this rule since."

After decades of brainwashing, the communist regime has successfully made the public believe that the law reflects the will of the ruling party and is created to protect the interests of the ruling party. As a result, "following politics but not the law" has become the unspoken rule within the political and legal system in China.

Party committees at different levels, including provinces, municipalities, counties and autonomous regions, each have their respective Political and Legal Affairs Committee (PLAC), which oversees law enforcement and judicial agencies. Most Party committee secretaries simultaneously head the PLAC, creating an intricate power network.

After Jiang Zemin ordered the persecution of Falun Gong in 1999, he further empowered the PLAC to implement the suppression campaign. The PLAC and the 610 Office work hand in hand (often sharing the same offices and leaders) to command government resources to arrest, detain, sentence, and brainwash Falun Gong practitioners, as well as to coordinate the harvesting of organs from living practitioners to supply China's organ transplant system. At each level, the PLAC sets the persecution strategy to be executed by the 610 Office.

§10.1 Shared Leadership and Resources

After Jiang established the 610 Office in June 1999, many deputy secretaries of PLACs were appointed to head the 610 Office in addition to their existing roles. For example, Xiao Xiangxin, the deputy secretary of the PLAC in Wan'an County, Jiangxi Province, was also the director of the 610 Office.

Both the PLAC and the 610 Office sometimes use different public-facing names to hide their illegality. For example, in Daqing City, Heilongjiang Province, the PLAC's doorplate read "Municipal Social Security Comprehensive Governance Committee Office," and the 610 Office was known as the "Municipal Government Office for the Prevention and Handling of Cults."

At an annual experience-sharing meeting of the 610 Office in Wuhan City, Hubei Province, in the summer of 2010, Zhou Yongkang, the former head of the Central PLAC, repeated Jiang Zemin's order to eradicate Falun Gong in China. Zhou also allocated more funds to the 610 Office to continue the persecution.

§10.2 Control Over the Police, Judiciary, and Penal System

In most democratic countries, the police, prosecutors, and courts work independently of each other while serving as mutual supervision. However, this is not the case in China. While law enforcement and judicial agencies were already under the Party's supervision before the persecution of Falun Gong started in 1999, Jiang Zemin and the 610 Office tightened this control in order to carry out his persecution policy while overriding the rule of law.

For example, the presidents of the Supreme People's Procuratorate and Supreme People's Court, as well as the Minister of Justice, all of whom were members of the PLAC, had to report to Zhou Yongkang and Meng

Jianzhu, the two former heads of the Ministry of Public Security and the PLAC. The same is true with many local prosecutors and judges, who must report to police officials, who also head the local PLAC. This increased control also contributed to a rapid expansion of the power of the public security system in China.

This structure makes it impossible for the law enforcement and judicial systems to operate with fairness and justice. In the persecution of Falun Gong, practitioners are subjected to show trials while the sentences are pre-determined by the PLAC and the 610 Office.

In one example, Ms. Gao Deyu, 68, from Xichang City, Sichuan Province, was arrested in September 2009 for practicing Falun Gong. Her lawyer had tremendous difficulty visiting her. Liu, the deputy director of the Xichang City PLAC, said to her lawyer, "Don't discuss the law with me. We don't follow the law." A year later, a Xichang Court judge sentenced Ms. Gao to 12 years in prison.

In Hebei Province, six Falun Gong practitioners were sentenced to between 7 and 8 years by the Qian'an City Court on December 6, 2009. Presiding judge Feng Xiaolin told the practitioners' families, "We don't follow the law when it comes to Falun Gong cases."

Another judge in Yiyang City, Hunan Province, said to Falun Gong practitioner Ms. Zhang Chunqiu, "Now it's the power of the Party overriding the law to suppress Falun Gong. We're only going through the formalities [in the sentencing process]. We can't do anything about it. You can't blame us for it."

Judge Gu Yingqing from Suzhou Court in Jiangsu Province once said to the daughter of Mr. Lu Tong, who was sentenced to four years in prison on December 17, 2008, "You should not expect the law to be above politics. It's useless to talk about the law with me because I'm talking to you about politics."

Director Ma of the 610 Office in Nong'an County, Jilin Province, said to a practitioner, "We make the decisions here. We talk about politics, not the law. You can go ahead and file complaints against us wherever you want."

When practitioners are imprisoned, the PLAC and the 610 Office order guards to brainwash them and force them to renounce their faith. The transformation rate, i.e., the number of practitioners renouncing their faith, is tied to the guards' promotions and bonuses. As a result, the guards use severe torture in order to increase their transformation rates for personal gain. Some guards even threatened practitioners, "It's either transformation or cremation."

§10.3 The 610 Office

The 610 Office was created as an organization within the Communist Party exclusively to coordinate and carry out the suppression and eradication of Falun Gong. It is an illegal spy organization that remains secretive at high levels while clearly evident at low levels. Its functions include strategizing, planning, and directing all activities related to suppressing Falun Gong. To carry out these tasks, it is effectively authorized to control government departments at all levels, including the justice system (police, procuratorates, and courts), in violation of Chinese law and the Chinese Constitution.

610 Offices have been set up not only at every level of government but also in state security bureaus, police departments, universities, schools, government agencies, and large businesses. Agents from the 610 Offices have been active in foreign relations, internet surveillance, foreign firms, the travel industry, and criminal activities.

After several rounds of adjustments, strengthening, and renaming, the 610 Office remains above the law. Its scope has expanded to include underground churches as well as other religious and qigong organizations.

§§10.3.1 Creation and Expansion

In a CCP Politburo meeting on June 7, 1999, Jiang Zemin gave a speech on the urgent need to "deal with Falun Gong." He announced that the Central Committee would launch a task force to quickly formulate strategies to eradicate Falun Gong. It would be led by Li Lanqing, a member of the Politburo Standing Committee, and assisted by Luo Gan and Ding Guangen, two other Politburo members.

The "Central Leading Group for Handling the Falun Gong Issue" was thus formed three days later, on June 10, 1999. Its members included officials of the Supreme People's Court, Supreme People's Procuratorate, Ministry of Public Security, Ministry of State Security, Propaganda Department, and Ministry of Foreign Affairs. Its operations arm was called the "Office of the Central Leading Group for Handling the Falun Gong Issue," or the Central 610 Office.

Lower CCP committees at the provincial, city, county, town, and even neighborhood levels mirrored this structure with their own Leading Group for Handling the Falun Gong Issue, along with an Office of the Leading Group for Handling the Falun Gong Issue (610 Office). The majority were attached to their respective CCP Committee's PLAC, and a few were attached to the Office of the Party Committee at their level.

While no documents were made public for when the Leading Groups were formed at the provincial and city levels, many documents record the establishment and functions of the Offices at county, district, and lower levels. These local 610 Offices follow the Central 610 Office. In urban areas, 610 Offices were established in neighborhood committees with dedicated officers. Rural areas also saw the establishment of working groups headed by village Party secretaries as well as the creation of 610 Offices.

Neither the CCP Central Committee nor the State Council has openly acknowledged the existence of this organization in either publicly accessible organization structures or official press releases, but it does appear in media reports and local government websites. The existence of the Central 610 Office can also be verified through documents of the State Council, ministries, and local governments, as well as media reports. The secrecy of the organization is similar to that of the "CCP Central Committee Leading Group for the Cultural Revolution" in the 1960s, which answered only to Mao Zedong and exercised vast extralegal powers.

§§10.3.2 Illegality

The 610 Office was established without following legal procedure or gaining approval from the National People's Congress, the highest organ of power in China. It also violates the Chinese Constitution, specifically Article 36 (freedom of religious belief) and Article 89 (enumerated powers of the State Council).

Due to its confidentiality, many details of 610 Offices are not known to the public. Although the 610 Office was mentioned in early news coverage, it did not appear in public policies from the CCP Central Committee, legal documents, or government documents. A screenshot of the government website of Changde City, Hunan Province, indicates that the Changde 610 Office began operations in July 1999, though its establishment was not officially approved by the Hunan Province Party Committee until March 2001. For almost two years, the Changde 610 Office operated as an unregistered entity within the provincial Party Committee. Its activities during that time can be seen in the example below:

Mr. Ou Keshun, born in 1962, was a Falun Gong practitioner from Linli County in Changde City. Linli police arrested him on January 12, 2001 and held him in a brainwashing center inside the Changde Drug Rehabilitation Center. Officers from a working group of the Changde 610 Office and PLAC forced Mr. Ou and a number of other practitioners to renounce their faith. They held him with drug addicts and instigated them to torture him. After being beaten severely and vomiting blood, Mr. Ou died eight days later, on January 20. To cover up the cause of death, officers of the working group ordered his cremation in Changde before his family arrived.

§§10.3.3 Organizational Structure

When it was created, the Central 610 Office fell directly under the CCP Central Committee as a temporary bureau-level organization but was later elevated to a permanent ministry-level agency. As of 2010, its code in China's civil service system was 959.

The first director of the Central 610 Office was Wang Maolin, who was later replaced by Liu Jing, Deputy Minister of Public Security. In 2009, Liu was replaced by Li Dongsheng, Deputy Minister of the Central Propaganda Department and Deputy Director of the Central 610 Office. Other former directors and deputy directors include Xu Haibin (Executive Deputy Director, former secretary for Luo Gan), Gao

Yichen (former Deputy Minister of State Security), Yuan Yin, Wang Xiaoxiang, and Dong Jufa. Li Anping was Secretary General of the Central 610 Office.

Below is the known structure of the Central 610 Office:

- **Secretary Office** (also known as the General Office). Director: Wang Tixian
- **First Office** (could be the same as Secretary Office). Director: Wang Tixian; Deputy Director: Li Xiaodong; Inspector: Song Quanzhong.
- **Second Office**: Director: Shao Hongwei; Deputy Director: Gao Xiaodong.
- **Third Office**: No additional information available.

The exact functions of these three offices are currently unknown to the outside, but one can reference the internal structure of lower 610 Offices. These local offices vary from place to place, but they normally have a secretary branch, a general branch, and an education branch. A county-level 610 Office normally consists of a general group and an education group. A city-level 610 Office usually comprises a general section and an education section. In a specific example, the structure of the Luhe District Party Committee 610 Office in Nanjing City, Jiangsu Province, contains the General Coordination Section, Education and Transformation Section, and Prevention and Control Section. It is not common for a district-level 610 Office to have three branches. Nonetheless, they could correspond to the three branches of the Central 610 Office.

The responsibilities of these branches are as follows:

- **Secretary branch**: processing daily work and coordinating administrative affairs; sending/receiving/circulating messages; drafting documents; managing the official seal, confidentiality, and archival of files; arranging and organizing meetings.
- **General branch**: processing files and intelligence information, comprehensive research, trend analysis, review of work, and

meetings; responsible for confidentiality, political work and human resources, administrative logistics, and daily routine.

- **Education branch**: defamatory propaganda against Falun Gong, brainwashing Falun Gong practitioners, forcing practitioners to renounce their belief (referred to as "education and transformation"), contact, coordination, supervision, inspection, coordinating other agencies on handling so-called Falun Gong issues.

In summary, the general branch focuses on collecting intelligence, analyzing information, and formulating persecution strategies, while the education branch conducts operations and forces practitioners to renounce their belief.

After the 610 Office name gained notoriety, it was changed to the "Office of Preventing and Handling Cult Issues." In some places, it is called the "Stability Maintenance Office." For example, a document from the Organizational Structure Committee of Tongling County, Shanxi Province, shows two titles for the 610 Office: the "Tongling Party Committee Office of Preventing and Handling Cult Issues" and the "Tongling Office of Preventing and Handling Cult Issues." However, its function remains the same, and internally it is still referred to as the 610 Office.

§§10.3.4 Staffing Composition

Because the 610 Office was originally intended to be a temporary agency, authorities pulled staff members from the political and legal system to run the organization in addition to their existing jobs. For example, if a police officer was moved to the 610 Office, he retained his position and law enforcement power in the police department. Such personnel were sometimes referred to as "610 police officers." If the person was a Party secretary or director of a certain agency, he remained a director; while he did not have law enforcement power, he did gain the authority to order the police force to carry out a specific task against Falun Gong practitioners. Other staff members were reportedly pulled from agencies such as procuratorates, courts, propaganda departments, judicial bureaus, finance bureaus, and appeals offices.

As the persecution continued well past the three months Jiang Zemin had predicted, the 610 Office became a permanent organization with full-time staff members. Despite the high degree of secrecy surrounding it, limited public information reveals this "modern Gestapo" has detailed and complete organizational charts, from the central government in Beijing to different regions in every corner of the country.

While it's impossible to ascertain how many people work in the 610 Office system throughout China, the number is no doubt high, considering its presence in all the government and non-government agencies, as well as Party committees, at the provincial, city, county, township, and district levels. The extensive presence of 610 Offices across the country also reflects the depth and scale of the persecution of Falun Gong.

§§10.3.5 Control Over Government Departments and Commercial Enterprises

The 610 Office has branches embedded in the police and education systems, as well as large state-owned and private businesses, to enable it to monitor and order the arrests of Falun Gong practitioners in all areas of society.

› 10.3.5(a) The Police System

After the 610 Office and other agencies failed to eradicate Falun Gong within three months as Jiang Zemin had originally envisioned, he ordered the 610 Office to be expanded into the Ministry of State Security, the Ministry of Public Security, and local police departments during an internal meeting in late 2000 or early 2001.

The Ministry of Public Security issued Notice No.157 in 2001 about setting up a specific department within the public security system to handle cases about Falun Gong and other "harmful qigong organizations." This notice marked the establishment of the 610 Office in the public security system.

The Ministry of Public Security also added an additional department, the 26th department, as the formal home of the 610 Office. In some regions, the 610 Office falls under the Ministry of Public Security's first department, the National Security Department, and shares the same office building with two different door plates. The head or deputy head of the National Security Department also became the head of the 610 Office.

In addition to the police system, the 610 Office also permeated every government agency and department, including the procuratorates, courts, justice departments, prison system, finance bureau, National Food Administration, Bureau of Commerce, Propaganda Department, and United Front Work Department.

› 10.3.5(b) The Education System

To advance the persecution policy and promote Party propaganda demonizing Falun Gong, the communist regime established the 610 Office within the education system, from the provincial level to the city level and from colleges and medical schools to middle schools and even elementary schools.

In late 2005, the 610 Office appeared on the campus map at Jilin University, marking its move from being affiliated with the university's Party Committee Office to being an independent operation. Such a move, however, wasn't common in universities in China, as most 610 Offices remain under the Party Committee on campus. In January 2006, new leadership at the Jilin University Law School announced the staff members of its 610 Office, making it the first law school in China to announce the existence of the 610 Office within its organization.

In Zibo City, Shandong Province, the Zhangdian District education bureau issued a notice in October 2006, ordering all schools in the district, including middle schools and elementary schools, to "perfect and implement the policy to set up 610 Offices according to each school's own situation."

› 10.3.5(c) The Postal Service

The 610 Office has pressured the postal service to inspect letters and packages for Falun Gong-related materials. In Yunnan Province, for example, post office employees were required to open envelopes to check for letters written by Falun Gong practitioners to raise awareness of the persecution.[278] Post offices throughout China have also withheld criminal complaints against Jiang Zemin sent by Falun Gong practitioners to the Supreme People's Court and Supreme People's Procuratorate (to be discussed further in Chapter 12).

This type of policy violates Article 40 of the Chinese Constitution (freedom and privacy of correspondence). It also violates the Chinese Postal Law, specifically Article 35 (prohibition on opening, concealing, or destroying mail belonging to others) and Article 38 (abuse of power by postal employees). Finally, it violates articles 252 and 253 of Chinese Criminal Law, which address the opening, concealment, and destruction of others' mail by citizens or postal workers.

› 10.3.5(d) Large Companies

Because many state-owned enterprises and public and private companies have their own Communist Party Committees, 610 Offices were naturally created within these organizations as well. Documented examples include the Shuicheng Mining Group in Liupanshui City, Guizhou Province and the Xinkuang Mining Group in Taian City, Shandong Province. In another example, the 10th Division of Xinjiang Production and Construction Corps, a unique economic and paramilitary organization, listed the phone number of its 610 Office director in its address book.

Case 1: Daqing Oilfield Has Persecuted at Least 27 Practitioners to Death

Among large enterprises in China, Daqing Oilfield Company (a subsidiary of PetroChina) has been responsible for the most deaths of Falun Gong practitioners since the persecution began. As of April 2013, at least 27 employees of this state-owned enterprise have been persecuted to death for practicing Falun Gong, accounting for 40% of practitioner deaths in Daqing and 5% of practitioner deaths in Heilongjiang Province.[279]

The 610 Office in the Daqing Oilfield Company has set up brainwashing centers, forced units in the company to pay to send their employees who practice Falun Gong to brainwashing centers to be tortured, withheld wages and bonuses from Falun Gong practitioners, directed the Daqing police and judiciary to arrest and imprison practitioners, and distributed propaganda materials defaming Falun Gong. Many of the targeted practitioners were model workers, and in some cases their leaders allowed them to continue working their jobs despite pressure from the 610 Office to demote them.[280]

Case 2: 610 Office Agents at the Gezhouba Group Corporation Persecute Practitioner to Death

Falun Gong practitioners employed by the Gezhouba Group in Yichang City, Hubei Province, have been assaulted, followed, intimidated, and subjected to brainwashing by the 610 Office and the Security Section of Gezhouba's eight subsidiary companies.

One of them was Ms. Shen Ju, who began practicing Falun Gong in May 1998 and saw her health improve as a result. After the persecution began, she went to Beijing three times to appeal for justice for Falun Gong. She was arrested and taken back to Yichang City, where agents from the 610 Office and officer Xu Hong of the Second Corporation of Gezhouba Group extorted a large sum of money from her and kept her prisoner. In the next few years, police and company officers repeatedly detained Ms. Shen and held her in brainwashing centers.

After years of physical and psychological abuse, Ms. Shen went into a coma for 24 hours and died in a hospital on January 10, 2006. She was 34 and is survived by her six-year-old child.[281]

Chapter 11: Accomplices to the Persecution

As discussed in Chapter 9, Jiang Zemin used his control of the Party, government, and military to drive the persecution of Falun Gong. Through the Political and Legal Affairs Committee (PLAC) and the 610 Office, Jiang successfully made the persecution a part of every Chinese citizen's life and work. People throughout the society have been compelled to participate in the persecution, either willingly through enticements of personal gain or unwillingly through political pressure and intimidation. These include nearly every Party, government, and military organization, as well as those related to education, health and medicine, finance, and foreign relations.

§11.1 Community-Level Authorities

Neighborhood committees are unique to the CCP and are used to monitor citizens at the district level. These local offices historically enjoyed low prestige as a source of employment. When the persecution of Falun Gong began in 1999, however, they became an integral part of the CCP's campaign and were steadily elevated. Staff members were made public servants and required to take civil service exams. They also began to receive stipends of more than 10,000 yuan per year, as well as retirement and medical benefits.[282] Some neighborhood committees have their own 610 Offices and have openly listed the suppression of Falun Gong as part of their job responsibilities.

In the Kuiwen District of Weifang, Shandong Province, the neighborhood committee carried out a defamation campaign against Falun Gong. Staff members posted and distributed propaganda materials throughout the district and even entered residents' homes to deliver the message verbally. In the same district, the Yingyuan Community Association held an anti-Falun Gong exhibition in which more than 200 residents and students were shown 76 display boards defaming Falun Gong and forced to sign denunciations. For holding these activities and setting up policing and monitoring facilities within the community, the Yingyuan Community Association was named a "model community" and given city-level awards.

These neighborhood committees were also incentivized by monetary awards. The Shandong provincial Party committee and government named its anti-cult association an "advanced" organization. The association awarded every community that participated in the persecution 5,000 yuan and every township 10,000 yuan. Between 2000 and 2009, it disbursed a total of 345,000 yuan in such awards.

In addition to defamation campaigns, neighborhood committees also cooperated with police and judicial agencies to investigate and monitor practitioners. Committee staff often harass and intimidate practitioners at home, photograph and videotape them, confiscate their Falun Gong books, and coerce them into signing statements renouncing their faith.

§11.2 Foreign Firms and Media Organizations

From self-censorship to active cooperation, many foreign firms and news media have directly and indirectly assisted the Chinese regime in persecuting Falun Gong.

§§11.2.1 Technology Firms Help Build Censorship and Monitoring Infrastructure

In 2000, the Chinese regime began to implement an online information filtering and monitoring system known as the Great

Firewall (GFW). Its requirements were defined by the Politburo, the Political and Legal Affairs Committee, Ministry of State Security, and the 610 Office.

Major technology companies that contributed to the development of the Great Firewall included Cisco and Nortel. A leaked internal presentation from Cisco revealed that it was aware that its products would be used for this purpose, and one slide stated a goal of the project as "Combating 'Falun Gong' Evil Cult and Other Hostile Elements," parroting the Chinese regime's defamatory rhetoric against Falun Gong.[283]

According to a 2005 study by Professor John Palfrey of Harvard University, the Great Firewall blocked 100% of information reporting positively on Falun Gong, 60% of information related to opposition political parties, close to 50% of information on the Tiananmen Square massacre of June 4, 1989, and 10% of pornography websites.[284]

§§11.2.2 Foreign Firm Complies with CCP Demands to Censor and Terminate Practitioners

In September 2003, a Falun Gong practitioner discussed her positive experience with the practice while giving a speech for the Chinese subsidiary of the cosmetics firm Mary Kay in Shenzhen. After a reporter tipped off the authorities, three Falun Gong practitioners were arrested. The 610 Office pressured Mary Kay to follow the Party line on Falun Gong, under the threat of having their business operations in China interrupted or discontinued.

Mary Kay complied with the demand and required all employees to sign a statement that they would not practice or advocate for Falun Gong; otherwise, their employment would be terminated. Several Mary Kay employees subsequently lost their jobs for refusing to sign the statement. Another employee who spoke in favor of Falun Gong was detained by Chinese authorities.

On November 17, 2003, U.S. Members of Congress Chris Smith, Tom Lantos, and Ileana Ros-Lehtinen wrote to Mary Kay CEO Richard R. Rogers, requesting that the company void its Chinese subsidiary's requirement for employees to sign a statement related to religious, spiritual, and political participation. A spokesperson for the company told Agence France-Presse (AFP) that Mary Kay was already in the process of retracting the requirement and denied that any employees had been terminated for refusing to sign the statement.[285]

§§11.2.3 International Media Outlets Repeat Chinese Communist Party Propaganda

Unlike prior political campaigns in which the CCP closed China's doors, the regime engaged the foreign press from the start of its campaign against Falun Gong, with the goal of propagating its anti-Falun Gong rhetoric worldwide to gain international support for the persecution. In the early days of the persecution, many major news organizations around the world rebroadcast the CCP's propaganda aired on Chinese state-controlled media, such as CCTV. Even today, Western media still often use the Chinese regime's derogatory language, such as "cult," "followers," and "threat" to refer to Falun Gong and its practitioners.

In the years that followed, some international media organizations continued to repeat the CCP's disinformation about Falun Gong or stayed silent on the issue, due to either economic incentives or intimidation by the Chinese regime. In one example, Talentvision TV, a Mandarin station in Canada, rebroadcast a CCTV program that falsely accused Falun Gong practitioners of a murder in Beijing. The Canadian Radio-television and Telecommunications Commission decided on August 16, 2002 that Talentvision's claim that Falun Gong was connected to the murder case in Beijing without factual evidence violated multiple policies of the Commission's code of professional ethics and constituted an attack on Falun Gong. The Commission required the station to broadcast its decision during primetime.[286]

The Chinese regime is also believed to use financial ties and advertising dollars as leverage to keep foreign media outlets from covering Falun Gong. At the same time, it has made deals with major newspapers to carry inserts of *China Daily* as a way to increase the reach of the Communist Party's propaganda campaigns.

§11.3 Chinese Officials Who Helped Implement the Persecution

Compared to the key perpetrators listed in Section 9.2 who were primarily responsible for launching the persecution, the officials below were recruited into the campaign later and played less central roles. Nevertheless, they actively pushed forward the persecution to build their own political capital and caused Falun Gong practitioners within their jurisdictions untold suffering.

§§11.3.1 Li Dongsheng

As the deputy director of China Central Television (CCTV) between January 1993 and July 2000, Li Dongsheng (李东生) carried out the CCP's nationwide propaganda campaign against Falun Gong. When the 610 Office was first established in June 1999, he was appointed deputy director and put in charge of propaganda. After Liu Jing retired in October 2009, Zhou Yongkang appointed Li Deputy Minister of Public Security and to head the 610 Office.

Li influenced public opinion through "Focus," a popular prime-time program on CCTV about current affairs. The program featured 102 anti-Falun Gong programs in the six and a half years between July 21, 1999 and late 2005. There were 70 such episodes between July and December 1999 alone.

Li also played a major role in orchestrating the self-immolation hoax on Tiananmen Square, pushing the propaganda campaign to a new level.

§§11.3.2 Bo Xilai

Once the mayor of Dalian City, Liaoning Province, Bo Xilai (薄熙来) actively implemented Jiang Zemin's suppression campaign against Falun Gong. He expanded the prison and labor camp system while building new ones.

Many of the Falun Gong practitioners who went to Beijing to appeal for the right to practice their faith were taken to the newly established camps and prisons. Bo gave orders to all levels of law enforcement to beat and kill practitioners. He also led the process of using practitioners for organ harvesting and body plastination in Dalian through his implementation of Jiang's directive to "destroy them physically." Bo was quickly promoted to Governor of Liaoning Province.

After Bo was appointed as the Party Secretary of Chongqing in 2007, wave after wave of practitioners in the city were arrested, detained, or taken to brainwashing centers.

§§11.3.3 Wen Shizhen

Wen Shizhen (闻世震), Party Secretary of Liaoning Province from August 1997 to December 2004, also used his stature and influence to implement Jiang Zemin's orders to "douzheng" Falun Gong. In July 1999, he instructed other Party leaders to "follow the orders of Jiang's CCP Central Committee to eliminate Falun Gong . . . in our province" through ideological conversion using torture ("transformation") to prevail against them. Again in October 1999, after Jiang Zemin misinformed the French newspaper Le Figaro and the People's Daily published Jiang Zemin's lies just one day later, Wen urged Liaoning provincial Party leaders to advance the "douzheng" campaign based on Jiang Zemin's slander of Falun Gong.

§§11.3.4 Wang Maolin

The first to head the Central 610 Office, Wang Maolin (王茂林) actively implemented Jiang Zemin's campaign against Falun Gong. For example, in his preface to the influential Party-authored book *Falun Gong and Evil Cults*, Wang argues that the book "captures the importance and necessity of the battle against Falun Gong."

§§11.3.5 Ding Shifa

As Secretary of the Liaoning Province PLAC, Ding Shifa (丁世发) reinforced Wen Shizhen's remarks to promote the suppression of Falun Gong. In October 1999, he urged his fellow comrades in Liaoning Province to "diligently participate in the [anti-Falun Gong] 'douzheng' with full political enthusiasm and to prevail."

Earlier, in July 1999, Ding led staff members from the Liaoning Party Organization Department, Propaganda Department, and Public Security Bureau to Huludao City and demanded that local officials strictly carry out the CCP central leadership's strategies (issued by Jiang Zemin) to succeed in the campaign against Falun Gong.

§§11.3.6 Zhang Xinxiang

While serving as Deputy Secretary of the Liaoning Provincial Party Committee, Zhang Xinxiang (张行湘) urged fellow officials, especially those in Huludao, to "be prepared for a lengthy 'douzheng' campaign against Falun Gong," who he characterized as "enemies of the Party."

明慧網
MINGHUI.ORG

Chapter 12: More than 200,000 Legal Complaints Filed Against Jiang Zemin

While several practitioners in China tried to file the first lawsuit against Jiang Zemin in August 2000, the authorities simply refused to register their complaint.[287] Though several lawsuits were independently filed outside of China in the years that followed, practitioners in China had always faced obstacles in getting their complaints lodged with the court system.

On May 1, 2015, the Supreme People's Court implemented a new "Registration System Reform," which stipulates that all criminal complaints must be registered with the court once received. Many Falun Gong practitioners began to exercise their legal right to sue Jiang Zemin for launching the persecution of Falun Gong and causing them great harm and tremendous suffering.

Key Highlights

By directing the persecution of Falun Gong, Jiang Zemin has violated the Chinese Constitution, Chinese criminal law, and international laws on torture, genocide, and crimes against humanity. Jiang also ordered government ministries to carry out actions for which they did not have legal authority.

209,908 lawsuits against Jiang have been filed with the Supreme People's Court and Supreme People's Procuratorate. Between the end of May and December 31, 2015, 201,803 individuals filed criminal complaints against Jiang, 171,059 of them submitted copies to Minghui.org, and 134,176 (78.4%) of mailed complaints were confirmed to have been delivered. Local authorities in many regions have retaliated against plaintiffs for filing lawsuits against Jiang. Cases of retaliation include harassment, interrogation, arrests, or even prison sentences. In late 2017, the CCP launched a "knocking on doors" campaign to keep track of practitioners who had sued Jiang and/or still practiced Falun Gong.

§12.1 Examples of Criminal Complaints Against Jiang Zemin

Legal complaints against Jiang Zemin are mailed to the Supreme People's Court and Supreme People's Procuratorate. Minghui.org also receives copies of criminal complaints against Jiang from many Falun Gong practitioners.

The following accounts, taken from these legal cases, describe repeated and brutal abuse simply for practicing Falun Gong and petitioning to the government for their right to freedom of belief. All three of the plaintiffs could have easily died from the torture, and one of them, Mr. Yang Zhiqiang, lost his wife as a result of relentless abuse in police custody.[288]

Case 1: Luo Zhihui

Hometown: Shijiazhuang City, Hebei Province

Date filed: June 8, 2015

Ms. Luo Zhihui, 64, used to work for the Qiaoxi Grain Supply Center in Shijiazhuang City. She started to practice Falun Gong in 1997, which helped her to completely recover from severe anemia. Grateful for the improvement in her health and for the spiritual guidance she derived from Falun Gong, Ms. Luo repeatedly appealed to stop the persecution. She was arrested more than 20 times. She was tortured and poisoned while being held in labor camps, a mental hospital, and brainwashing centers.

Ms. Luo was first detained in October 1999, when she visited Beijing to appeal for Falun Gong. She was detained in multiple police stations and detention centers for a total of at least 55 days. Police tortured her with "Flying an Airplane" and "Carrying a Sword on One's Back" (handcuffing behind the back with one hand crossed over a shoulder). She was restrained in a chair for eight days in a row and had to carry the chair with her even when she used the bathroom.

In March 2000, Ms. Luo was taken from her home and detained in a mental hospital for more than 10 days. She was tortured with the "Death Bed" and force-feeding.

Ms. Luo visited Beijing again in May 2000 and July 2001 to petition the government on behalf of Falun Gong. She was arrested both times. The first time, she was sentenced to one year of forced labor and the second time, to three years. In the labor camp, guards slapped her repeatedly, knocked her head against the wall, and pulled out her hair. They chained her to a heater to prevent her from sleeping. The long-term sleep deprivation led to hypertension.

The guards also instructed prisoners to put drugs into Ms. Luo's food, which made her dizzy and forgetful.

Ms. Luo was forced to do intensive labor. She was once forced to work for 48 hours without sleep.

Her health deteriorated so much that she was temporarily released for several months for medical treatment. The police put her back in the labor camp when she went to Beijing to appeal for Falun Gong again while on parole.

Before the 2008 Beijing Olympics, the police broke into Ms. Luo's home, arrested her, and sentenced her to three and a half years in prison. However, Ms. Luo's health was so poor that no prison would accept her. The police had to let her go.

Case 2: Dong Ming

Hometown: Changchun City, Jilin Province

Date filed: July 17, 2015

Mr. Dong Ming, 45, used to work for the Technology and Information Institute in Jilin Province. Because he practiced Falun Gong, he was fired by his employer, arrested six times, and taken to forced labor camps three times for a total of three years and nine months.

Mr. Dong went to Beijing on December 23, 1999, to appeal for Falun Gong. He was detained for 15 days. After he was released, he was fired from his job because he refused to renounce Falun Gong. However, this did not stop Mr. Dong from speaking out. He went to Beijing again on December 31, 2000, to appeal for Falun Gong. This time he was detained for eight days. The police hit his ribs and face, used chopsticks to squeeze his fingers until the skin was rubbed raw, and violently force-fed him, causing injuries to his mouth and gums.

Mr. Dong was arrested for a third time in March 2001 while he was attending a Falun Gong experience-sharing conference in Guangxi Province. He was detained for more than one month in the police station and brainwashing center. He was force-fed after he held a hunger strike. Then he was detained in isolation and forced to watch videos slandering Falun Gong. He was not allowed to see his family.

On March 13, 2002, Mr. Dong was arrested and taken to a labor camp for 16 months. Guards hit him with a board until the board broke into three pieces. He was forced to sit on a "small stool" for long periods of time and his use of the restroom was restricted. He was kicked in the lower back, causing severe pain that lasted for a month. He was deprived of family visits. Right after his term ended, he was taken to a brainwashing center.

On May 27, 2004, Mr. Dong was arrested when he visited another Falun Gong practitioner's home. He was taken to a labor camp for another 16 months. He was tortured with the "Tiger Bench." Guards poured ice-cold water on him repeatedly until he passed out. They also put wasabi oil into his nose. Right after that labor camp term ended, he was taken to a brainwashing center again, but released soon after he held a hunger strike to protest.

In July 2007, the police arrested Mr. Dong in his own store and confiscated his belongings. Some of them were never returned. The police punched him and struck him in the head with unopened bottles of water. Mr. Dong was taken to a labor camp for one year and 28 days.

Case 3: Yang Zhiqiang

Hometown: Tianjin

Date filed: August 15, 2015

Mr. Yang Zhiqiang, 61, filed a lawsuit for his wife and himself. His wife Dong Yuying died after spending three years and ten months in the Tianjin Women's Labor Camp for her belief in Falun Gong. In the camp, police tortured and sexually assaulted her by inserting four toothbrushes into her vagina. She was beaten and force-fed, causing her to lose three teeth. Her weight went from 80kg to 40kg. Ms. Dong died on March 17, 2005, four months after she returned home from the labor camp.

Mr. Yang was arrested three times and detained for a total of 19 months and 15 days. He was first arrested and detained for 15 days on July 20, 1999, when he and his wife went to Beijing to appeal on behalf of Falun Gong.

The couple went to Beijing again on October 1999. The wife was detained for more than a month and forced to pay 10,000 yuan before she was released. Mr. Yang was sent to a labor camp for 18 months. He was subjected to forced labor and beaten with rubber batons. Guards shocked his head and body with electric batons for long periods of time. Mr. Yang still has scars all over his body 15 years later.

While his wife was in a labor camp between 2000 and 2004, Mr. Yang was taken to a brainwashing center for a month, leaving their children unattended.

Case 4: Former Chinese Judge Files Criminal Complaint Against Jiang Zemin[289]

Ms. Sun Linghua, a former judge from Jinzhou City, Liaoning Province, filed a complaint against Jiang on June 8 with the Chinese Supreme People's Procuratorate. Ms. Sun was fired from her job and tortured in labor camps and prison because of her belief in Falun Gong.

Ms. Sun was appointed as an economic division chief judge and an administrative division chief judge of the Yixian County Court in Jinzhou City. In 1995 and 1996, she was given an award for being a model employee in the Jinzhou City legal system.

Ms. Sun was incarcerated in the notorious Masanjia Forced Labor Camp in Liaoning Province three times. In June 2003, she was sentenced to seven and a half years and sent to Dabei Prison, where she was forced to do hard labor, all while being pressured to give up her belief. When Ms. Sun was sentenced, she was fired from her job and has been unemployed ever since.

In her complaint, Ms. Sun recalled a woman whose case she had handled, who visited her when she was being held in a detention center. Ms. Sun wrote, "This woman told the detention center police, 'There are about 100 judges and court officials in this area. Sun Linghua is probably the only one that refuses to take bribes. An honest person like that should not be jailed.'"

Many people have supported her and condemned the persecution, Ms. Sun recalled. "A detention center police officer once told me that he respected me for my moral standards. A supervisor where I worked cried when she visited me in the detention center. She promised to try her best to get me out."

Before practicing Falun Gong, Ms. Sun had numerous health problems, including lumbar spondylosis, neurasthenia, rheumatic heart disease, mastitis, and colitis. That year, a doctor introduced her to Falun Gong. After a year of practice, all of these ailments were cured. She has never had to go to a hospital since 1996.

In the complaint, Ms. Sun also accused Jiang Zemin of creating defamatory propaganda to deceive people and stir up public hatred towards Falun Gong, as well as forcing and tempting government officials to get involved in the persecution.

Case 5: Retired Navy Commodore Sues Former Chinese Dictator[290]

A retired PLA Navy Commodore mailed a criminal complaint to the Supreme People's Procuratorate, charging former Chinese dictator

Jiang Zemin with launching the brutal suppression of Falun Gong that led to his tremendous suffering.

Commodore Zhou Yi, 79, retired as an associate professor at the Naval Aeronautical and Astronautical University. He alleges that Jiang violated his constitutional right to freedom of belief and opened the door to his illegal arrest and false imprisonment for doing nothing wrong. As for the persecution of Falun Gong in general, Zhou says Jiang has committed genocide, torture, and crimes against humanity.

Mr. Zhou asks the Supreme People's Court to order Jiang to issue an open apology for slandering Falun Gong to incite public hatred and to redress the suffering inflicted upon the founder and practitioners of Falun Gong, including Mr. Zhou and his family.

§12.2 Summary Statistics

Between the end of May and December 31, 2015:

- 201,803 Falun Gong practitioners and their family members filed criminal complaints against Jiang with China's highest court.
- 171,059 of them submitted copies to Minghui.org.
- 134,176 cases were confirmed to have been delivered to the Supreme People's Procuratorate and the Supreme People's Court, accounting for 78.4% of all complaints mailed.

Among the plaintiffs, 2,189 are from Taiwan and 28 other countries, including the United States, Canada, Australia, South Korea, New Zealand, Thailand, Japan, the United Kingdom, Malaysia, Germany, the Netherlands, Sweden, Singapore, France, Spain, Indonesia, Ireland, Denmark, Finland, Norway, Italy, Portugal, Switzerland, Poland, Romania, Belgium, Peru, and Hungary.

The plaintiffs in China come from 33 provincial-level administrative divisions, including 22 provinces, 4 municipalities (Beijing, Tianjin, Shanghai, Chongqing), 5 autonomous regions (Guangxi, Inner Mongolia, Tibet, Ningxia, Xinjiang), and 2 special administrative regions (Hong Kong, Macau).

As of October 25, 2016, a total of 209,908 legal complaints had been filed against Jiang Zemin.

§12.3 Retaliation Against Practitioners

Many practitioners have been harassed, interrogated, arrested, or even sentenced for filing criminal complaints against Jiang Zemin. In late 2017, the CCP also launched a "knocking on doors" campaign to keep track of practitioners who had sued Jiang and/or are still continuing to practice Falun Gong.

Among the 19,095 cases of harassment and arrests of Falun Gong practitioners, 7,056 were in retaliation for filing lawsuits against Jiang Zemin.[291]

§§12.3.1 Examples of Retaliation

› 12.3.1(a) 36 Sentenced in Chaoyang, Liaoning Province[292]

More than 300 locals from Chaoyang City and its subordinate regions were arrested in November 2015. The practitioners had filed criminal complaints against Jiang Zemin, accusing the former Chinese dictator of launching the persecution of Falun Gong, which resulted in their repeated arrests and detention. Local authorities quickly moved to prosecute the arrested Falun Gong practitioners in the following few months. To date, 36 of the arrested are confirmed to have been sentenced to prison, with terms ranging from 6 months to 12 years.

Below are the practitioners and their prison terms:

1. Jiang Wei, 12 years
2. Liu Dianyuan, 11.5 years

3. Li Guojun, 11 years
4. Lin Fengfen, 10 years
5. Chen Suying, 9 years
6. Ma Yanhua, 7 years
7. Lin Jiangmei, 7 years and fined 20,000 yuan
8. Wu Jinping, 7 years
9. Xie Jianping, 7 years
10. Xu Jinfeng, 7 years
11. Yin Xiuzhu, 7 years and fined 20,000 yuan
12. Zhou Ruixue, 6.5 years
13. Song Zhifu, 6 years
14. Liu Shuhua, 5 years
15. Wang Guojun, 5 years
16. Wang Qing, 5 years
17. Wang Yuhua, 5 years
18. Chi Shuhua, 4 years
19. Wang Zhiguo, 4 years
20. Zhao Hongjun, 4 years
21. Zhang Yongkui, 3 years
22. Zhang Haifeng, 3 years
23. Li Zhihong, 3 years with 4 years' probation
24. Liu Yaping, 3 years with 3 years' probation
25. Sun Liancheng, 3 years with 3 years' probation
26. Xu Xiuhua, 3 years with 3 years' probation
27. Yang Zemei, 3 years with 3 years' probation
28. Zhang Weimin, 3 years with 3 years' probation
29. Zhao Hongxue, 3 years with 3 years' probation
30. Yang Qinghua, 3 years with 4 years' probation
31. Lv Xin, 2 years with 3 years' probation
32. Jing Fei, 1 year, fined 2,000 yuan
33. Ren Man, 1 year
34. Huo Huixian, six months
35. Sha Jingtang, probation (exact sentence unknown)
36. Huang Lixin, probation (exact sentence unknown)

› 12.3.1(b) Couple Sentenced for Suing Former Chinese Dictator[293]

A married couple in Binchuan County were both sentenced to prison for filing criminal complaints against Jiang Zemin and holding the former Chinese dictator responsible for initiating the persecution of Falun Gong.

Both Mr. Shi Jianwei and his wife Ms. Xiao Zhu were repeatedly persecuted over the course of 17 years for refusing to renounce Falun Gong. After filing a legal complaint, Mr. Shi was sentenced to six and a half years and Ms. Xiao to five years. They are now in the process of appealing their sentences.

Case 1: Neighboring County Takes Over after Lawyer's Complaint

The couple was arrested on October 16, 2015. Mr. Shi was taken to Binchuan County Detention Center and Ms. Xiao to Dali City Detention Center.

Their lawyer encountered many obstacles in his quest to defend their constitutional right to seek justice against Jiang for infringing upon their right to freedom of belief.

The two detention centers denied the lawyer's request to meet with his clients a total of four times. Yang Yu, head of Binchuan County Domestic Security Office, claimed that the couple's case concerned national security and that no meetings with lawyers were allowed.

The lawyer then filed a complaint against Yang with the appropriate government agencies.

A deputy prosecutor with the Binchuan Procuratorate later denied the lawyer's request to review the couple's case. The lawyer proceeded to file a complaint against the prosecutor and requested that the case be moved to a different jurisdiction.

Dali City Procuratorate, the administrative supervisor of Binchuan Procuratorate, then ordered neighboring Xiangyun County Procuratorate and Xiangyun County Court to take over.

Case 2: Access to Hearing Restricted

The Xiangyun County Procuratorate indicted the couple, who were tried by the Xiangyun County Court on June 23 of this year.

Only a few of the couple's family members were allowed in the gallery. Local Falun Gong practitioners who showed up to support the couple were barred from entering the courthouse.

Case 3: Unlisted Prosecutors

As soon as the hearing began, Mr. Shi requested that judges and prosecutors who were also members of the Chinese Communist Party be recused, because he deemed them unfit to try him and his wife. The presiding judge ordered a recess in response.

The lawyer next noticed two more prosecutors present when the indictment listed only one. He demanded to know the identities of the two additional prosecutors.

The presiding judge initially ignored the request, but he relented and announced a second recess when the lawyer kept protesting the procedural violation. The additional prosecutors revealed their identities when the hearing resumed. They were special agents from the Dali City Procuratorate.

Case 4: Couple Testifies Against Police

Mr. Shi said Yang Yu, the aforementioned Domestic Security officer, ordered more than a dozen of his officers to beat him a total of three times. They twisted his arms behind his back, kicked him on the back and abdomen, and pushed him down to stomp on his head.

Ms. Xiao said she was also brutalized during police interrogation. She also testified that the police threatened her with the safety of the couple's daughter.

The couple explained that they feel compelled to do everything they can to stop the persecution of Falun Gong, and that suing Jiang Zemin is a step forward.

They were sentenced on August 5.

› 12.3.1(c) Police Launch "Knocking on Doors" Campaign to Harass Falun Gong Practitioners[252]

Police in many regions of China went to the homes of Falun Gong practitioners in advance of the Chinese Communist Party's 19th National Congress in October 2017. Officers said they were carrying out a "Knocking on Doors" directive.

Practitioners were questioned as to whether they still practiced Falun Gong. Officials also inquired about their occupations and other aspects of their lives. Some said they did not have bad intentions but had to have something to report to their supervisors.

In some areas, the police tried to get practitioners to sign a "guarantee statement" not to practice anymore, not to participate in activities related to Falun Gong, and not to appeal to higher courts. Others checked for computers or printers in the home and whether practitioners were using the Internet. Some confiscated their Falun Gong books.

Officers often had a list of practitioners who were known to them before the Communist Party's persecution of Falun Gong began in 1999, as well as the names of practitioners who had filed criminal complaints against former Chinese leader Jiang Zemin, who directed the persecution.

» A Nationwide Campaign

Police in Lechang, Guangdong Province, harassed practitioners who had been recorded by police in 1999 or had participated in the movement to sue Jiang Zemin. Officers even questioned the family members of practitioners who had passed away.

Police and domestic security officers in the Kuiwen District of Weifang City, Shandong Province harassed practitioners who had submitted criminal complaints against Jiang. They brought audio and video recording equipment to check on these practitioners, who then talked to them about Falun Gong and the persecution.

Around 100 practitioners in the Fushun District in Liaoning Province were harassed. Local police and community personnel went to practitioners' homes or called them by phone, stating that they were acting on their supervisors' orders to investigate. Some officers took pictures or videos of practitioners, confiscated their Falun Gong books and written materials, and checked to see if they were using the Internet.

Guanshan Town, Shanxi Province, police officers questioned practitioners about whom they had recently contacted and whether they still practiced Falun Gong. They tried to get practitioners to sign a document denouncing Falun Gong but were not successful.

Some practitioners in Henan, Jiangsu, Jiangxi, and Ningxia were threatened during attempts to get them to sign letters stating that they would give up practicing Falun Gong. Practitioners in some areas did sign their names, however, including many who gave up their practice at the start of the persecution.

§12.4 Increasing Public Support

The wave of lawsuits against Jiang has received widespread support both inside and outside China.

§§12.4.1 2016 Report: Over 14,000 More People Call for Jiang's Prosecution[294]

Many non-practitioners have also joined forces in calling for the former Chinese dictator to be brought to justice for his crimes against Falun Gong practitioners. They have showed their support by signing petitions prepared by practitioners.

According to information compiled by the Minghui website, a total of 14,408 more people are confirmed to have either filed criminal complaints against Jiang or signed petitions as of May 2016.

They include: 7,484 people in Yueyang, Hunan Province; 1,522 in Linquan, Anhui Province; 1,207 in Wuhan, Hubei Province; 2,707 from Laizhou, Shandong Province; and 1,488 in Teiling, Liaoning Province.

§§12.4.2 Taiwan: New Taipei City Council Passes Resolution Supporting Prosecution of Former Chinese Leader[295]

The New Taipei City Council unanimously passed a resolution "supporting lawsuits against Jiang Zemin and calling for an immediate end to the persecution of Falun Gong."

On October 20, 2016, New Taipei became the 13th city in Taiwan to pass a resolution supporting the movement by hundreds of thousands of victims and supporters to prosecute former Chinese Communist Party (CCP) leader Jiang Zemin for launching the persecution of Falun Gong.

"The CCP's 17-year-long persecution of Falun Gong and live organ harvesting cannot be tolerated," said council member Cheng Chin-long, who sponsored the resolution. "Democratic governments, including New Taipei, Taichung, and other cities, respect basic human rights. It is a universal value of Taiwan."

He said that despite China's rapid development, the country is way behind when it comes to human rights. "Freedom and human rights are universal values. The passage of the resolution represents the voices of four million New Taipei citizens. This calls on the Chinese government to respect human rights, especially for Falun Gong practitioners," added Cheng.

Council member Hsu Chao-hsing said in an interview, "We stand in support of Falun Gong practitioners against the unfair treatment. I hope they keep up their fight for freedom, as it is the right thing to do."

"Forced live organ harvesting is inhuman and against the basic right to life," said council member Lin Chiu-hui in an interview. "Freedom of belief is a part of life. Damaging it would bring condemnation around the world."

He stressed, "Jiang must be held responsible for his crimes. Rights must be returned to Falun Gong practitioners and their name cleared."

§§12.4.3 More Than 2.6 Million Sign Petition Supporting Legal Action Against Jiang

As of December 8, 2017, over 2.6 million people had signed petitions calling for Jiang Zemin to be brought to justice for initiating the persecution of Falun Gong. These include 770,000 signatures collected in seven Asian countries (excluding China) in 2015 alone.

One person in China who signed such a petition explained:[296]

> *My mother recovered from her diseases and was in good health after practicing Falun Gong before July 1999. However, she gave up the practice out of fear after Jiang Zemin started the persecution of Falun Gong. After that, she no longer had tolerance and often scolded others. Her illnesses then returned, and she had to undergo surgery. I know my mother would not be in such condition if there were no persecution. It's Jiang Zemin who brought harm to my mom. So, I too wanted to sue Jiang and hope the Supreme Procuratorate will bring him to justice."*

A Taipei resident said after giving his signature, "Signing the petition is the right thing to do. [The CCP] harvesting and selling [practitioners'] organs is a terrible mistake, and anyone can stand up, condemn [the perpetrators], demand Jiang be prosecuted, and stop the persecution."[297]

Part 3: Current Status of Falun Gong

Part 3: Current Status of Falun Gong

世界需要真善忍

Key Highlights

Inside China, practitioners continue to use nonviolent means to resist the persecution. To make sure people around them understand Falun Gong and the mistreatment of practitioners by the authorities, they talk to people on the street, print and distribute informational materials, hang banners and posters in their communities, write letters, and make phone calls. Some have reached out to perpetrators in the police and judiciary to dissuade them from following unlawful orders to persecute practitioners.

Outside China, practitioners raise awareness of the persecution by hosting and participating in community events. They also hold rallies and peaceful protests on major anniversaries, and they reach out to all levels of government for support. To rescue practitioners facing persecution in China, they coordinate efforts to make phone calls to perpetrators. In addition, artists among practitioners have created paintings, produced documentary films, and formed performing arts groups that display the spirit and essence of Falun Gong.

More people are learning about Falun Gong around the world. Some learn the exercises from practitioners at group exercise sites in public parks and community events. Others attend local workshops, including those held at Tianti Bookstores in New York and Seoul. Practitioners have taught the Falun Gong exercises at many schools in India, Indonesia, and elsewhere. More Chinese tourists are stopping at practitioners' booths at major destinations to learn about the persecution, which is heavily censored in their home country. Falun Gong is now practiced in more than 80 countries, and its teachings have been translated into over 40 languages.

The international community continues to support practitioners' efforts to end the persecution in China. Both governments and non-governmental organizations have called for the release of Falun Gong practitioners imprisoned for their faith in China. Key perpetrators of the persecution have been sued outside of China for crimes of genocide and torture. The U.S. now plans to tighten visa vetting to deny entry to human rights violators, including Chinese officials who have participated in the persecution of Falun Gong.

法 輪 大 法 好

Chapter 13: Countering the Persecution Inside China

Since the persecution began in July 1999, practitioners in China have used a variety of means to resist the persecution and counter the defamatory propaganda spread by Party-controlled media. Because all legal channels of appeal have been closed off to them and independent sources of information have been censored, practitioners have often resorted to creative methods to spread information about the persecution.

For example, some have printed messages such as "Falun Dafa is good" on paper currency. In the first few years of the persecution, practitioners intercepted TV signals to broadcast programs exposing the Party's propaganda (one such case is detailed in Section 1.4.7).

The following sections cover the main methods practitioners in China have used to counter the persecution.

§13.1 Early Appeals and Protests

Shortly after the arrests started overnight on July 20, 1999, practitioners from all over the country traveled to government appeals offices and the National Appeals Office in Beijing under the impression that the government was suppressing Falun Gong as the result of a misunderstanding. They sought to tell public officials about their own positive experiences practicing Falun Gong and of its benefits to society.

A noteworthy characteristic of these appeals was that they were acts of individuals, not centrally organized, as Falun Gong has no formal membership or organizational structure. Most practitioners had to do some amount of soul-searching before making up their minds to go to Beijing, as they knew that doing so could jeopardize their personal safety and livelihoods.

As one practitioner recounted:[298]

The entire country was suddenly blanketed by lies. Seeing the upright and compassionate Master and Dafa being treated this way, as a Dafa disciple, I had to make the government understand our cultivators' voices. I decided to go to petition the provincial government first.

He arrived in the provincial capital to find the streets full of police and under martial law:

Officers forcibly put us in vehicles and took us to a stadium. It was already full of Dafa practitioners who had been arrested.

We sat there quietly, waiting to speak to a provincial government official to tell him about Dafa and how it had improved cultivators' health and uplifted their morality.

...

Police vans started gathering at around eight or nine in the morning. Another wave of officers came over and started arresting people.

The first to be taken away were professors and students. The police gave practitioners no opportunities to explain. One professor—an elegant, refined woman who appeared to be in her 40s—was roughly pulled by the arm into a police vehicle. The men were treated even worse: teams of four officers simply picked them up and threw them in. At that moment, I knew that the provincial government would not hear our petitions.

...

I went to petition in Beijing before July 20, 2000. When I arrived, I saw that the National Appeals Office was only arresting people, without giving practitioners a chance to speak. I decided to go to Tiananmen Square to hold up banners and tell the world, "Falun Dafa is good!"

An American exchange student in China recalled his first encounter with Falun Gong:[299]

My friends and I were taking photos at Tiananmen Square. We saw some Falun Gong practitioners raise their banners quietly and peacefully. The Chinese police immediately jumped on them, punching and kicking, then dragged them into police vans and to the police station. My two friends took some pictures of police beating practitioners, but the film was confiscated. Both of them were also detained.

This scene unfolded on a daily basis in the first few years of the persecution: after a Falun Gong practitioner unfurled a banner on Tiananmen Square, police would descend on the protester and take him or her into a waiting van, often punching and kicking the practitioner in the process.

Even though petitioners traveled to Beijing of their own accord, the sheer number of Falun Gong practitioners in China at the time—70 to 100 million according to government estimates—meant that even if a small percentage of all practitioners chose to make the trip, the number of petitioners would be large.

At the peak of the appeals in 2000 and 2001, the Beijing Public Security Bureau estimated that more than one million Falun Gong practitioners were petitioning in Beijing.[300] Internal police records indicated that there were more than 830,000 arrests of practitioners for petitioning in Beijing as of April 2001, not including practitioners who refused to provide their identities to protect their families and colleagues.[301]

Some practitioners outside China also traveled to Beijing to join the appeals. These included a group of more than 40 practitioners from Japan who went to Tiananmen Square and did the Falun Gong exercises on the eve of the new millennium.[302] On November 20, 2001, 36 Western practitioners from 12 countries (including the United Kingdom, Switzerland, Germany, United States, Canada, and Australia) staged a peaceful appeal for Falun Gong on Tiananmen Square. They displayed a banner that read "Truthfulness-Compassion-Forbearance" and sat in meditation. One of them called out, "Falun Dafa is good!" to tourists and was beaten by police. All 36 were arrested a few minutes later.

One practitioner made a brief phone call to a friend from a police station near Tiananmen Square about their situation and said that reporters from CNN and other overseas media had been arrested along with them.

§13.2 Talking to People Face-to-Face

Practitioners take many opportunities in their daily lives to talk to people about Falun Dafa and the persecution, including those they meet on the bus, on the street, in parks, or other public places. At the workplace, they talk to their bosses, coworkers, clients, and business partners. Some go door to door in the countryside, where residents have even less access to independent sources of information.

If a practitioner's bosses and coworkers have a bad impression of Falun Gong as a result of the Communist Party's propaganda campaign, practitioners have to work hard to turn these attitudes around.

One practitioner in Henan Province said:[303]

As a Falun Dafa practitioner, I use the principles of Truthfulness-Compassion-Forbearance (真善忍) to measure myself and to clarify the facts to my colleagues in my company. Many people have understood the truth after coming into contact with me, and some of them now also use the principles of Falun Dafa to measure themselves in their daily lives.

I started out as a general clerk... and was promoted to a department manager in three months. I was tolerant of my supervisor when he made things difficult for me, and I resolved our conflicts. My boss said, "You are so honest. I feel confident when I hand several hundred million in assets to you."

Outside of urban areas, some practitioners have taken the initiative to go from village to village and home to home:[304]

In those villages, we went from house to house and discovered that the people there only knew about what happened on July 20, 1999, when Dafa was banned by the Communist Party. They only knew what the media had said about Dafa. I regretted that we had not visited them earlier. We clarified the truth door to door, as well as to a group of people chatting in front of a house.

We patiently answered their questions and told them that people all over the world now practice Falun Dafa. We told them that the Tiananmen self-immolation incident was staged by the CCP to justify the persecution. We also let them know about the state-sanctioned harvesting of organs from living Dafa practitioners.

When we told them that more than 200,000 people had filed criminal complaints against Jiang Zemin, the former head of the CCP who initiated the persecution, one elderly woman said, "Jiang Zemin, that evil old man, has never done one good thing. He is so bad. Do you have the petition? I also want to sign it to support the lawsuit."

Even when they are imprisoned for their faith, practitioners take opportunities to talk to inmates and guards about Falun Gong and the persecution. As a result, many criminal inmates and officers have come to sympathize with practitioners and take inspiration from them. Some have even decided to start practicing Falun Gong themselves.

A practitioner who was imprisoned wrote:[305]

A violent inmate named Xiao Ping (alias) was transferred to my prison cell in 2005. She and I wound up sharing the same bunk bed.

A guard named Wang Ling (alias), who knew the facts about Falun Gong, told her while pointing at me, "You should learn from her; she can teach you how to be a good person."

Xiao Ping had a hot temper and rough manners, which is why no one liked her. She also shouted and cried whenever she faced trying circumstances. I truly wondered if she could learn Falun Gong. Sometimes I'd talk to her about the practice, but she was very restless and found it hard to listen. Then one day she asked, "Can you teach me how to practice Falun Gong?" I then explained what Falun Gong is and how the Chinese Communist Party (CCP) persecutes the practice. I also wrote down several short scriptures and suggested that she read them.

Several days later I asked, "Do you understand what Master is saying?" She answered, "Yes. I do."

Her only wish after being released was to find a Falun Gong practitioner to help her continue her cultivation.

I was released from prison ten years ago, yet Xiao Ping has not stopped practicing Falun Gong. She is now widely praised in prison, just like I was when I was there.

An inmate who had been repeatedly jailed for thievery wrote about his encounter with Falun Gong practitioners in a detention center:[306]

They got detained because they had gone to Beijing to appeal for Falun Gong or practiced Falun Gong in the parks. They did not look down on me just because I was a convicted thief. Instead, they told me to be a good person and not to be a thief and not to do wrong anymore.

I was deeply touched by their words. In particular, they had no hatred or complaints when they were being cursed at or beaten up by the guards. They always treated those guards kindly and told them the principles of becoming a good person. I was very surprised and also perplexed. The TV had been saying how bad Falun Gong was. Then how came so many people had become so good after learning Falun Gong? I had to admit that they were really good people from what I saw.

I was suddenly full of regret that in the past ten years I had done so many bad things. How wonderful it would be if I could be a good person like these Falun Gong practitioners!

In addition to showing how practitioners uphold their faith in harsh environments, the above accounts highlight Falun Gong's effectiveness in rehabilitating criminals. This is in stark contrast to the abuses perpetrated in the Chinese's prison system, which instigates inmates to torture practitioners, thereby encouraging bullying and violence.

§13.3 Distributing Information and Displaying Banners and Posters

With great difficulty, I finally found a copy shop. I asked the owner, "Do you make copies of Falun Gong materials?" He replied, "The material must criticize Falun Gong." I hesitated but still handed the [materials] to him... Later he discovered that the materials were clarifying the facts about Falun Gong, so he secretly reported me to the police. Soon after, I was arrested... [and] lost my job and Dafa books.

A practitioner in China recalled the above experience in 2001, when he had just moved to a new province and wanted to make more people aware of the persecution.[307]

In an environment where no truthful information about Falun Gong is allowed to be disseminated, informing the public of human rights abuses around them is all the more valuable and necessary. Practitioners all over China have taken on this monumental challenge by turning their homes into small production sites, printing pamphlets, books, CDs/DVDs, posters, calendars, keepsakes, and other materials to tell people about Falun Gong.

These production sites are entirely funded by practitioners themselves using their income and savings, and they distribute the materials for free, often at the risk of personal safety. As can be seen in the many persecution cases in this report, the authorities in China routinely seize computers, printers, and flyers discovered in practitioners' homes as "evidence" with which to prosecute and imprison them.

Nevertheless, practitioners have found great demand when they distribute copies of the *Nine Commentaries on the Communist Party*, as well as journals, calendars, and DVDs. Below is one story shared by a practitioner in China:[308]

We go to the main market and nearby towns and villages every day regardless of the weather. So many people have come to know us. We saw one particular fellow repeatedly. We had clarified the truth to him and given him brochures many times. He said, "I appreciate you. You are all good people."

He would often help us distribute desk calendars and persuade people to withdraw from the CCP. He often yelled out, "Falun Dafa is good! Truthfulness-Compassion-Forbearance is good!"

When he saw us one day, he exclaimed, "Finally, I found you!"

He was out of desk calendars and wanted more. I had only a few left myself and did not want to give them up. But he pleaded, "I promised many people I would bring them a calendar. I don't want to let them down." I relented and gave him the few I had.

Practitioners have also put up large posters in public places with information about the persecution and calling for the prosecution of Jiang Zemin.

§13.4 Writing Personal Letters to Perpetrators

In addition to informing the general public, practitioners have also written letters to police officers and officials to dissuade them from participating in the persecution. The authors of these letters often address local cases connected to the recipient and clear up misinformation about Falun Gong propagated through government channels.

One practitioner shared his experience of working with others in his area to write letters to police and judicial officials, prisons, brainwashing centers, residential committees, school officials, and others:[309]

After a director of a city police department read the [letter], he stopped participating in the persecution. He said, "These Falun Gong practitioners are all kind, they don't hit back when hit or yell back when yelled at. They only want to hold on to their beliefs. I am really not cruel enough to continue to treat them unfairly like this. I received the letters every month, and I read them all. I am not cruel enough to do that! Many of the letters touched me, and the words between the lines shook my conscience! As long as I am in this position, I will do my best to protect practitioners and treat them kindly!"

In 2004, a senior official at a Procuratorate started to receive one truth-clarification letter every month. After reading the letters, his attitude towards practitioners changed dramatically. He questioned why those people were being sent to prisons or labor camps. He said that he no longer wanted to do such things that made him lose virtue. When any instructions or assignments from the CCP came, he would find excuses not to do them. He even secretly found practitioners to ask for a copy of Zhuan Falun to read.

While practitioners have found this to be an effective method for lessening the persecution of other practitioners and preventing perpetrators from committing more crimes, mailing such letters presents challenges and safety risks:

Since we mailed out a lot of letters, a practitioner needed to buy many postage stamps. The state security agents had connections in the post offices... We had to send the letters from different locations, and sometimes we had to walk a long distance to send out one letter.

Another practitioner in Liaoning Province noted:[310]

The post office changed their rules regarding stamp sales after the persecution of Falun Dafa began on July 20, 1999. Each person was only allowed to buy 20 stamps at a time, and they were asked why they were buying them. However, people were allowed to buy unlimited stamps without being questioned during the Chinese New Year. So that's when I would buy a lot of stamps to use during the entire year.

I posted letters to local judicial departments, the Political and Legal Affairs Committee, communities, prisons, detention centers, and village government officials. I also sent letters to practitioners who, according to Minghui, were in urgent need of help.

I wrote every letter with sincerity, as if I were talking to the person face to face. My letters were to the point and carried positive energy. When I was impatient, my handwriting was sloppy, so I would rewrite the letter.

§13.5 Disseminating Information Through Phone Calls and the Internet

In addition to talking to people face-to-face and distributing printed publications, practitioners in China have sent text and multimedia messages and made phone calls to both perpetrators and the general public.

One practitioner recalled:[311]

> *I targeted prisons, forced labor camps, 610 Offices, police departments, police stations, detention centers, brainwashing centers, courts, procuratorates, hospitals, and schools. Those that received the messages included a director, local chiefs, a court director, a chief justice, Party secretaries, political commissioners, team leads, police officers, and security staff. After receiving the message, some of them were regretful while others persisted in doing wrong.*

Another practitioner shared:[312]

> *We can use cell phones to spread our message to a large area in a very short period of time. There are always restrictions with other methods, it seems, but using cell phones we can reach out to anyone regardless of their social status, professional background, or age.*

Sending messages and making calls using cell phones also present safety risks, however, as Chinese authorities have invested heavily in phone surveillance and tracking capabilities. In 2014, four practitioners in Sanhe, Hebei Province, were arrested for sending group text messages about Falun Gong. It was revealed that several practitioners' cell phones were being monitored, even when they were turned off.[313]

Such surveillance also extends to other forms of electronic communication, including social media. In January 2019, a college professor in Guangzhou was sentenced to three and a half years in prison and fined 10,000 yuan after police found that he had shared information about the persecution of Falun Gong on the QQ platform between October 2014 and January 2017.[314] In Sichuan Province, a man was arrested and abused in a brainwashing center and his wife beaten after he sent messages on WeChat to inform judicial officials that the China Administration of Press and Publication had repealed its ban on the publication of Falun Gong Books in 2011.[315] There have been numerous other cases of practitioners being arrested after posting information about Falun Gong online.

To help people in China access news and information freely, practitioners have also given out software to circumvent online censorship, such as Freegate, Dynaweb, and UltraSurf. Two groups of practitioners developing anti-censorship software eventually formed the Global Internet Freedom Consortium, whose tools have also been used extensively in Iran, Myanmar, Cuba, North Korea, and Syria.[316] [317]

Chapter 14: Raising Awareness Outside China

While practitioners in China work to lighten the persecution and inform the Chinese public, often risking their personal safety in the process, those outside China have also actively worked to increase awareness of the persecution and clarify the misinformation propagated by the Chinese regime.

§14.1 Protests at Chinese Embassies and Consulates

Throughout the past two decades, Falun Gong practitioners have held banners and hosted activities in front of Chinese embassies and consulates around the world to tell the public about Falun Gong and the persecution in China.

Chinese officials often attempt to disrupt such events by denying the renewal of practitioners' Chinese passports, obscuring banners with obstacles or sprinklers, or threatening facility owners. Practitioners have occasionally sought help from the police to uphold their rights.

§14.2 Rallies and Petitions

Every year, practitioners gather at the U.S. Capitol to raise awareness of the persecution in China and call for action to end it. U.S.

lawmakers, human rights activists, and representatives from non-governmental organizations often take part in the annual rally to express their support for practitioners' peaceful resistance to the persecution. At one such rally on June 20, 2018, speakers condemned the Chinese regime's state-sanctioned forced organ harvesting from prisoners of conscience in China, highlighted Falun Gong's universal values of Truthfulness-Compassion-Forbearance (真善忍), and called on the public to see through the Communist Party's deceit.

Congressman Dana Rohrabacher (CA) addressed the practitioners with heartfelt remarks. He said he would be a longtime supporter of Falun Gong not merely based on people's rights to express their views; rather, he identified with the core principles of Falun Gong. "I am proud to stand with you and always have been," he remarked.

Following the rally, a large procession set off from Capitol Hill, traveled along Pennsylvania Ave. and Constitution Ave. and ended at the Washington Monument.

Practitioners in the procession carried portraits of those who lost their lives during the persecution in China, while others carried banners calling on the public to recognize that the Communist Party is responsible for the persecution of Falun Gong. A candlelight vigil was held at the Washington Monument on the evening of June 22, 2018, the third day of the practitioners' large-scale activities in Washington D.C. "Please sit by my side. Let us close our eyes in serenity. A voice is resounding from deep in our hearts: end the torture, end the killing, and end all suppression. Our compassion and perseverance will prevail," said the host.

Other rallies are also held around the world to raise awareness of the persecution in China.

§14.3 SOS Walk and Ride to Freedom

Besides these large-scale events, practitioners have also organized other types of activities to expose the persecution of Falun Gong in China. One example was the SOS Walk in 2001, when four practitioners walked from Ottawa to the United Nations Headquarters in New York.

Like their adult peers, young practitioners outside of China have also benefited from Falun Gong. Some participate in summer camps located all over the world, from New Jersey to San Diego, from France to Taiwan.

In 2015, a group of young practitioners participated in "Ride to Freedom," a 3,000-mile bicycle journey across the U.S. to raise awareness of and rescue five children orphaned by the persecution of Falun Gong in China.

The riders received commendations from U.S. Senator Patrick J. Toomey, Philadelphia Mayor Michael A. Nutter, and Philadelphia City Council members. The riders participated in a concert in Washington, D.C. held by Falun Gong practitioners. Local resident William Craig told them, "The performance is magical. Just the fact that we can hear these songs that have been sung in these prisons and from people who have gone through the Chinese torture system is remarkable. It is as if we're reaching out and touching them in a small way, though they are millions of miles away."

§14.4 Raising Awareness at Community Events and Tourist Attractions

Apart from exposing the persecution, practitioners also participate in community events to celebrate holidays and introduce Falun Gong to more people.

May is a busy month for Falun Gong practitioners, who hold activities in honor of World Falun Dafa Day on May 13 each year in honor of the anniversary of Falun Gong's introduction to the public in 1992. May 13 is also the birthday of its founder, Mr. Li Hongzhi. Below is a selection of these events held in different corners of the world in 2019.

§§14.4.1 Ottawa, Canada

Practitioners from the Ottawa area attended the 67th International Tulip Festival on May 20, 2019. This popular festival attracted approximately 650,000 visitors, and many expressed interest in learning the Falun Gong exercises.

As he watched the practitioners demonstrating the exercises, college freshman Mudar Ayouby said he wanted to join them because he knew that meditation can relieve stress. Mudar said he appreciated Falun Gong's guiding principles Truthfulness-Compassion-Forbearance (真善忍). He remarked, "Everybody should try it. It would help everyone worldwide feel peace and experience a reduction in stress. Their lives would be more meaningful."

§§14.4.2 New York, United States

Nearly 10,000 practitioners from dozens of countries held a parade through Manhattan, New York on May 16, 2019. The Tian Guo Marching Band led the parade, followed by a dragon dance, a lotus flower boat, practitioners demonstrating the Falun Dafa exercises, and practitioners of different nationalities in traditional dress.

The two-mile route started at United Nations Plaza, wound through Times Square, and ended near the Chinese Consulate. Jane, a retired social worker, watched almost the entire parade with her husband. She said it was "exhilarating" and added, "We will remember truthfulness, compassion, and forbearance. Everyone in this world needs these values."

§§14.4.3 Hamburg, Germany

May 18, 2019, practitioners from Hamburg, Germany, held a Falun Gong Information Day. They introduced the practice and called for an end to the persecution in China. Many people signed a petition condemning the Chinese regime's forced organ harvesting from prisoners of conscience.

Rosemarie Gohlke compared the persecution of Falun Gong to the Nazi genocide. She found the persecution of a peaceful group unbelievable, and she thanked practitioners for telling her about this atrocity. Three students from Africa said they hoped to bring up the issue of the persecution in China during an upcoming class discussion.

§§14.4.4 Antalya, Turkey

At the end of April 2019, Turkish practitioners in Antalya participated in a two-day Tourism Festival.

Begüm Borçetin was moved to tears when she heard about Falun Gong's principle of Truthfulness-Compassion-Forbearance (真善忍). She learned the five Falun Gong exercises and hoped to join the local group exercise site.

Iffet and Nimet felt that their bodies were "light like birds" when they learned the exercises. "All the stress has disappeared," said Iffet.

The organizer of the event, Hatice Bozkurt, told practitioners that the festival would not have had the diversity or rich culture if it wasn't for Falun Gong's participation. She invited practitioners to attend another local community event.

§§14.4.5 São Paulo, Brazil

May 11, 2019, practitioners from São Paulo traveled to Bras, a local Chinatown-like business district, to hand out fliers and talk to the people to clear up the misinformation spread by the Chinese Communist Party (CCP) to slander Falun Gong. They also demonstrated the exercises and held up banners and display boards.

Practitioners from Brasilla held a similar activity the following day.

§§14.4.6 Miaoli, Taiwan

A waist drum troupe made up of local Falun Gong practitioners performed at the annual Toufen Parade on May 11 in Toufen City, Miaoli

County. Their performance was warmly welcomed by the spectators and local community leaders. Many people called out "Falun Dafa is good!" as the group approached.

§§14.4.7 Sydney, Australia: Chinese Tourists Learn about Falun Gong and Renounce the CCP[318]

Every weekend Falun Gong practitioners throughout Australia hold activities to raise awareness about Falun Gong and the persecution of the practice in communist China. One event venue has been the popular tourist attraction in Sydney, Mrs. Macquarie's Chair. Due to its scenic location overlooking Sydney Harbor, many tourists from other countries, including Chinese tourists, visit it.

The practitioners distribute information about Falun Gong, demonstrate the exercises, and encourage Chinese tourists to renounce the Chinese Communist Party (CCP) and its affiliated organizations.

Because the practice is being persecuted in China, many Chinese tourists come to watch the exercise demonstration. They read the materials and talk with practitioners. When one tourist said that he had seen Falun Gong practitioners in Hong Kong, a practitioner asked if he had quit the CCP yet. She explained that the practitioners were there to answer questions and dispel any misunderstandings people had as a result of the Party's propaganda against it.

The man immediately said that he wished to quit the Youth League and the Young Pioneers. When another Chinese tourist said that he was not allowed to take the Falun Gong informational materials back to China, a practitioner said, "You can download software from *The Epoch Times* website to get around the Party's censorship," and she gave him the information. The man was very pleased and thanked her.

› Scientist Couple Quit the CCP

One man told practitioners he was a scientist and said, "I'm an atheist and I don't believe in spirituality. I'm a professor at a well-known university in Beijing. I'm also in charge of a research institute. My wife is my colleague. I'm also the chief executive officer of a company. What can you say to convince me?"

A practitioner told him, "Famous scientists like Newton and Einstein believed in religion. Why? They knew that only gods could explain the complexities of the universe. Falun Gong is practiced worldwide. Many people who practice it are scientists. Many national leaders practice, as well as people of different ethnic groups."

When the practitioner offered to help them quit the CCP and its affiliated organizations, they agreed.

§14.5 International Art Exhibitions

The Truth-Compassion-Forbearance International Art Exhibition has been displayed all over the world. The paintings that make up the exhibition were created by a group of accomplished artists who are also Falun Gong practitioners. The works highlight the beauty and serenity of Falun Gong and the brutality of the Chinese Communist Party's persecution. The exquisite paintings and the true stories behind each image touch viewers.

The exhibition was held in Toronto City Hall from August 26 to September 1, 2019. Former Canadian senator Consiglio Di Nino said at the opening ceremony, "I'm impressed with the very high artistic level of these works. They display the spiritual values that can guide us. This is particularly important." Mr. Sharpe, a government employee who visited the exhibition, told the hosts, "These paintings are so beautiful ... Thank you for bringing such great artworks to Toronto."

On August 17, 2010, the art exhibition was displayed at the Galeria Caminul Artei Gallery in Bucharest, Romania. The exhibition was held in Romanshorn from August 20 to 29, 2010. News of its arrival was published four times in a local newspaper and caused a stir among the local residents. One gentleman said to the practitioners after viewing the paintings, "I support you and will stand with you." He wrote in the visitor's book, "I express my deepest sympathy and stand with you because I believe that universal love and truth will prevail."

An older couple praised the accomplished technique in the paintings and said that the painting "Fulfilling Vow" provided an answer to all problems: as long as all people of different backgrounds live together peacefully, all problems will be solved. The gentleman said that the CCP made the wrong decision to suppress Falun Gong and should instead encourage people to practice it. The lady was touched to learn about the iconography of lotus flowers, which emerge clean from the mud.

§14.6 Documentary Films

A few documentaries have been produced about the persecution of Falun Gong. Below are two high-profile films on this subject.

§§14.6.1 Free China: The Courage to Believe

The award-winning documentary *Free China: The Courage to Believe* tells the story of two practitioners of Falun Gong who were imprisoned and tortured by the Chinese regime. Falun Gong practitioners have hosted more than 1,500 screenings of the film, including on Capitol Hill in the U.S., the European Parliament, and cinemas around the world.

An audience member in Turin, Italy said that Falun Gong practitioners are "modern-day saints." He added: "I see history being repeated. The firm resolve that Falun Gong practitioners continue to show is as sacred as that of the Christians who had been persecuted during the Roman Empire."

§§14.6.2 Letter from Masanjia

"What begins as an unusual 'message in a bottle' story builds to a powerful tale of human suffering, compassion and perseverance," wrote Kevin Crust of the *Los Angeles Times* in his review of the documentary *Letter from Masanjia*. Based on a true story, the SOS letter found in a box of "Made in China" Halloween decorations at an Oregon Kmart soon set off a chain of events that eventually led to the shutdown of the entire labor camp system in China.

The letter's author, Falun Gong practitioner Sun Yi, was imprisoned for his faith at the notorious Masanjia Forced Labor Camp. Learning filming techniques from the film's director through Skype, Sun secretly captured harrowing footage of his daily life in his quest to expose the horrendous human rights atrocities inside China.

The film won more than a dozen awards in 2018, including at the Calgary International Film Festival, Atlanta DocuFest, and Milano International Film Festival Awards. It is also a contender in the Feature Documentary category of the 91st Academy Awards.

"We need to have open dialogues with China about these problems. One of the problems was and still is the (forced) organ harvesting. We cannot stop our open dialogues. We cannot say that this problem doesn't exist," said Tomas Zdechovsky, a Member of the European Parliament (MEP) from the Czech Republic, after a screening of the film at the European Parliament on December 4, 2018.

§14.7 International Parties Working to Secure the Release of Practitioners in China

"If you did not have people, plus their media, supporting you abroad, your situation would be tragic," a police officer once told a practitioner in Beijing.[319] Numerous practitioners in China have written about the effectiveness of phone calls made by practitioners and governments outside of China, as well as inquiries by overseas journalists.

Below is one such account:[320]

A practitioner was arrested on May 15, 2013, while she was distributing Falun Dafa informational materials. She was taken to a detention center. Local practitioners quickly organized to rescue her by publishing the phone numbers of the perpetrators on the Minghui website.

The police officers who participated in the arrest grew fearful after receiving phone calls from practitioners outside of China. They tried to figure out who had disclosed their phone numbers, and they expressed regret that they had participated in the arrest.

The arrested practitioner was released on May 22, 2013, which was unprecedented. The police had never released a practitioner after such a short period of time.

This type of public exposure and phone calls have effectively counteracted the impunity Chinese officials have in persecuting Falun Gong practitioners. For example, a deputy secretary of the Political and Legal Affairs Committee in Henan Province who actively persecuted practitioners for personal gain was dissuaded from doing so after his information was posted on Minghui.org. His wife recalled:[321]

There are so many people who practice Falun Gong overseas. I received ten calls every day. Every time I answered the phone, my heart beat faster. Because of this, he had to transfer out. When I think about it carefully, what these Falun Gong practitioners said is very reasonable. The CCP is not invincible; we have to plan for our futures.

Some timely phone calls from overseas have even stopped perpetrators just before they were about to torture practitioners. One report described what a practitioner in a forced labor camp experienced:[322]

In the camp, a police officer was about to torture this practitioner to try to force him to renounce Falun Gong. Right as the practitioner entered the office, the officer got a phone call from overseas.

During the call, he said the word "cult" five times and taunted the caller, "If you have the ability, come fly over here and see me, then I will believe you." The practitioner calling him was not moved by his words and kept talking to him for about five minutes. As the officer listened, his eyes had a blank stare and he seemed to have little energy left. He turned to the practitioner in his office and said to him, "You—go home!"

After that phone call, this police officer requested a transfer from the brigade that tortures Dafa practitioners to one that produces materials.

Chapter 15: Newcomers Discover, Take Up Falun Gong Despite Persecution

Despite the ongoing persecution in China, a steady stream of newcomers has taken up Falun Gong after learning it from their friends and family, coming across practitioners meditating in public parks and community events, or searching online.

This chapter provides a selection of personal accounts of new practitioners' experiences and reactions of Chinese tourists who encounter practitioners while traveling abroad.

§15.1 China: A Former Prisoner's Account of Learning Falun Gong During Her Detention[323]

I was detained in Heizuizi Women's Prison in Changchun for my involvement in a pyramid scheme in 2008. I got to know several Falun Gong practitioners who were detained there for their belief. Due to the Chinese Communist regime's propaganda, I refused to listen to them at first. But I wondered why they were in prison. If Falun Gong was bad, why would so many people practice it? But if it was good, why had they been arrested? I doubted what was said about Falun Gong on TV. These practitioners seemed to be good people. Were they deceived by Falun Gong? Otherwise, why did they refuse to give up the practice despite arrest?

These practitioners told me they were tortured by police officers for refusing to give up their belief. They said that practitioners were even killed for their organs. I did not believe them. Since I was young, I had been indoctrinated by the Chinese Communist Party's books and TV programs and believed that police officers were good. At that time, I had a lot of respect for the police and thought that they were there to change the world. I could not believe that they could treat Falun Gong practitioners so cruelly.

One day a practitioner was beaten and shocked on the chest with an electric baton. Before she became a practitioner, her leg was disabled, and she had suffered a heart attack. Yet the guards disregarded her condition. This got my attention. Those I thought were bad people were the good ones. Those I regarded as good were actually the bad guys!

I decided to learn more about Falun Gong. I asked practitioners all kinds of questions every day. Later, I asked them to recite Master Li's poems in *Hong Yin* for me and I learned them by heart. One day, as I recited one of the poems, I sensed the profoundness of Dafa.

Although I was just a new practitioner, I experienced a few extraordinary incidents. In prison, you cannot change cells without permission. Whenever the practitioner next to me had taught me everything she knew, the guards would move me to another cell where another practitioner could teach me something different. One day, I finally got to read *Zhuan Falun*, the main book of Falun Gong teachings. After I finished reading the first lecture, I knew that this was what I'd been searching for. I'd always wanted to practice cultivation, and at last I found Dafa!

I'm grateful to Master Li Hongzhi (the founder of Falun Gong) for not giving up on me. During my one-year prison sentence, I learned some of Master's teachings. I have been practicing for nearly 10 years now. I've experienced many miracles and have unwavering faith in Dafa. I want everyone to know that Falun Dafa is good.

§15.2 Tibetan Schools in India Welcome Falun Dafa[324]

I am a Western practitioner who lives in India. I went to two northern, mountainous states in India for six weeks.

Most of the 23 different institutions I visited were schools, with the youngest kindergarten children being around 2–3 years old. I also went to two hostels, a college, and a private industrial training institute.

The emphasis of this trip was on introducing Falun Gong to Tibetan schools. During the past 60 years, many thousands of Tibetan refugees have fled to India due to increasing repression and severe human rights abuses in Tibet. Most of them have remained in India.

The journey was made challenging by my having to move 11 times, the many bags containing brochures and displays about Falun Gong and the persecution of the practice in China, the unexpected heat, and early rains. Despite the expected and unexpected tribulations, the trip was very successful. I was able to introduce Falun Gong to many more schools than originally planned.

Most of the places I visited were completely new to me. Nearly everywhere I went I ran into people—teachers, children, and others—I had met previously, mostly during my many visits to Ladakh and other parts of India. Some had practiced Falun Dafa in their schools, received flyers at displays, or seen posters. Several times when I met new people, I felt a deep connection, as if I was seeing long-lost friends again. The feeling often seemed mutual. The principal of one school wrote me a letter that said, "This is to express my deepest gratitude and heartfelt thanks to you for sharing the five exercises of the Falun Gong practice with the staff and the students of our school."

It is always heartening when children, even if they had Falun Dafa sessions in their schools years ago, say "Falun Dafa" or "Falun Dafa is good" with delight when they see me on the street or at their new school. When it was crowded, hot, or a Saturday, the students were sometimes restless while doing the standing exercises. But they calmed down fully during the fifth exercise, which is a sitting meditation. Indeed, it was almost pin-drop silence, after which all repeated with much heart, "Truthfulness, compassion, and forbearance are good, Falun Dafa is good."

The above-mentioned principal also wrote, "I really admire your spirit and dedication... Through these exercises, the students' ability to concentrate, which is lacking these days, will improve. I thank you for your dedication and concern."

(1) Displays of Persecution in China

Many children were mesmerized by the posters and captions depicting the persecution that practitioners of Falun Dafa, including young children, face in China. One young girl looked at each picture for a long time.

A headmistress wrote, "This is definitely a pure and unconditional service to humanity. I appreciate your kind service for the cause of humanity."

When talking about these human rights abuses and showing the posters, I noticed that some eyes were wet, with tears falling silently or wiped away. Some of them could have been remembering the severe human rights violations the Tibetans have been facing, such as leaving behind family members and friends, who are often tortured or even killed. Their experiences are very similar to what Falun Dafa practitioners and many other people of different faiths suffer in China. Many Tibetans commented that, concerning these atrocities, we—Tibetans and Falun Dafa practitioners—"are all sitting in the same boat." The many letters of appreciation I received expressed not only a deep appreciation of Falun Dafa but oftentimes a clear understanding of the persecution as well.

A headmistress wrote, "We owe much appreciation and admiration for your work to promote these messages of peace and wellness, while also highlighting the cruel persecution of Falun Gong by the communist regime in China of their own people, much in the same line as they are persecuting Tibetans in Tibet.

"It is our hope that you get to talk about the Tibetan issue along with Falun Gong and help create awareness in the many places you travel to. So, a big 'Thank you' on behalf of all Tibetans inside and outside Tibet."

The principles of Falun Dafa resonate with the secular ethics now taught in all Tibetan schools. The same headmistress wrote, "The session was also meaningful for us, as the three principles of Truthfulness-Compassion-Forbearance (真善忍) fall in line with what we are trying to inculcate in our students through the secular ethics lessons our school is carrying out as directed by the Department of Education, Tibetan Administration in Exile."

Since the first arrival of Tibetan refugees in India some 60 years ago, it became apparent that one of their most critical needs was finding a means to care for the many children who had been orphaned or separated from their families during the arduous escape from their homeland. The reason for establishing separate schools for Tibetans in India was to provide them with an excellent education and at the same time help preserve the Tibetan language and culture. All these schools, big or small, are amazingly well-managed, with many dedicated teachers and staff staying true to the motto of their schools, "Others before self."

One school principal wrote in an appreciation letter that the staff and students "cherish that extraordinary event and adopt the Falun Dafa principles of 'Truthfulness-Compassion-Forbearance (真善忍)' as our guiding ethical standards.

"We earnestly express our solidarity with the Falun Dafa practitioners and pray for the revival and the flourishing of this ancient spiritual practice. May Peace Prevail on Earth. In deep appreciation."

The director of a private industrial training institute wrote after a Falun Dafa session, "We sincerely acknowledge and greatly appreciate your awareness program on the importance of Truthfulness, Compassion, and Tolerance, which are of prime importance in today's world. We express our solidarity with the members of Falun Dafa and wish them success in their contribution towards world peace."

In addition to giving out flyers, magazines, books, DVDs, Ancient Tales of Wisdom stories, posters, etc., to school libraries, I recommended the *Nine Commentaries on the Communist Party*. Although most Tibetans are fully aware of and have experienced the evil of the CCP, many do not know the details or the CCP's history.

Besides schools, I visited many other places and people and put up posters in shops.

When I talk about the persecution in China, I mention that China is just a country and has a very old history, just like India, and that Chinese people are just like people everywhere in the world: some are good, some are bad, and who is who may change. Some good ones might become bad, and bad ones might become good.

In the Falun Dafa sessions, the children were advised to rationally and compassionately understand what is good, what is bad, and why.

Another principal wrote, "These body and mind exercises that you demonstrated today will certainly help in the long run to promote a better society and a more harmonious world as students are the seeds, and our future solely depends upon how we raise them and what values we teach them.

"I would also like to express my gratitude to you for standing up to the Chinese communist government's persecution of its own innocent people. I appreciate the valuable lesson that you conveyed to the students that we should be rational and make a distinction between what is good and what is bad."

Many teachers already knew of *The Epoch Times*, NTD India, and different Falun Dafa websites, but those who did not were made aware of these independent media outlets. Surely, in the time to come, and with the help of all these informational channels, more awareness will spread among the children and many others.

(2) Ideas and Initiatives

Many thanks go to the many "helping hands," without whom this endeavor would not have been possible: the directors, principals, headmasters and headmistresses, teachers, staff, children, and so many more.

I am very fond of the Tibetans and my many connections to my good Tibetan friends from my 28-year stay in India. Several times, it happened to be Tibetans who gave me ideas and suggestions on how to move ahead on my path as a practitioner.

In Ladakh, which is located in the northernmost part of India, more than 15 years ago, I first heard about Falun Dafa from a visiting Chinese-American practitioner accompanied by a local Tibetan. Both of them were doing the Falun Dafa exercises at a local women's festival. This was my very first contact with Falun Dafa.

In August 2007, when I was putting up posters in a local restaurant in Leh, Ladakh, a Tibetan teacher suggested that I come to his school. The principal of the school agreed, and I held the first-ever Falun Dafa session in a school in Ladakh, followed in subsequent years by sessions in this same school and many of its branches and many other schools.

In 2008, when the first-ever display was done in Leh to commemorate July 20, 1999, the day the persecution started in China, another young Tibetan man voluntarily vacated his outdoor "shop" for the occasion. Many other displays followed over the years.

Years ago, a relative of a close Tibetan friend had the idea to display the posters and banners on the long wall of her house on special occasions. Thousands of locals and tourists have since received flyers during these displays. Even where I live, I was inspired to hold weekly displays, usually from October through April, after seeing a young Tibetan man selling his merchandise there on a foldable bed. I have been doing this for many years and have reached people from the local community as well as from all over India and the world.

All these ideas and initiatives, and many more, were suggested by Tibetans. Therefore, in a way, this trip to Tibetan schools in India was something of a return of these "favors," not to the individuals involved but at least to many members of their community.

India is a vast country with many different cultures, traditions, tribes, religions, castes, etc. Several practitioners in India had previously visited schools and universities and in the process taken many photos and received many letters of appreciation. In this vast country with so many young people, we hope to visit many more schools in different parts of India in the time to come.

Looking back, the success of this astounding trip was possible only due to Master's arrangements—the right timing, strong karmic connections, and many other factors.

Some schools put video clips, news articles, and photos about their Falun Dafa event on Facebook and other social media. Some had already seen the three-minute video "A Way to the Heart" or had previously circulated this video and its related article on NTD India.

§15.3 Indonesia: 500 Secondary School Students and Teachers Learn the Falun Gong Exercises[325]

The principal of the No.38 Public Secondary School on Batam Island, Indonesia, had seen students practicing Falun Gong on a social media website and wanted to learn more about this mind-body cultivation practice from China. So, he invited Falun Gong practitioners to introduce the practice to teachers and students on February 16, 2019. About 500 students and teachers turned out to learn the Falun Gong exercises as well as the principles of this traditional Chinese cultivation practice.

Practitioners explained that the exercise movements are relaxing and easy to learn. The principles of Falun Gong are Truthfulness, Compassion and Forbearance—principles that resonate in the minds of many people. The practitioners further explained that anyone, regardless of age or background, can learn Falun Gong.

Indonesia's Falun Gong practitioners often visit area schools to share the goodness of Falun Gong with the local community. Their hope is that more people can enjoy the benefits of the practice. After doing the exercises, the principal said, "The music and exercise movements keep one focused. My whole body, especially my torso, joints, and back, feels so comfortable after doing the exercises." An art teacher remarked, "When I closed my eyes and listened to the music, I could feel the presence of light. I had injured my arm and could not lift it very high. However, after the fourth exercise, I can now lift my arm above my head—what a wonderful experience!"

§15.4 United States: Spiritual Journey of a Software Developer[326]

By some people's reckoning, Santhosh had it all: a good

education, caring parents, and a promising career that led him to move to the United States and his current job as a software company manager. He had a loving wife and two beautiful daughters. "I was at the peak of fitness. I had no health issues," he recalled. But the sudden onset of an autoimmune disease changed all that. Santhosh consulted with doctors, but they couldn't identify the root cause. In the end, his doctors recommended strong steroids. They warned of side effects and advised him that he would need to be on them for the rest of his life.

"The prognosis hit me like a bolt of lightning. I always thought that I had all the answers for a happy life with friends and family. But when this struck, I soon became frustrated and depressed.

"The situation would deteriorate, and in my case, it would affect my eyes. So, if I were not careful, I could become totally blind."

Santhosh had already developed pain in his wrists and knees and was having difficulty lifting everyday objects. "It got to a point where I felt that there was no hope, because I was unable to do any physical exercise."

Searching for a solution, he began to think more deeply about life itself, searching online about God and the universe. "But as I sought spiritually, I was literally lost. I was born into a religious family, but now I couldn't figure out what was happening and what was going on."

And then, one day, a coworker told him about Falun Gong. "I was very interested. It came at exactly the right moment." His coworker gave him a link to the Falun Dafa website (FalunDafa.org), saying that the teachings and exercise instructions were available online for free. One weekend, Santhosh downloaded the books *Falun Gong* and *Zhuan Falun*.

"The minute I started reading, I knew this was something very special," he said. "It was very clear and explained things, answering the many questions I had in my mind. So, I immediately knew that this was very different from things that I'd learned in the past."

(1) Health Quickly Restored

Within just a few days, Santhosh experienced tremendous improvements in his health. The pain and discomfort slowly faded away until they were completely gone—as if they'd never existed.

"I couldn't believe it. These are the changes I experienced from doing the exercises on a daily basis. This is firsthand experience – it's undeniable!

"My viewpoint changed because the main teaching of Falun Dafa is Truthfulness-Compassion-Forbearance (真善忍). What really hits me hard is the purity in the core teachings—you have to be truthful and you have to be compassionate, even if others are angry or insulting you. This is the ultimate thing and it really touches my heart."

Santhosh found himself no longer easily irritated or angry like he used to be. "I used to be very short-tempered and extremely sensitive. That is all changing, and I am now predisposed to be kind to people," he added. His parents were living with him at that time, and they both saw the positive changes in him. His father was very impressed, saying that Santhosh was a new and better person.

(2) A Happier Family

Santhosh used to argue with his wife, as many couples do. "If I had to do chores around the house such as washing the dishes, I sometimes thought, 'I did them yesterday, today it's her turn. Why should I do the dishes every day?' That is, I thought that everything had to be spelled out."

After he started practicing Falun Gong, his thoughts completely changed: "Now, it's no longer that she needs to do it or that it's her thing. Whenever I can help, I will help and just do it."

His wife quickly noticed. She found that Santhosh stopped arguing and instead quietly helped get things done. He stopped complaining. So, she asked him about Falun Dafa and became interested and sometimes read the books, too.

His daughters also felt the positive impact. Their dad used to get agitated over many things. Now he is calmer and more patient. "It seems that you haven't yelled at us for quite a while," his eight-year-old daughter reminded him.

(3) Better at Work

Santhosh is goal-oriented and often set targets that his team had to reach. After he started practicing Falun Dafa, he found that this approach was somewhat selfish. "In my heart, I was not caring about my team members. So, I was a bit pushy and put lots of pressure on the team to deliver," he recalled.

"But the team's view of me changed as I became less demanding and more helpful. Their connection with me has become much stronger," he said. Sometimes, even before he asks them to do something, Santhosh discovers that the team has already gone beyond expectations and met the objectives. "One of the team members actually told me that he saw tremendous improvement in my overall management style, especially with meetings and deadlines," he added.

"Incorporating the core teachings of truthfulness, compassion and forbearance (真善忍) at work has really brought about great benefits—not just for me, but for the entire company," he concluded.

(4) A Benefit to All of Society

It took him some time to understand the persecution that Falun Dafa faces in China. Why would someone persecute Falun Dafa, which teaches someone to be a better person, develop higher moral values, and be truthful and kind?

"It is a real tragedy, because on the one hand, you have the positive teaching you to be good; on the other side, you have the negative, or evil, trying to suppress the good. The real victims, as I see it, are the Chinese people who are deceived by the Communist Party with its slanderous propaganda. I really hope the persecution ends soon and that every single person in China will be able to see the magnificence and the truth about Falun Dafa.

"In my experience, I would say that Dafa is the most righteous and straightforward, very simple, yet convenient cultivation practice that I have ever encountered in my entire life. I have been quite a spiritual person and was raised in a family with highly traditional values, but I have never come across such an elegant, positive, simple way of practice that can take you to a really high spiritual level. It is a practice that really benefits your mind and your body.

"In fact, it really helps you to live your life in a complete, wholesome manner, be it in terms of your family, your friends, relatives, work, and everybody else, even strangers. You always present yourself as a very good and kind person, which is a very positive thing. This is something very precious."

§15.5 Chinese Tourists Seek the Facts about Falun Gong During Trips Abroad

"I know that of all the groups the Chinese Communist Party has suppressed, the persecution of Falun Gong is the most brutal. You [practitioners] have suffered so much. I feel very bad," a Chinese tourist said to a practitioner raising awareness of the persecution during his trip in Switzerland. "You [practitioners] are mistreated so badly, but you still do this to help others."

Major tourist destinations around the world have become nerve centers where the public can learn about the persecution, especially state-sanctioned forced organ harvesting from Falun Gong prisoners of conscience, which is covered up in China, and learn what the Chinese public really thinks, which is inaccessible to most outside of China due to the Party propaganda exported to the West. Some Chinese tourists have sent greetings to the founder of Falun Gong and hope that he can return to China soon. They engage in discussions with Falun Gong practitioners at tourist sites to learn about the self-immolation hoax and the atrocities of live organ harvesting.

Overseas trips also present opportunities for Chinese citizens to quit the CCP and its youth organizations, the Youth League and the Young Pioneers. Volunteers from the Global Service Center for Quitting the CCP have been helping Chinese people all over the world.

The tourists not only quit the Party themselves but also bring the information to their friends and family back in China.

The number of tourists who choose to renounce their Party memberships has steadily increased across North America and Europe. Ms. Zhou, a Falun Gong practitioner volunteer at a tourist site in England, described in the summer of 2014 a trend she noticed:

> *In 2008 and 2009, I could help a few hundred Chinese people quit the CCP in a year. In 2010, it increased to about one thousand a year. After 2012, it has doubled and tripled, to a few thousand a year. Since the beginning of this year, it's about a thousand a month.*

§15.6 Taiwan: Falun Dafa Helps a New Practitioner Recover a Vibrant Life[327]

I was a very unreceptive and fragile person three years ago. The stress from my pursuit of 'fame and gain' impacted my health and I was frequently sick. I suffered from headaches, dizziness, palpitations and chest pain. Although I was academically successful and had a solid resume, I was not happy. I thought I had reached a dead end and felt trapped. Life had no meaning and I had no hope for the future.

I was fortunate to be able to learn about Falun Dafa and start on my path of cultivation. Cultivation has helped me to be more content and peaceful, and I gradually recovered a vibrant life.

(1) Searching for Answers

I just graduated from university this year. Since my youth, I was always at the top of my class. I studied in the best schools and went for lessons to become skilled in many areas. However, few people knew the hardship behind all my academic success. The acknowledgments and benefits I reaped as a result of my great success caused me to unknowingly suppress my real thoughts and emotions. I always worked hard at my studies to get good results and I strove to accommodate everyone in my life so I would always be seen in the best light.

Deep in my heart, I knew that all this was meaningless and I was not truly happy. However, I still allowed myself to indulge in this endless pursuit. Even with my parents I suppressed my true feelings. I continued to present an increasingly glamorous appearance on the outside but it was getting increasingly dark on the inside.

"What is the meaning of life?" I often asked myself. I could not find the answer in my pursuit of academic recognition and good interpersonal relationships, nor in my favorite readings about supernatural happenings that science could not explain.

Often, while lying in bed, I thought about the vastness of the universe and how my thoughts, or even the existence of human beings, would disappear thousands of years later. How empty and lonely would a space like that be? An unimaginable sense of fear sent shivers down my spine and made it hard to sleep. Although I was always trying to be at my best, I did not have standards or principles of my own that guided me. I always changed according to the person I was with, so much so that it affected my thoughts and the way I expressed myself. I found it difficult to honestly express myself and feared I might be too critical of someone or hurt their feelings.

The stresses of life and my studies took a toll on my body, too, and I had headaches, chest pain, and low-grade fevers. I often had to visit the big hospitals and take medical leave to rest at home or at the school's medical center. All these conditions occurred because there was a problem with my mental health. But I did not notice that and was also not willing to face that fact. Once, as a senior in high school, I even painted a picture depicting my memories of my life so far as totally black.

(2) Finding Falun Dafa and Cultivation Practice

During my time at the university, I joined a training program where the teacher functioned as a counselor and mentor and assisted students with life problems or issues. Topics such as the concept of life and death or family problems were brought up for discussion during the program. Feeling lost and helpless about different aspects of life, I often approached the program teacher to talk.

This teacher appeared to be very wise. She seemed to be able to grasp everything that happens in life. Once, during a conversation, she mentioned Falun Dafa and cultivation and recommended I read *Zhuan Falun*. She told me this was a book that I would not stop reading once I started it. I was very curious as to what kind of book could make such a wise teacher believe in it.

With a skeptical attitude, I clicked on the link to *Zhuan Falun*, only to be shocked by such a heavenly book. My emotions were very complex. I was excited, touched, and sad. I was excited because I'd discovered that a universal law based on Truthfulness-Compassion-Forbearance (真善忍) really existed!

This book answered all the questions I had about science and beliefs and taught me about the meaning of life, the presence of gods and higher-level beings, and how I should live as a human being from then on. I shouted in my heart, "Why did I only come across such a precious teaching now?" At the same time, I felt like crying from the bottom of my heart. I realized that I was sad because my earlier life had deviated from this Fa teaching so much!

After that, I started to cultivate my character based on the tenets of Truthfulness-Compassion-Forbearance (真善忍), and I also started to do the five Falun Dafa exercises. In terms of my studies, for the first time, I felt the joy of studying with my heart rather than merely caring about the results. When I changed my attitude towards my studies, studying became a relaxing and happy thing to do and I actually did even better!

The logic that I learned in Falun Dafa even helped me to answer some scientific questions that sometimes shocked the professor. In terms of health, I no longer had any ailments and I could feel the lightness and healthy state of my body. Because I have the Fa in my heart, I just have to reflect on my behavior based on the tenets of Truthfulness-Compassion-Forbearance (真善忍). Therefore, I no longer feel awkward when I interact with people or express my thoughts. I can talk to people very openly.

As my xinxing (moral character, or "heart/mind nature") improves, I am also more able to face the problems and setbacks in my life calmly, maintaining a placid and stable mental state. With that, I am able to lead an unrestrained and satisfying lifestyle and I feel that I have actually recovered the vibrancy in my life!

Not long ago, my boyfriend ended our relationship of many years. By the time I knew about it, he already had another girlfriend. When my friends and relatives found out, they were angry about it and sad for me. Even my ex-boyfriend worried about me.

Although it came up very suddenly, I almost had no negative emotions. Instead, I pondered it quite calmly and even put myself in his shoes and thought about him. He felt my calmness and kindness, too. In cultivation, we talk about compassion. We need to be kind to others and always think about others first. I understood that the purer the compassion, the greater its strength, and that others can feel it, too. In cultivation, we also talk about the principle of tolerance.

Master Li said, "Forbearance is the key to improving one's xinxing. To endure with anger, grievance, or tears is the forbearance of an everyday person who is attached to his concerns. To endure completely without anger or grievance is the forbearance of a cultivator." ("What is Forbearance (Ren)?" from *Essentials for Further Advancement*)

Before my cultivation, I would definitely not have been able to truly be so calm.

(3) Master and Dafa Guided Me Out of the Swamp to Recover My Vibrance

Guided by the Falun Dafa principles and teachings I have straightened out my attitude towards life and regained my health. I now speak with confidence from the bottom of my heart and know that I have truly found purity and satisfaction in my life. I have found the meaning of life in all these achievements which I did not dare to think about before. I am very thankful that I chose to read *Zhuan Falun* three years ago and start on my path of cultivation. I can still remember the image of myself in the past, struggling in the swamp all alone. It was suffocating and the future was nowhere in sight. After three years of cultivation, I am a totally new person through and through.

I am sharing my experiences before and after I started cultivating in the hope that everyone can know the deep meaning of these two phrases: "Falun Dafa is good. Truthfulness-Compassion-Forbearance (真善忍) is good." Thank you, Master! Thank you, Dafa!

§15.7 Seoul, South Korea: New Practitioners Share Their Experiences[328]

The first nine-day Falun Gong seminar of 2019 at the Tianti Bookstore in Seoul was held on January 31. At the end of the nine days, the new practitioners held a roundtable discussion to share how they found Falun Gong and discuss their experiences with the practice.

(1) Finding the Meaning of Life

During the 2007 economic crisis in South Korea, Kang, one of the seminar attendees, lost his property. As he struggled financially, he was worried about how he would survive. Then he thought, "Human beings enter the world naked and leave the world naked. What should I be attached to?"

He tried to stay cheerful by reading books, climbing mountains, doing exercises, and going to church. He hoped to find the true meaning of life.

"Although I am just a tiny speck of dust in the universe," Kang thought, "I can accept the energy of the universe and become healthy. It is more important to assimilate to the universe than worry about wealth."

One evening, he saw Falun Gong practitioners doing the exercises near his residence. After reading the Falun Gong flier, he thought, "I should practice Falun Gong."

He went to the Tianti Bookstore, where he was told that he should read the book *Falun Gong*, the introductory book about the practice. Kang said, "It was as if I found the purpose of life after reading that book." So, he decided to explore the practice further by participating in the nine-day seminar.

The seminar involves watching recorded lectures of Mr. Li Hongzhi, the founder of Falun Gong, giving nine foundational lectures and learning the exercises. As Kang listened over the course of the nine days, he found that the teachings touched his heart. He understood that, through cultivation, the body will be purified, any toxins will be removed, and one's xinxing must improve. He realized how important it is to follow Falun Gong's principles of Truthfulness-Compassion-Forbearance (真善忍) throughout life.

"I felt that cultivation is not simple," Kang said. "It won't work without being able to endure. I need to practice with a pure mind."

He used to think about deities. "Now, I feel that I can become a spiritual being by practicing Falun Gong."

Kang said that he planned to come to the store during his free time to learn more about cultivation practice, read more, and practice hard.

(2) Becoming Healthy and Feeling Strong Energy

Another new practitioner, Kim, saw a woman practicing the Falun Gong exercises in a park one morning. He said, "I felt a strong energy emanating from her, and her hand gestures were so beautiful."

Kim accepted a flier and started practicing Falun Gong. He went to the practice site to do the exercises daily. He has gained a deep understanding of life and cultivation practice over the past year and a half of practicing Falun Gong. He said that he became healthy after he took up the practice. He used to be very thin, but now his body weight is back to normal.

"Falun Gong not only benefits one's health," Kim said, "but it's also a high-level teaching. I think one can return to good health if one improves one's xinxing when cultivating."

Kim has experienced a strong sense of spirituality on his cultivation path. He said, "I felt like a divine being when I entered tranquility while doing the fifth exercise, the sitting meditation."

Seeing the positive changes in her husband, Kim's wife became interested in Falun Gong. She also attended the nine-day seminar. Although she initially thought she'd go for just one day, she attended all nine sessions. She remarked that she looked more beautiful after the nine-day seminar. In addition, she no longer felt discomfort in her back.

(3) Happily Living by Truthfulness-Compassion-Forbearance

Ms. Kang said that she saw Falun Gong practitioners doing the exercises when she was mountain climbing last year. She participated in a nine-day seminar two months later but felt that she needed to learn more. So, she attended another nine-day seminar, then decided to attend a third seminar this past January in Seoul.

Ms. Kang said, "I felt that my body had become very relaxed after practicing the exercises. Especially after practicing today, I feel so good!"

She enjoys reading the Falun Gong books during her free time, and when she travels on the subway. She said she has read Master Li's book *Zhuan Falun* 30 times.

"I feel very happy when reading the Falun Gong books," she said. "They help me assimilate to Truthfulness-Compassion-Forbearance (真善忍)."

§15.8 Manhattan: Tianti Bookstore Offers a Convenient Way to Learn Falun Gong

Tianti Bookstore has operated online for over ten years. Due to increasing demand in the New York area, it opened a physical location in midtown Manhattan on October 10, 2013. Tianti, as the name implies (*tian* in Chinese means "sky" or "heaven," and *ti* means "ladder"), aims to provide readers with a way of self-improvement through the practice of Falun Gong.

Tianti opened its second store in Toronto on July 1, Canada Day, 2013. Located in the predominantly Chinese York region of Toronto at the Pacific Mall—the largest Chinese indoor mall in North America—the store is dedicated to providing books and multimedia on Falun Gong.

Last but not least, Tianti Bookstore opened a new branch in Seoul, making it easier for people to access Falun Dafa books and instructional materials and learn the meditation practice. Holly, who attended a nine-day video seminar at the Manhattan store, told other attendees that she had practiced other meditation disciplines before but had never reached such a peaceful state of mind as she had with Falun Dafa.

Chapter 16: Support from the International Community

Human rights organizations, public officials, and legislative bodies around the world have spoken out to call for an end to the persecution in China. Courts in Spain and Argentina have indicted top CCP officials for torture and genocide. The U.S. Department of State and Congressional-Executive Commission on China (CECC) have highlighted the persecution of Falun Gong in their annual reports, and the former is now tightening its visa vetting process to deny entry to human rights violators, including perpetrators in the persecution of Falun Gong.

§16.1 Chinese Officials Sued in Other Countries

Courts in various countries have taken up cases against the main perpetrators of the persecution, including Jiang Zemin, under the legal principle of universal jurisdiction, which allows domestic courts to hear cases of genocide and crimes against humanity regardless of where they occur.

§§16.1.1 Spanish Court Indicts Top Communist Party Officials for Torture, Genocide

In an unprecedented decision, a Spanish judge indicted five high-ranking Chinese Communist Party (CCP) officials for their role in crimes of torture and genocide committed against Falun Gong practitioners. The court announcement in 2009 indicated that if they are convicted, the defendants would face at least 20 years in prison and financial penalties. The five defendants, Jiang and his four followers who were primarily responsible for implementing the persecution, had four to six weeks to reply and could subsequently face extradition if they travel to a country that has an extradition treaty with Spain.

Following a two-year investigation, Spanish National Court Judge Ismael Moreno notified attorney Carlos Iglesias of the Human Rights Law Foundation (HRLF) that the court had granted a petition to send rogatory letters (letters of request) to the five defendants in China with questions relating to each individual's involvement in the persecution of Falun Gong. The decisions favoring the plaintiff followed a series of submissions to the court by Iglesias and other HRLF staff.

Attorney Iglesias said, "This historic decision by a Spanish judge means that Chinese Communist Party leaders responsible for brutal crimes are now one step closer to being brought to justice. When one carries out the crime of genocide or torture, it is a crime against the international community as a whole and not only against Chinese citizens. Spain is emerging as a defender of human rights and universal justice."

Among the accused, Jiang Zemin was widely acknowledged as the primary instigator of the campaign launched in 1999 to "eradicate" Falun Gong. Also facing charges is Luo Gan, who oversaw the 610 Office, a nationwide secret police task force that has led the violent campaign. Chinese lawyers have compared the 610 Office to Nazi Germany's Gestapo in its brutality and extra-legal authority.

The other three accused are Bo Xilai, former Party secretary for Chongqing and former Minister of Commerce; Jia Qinglin, the fourth-highest member of the Party hierarchy; and Wu Guanzheng, head of an internal Party disciplinary committee. The charges against them are based on their proactive advancement of the persecution against Falun Gong when they served as top officials in Liaoning Province, Beijing, and Shandong Province, respectively.

In a Pulitzer prize-winning article, *The Wall Street Journal*'s Ian Johnson describes how Wu imposed fines on his subordinates if they did not sufficiently crack down on Falun Gong, leading officials to torture local residents, in some cases, to death.

Other evidence considered by the judge during his investigation included written testimonies from 15 Falun Gong practitioners and oral testimonies from seven practitioners, including torture victims and relatives of individuals who had been killed in Chinese custody. The judge also relied on reports by Amnesty International, Human Rights Watch, and the U.N. Human Rights Commission to reach his decision, attorney Iglesias said.

§§16.1.2 Federal Judge in Argentina Orders Arrest of Perpetrators Jiang Zemin and Luo Gan

After a four-year investigation, Judge Octavio Araoz de Lamadrid of the Argentina Federal Court No.9 made a historic decision on December 17, 2009. Judge Lamadrid has issued arrest warrants for former leader of the Chinese Communist Party (CCP) Jiang Zemin and Luo Gan, former head of the 610 Office, for their role in the persecution of Falun Gong. The two high-ranking CCP officials were charged with crimes against humanity. Judge Lamadrid ordered the Interpol Department of the Federal Police of Argentina to carry out the arrests.

In a 142-page legal document, the judge elaborately assessed the CCP's persecution of Falun Gong practitioners in China, and the roles that Jiang and Luo played.

Judge Lamadrid explained in his decision that "the strategy of genocide that has been designed encompassed all range of actions with a total contempt for life and human dignity. The end devised—the eradication of Falun Gong—justified all utilized means. In this way, torment, torture, disappearances, deaths, brainwashing, and psychological torture were the currency of the persecution of its practitioners."

Judge Lamadrid said in his ruling, "I understand that in the present case the principle of universal jurisdiction must be applied in view of the [severity of the] crimes, the number of victims affected, and the ideological nature of the actions taken against members of the Falun Gong religious group."

› 16.1.2(a) Jiang and Luo became the accused

During Luo Gan's visit to Argentina on December 12, 2005, Argentina Falun Dafa Association Chairperson Ms. Fu Liwei entrusted lawyers Adolfo Casabal Elas and Alejandro Guillermo Cowes to file a lawsuit against Luo Gan with the Federal Court for Criminal Punishment, No.9 Court. The charges against Luo were crimes of genocide and torture. The Argentine Federal Court accepted the suit, and Judge Octavio Araoz de Lamadrid handled the case.

While handling the case, the judge found Jiang Zemin, Luo Gan's superior, was the initiator of the persecution of Falun Gong. He, therefore, included Jiang Zemin in Luo's case and handled the two cases together. The persecution facts about Jiang were also added to his documents. He charged Jiang with the same crimes as Luo Gan.

The CCP has repeatedly interfered with the case, including exerting pressure on the plaintiff's lawyers, but all its attempts failed to prevent the case from proceeding. Judge Lamadrid spent four years investigating and collecting evidence and then decided to order the arrest of Jiang and Luo and have them brought before the court.

› 16.1.2(b) To investigate the facts about the persecution, the judge traveled in person to the U.S. to collect evidence

The Argentine Federal Criminal Court No.9 began investigating Luo Gan's crimes against Falun Gong in China early 2006. Judge Lamadrid collected evidence from multiple sources regarding the case.

During this time, Falun Gong practitioners from different countries went to Argentina to testify; non-practitioners also went to Argentina to testify, including David Kilgour, former Canadian Secretary of State for the Asia-Pacific Region, and David Matas, human rights attorney. The judge gathered testimony from nine witnesses in the federal court in Buenos Aires between April 3, 2006 and March 26, 2008.

Judge Lamadrid went to New York to meet with more victims in April 2008 with the approval of and financial assistance from the Supreme Court of Argentina. Because most of the victims were seeking asylum after fleeing China, they did not have passports to go to

Argentina to testify. On April 28 to May 5, 2008, the Judge went to the Consulate General of Argentina in New York and collected evidence from ten witnesses who lived in the U.S.

During the investigation, the judge also included investigative reports by the United Nations and many organizations regarding Jiang and Luo's persecution of Falun Gong in his files. The CCP repeatedly attempted to stop the case from proceeding, but Judge Lamadrid persisted and ultimately completed his investigation and made an official decision to order the two defendants arrested.

§16.2 Actions by National Governments

§§16.2.1 Australian Government Assists in Rescue of Falun Gong Practitioners

On December 1, 2003, the Australian Senate passed Motion No.704, which indicated Australia's commitment to supporting the close relatives of Australian citizens who are detained on the basis that they practice Falun Gong, and calls on the Australian Government to raise the issue in the context of the human rights dialogue.[329]

Australian Democrats' Foreign Affairs spokesperson Senator Stott Despoja said, "The Democrats appreciate the importance of the relationship between the Australian Government and the Chinese Government. However, we should never sacrifice human rights issues for trade opportunities. Australia's relationship with China, while significant, must be qualified by our firm opposition to any conduct which violates fundamental human rights. The Democrats will continue to highlight human rights abuses in China, in particular the persecution and killings of Falun Gong practitioners."

Despoja continued, "The stories of murder, torture and imprisonment of Falun Gong practitioners are truly horrifying. Many Australian citizens have relatives in China who are being subjected to such persecution and it would be wrong not to use the Parliament to speak out on their behalf and highlight their situation.

"Motions, such as that passed by the Senate today, not only send a message to the Chinese Government but also to the Falun Gong community in Australia—that their struggle is recognized and supported," she concluded.

On the day the motion was passed, about 200 Falun Gong practitioners from all over Australia gathered in front of Parliament House in Canberra. They handed in 21,700 petition signatures from the Australian public in support of the motion.

While expressing appreciation to the Australian government, Members of Parliament, non-governmental organizations, and the public for their efforts to rescue Ms. Li Ying, the fiancée of Australian citizen Li Qizhong, they also extended condolences to Ouyang Ming, the younger brother of Australian citizen Ouyang Yu; Ming had died from torture in a Chinese labor camp despite his name being included four times in lists of family members that the Australian Department of Foreign Affairs and Trade presented to the Chinese government during bilateral Australia-China Human Rights Dialogues.

Speakers at the rally included Democratic leader Andrew Bartlett; Chairman of the Federation for a Democratic China Mr. Qin Jin; and Secretary of Chinese Labor Party Australian Branch, Mr. Ruan Jie.

Other rescue efforts assisted by the Australian government include that for Falun Gong practitioner Nancy Chen, who was released by Chinese authorities on January 30, 2003, as a result of joint efforts of the Australian Department of Foreign Affairs and Trade, the "Nancy Chen Urgent Rescue Team," and many other concerned parties.[330] When Ms. Chen was taken into custody eight days earlier, practitioners all over the world made phone calls and sent faxes to all levels of government in Sichuan Province, China. Media outlets in Australia frequently reported on her case, and ABC Radio broadcast several stories on its news program.

Officials from the Australian Department of Foreign Affairs and Trade in Canberra called Ms. Chen's husband immediately after receiving updates from China. In addition, the Australian Embassy in Beijing contacted Ms. Chen's parents in Sichuan to inform them of the progress of the rescue effort and flew to Chengdu City in person to mediate with the relevant authorities in China.

The Australian government also aided in the rescue of Ms. Xie Yan, the fiancée of Australian citizen Philip Law.[331] Xie was tortured in the notorious Chatou Forced Labor Camp in Guangzhou at the age of 24. NSW Liberal Party Member Anthony Roberts said that he would tell his colleagues about Xie's situation. Chief Minister Jon Stanhope, MLA from Canberra, made an inquiry with the Chinese Embassy regarding Xie and the details of their refusal to grant Philip Law a visa to China.

MP John Murphy wrote to Foreign Minister Alexander Downer, requesting the Department of Foreign Affairs and Trade to raise the matter with the Chinese authorities. Mr. Downer pointed out to the Chinese authorities that they had violated the human rights convention. Mr. Murphy further contacted the Australian Consulate in Guangzhou, asking them to help with Xie Yan's application to Australia and to assist her in getting to Australia as soon as possible. The young couple was reunited on July 31, 2004, when Xie Yan safely arrived at Sydney International Airport.

§§16.2.2 Canadian Government Helps Rescue Two Brothers Imprisoned in China[332]

In 2002, the Canadian Parliament passed Resolution M-236 proposed by MP Scott Reid, requesting the Prime Minister to rescue 13 Falun Gong practitioners in China. One of them was Lin Shenli, who was successfully rescued with help from the Canadian government and Amnesty International in 2002. His brother, Lin Mingli, was later freed in 2011. The siblings were reunited in Toronto after being separated for 13 years, having been arrested in 1999 for practicing Falun Gong.

"I am grateful to the Canadian government, to the Minister of Immigration, and to Member of Parliament Mr. Scott Reid, who helped to rescue me from China," said Lin Mingli after landing in Toronto. He also thanked Falun Gong practitioners in Canada for their efforts to rescue him.

In the two weeks prior to Lin Mingli's release, two Canadian MPs wrote to the labor camp where Mingli was held to urge the camp to free Mingli immediately.[333]

On March 20, MP Rob Anders held a news conference at the Parliament in Ottawa together with Lin Shenli and said that he would try his best to help rescue Mingli.

MP Liza Frulla wrote in her letter, "While I appreciate that it is a sensitive issue to comment on the internal affairs of another country, I would like to add my voice to my colleague, Mr. Irwin Cotler, M.P. for Mount Royal, and other Canadians from across the country who are demanding the immediate release of all illegally held Falun Gong practitioners in China and to decry the continuing violation of human rights that Mingli Lin's imprisonment represents."

In 2000, Mr. Lin Mingli was sent to a brainwashing center for the first time, where he was told to renounce Falun Gong. He refused. In 2001, he was sent to a forced labor camp, where he was confined until March 2003.

In October 2005, he was arrested again. This time, he was sentenced to six years. "In the prison, they took off my clothes, hung me up with five ropes, and beat me with bamboo sticks," Mr. Lin said. "They often beat me and wouldn't let me fall asleep. They often told me to renounce Falun Gong and beat me when I said I wouldn't.

"They also played audio recordings that attacked Falun Gong and forced me to listen to them.

"I saw them beating a Falun Gong practitioner in prison until he passed out. Then they took him to the hospital. Once, I saw them beating another practitioner. His head was bleeding, but they didn't take him to the hospital."

More than 20 practitioners and supporters welcomed Mr. Lin at the airport. He said: "I am very happy today. Thank you all. There are still many practitioners who are suffering unimaginable torture. They still solidly uphold their belief despite all the torture."

§§16.2.3 Taiwan Denies Entry to Chinese Officials Involved in Persecution

In 2017 Taiwan denied entry to at least three Chinese officials who have been involved in the persecution of Falun Gong. The delegates led by the officials were also denied entry.

Chiu Chui-Cheng, deputy chief of the Mainland Affairs Council, confirmed that the council is restricting permits for human rights violators from China. Chinese officials are immediately denied entry if they have a record of persecuting Falun Gong practitioners and belong to the 610 Office, an extralegal Party organization that oversees the persecution of Falun Gong. This is to emphasize and carry out Taiwan's policies, which value and protect human rights, according to Chiu.

§§16.2.4 Actions by the U.S. Government

› 16.2.4(a) U.S. Department of State Expresses Concern in Annual Report

China is in "a league of its own when it comes to human rights violations," Secretary of State Mike Pompeo said when he presented the State Department's annual Country Reports on Human Rights Practices on March 13, 2019.

The report documents violations in nearly 200 countries and territories; 120 pages were about China. The persecution of Falun Gong was mentioned six times.

The report identified the issue of forced organ harvesting in China, about which the House of Representatives unanimously passed Resolution 343 in June 2016, "Expressing concern regarding persistent and credible reports of systematic, state-sanctioned organ harvesting from non-consenting prisoners of conscience in the People's Republic of China, including from large numbers of Falun Gong practitioners and members of other religious and ethnic minority groups."

According to the report, "Some activists and organizations continue to accuse the government of involuntarily harvesting organs from prisoners of conscience, especially members of Falun Gong."

Two Falun Gong practitioners, Bian Lichao and Ma Zhenyu who are currently imprisoned in China, were mentioned in the report.

Bian Lichao is an award-winning teacher at the 10th High School in Kailuan, Tangshan City, Hebei Province. He was sentenced to 12 years' imprisonment in 2012. Ma Zhenyu was an engineer at the 14th

Research Institute of the China Electronics Technology Group. He was sentenced to three years in prison by the Nanjing Intermediate Court in 2018.

The report lists several serious human rights abuses in China, including those carried out by the government: "arbitrary or unlawful killings by the government; forced disappearances by the government; torture by the government; arbitrary detention by the government; harsh and life-threatening prison and detention conditions; political prisoners," and many others.

The report also detailed how practitioners of Falun Gong have been victims of "systematic torture in custody" by the Chinese Communist Party.

The report points out that political activists and religious believers, including Falun Gong practitioners, have been detained at addiction treatment centers; the longest detention was two years.

It was also reported that some lawyers who help political activists and spiritual followers were stripped of their professional licenses. Some of them were detained, harassed, threatened, or banned from meeting with their clients. A few lawyers who have helped Falun Gong practitioners have even disappeared. It is believed that they have been secretly imprisoned. One example is Gao Zhisheng, who has not been seen since August 2017.

The State Department's Bureau of Democracy, Human Rights, and Labor publishes the human rights report every year. This is its 43rd report.

› 16.2.4(b) 2018 CECC Annual Report: The Persecution of Falun Gong Continues in China

The Congressional-Executive Commission on China (CECC) issued its 2018 annual report on October 10, highlighting the worsening human rights conditions in China. In particular, the communist regime continues to suppress Falun Gong practitioners, human rights lawyers such as Gao Zhisheng, and ethnic minorities.

Forced organ harvesting was also mentioned. "Several international organizations expressed concern over reports that numerous organ transplants in China have used the organs of detained prisoners, including Falun Gong practitioners," cited the 324-page report, which is available on the CECC website.

"Audaciously Repressive"

U.S. Senator Marco Rubio and U.S. Representative Chris Smith, chair and co-chair of CECC, presented the report at a press conference. "The Communist Party has dramatically increased its control over government, society, and business and is ruthlessly employing technology to further its aims. As American policymakers increasingly reexamine the misguided assumptions that have informed U.S.-China relations, we must be clear-eyed about the global implications of China's domestic repression," remarked Sen. Rubio.

He said repression of religious groups by the Communist Party also impairs the relationship between China and the U.S. The Communist Party needs to adhere to universal values, not only for U.S. security, national interests, and moral values, but also to be consistent with the hopes of Chinese citizens who seek protection for their basic rights and real political reforms.

Sen. Rubio called for sanctions against the communist officials responsible. He said the committee's censure is aimed at the Chinese Communist Party, not the Chinese people. In fact, the Chinese people and Chinese culture have made great contributions to human civilization, Rubio said.

Rep. Smith explained, "This report shines a light on the Chinese government's failures to abide by universal standards, shines a light on the cases of tortured and abused political prisoners." "Even by the Chinese Communist Party's low standards, this year has been audaciously repressive." He said the suppression of religious groups, ethnic minorities, and human rights lawyers is the most severe since the Cultural Revolution.

Rep. Smith said that including organ harvesting in the annual report means action needs to be taken against the deplorable practice.

The report states,

> *As in previous years, authorities continued to detain Falun Gong practitioners and subject them to harsh treatment, Human rights organizations and Falun Gong practitioners documented coercive and violent practices against practitioners during custody, including physical violence, forced drug administration, sleep deprivation, and other forms of torture.*

The CECC report noted figures from the U.S.-based non-profit organization Dui Hua Foundation that Falun Gong practitioners made up the majority of the 800 people convicted under Article 300 of China's Criminal Law. These cases from 2017 are available in judicial databases.

Among them, Deng Cuiping of Yuxi City, Yunnan Province, was in prison with a term of six years. Bian Lichao of Tangshan City, Hebei Province, was sentenced to 12 years of imprisonment. Zhang Ming and Li Quanchen of Dandong City, Liaoning Province, were also arrested in late June.

Even citizens of other nationalities were affected. On January 5, 2018, the Shenzhen Intermediate Court in Guangdong Province upheld the sentence on the appeal of Miew Cheu Siang (one year and six months), a Malaysian citizen, and his wife Yu Linglan (five years). They are charged with possession and distribution of Falun Gong materials.

In December 2017, *The Epoch Times* reported 29 confirmed deaths of Falun Gong practitioners in 2017 due to abuse by officials.

Calling for an FBI Investigation

The report also found the Communist Party was "re-inserting itself into the private lives of Chinese citizens through the expanded collection of biometric data, growing surveillance networks, and continued development of the social credit system."

Sen. Rubio and Rep. Smith also released a letter asking the FBI to report on how it addresses "unacceptable" intimidation and threats targeting Chinese communities living in the United States.

"China's authoritarianism at home directly threatens our freedoms as well as our most deeply held values and national interests," noted the report in its Executive Summary.

› 16.2.4(c) Department of State Imposes Stricter Visa Vetting for Human Rights Violators

Minghui.org issued a notice on May 31, 2019, that an official from the U.S. Department of State had told various religious groups that the U.S. government might deny visas to human rights violators and perpetrators of religious persecution.[334] This includes both immigration visas and non-immigration visas, such as tourism and business visas. Those who have already been granted visas (including "green card" permanent visas) may also be denied entry.

The official specifically told Falun Gong practitioners that they could submit a list of perpetrators involved in the persecution of Falun Gong. Minghui.org has begun to compile information about such perpetrators, including their identities, family members, and assets, to be submitted to the U.S. government.

The perpetrators include both officials in China and individuals in the U.S. who have attempted to interfere with Shen Yun Performing Arts, Shen Yun Symphony Orchestra, Falun Dafa experience sharing conferences, and Falun Dafa practitioners' public activities. They also include those who spread CCP propaganda against Falun Dafa on various websites.

News of the tightened visa vetting has deterred some officials in China from participating in the persecution.[335] In Heilongjiang Province, domestic security police released four Falun Gong practitioners after 15 days of detention and returned their personal belongings. One officer said, "We didn't hit you, right? We didn't swear at you. Don't report me. I can't have my kids not be able to go overseas." In Shandong Province, police arrested two practitioners and confiscated their Falun Gong books; after officers discovered flyers about the Minghui notice among the confiscated items, they released the practitioners the next day and returned their electric bike.

Canadian Member of Parliament Judy Sgro, who previously served as Minister of Citizenship and Immigration, called for similar measures to be adopted in Canada.[336] She suggested using the Magnitsky Act to sanction Chinese officials, especially those who have participated in the harvesting of organs from Falun Gong practitioners.

› 16.2.4(d) U.S. Leaders Address Religious Freedom and Meet with Falun Gong Practitioners

(1) President Trump Meets Falun Gong Practitioner in White House

Ms. Zhang Yuhua was one of 27 survivors of religious persecution from 17 countries who met with President Donald Trump in the Oval Office in the White House on July 17, 2019.[337]

The 27 survivors were in town to attend the Second Ministerial to Advance Religious Freedom held by the U.S. Department of State in Washington, D.C. on July 16-18, 2019.

Ms. Zhang, 59, told President Trump about the persecution of her husband, Mr. Ma Zhenyu, who is currently serving a three-year term in Suzhou Prison in Jiangsu Province, China.

Mr. Ma, 56, was arrested in September 2017 and sentenced to prison in June 2018 for "writing seven letters to central government leaders to appeal for Falun Gong," as stated in the verdict.

Ms. Zhang told President Trump that she is very worried about her husband. She knew another practitioner who was imprisoned for three years at the same facility. That practitioner vomited a lot of blood and died two days after being released. She urged President Trump to take solid action against China for the human rights abuses and the forced organ harvesting. The President said, "Yes, I understand."

During his opening remarks at the Oval Office meeting, President Trump expressed his solidarity with the survivors and reaffirmed his commitment to protecting religious freedom.

"Each of you have suffered tremendously for your faith. You've endured harassment, threats, attacks, trials, imprisonment and torture. Each of you has now become a witness to the importance of advancing religious liberty all around the world," he said.

"In America, we always understood that our rights come from God, not from government. In our Bill of Rights, the first liberty is religious liberty. Each of us has the right to follow the dictates of our conscience and the demands of our religious conviction.

"For everyone here, you've been through a lot more than most people could ever endure and I want to congratulate you. It's really an honor to be with you and I will stand side by side with you forever."

(2) Falun Gong Persecution Presented at Second Ministerial to Advance Religious Freedom

Earlier that day, Ms. Zhang spoke at the Ministerial to Advance Religious Freedom about the persecution she and her husband are enduring. Ms. Zhang is a former professor of Russian Language at Nanjing Normal University. She was arrested four times and sentenced to seven years and seven months for practicing Falun Gong. She was severely tortured in the prison, including being shocked with electric batons, deprived of sleep, given forced injections of unknown drugs, and made to run under the baking sun for hours.

Her husband, Mr. Ma, a radar design engineer, was arrested multiple times and served seven years in prison prior to his latest term. Because the authorities are preventing his lawyers from meeting with Mr. Ma and several lawyers who represented him before were retaliated against, Ms. Zhang said that she worries about him day and night: "He could be tortured to death like thousands of other Falun Gong practitioners have been. He could be killed for his organs like an unknown number of Falun Gong practitioners have been."

She called on the U.S. government to impose sanctions under the Global Magnitsky Act on Chinese officials "known to have illegally detained, tortured, and killed Falun Gong practitioners." "I hope that the U.S. government, international media, and human rights groups can help free my husband and the hundreds of thousands of other innocent but jailed Falun Gong practitioners," she said.

(3) House Speaker and Former Lawmaker Condemn Human Rights Violations in China

U.S. House Speaker Nancy Pelosi also attended the conference. She had an hour-long discussion with former Congressman Frank Wolf, focusing on human rights violations in China.In the discussion, Ms. Pelosi called the suppression of religious freedom in China "a challenge to the conscience of the world." She said, "Violations are of such scale and so big, and the commercial interests are so significant, that it sometimes tempers our values as to how we are to act on it."

Former Congressman Frank Wolf expressed his concerned about the escalating repression of religious freedom in China and how companies in Western countries are working with the Chinese regime to repress faith groups by developing technologies such as mass surveillance and artificial intelligence.

"No company in the West ought to be cooperating with the Chinese to do this," Mr. Wolf said. "I think they ought to be sued." He said people should bring lawsuits against such companies, and damages should be then awarded to victim groups, such as Uyghurs, Tibetans, and Falun Gong practitioners.

(4) Vice President Mike Pence Meets with Representatives of Religious Groups Persecuted in China, Including Falun Gong

Representatives of three religious groups persecuted in China met with Vice President Mike Pence and representatives of the National Security Council on August 5, 2019 to discuss the suppression of religion in China and ways to address the issue.[338]

A member of the Falun Dafa Association of Washington D.C. spoke about the persecution of Falun Gong and told Pence, "The persecution is still severe. In the last 20 years, we have identified over 4,000 people who died of torture or other physical abuses. Due to the information blockade, the actual number would be many times higher. Organ harvesting has been going on for nearly 20 years also. The number of the victims is really high." He recalled Pence's response: "We won't forget you [Falun Gong]. I promise."

Pence has stressed the importance of addressing religious persecution in trade talks with China. At the Second Ministerial on July 18, 2019, Pence said, "...whatever comes of our negotiations with Beijing, you can be assured, the American people will always stand in solidarity with the people of all faiths in the People's Republic of China."[339]

§16.3 Actions by Non-Governmental Organizations

§§16.3.1 Freedom House Publishes Report on Persecution of Falun Gong

Twenty-two pages of a 142-page report from Freedom House highlighted and analyzed the persecution of Falun Gong and other faith groups in China.[340] "[The Communist Party initiated] the worst instance of religious persecution since the Cultural Revolution, with the clampdown against Falun Gong," cited in the report remarks from André Laliberté, a leading scholar from Ottawa University on religion in China.

Below are key findings of the report:

> **Survival:** *Despite a 17-year Chinese Communist Party (CCP) campaign to eradicate the spiritual group, millions of people in China continue to practice Falun Gong, including many individuals who took up the discipline after the repression began. This represents a striking failure of the CCP's security apparatus.*
>
> **Ongoing large-scale persecution:** *Falun Gong practitioners across China are subject to widespread surveillance, arbitrary detention, imprisonment, and torture, and they are at a high risk of extrajudicial execution. Freedom House independently verified 933 cases of Falun Gong adherents sentenced to prison terms of up to 12 years between January 1, 2013, and June 1, 2016, often for exercising their right to freedom of expression in addition to freedom of religion. This is only a portion of those sentenced, and thousands more are believed to be held at various prisons and extralegal detention centers.*
>
> **Cracks in the crackdown:** *Despite the continued campaign, repression appears to have declined in practice in some locales. President Xi Jinping has offered no explicit indication of a plan to reverse the CCP's policy toward Falun Gong. But the purge and imprisonment of former security czar Zhou Yongkang and other officials*

associated with the campaign as part of Xi's anticorruption drive, together with Falun Gong adherents' persistent efforts to educate and discourage police from persecuting them, have had an impact.

Economic exploitation: *The party-state invests hundreds of millions of dollars annually in the campaign to crush Falun Gong, while simultaneously engaging in exploitative and lucrative forms of abuse against practitioners, including extortion and prison labor. Available evidence suggests that forced extraction of organs from Falun Gong detainees for sale in transplant operations has occurred on a large scale and may be continuing.*

Response and resistance: *Falun Gong practitioners have responded to the campaign against them with a variety of nonviolent tactics. They have especially focused on sharing information with police and the general public about the practice itself, the human rights violations committed against adherents, and other content aimed at countering state propaganda. In recent years, a growing number of non–Falun Gong practitioners in China—including human rights lawyers, family members, and neighbors—have joined these efforts.*

§§16.3.2 Amnesty International Releases "Urgent Action" Notice

Amnesty International release dan "Urgent Action" notice on February 21, 2017, calling attention to Falun Gong practitioner Chen Huixia, who was facing imprisonment of three years to life for her faith, and asked the Chinese communist regime to release Chen immediately. Amnesty International also called for action to stop further persecution of Chen.[341]

"First taken away by the police on 3 June 2016, Chen Huixia was strapped to an iron chair at an unofficial place of detention for more than a month before being relocated to Shijiazhuang Municipal No.2 Detention Center in the northeastern province of Hebei on 15 July 2016," the Amnesty update stated.

Her family members had not been allowed to see her since her arrest. Chen did not have a lawyer until November 2016, "as many lawyers that her family approached refused to take up the case because they believed the authorities would not allow them to defend a Falun Gong practitioner."

The notice urged people to write a letter, send an email, call, fax or tweet to relevant officials to ask that they "immediately and unconditionally release Chen Huixia, as she had been detained solely for exercising the right to freedom of belief and expression and, pending her release, ensure that she has prompt, regular and unrestricted access to her family and lawyers of her choice."

Amnesty International also called for Chen to be protected from torture or other ill-treatment during detention. "According to her daughter, Chen Huixia started practicing Falun Gong in 1998 to heal her chronic illness and poor health. She was consequently detained for approximately three months in 2003, and following her release, her family has been subjected to persistent harassment and intimidation by authorities," the update stated.

The notice further described the CCP's torture, detention and imprisonment of hundreds of thousands of Falun Gong practitioners.

§16.4 Resolutions, Proclamations and Support Letters

Falun Gong has received numerous proclamations and support letters from governments and NGOs around the world. These proclamations highlight the benefits Falun Gong has brought to various regions and communities and universally condemn the Chinese regime's persecution of Falun Gong.

§§16.4.1 Support from All Levels

To date, Falun Gong has been the subject of 2,025 proclamations, 409 resolutions, and 1,200 letters of support from elected officials and governments at the national, provincial, and local levels.

On August 3, 1994, the City of Houston in the United States appointed Mr. Li Hongzhi an Honorary Citizen and Goodwill Ambassador of the city. Two years later, it issued a second proclamation declaring October 12, 1996 "Li Hong Zhi Day."[342] The proclamation reads:

> *As the founder of Falun Dafa, an advanced system of spiritual cultivation, Li Hong Zhi has gained the respect and admiration of people around the world. Falun Dafa is based on the principles of Zhen, Shan and Ren (truth, compassion, and forbearance), the virtues of the universe. Falun Dafa emphasizes health improvements and leads sincere practitioners towards enlightenment.*
>
> *Falun Dafa transcends cultural and racial boundaries. It resonates the universal truth to every corner of the earth and bridges the gap between east and west...*

Over the past two decades, elected officials and governments have issued proclamations and letters of support in recognition of World Falun Dafa Day each year.[343] Canadian MP Judy Sgro wrote in a congratulatory letter on May 13, 2019:[344]

> *I am honoured to add my endorsement to your efforts, as you strive to help advance the values of openness, tolerance, and freedom of conscience and religion here and Canada and globally.*
>
> ...
>
> *Sadly, too many non-violent and devout practitioners live in darkness and under the constant threat of persecution and even death. As Canadians, we must do our part to help bring about the changes needed to right these terrible wrongs.*

The U.S. House of Representatives has passed resolutions calling on the Chinese government to end the persecution of Falun Gong, including House Concurrent Resolution 304 in 2004[345] and House Resolution 605 in 2010,[346] both sponsored by Rep. Ileana Ros-Lehtinen. Congressman Frank Wolf stated in his speech before voting, "China has become increasingly brazen in its human rights abuses. In the face of this repression, America has a responsibility to continually affirm that we stand with the defenseless—with those whose voices have been silenced."[347]

Around July 20, 2019, which marks the 20th year of the persecution, 22 U.S. Senators and Representatives sent letters commending practitioners' efforts to counter the persecution.[348]

§§16.4.2 Germany Condemns 20 Years of Persecution of Falun Gong in China

Dr. Baerbel Kofler, a federal Commissioner for Human Rights Policy and Humanitarian Aid, posted a news release on the German Federal Foreign Office website in which she condemned Beijing for its persecution of Falun Gong.[349]

The news release published on July 20, 2019 states:

> *During the past 20 years the Chinese communist regime viciously treated practitioners of the spiritual cultivation practice Falun Gong. Falun Gong practitioners are persecuted and detained without legal process. Many reports have shown that practitioners are tortured and even died during detention. At the 20th anniversary of the persecution I am deeply concerned that the practitioners in China are still in danger.*

Dr. Kofler demands that Beijing "follow international guidelines and Chinese laws to protect human rights, including the rights of Falun Gong practitioners." She asked Beijing to respond to "the serious accusations of its years of systemic organ harvesting from detained Falun Gong practitioners," and "immediately increase the transparency of its sources of organs for transplants, as well as allow free entrance by independent observers to its detention facilities."

§16.5 International Response to Forced Organ Harvesting

Following independent investigations starting in 2006, a number of government bodies have enacted stronger legislation against organ trafficking and passed resolutions calling for an end to the killing of prisoners of conscience in China.

Medical and professional organizations have also taken steps to uphold ethical standards, though Chinese transplant officials and surgeons continue to be welcomed at some international conferences.

§§16.5.1 Resolutions

› 16.5.1(a) European Parliament

The European Parliament passed a resolution (2013/2981(RSP)) on December 12, 2013 to express "deep concern over the persistent and credible reports of systematic, state-sanctioned organ harvesting from non-consenting prisoners of conscience in the People's Republic of China, including from large numbers of Falun Gong practitioners imprisoned for their religious beliefs, as well as from members of other religious and ethnic minority groups."

The resolution "[called] for the EU and its Member States to raise the issue of organ harvesting in China; recommends that the Union and its Member States publicly condemn organ transplant abuses in China and raise awareness of this issue among their citizens travelling to China; calls for a full and transparent investigation by the EU into organ transplant practices in China, and for the prosecution of those found to have engaged in such unethical practices..."

In 2016, 12 Members of the European Parliament issued a joint declaration requesting that the European Parliament investigate the illegal harvesting and trafficking of human organs by the Chinese communist regime. After a special hearing on June 29, more than half of the Members of the European Parliament (MEP) co-signed

Written Declaration (2016/WD48), requiring the European Parliament to take action to stop the state-sanctioned forced organ harvesting in China.[350 351]

› 16.5.1(b) U.S. House of Representatives

The U.S. House of Representatives unanimously passed Resolution 343 on the evening of June 13, 2016. The resolution calls on China's communist regime to immediately stop forced organ harvesting from Falun Gong practitioners and other prisoners of conscience.

The resolution also calls for an immediate end to the persecution of Falun Gong, which was in its 17th year. It further calls for the release of all incarcerated Falun Gong practitioners and other prisoners of conscience, and for a credible, transparent, and independent investigation into China's organ transplantation system.

H.Res.343 was initiated by representatives Ileana Ros-Lehtinen (R-FL), Chairman of the Subcommittee on the Middle East and North Africa, and Rep. Gerald Connolly (D-VA), as well as six other members of Congress: Rep. Dana Rohrabacher (R-CA), Rep. Ted Poe (R-TX), U.S. Reps. Mario Diaz-Balart (R-FL), Julia Brownley (D-CA), Sam Farr (D-CA), and David G. Valadao (R-CA). It garnered strong bipartisan support, with 185 co-sponsors.

(1) Rep. Ileana Ros-Lehtinen: "We Condemn this Continued Practice of Persecution of Falun Gong Practitioners"

Representative Ileana Ros-Lehtinen, who authored the measure, said in a press statement:

> *China has been perpetuating perhaps some of the most gruesome and egregious human rights violations against the Falun Gong and other prisoners of conscience, yet has hardly faced any criticism, let alone sanctions, for these abuses.*
>
> *The regime's ghoulish and inhumane practice of robbing individuals of their freedom, throwing them in labor camps or prisons, and*

then executing them and harvesting their organs for transplants is way beyond the pale of comprehension and must be opposed universally and ended unconditionally.

She said in her speech on the floor before the vote:

By passing this resolution, we can send a message to the Chinese regime that we condemn this continued practice of persecution of Falun Gong practitioners, and this sickening practice must stop, especially harvesting organs from non-consenting individuals.

(2) Congressman Eliot Engel: Forced Organ Harvesting Is "Gruesome and Shocking"

"What's particularly unsettling is that this practice allegedly targets prisoners of conscience, including practitioners of Falun Gong and other religious and ethnic minorities," said New York Congressman Eliot Engel regarding the practice of organ trafficking in China.

Congressman Engel said in his floor speech regarding H.Res.343:

Non-consensual organ harvesting under any circumstance represents a gross violation of human rights. But these allegations are particularly egregious: authorities at Chinese prisons targeting prisoners because of their religious beliefs and then making a profit by trafficking these victims' organs. I cannot think of hardly anything that's more disgusting than that.

Engel called the accounts of organ harvesting, "gruesome and shocking" and called for further investigations.

(3) Congressman Chris Smith: Persecution of Falun Gong "One of the Great Horrors"

Congressman Chris Smith from New Jersey said in his speech:

This legislation is an important step in bringing accountability and transparency to maybe the great crime of the 21st century.

The evidence is quickly mounting of the horrific crimes committed against Falun Gong practitioners, including this terrible practice of organ harvesting.

Shockingly, researchers David Kilgour, David Matas and Ethan Gutmann conducted detailed investigations and estimated that between 45,000 to 65,000 Falun Gong practitioners were killed for their organs which then were sold for profit.

Congressman Smith said he strongly believes that the communist regime's campaign to eradicate Falun Gong in China will be seen as "one of the great horrors."

› 16.5.1(c) U.S. State Legislatures

At least ten state-level legislatures in the U.S. have passed resolutions to condemn the state-sanctioned organ harvesting.

The Missouri State Legislature passed Senate Concurrent Resolution (SCR) No.6 on May 15, 2019, which calls on "the Chinese Government to end the practice of organ harvesting from prisoners as well as prisoners of conscience, specifically Falun Gong prisoners of conscience."

State Senator Jill Schupp, sponsor of SCR 6, said, "It is long overdue and the fight continues... Here in the state of Missouri, we cannot stand for these human rights violations."[352]

The Maine Legislature passed Joint Resolution S.P.574 on May 7, 2019, calling to end forced organ harvesting in China. The resolution also encourages the medical community in the State of Maine to educate its citizens about the risks of travel to China for organ transplants to prevent them from unwittingly becoming involved in murder in the form of forced organ harvesting from prisoners of conscience.[353]

The General Assembly of Pennsylvania unanimously passed House Resolution 1052 on October 8, 2014, urging the medical community to help raise awareness of unethical organ transplant practices in China.

Similar resolutions have been passed in the Georgia State Senate[354] and the Arizona State Congress.[355]

› 16.5.1(d) Italian Senate

On March 5, 2014, the Italian Senate's Human Rights Commission unanimously passed a resolution urging the Italian government to launch a thorough investigation into organ harvesting in China through diplomatic and other channels.

In the resolution, the Extraordinary Commission for the Protection and Promotion of Human Rights also requested the Italian government to reconsider training programs for Chinese doctors and prosecute, in accordance with international conventions, individuals involved in organ trafficking.

This resolution came after a Senate hearing on the same issue on December 19, 2013. Canadian human rights lawyer David Matas made a presentation at the hearing, urging Italy to revise its laws in order to keep the country from becoming an accomplice to the crimes of forced organ harvesting in China.

§§16.5.2 Strengthening Organ Trafficking Laws

Some countries have strengthened their organ trafficking legislation to include extraterritorial jurisdiction and forbid their citizens from traveling abroad, including to China, to receive an illicit transplant. Below are a few examples of such bills that have been passed by legislative bodies, though not all have ultimately been signed into law.

› 16.5.2(a) Israel

In 2008, Israel passed the Organ Transplant Act, which prohibits insurance companies from reimbursing transplants received in other countries in violation of Israeli law. Violators who buy, sell, or broker illicit organs—including outside of Israel—would face up to three years in prison and a large fine.[356]

› 16.5.2(b) Spain

The Spanish Penal Code was amended in 2010 as follows:[357]

1. Those who promote, facilitate, or advertise the procurement or illegal trafficking of human organs or their transplantation shall be punished with imprisonment from six to 12 years in cases of vital organs and imprisonment for three to six years in cases of non-vital organs.

2. Recipients consenting to receive a transplant knowing its illicit origin shall be liable to the same penalties as in the previous section, which may be lowered by one or two degrees attending to the circumstances of the crime and of the offender.

3. When in accordance with the provisions laid down in Article 31 bis, a legal person is responsible for the offenses covered by this article, he shall pay a fine of three to five times the profit made.

› 16.5.2(c) Italy

The Italian Senate unanimously passed a bill on March 4, 2015 that would punish those who illegally sell organs from living people with severe sanctions, including prison time.[358]

Under the new bill, any person who trades, sells, or manages illegally trafficked organs from living persons would serve a prison term of three to 12 years and pay a fine of 50,000 to 300,000 euros. The bill punishes whoever publicity encourages or advertises the selling of organs or presents propaganda and announcements to encourage transplant tourism to China. Doctors who promote or assist patients to travel to illegally obtain an organ would face lifetime disbarment for violating medical ethics.

Senator Maurizio Romani, who proposed the bill, said that it "establishes equivalence between the crime of trafficking human organs for transplantation and the crime of human trafficking." He explained, "This makes all participants guilty, the donors, the organizers, the surgeons who perform the transplants, and even those who buy the organs."[359]

› 16.5.2(d) Taiwan

Legislators amended Taiwan's Human Organ Transplant Act on June 12, 2015, forbidding illegal organ sales.[360]

The Act targets the trading of organs from unknown sources and prevents it from taking place by amending the law. It stipulates that organs must be provided or received without any form of compensation [free of charge]. If those who purchase transplant organs overseas are found guilty of receiving an illicit organ, the maximum sentence is five years, plus Taiwan levies a fine of no more than NT$1.5 million [approximately $49,000 USD] on the accused. Additionally, doctors involved in illegal organ transplants could lose their license. Legislator Yu Mei-nu of the Democratic Progressive Party said that the Chinese regime is actively involved in the organ trade, which depends heavily on the harvesting of organs from living Falun Gong practitioners.

"We hope to effectively deter organ trafficking and its sales with this amendment," said Yu.

› 16.5.2(e) Croatia

The Croatian Parliament voted unanimously on March 1, 2019, to adopt the Council of Europe Convention against Trafficking in Human Organs, becoming the eighth European nation to ratify the treaty.[361]

In addition to criminalizing the act of illegal organ extraction, the Convention also compels signatories to criminalize aiding and abetting in such acts and the solicitation of organ donors or recipients for illicit transplants.

Dr. Branimir Bunjac, Member of Parliament, stated during the parliamentary proceedings, "Our countrymen unwittingly participate as users of such services—they travel overseas, especially to China, to obtain organs quicker. One has to ask the question: how is it possible that there is no waiting period in China, as opposed to the European Union?"

He cited international organizations' findings that China has carried out up to 100,000 transplants per year for over a decade despite the lack of an organ donation system.

"When you ask Chinese authorities about the source of such organs, they justify it by saying they were obtained from death row prisoners," he said. "However, there are only 2,000 such prisoners in China annually, which is evidently not enough for such a large number of transplants.

"After those reports, the Chinese authorities have replied that those were black market figures. However, all transplants in China are conducted inside state hospitals, under state supervision. Therefore, such information just does not seem plausible," Dr. Bunjac added.

Pointing to laws passed in Italy, Spain, and the Czech Republic that prohibit their citizens from going to China to obtain illicit organs, Dr. Bunjac cautioned that adopting the Convention alone would not resolve the problem entirely.

"It is necessary to continue developing further legislation, especially bearing in mind that Croatia is at the very top of transplant medicine. As such, we should serve as an example, both in legislation and in practice," he said.The Croatian government has announced further initiatives to inform health professionals and the wider public about the magnitude of the issue, to enable them to recognize, prevent, and report unethical transplant practices.

› 16.5.2(f) The Czech Republic

The Senate of the Parliament of the Czech Republic passed Resolution No.131 No.131 on March 20, 2019, expressing support for persecuted groups in China, including Falun Gong practitioners, Christians, Uighurs, and Tibetans. It called for the Czech president and government to demand that China adhere to international human rights conventions by ending the persecution of these groups and releasing all prisoners of conscience. The resolution was a response to the nationwide petition regarding "The Chinese communist regime committing genocide of Falun Gong practitioners." Over 37,000 Czechs signed the petition.

› 16.5.2(g) Belgium

Belgium's primary legislative body passed a new bill on April 25, 2019, that would punish all parties involved in the buying and selling of human organs for commercial purposes.[362]

The bill is the first in Europe to refer directly to the European Parliament's 2013 resolution and 2016 written declaration that called on EU Member States to inform their inhabitants about practices of organ harvesting in China and to prosecute those who participated in these unethical practices.

Violators face up to 20 years of imprisonment with a €1.2m (USD$1.35 million) fine. If an organized criminal group is involved in such trade, all individuals in the group will face punishment.

The new law imposes punishment for both the organ seller and recipient, as well as any middlemen, doctors, and other medical workers who participate in the sale of organs for profit.

The law also applies to transactions that take place outside of Belgium.

› 16.5.2(h) Canada

S-240, a bill that targets human organ trafficking, was unanimously passed on the evening of April 30, 2019, in the Canadian House of Commons.[363] It was introduced by the Senate and was already approved by the Committee on Foreign Affairs and International Trade (AEFA) prior to voting in the House of Commons.

The Act amends the Criminal Code so that unauthorized overseas organ transplant will be treated as criminal activities and also amends the Immigration and Refugee Protection Act so that those involved in organ trafficking will not be granted immigration or refugee status.

§§16.5.3 U.S. Commission on International Religious Freedom Highlights Organ Harvesting in China

The U.S. Commission on International Religious Freedom (USCIRF) highlighted China as one of the world's most egregious persecutors of religious faiths in its 2019 annual report released on April 29, 2019. The report also states that the Chinese Communist Party is still harvesting organs from Falun Gong practitioners on a large scale.[364]

Gary Bauer, USCIRF Commissioner, relayed that the committee had recommended that the U.S. government quickly and decisively sanction CCP officials and institutions that commit or condone serious violations of religious freedom.

› 16.5.3(a) Persistent, Serious Violation of Religious Freedom

According to the report, due to the systematic and persistent serious violation of religious freedom by the CCP, China was once again listed as a "country of particular concern" for violation of religious freedom by the USCIRF in 2019. This is the second consecutive decade in which China has been classified as a country of particular concern. The report documents a large number of records of the CCP's systematic, persistent, and serious violation of religious freedom in 2018.

› 16.5.3(b) Persecution of Falun Gong Practitioners Ongoing

The report mentions that Jiang Zemin, former head of the CCP, launched the persecution of Falun Gong in 1999 and founded the 610 Office, an institution that is above the law and that is charged with eliminating Falun Gong. The report states that Falun Gong practitioners are arbitrarily detained, shocked with electric batons, and forced to become subjects of medical and psychological research.

In 2018, the Chinese authorities continued to harass, detain, and intimidate Falun Gong practitioners because of their belief. It has been reported that many practitioners who were detained were beaten, subjected to mental abuse, sexually assaulted, forced to take unknown drugs, and deprived of sleep.

According to information provided by Falun Gong practitioners, the CCP arrested and detained at least 931 practitioners in 2018. Last summer, several practitioners who sent messages calling for support for Falun Gong through social media, or who passed out Falun Gong informational materials in public, were arrested.

The report discussed the CCP's claims that as of January 1, 2015, it had ended the practice of harvesting organs from prisoners (many detainees are believed to be Falun Gong practitioners). However, in 2018, human rights activists, medical professionals, and investigators provided more evidence that the CCP is still continuing the organ harvesting on a large scale. The report stated that last November, the Changsha Judicial Bureau in Hunan Province, China, barred two lawyers for six months because they defended Falun Gong practitioners in court.

› 16.5.3(c) Continued Deterioration of Religious Freedom

In November 2018, during the United Nations periodic review of China, the United States questioned the issue of the persecution of Falun Gong and the closure of Christian churches in a written questionnaire, which was submitted in advance.

Gary Bauer, USCIRF Commissioner, said at the press conference for the annual USCIRF report that the situation in China is still deteriorating. To this end, the Commission made a series of recommendations to the Administration, including that all bilateral negotiations between the United States and China, especially in ongoing trade negotiations, place religious freedom and human rights issues on the table.

The commission also recommends that the U.S. government promptly and decisively sanction Chinese officials and institutions that commit or condone serious violations of religious freedom. Finally, the commission urges the U.S. and other governments to pressure the Chinese communist regime to unconditionally release prisoners of conscience.

§§16.5.4 People's Tribunal Concludes Forced Organ Harvesting Continues Today

An independent people's tribunal in London, established to inquire into forced organ harvesting from prisoners of conscience in China, announced its findings on June 17, 2019.

The panel concluded that the Chinese Communist Party (CCP) has been harvesting organs from living Falun Gong practitioners in China for many years and that this brutality still continues today:[365]

> *Forced organ harvesting has been committed for years throughout China on a significant scale and that Falun Gong practitioners have been one—and probably the main—source of organ supply. The concerted persecution and medical testing of the Uyghurs is more recent and it may be that evidence of forced organ harvesting of this group may emerge in due course. The Tribunal has had no evidence that the significant infrastructure associated with China's transplantation industry has been dismantled and, absent a satisfactory explanation as to the source of readily available organs, concludes that forced organ harvesting continues till today.*

Chaired by Sir Geoffrey Nice QC, who worked at the International Criminal Tribunal for the Former Yugoslavia—the ICTY—and led the prosecution of Slobodan Milosevic, the seven-member tribunal reached its conclusion after questioning "over 50 fact witnesses, experts, investigators, and analysts over five days of public hearings in December 2018 and April 2019, the review of written submissions, investigative reports, and academic papers."

Appendices: Three Key Facts about the Persecution of Falun Gong

世界需要真善忍

Appendices: Three Key Facts about the Persecution of Falun Gong

In totalitarian China, "news" is carefully crafted by state-controlled media to promote the interests of the Communist Party. This vast propaganda machine has played a leading role in the persecution of Falun Gong.

By flooding the airwaves, newspapers, and magazines with countless stories vilifying Falun Gong and its founder, Mr. Li Hongzhi, the Communist Party drafted the entire society into the ranks of persecutors. People hear the lies so often repeated that in the end, they grow to believe them. This created an environment in which practitioners had no rights and no security. They could be attacked with impunity, and it became easy for the Chinese people to shut their ears to the cries of the tortured innocents.

The propaganda has also deceived many in the West, who have developed inaccurate perceptions of Falun Gong as a result. The following three chapters debunk the most common lies the CCP has employed to turn public opinion against Falun Gong.

Key Highlights

A peaceful appeal by more than 10,000 Falun Gong practitioners on April 25, 1999 was mischaracterized as a "siege of the central government compound" by Jiang Zemin, who used the event to justify the subsequent persecution. The demonstrators were appealing on behalf of 45 practitioners who were beaten and arrested in Tianjin, and they had been instructed to go to the national appeals office in Beijing to do so. The quiet, orderly appeal was peacefully resolved after practitioners' representatives met with Premier Zhu Rongji.

On January 23, 2001, five individuals allegedly set themselves on fire in Tiananmen Square, but they were not Falun Gong practitioners as claimed by state-controlled media. The event was planned ahead of time, filmed from multiple angles in a secured area, and broadcast throughout China immediately after it took place. Even though the self-immolation was later found to be staged, it was successfully used to turn public opinion against Falun Gong.

Chinese authorities have alleged that Falun Gong has "led to more than 1,400 deaths" of its followers, but the cases were found to be fabricated. The alleged victims who were investigated either did not practice Falun Gong or simply did not exist. Chinese authorities falsely claim that Falun Gong teachings forbid practitioners from taking medicine and seeking medical treatment.

法 輪 大 法 好

Appendix 1: Peaceful Appeal of April 25, 1999

§A1.1 Overview[366]

§§A1.1.1 Background

On April 23 and 24, 1999, police in Tianjin, a city near Beijing, assaulted and arrested dozens of Falun Gong practitioners who had gathered outside a magazine office to discuss errors in a recently published article attacking Falun Gong. As word spread of the arrests and more Falun Gong practitioners inquired with officials, they were told to take their appeals to Beijing. The following day, April 25, more than 10,000 Falun Gong practitioners spontaneously gathered at the central appeals office in Beijing as they had been instructed to do by Tianjin officials. The gathering was peaceful and orderly. Several Falun Gong representatives were called in to meet with Chinese Premier Zhu Rongji and members of his staff. That evening, the concerns of Falun Gong practitioners were addressed, the detained practitioners in Tianjin were released, and everyone went home.

§§A1.1.2 The Problem

According to several sources within the Chinese government, in the months following the April 25th gathering, a fierce political struggle ensued within the top levels of the CCP brass. Then CCP leader Jiang Zemin called upon the government to "crush" Falun Gong, while other members of the Politburo saw no threat in the practice. CNN senior analyst Willy Lam quoted senior officials who said the suppression of Falun Gong had become very "personal" for Jiang Zemin. In July, Jiang formally ordered the suppression of Falun Gong. The April 25th gathering was quickly re-characterized not as the peaceful appeal that it was, but rather as "laying siege" to the central government compound and "evidence" as to how Falun Gong was a threat.

§§A1.1.3 Why It Matters

The misrepresentation of April 25th as a "siege" of the central government compound politicized Falun Gong, both in China and abroad. Thus, rather than seeing the CCP's persecution as the violent suppression of a religious minority, a narrative that Falun Gong and the CCP were vying for power began to evolve. Furthermore, some China watchers in the West believed Falun Gong brought the persecution on themselves by "challenging" the government on April 25th. This narrative has eroded the enthusiasm of many would-be supporters of human and religious rights, and it remains the single greatest factor in the blame-the-victim phenomenon that surrounds the investigation of and reporting on the persecution of Falun Gong more broadly.

§A1.2 Quick Facts[367]

§§A1.2.1 Why did Falun Gong practitioners appeal to the CCP Central Committee?

As early as June 1996, the Central Propaganda Department instructed various levels of government to criticize Falun Gong. *Guangming Daily* launched the first salvo with the article "Alarm Bell Keeps Ringing." The News Publishing Bureau subsequently prohibited the publication, distribution and sale of Falun Gong books.

Before April 25, police all over China had already begun to seize Falun Gong books and interfere with group exercise sites. The arrests of practitioners by the Tianjin police were an escalation of the persecution.

§§A1.2.2 How many people went to appeal on April 25, 1999?

From Beihai Park's South Gate to the west side of the Xi'an Gate, and from Fuyou Street to the alley west of it–in these two places alone, there were 30,000 people. Practitioners who came later were stopped on the outer peripheries. Practitioners from out of town were not allowed to leave the train stations or were blocked at highway checkpoints and not allowed to get into Beijing. The Chinese government only acknowledged the greatly reduced figure of 10,000, but the actual number far exceeded that.

§§A1.2.3 What did the practitioners ask for?

They had three requests at the time:

1. For Tianjin police to release the Falun Gong practitioners who were taken into custody.
2. That Falun Gong practitioners be accorded a non-hostile environment in which to practice.
3. That the printing of Falun Gong books be permitted.

§§A1.2.4 How did those who appealed conduct themselves?

On the main thoroughfare from Beihai Park to Xi'an Gate, traffic flowed smoothly the entire day. Some practitioners took the initiative to ensure the smooth flow of vehicular and pedestrian traffic. The practitioners walked along the edge of the road, allowing pedestrians to use the sidewalk. They were calm and peaceful.

§§A1.2.5 How did the appeal end?

At around 10 p.m., a message came from the West Gate of Zhongnanhai: "The representatives have returned, and they have conveyed the practitioners' requests to the leaders of the Central Committee. All practitioners arrested by Tianjin police have been released. Everybody can now go home." The practitioners cleaned up their surroundings and even picked up cigarette butts dropped by the police. In less than 20 minutes, all the practitioners had left.

§§A1.2.6 One unsettled case:

Premier Zhu Rongji asked the representatives at the time if they had ever read his commentary on Falun Gong. The Falun Gong representatives said they had never seen it. Many wondered who had withheld the commentary and why it was withheld. This remains unknown to this day.

§A1.3 Analysis[368]

§§A1.3.1 Sequence of Events

A scholar named He Zuoxiu from the Chinese Academy of Sciences published an article titled "I do not agree with adolescents practicing qigong" in *Science and Technology for Youth* (a magazine published by Tianjin Education College). In the article, he fabricated stories about Falun Gong leading to mental illness and implied that Falun Gong could become an organization similar to the Boxers, who led a rebellion in the 19th century that destroyed the nation.

Some practitioners went to Tianjin Education College between April 18 and April 24 to talk to the magazine editors to clear up the slander and convey their own experiences of practicing Falun Gong. The conversations were calm and peaceful. However, the Tianjin Public Security Bureau dispatched riot police on April 23-24, who beat the practitioners and arrested 45 of them.

When other practitioners went to the Tianjin city government to seek their release, they were told that the Ministry of Public Security was involved and that they could not release the practitioners without approval from Beijing. Tianjin police told practitioners, "Go to Beijing. Only going to Beijing can solve the problem."

On April 25, practitioners gathered outside the national appeals office in Beijing to ask for 1) the release of practitioners detained in Tianjin, 2) an open and legal environment in which to practice the Falun Gong exercises, and 3) the lifting of the ban on the publication of Falun Gong books.

Several police officers told practitioners at the appeals office that one place was not safe and that another place was off limits. Following police instructions, the practitioners divided into two groups alongside Zhongnanhai. Later, He Zuoxiu arrived and tried to provoke the practitioners, who did not respond to him.

According to a witness, on the evening of April 24, some practitioners working in the Public Security Department had already submitted their name cards to Zhongnanhai, asking for a chance to discuss the situation. There was no response. At 9 p.m., practitioners started to gather on Fuyou Street near Zhongnanhai, some with luggage, some with meditation mats.

At 6 a.m. on April 25, a witness went to the north entrance of Fuyou Street and discovered that the police were blocking the way to Zhongnanhai. None of the practitioners attempted to force their way through. The police first led the practitioners from the east side of the street to the west side, and then directed them to walk south towards Zhongnanhai. Meanwhile, another group came from the opposite direction, also led by police, and both groups met right outside the main entrance of Zhongnanhai. According to the media, there were over 10,000 practitioners gathered outside Zhongnanhai.

Soon, there were practitioners approaching from all directions. They filled all the sidewalks outside of Zhongnanhai. But the traffic was not blocked at all; even the route for the disabled remained clear. There were men and women in their eighties, pregnant women who were near the end of their terms, and mothers holding their newborn babies. Practitioners did not wander up and down the streets, chant slogans, wave signs, or start fights.

In China, appealing to the government does not require a permit from the Public Security Bureau. Each practitioner went to represent his or her own views and to report the mistreatment that they and their friends had been experiencing. They did not violate any laws or regulations. Once practitioners thought that they had achieved the goal of expressing their concerns and seeking understanding and support from the government, they quietly dispersed.

§§A1.3.2 Causes of the Gathering

On the surface, the April 25 appeal appeared to be triggered by the Tianjin arrests and an anti-Falun Gong article by He Zuoxiu. The underlying reason stemmed from the central authorities' anxiety about the unprecedented popularity of Falun Gong. Seven years after Mr. Li Hongzhi's first public lecture in 1992, there were about 70 to 100 million Falun Gong practitioners in Mainland China. A full understanding of the incident is very complex, as it had both long-term and short-term causes and was related to political struggles inside the Communist Party.

(a) Long-Term Cause

The long-term cause of the April 25 appeal was the ongoing suppression of Falun Gong. With the rapid spread of Falun Gong, the central Party leadership feared that it would lose ideological control over the people. The government had therefore been attempting to undermine Falun Gong through the media, by banning books, by conducting underground investigations, and by disrupting exercise practice sites the preceding few years. The government had already been attempting to destroy the practitioners' environment for practicing Falun Gong. Practitioners had no other way to let the facts about the repression be known than to appeal to the central authorities. The April 25 gathering aimed to do just this.

The central authorities began to criticize Falun Gong on June 17, 1996. That day, *Guangming Daily* (the official voice of the State Council with articles that reflect only the opinions of government officials) published an article criticizing Falun Gong as "anti-science" and "superstitious" and labeled its practitioners "stupid."

On July 24, 1996, the Chinese News Publishing Office issued a notice to immediately confiscate five books nationwide, including Falun Gong (formerly titled China Falun Gong). Dozens of newspapers and magazines soon joined the campaign against Falun Gong. Some official scholars such as He Zuoxiu were also active in the campaign. The Central Office of National Publication and Central Propaganda Department also ordered all publishers not to publish books related to Falun Gong.

At the beginning of 1997, Luo Gan (member of the Politburo Standing Committee and Secretary of the Political and Legal Affairs Committee) ordered the Ministry of Public Security to conduct a nationwide investigation into Falun Gong to collect evidence that it was an "evil cult." The investigation ended after public security departments found no criminal activity in Falun Gong.

In May 1998, Beijing TV Station (BTV)'s Beijing Express show broadcast a segment by He Zuoxiu that defamed Falun Gong using material unrelated to the practice. Following the broadcast, hundreds of Falun Gong practitioners in the Beijing and Hebei areas wrote to the station to point out false information that was shown in the program. On June 2, 1998, BTV broadcast a correction acknowledging the mistakes in the earlier program. It is worth noting that He Zuoxiu later used the same defamatory content in his magazine article.

Also in May 1998, the General Administration of Sport of China initiated a comprehensive investigation of Falun Gong. On October 20 of the same year, the head investigator for the cities of Changchun and Harbin stated that Falun Gong was effective in improving health and spiritual civilization. Investigations in Beijing, Guangdong, Dalian, and Wuhan reached similar conclusions.

In July 1998, under orders from Luo Gan, the Ministry of Public Security issued Notice [1998] No.555 to investigate Falun Gong. The notice first concluded that Falun Gong was an "evil cult" before ordering local public security and political protection departments to look for evidence of criminal activity by Falun Gong practitioners. In other words, the Ministry proclaimed guilt before conducting the investigation.

After this document was issued, many local public security bureaus announced that Falun Gong activities were considered illegal assemblies. They dispersed exercise groups, confiscated practitioners' personal property, and detained, arrested, beat, and verbally abused them. In some areas, practitioners were fined, and Falun Gong-related books were banned. Practitioners tried many times to appeal through normal channels but were not successful.

The CCP allows only the official voice in the public sphere. By this point, many articles had been published that criticized, cursed, and slandered Falun Gong. No articles defending Falun Gong were allowed to be published. Under these conditions, Falun Gong practitioners were left with no other options but to go to Beijing and petition the government to give them an unrestricted environment in which to practice their faith.

(b) Political Causes

The government's suppression campaign, which led to the April 25 appeal, was likely related to political struggles among high-level officials. Different groups within the central government held a variety of views on Falun Gong. Among them, a few tried to capitalize on destroying Falun Gong in order to advance their political careers. According to a report from the Central News Agency (5/4 from Taipei), the government's political scheme behind the April 25 incident could be described as a "release before capturing" and a "ruse of suffering [by the government] before charging [against Falun Gong]." The purpose was to make Zhongnanhai appear to have been under pressure and then to outlaw Falun Gong, allowing the government to demonstrate its might in demolishing this so-called threat.

As early as 1996, the rapid development of Falun Gong caught the attention of the central Party leadership. Luo Gan, Secretary General of the State Council at the time, ordered the Ministry of Public Security to conduct a secret investigation. Public security personnel participated undercover in various Falun Gong activities but found no evidence of criminal conduct.

Even with the lack of evidence, there were still two opinions inside the government about how to deal with Falun Gong. One side thought that Falun Gong was not a political problem and therefore should not be banned. The other side worried about Falun Gong's increasing popularity and influence, which they thought could potentially become a force opposing the Communist Party. Luo Gan advocated the banning of Falun Gong, Premier Zhu Rongji rejected the idea, and President Jiang Zemin did not express an opinion.

Luo Gan is a relative of He Zuoxiu, who used the media to slander Falun Gong and create incidents that would lead all factions in the Communist Party to agree to outlaw Falun Gong. After the April 25 incident, Luo Gan reported that Falun Gong had tens of millions of followers, that it was "religious and superstitious" in nature, and that Mr. Li Hongzhi, who was living in New York, was suspected of having a complex network of international connections. He reported that Falun Gong was therefore a potential threat to social stability. These opinions were widely distributed to Hong Kong and international media to exaggerate the potential threat of Falun Gong.

In fact, Falun Gong is a loosely organized practice with no membership or hierarchy, and its practitioners could not have been "well organized and directed" as alleged.

§§A1.3.3 Some Clarifications

(a) Practitioners Were Tricked into Surrounding Zhongnanhai by the Authorities

The CCP claimed that Falun Gong practitioners "surrounded" Zhongnanhai. As discussed earlier, this arrangement was set up by the police, who led the Falun Gong practitioners to take two routes that converged at the front entrance of Zhongnanhai and formed a circle. Even as the witness was describing what he saw, he did not realize the outcome of the setup.

Three days before the April 25 appeal, the police had received information about the impending gathering and were closely monitoring the situation. They chose not to report the information, however. When He Zuoxiu was asked to comment on the incident, he said, "For the time being, I will not comment because I do not want to mess up the whole arrangement."

(b) Practitioners Went to Beijing Only to Appeal

Practitioners went to Beijing and Tianjin because there was no other way to report the facts and seek redress for the slander being spread against them.

Article 41 of the Chinese Constitution grants citizens the right to criticize and make suggestions regarding any state organ or functionary. The 10th Code of the Chinese "Codes of Appeal" states that issues in the appeal process should be submitted to the appropriate executive departments or to one level higher, as these departments have the legal right to make decisions.

After the practitioners were arrested in Tianjin on April 23, other practitioners gathered at the Office of Appeals of the Tianjin city government. The appeal was not well received, and about 40 more practitioners were arrested instead. As a result, practitioners had to appeal to the level above the Tianjin city government, which is the central government in Beijing. The appeals in Tianjin and Beijing did not violate any government regulations.

(c) The April 25 Gathering Was Not Masterminded by Mr. Li Hongzhi

In a 10,000-word report by the Ministry of Public Security, Mr. Li Hongzhi, the founder of Falun Gong, was accused of orchestrating the April 25 appeal behind the scenes. In fact, Mr. Li was on a layover in Beijing on his way to Australia to attend a Falun Gong conference, but he was not in Beijing on April 25. To reduce the cost of his airline ticket, he had layovers in Beijing and Hong Kong. He was in Beijing for 48 hours before leaving on April 24 for Hong Kong.

(d) How 10,000 Can Gather Without Being "Organized"

The Chinese government questioned how, without any organization, so many people arrived at Zhongnanhai at the same time. News of the Tianjin arrests spread by word of mouth, just as Falun Gong itself spread quickly by word of mouth as individual practitioners told their friends and families how they had benefitted from it. This network allows information to flow to many people without an organization or planning by a central figure.

Some observers have noted that the practitioners outside Zhongnanhai were more disciplined than the police, suggesting that the crowd was extensively trained. However, we should note that the teachings of Falun Gong encourage practitioners to discipline themselves, avoid impulsive emotional responses, and consider others before themselves. This calm behavior is the standard they maintain on a daily basis. Rather than a disciplined crowd, this was a crowd of disciplined individuals.

(e) Summary: Who Has Actually "Disrupted Social Stability"?

As mentioned above, practitioners of Falun Gong are taught to be exemplary citizens and diligent, honest workers while taking personal gain lightly. In the city of Changchun, there was a saying among employers, "We will hire whoever practices Falun Gong because it puts our minds at ease." At home, practitioners strive to be good husbands, good wives, and good children, working to ensure a peaceful and harmonious family life. They are taught to examine themselves for shortcomings when they encounter interpersonal conflicts.

These qualities do not disrupt social order but instead ensure it. This agrees with the Chinese regime's stated desire to have "stability above all else."

Rather than embracing these values, however, the government has alienated tens of millions of innocent people. Parents have been arrested and taken to labor camps or prisons, leaving their children behind, sometimes even unattended. Families and communities have been ripped apart. Mothers have been made to slander their daughters, sons to turn in their fathers, and neighbors to police and report on one another. Students have been kicked out of school for practicing Falun Gong, and workers have been fired from their jobs and heavily fined for not renouncing their faith. No one has been allowed to remain neutral, and the persecution has achieved the opposite of social stability.

Appendix 2: Self-Immolation Hoax on Tiananmen Square

§A2.1 Overview[369]

§§A2.1.1 Background

By the end of 2000, a year and a half after the Chinese Communist Party (CCP) launched the suppression of Falun Gong, the campaign had failed to garner support among many of the CCP's rank and file. Party leader Jiang Zemin had toured southern provinces earlier in 2000, hoping to shore up more support for the campaign among local leaders. Meanwhile, public support for the campaign had waned. On January 23, 2001, five individuals allegedly set themselves on fire in Tiananmen Square in Beijing. The entire event was caught on camera from multiple angles. Beginning just hours after the event, state-controlled media was flooded with reports that the self-immolators were Falun Gong practitioners. These reports included grisly footage of the victims, portraying Falun Gong teachings as directly responsible for the tragedy.

§§A2.1.2 The Problem

In the weeks following the event, a wealth of evidence that was uncovered (including a Washington Post article finding that two of the self-immolators never practiced Falun Gong) indicated that the entire incident was staged. While people inside China had no access to this information, Chinese state-run media continued its blitz campaign to portray the "self-immolators" as Falun Gong practitioners. People across China went from respecting and sympathizing with Falun Gong to becoming infuriated with and attacking the practice. Hate crimes targeting Falun Gong practitioners increased, and the CCP escalated its persecution with increased arrests, torture, killing, and forced organ harvesting.

§§A2.1.3 Why It Matters

With 70 to 100 million practicing Falun Gong in China, by 1999 the traditional discipline was largely a household name and a respected one at that. The staged "self-immolation," however, changed everything overnight, and to this day remains the single most influential factor in the Chinese people's hatred and fear of the practice. The resulting apathy and hostility toward Falun Gong in China have greatly facilitated the regime's attempt to eradicate the practice.

§A2.2 Quick Facts

False Fire: China's Tragic New Standard in State Deception, a documentary produced by NTD Television that showed how the self-immolation was staged, won a Certificate of Honorable Mention at the 51st Columbus International Film & Video Festival.

The International Education Development (IED) organization condemned the persecution of Falun Gong practitioners in China and referred to it as "state terrorism." "We have obtained a video of that incident that, in our view, proves that this event was staged by the government. We have copies of that video available for distribution," said a statement from IED to the United Nations on August 14, 2001. Numerous witnesses also testified independently that martial law was enforced on Tiananmen Square that day, which would have prevented Falun Gong practitioners from entering the square.

Based on these pieces of evidence, the United Nations Educational, Scientific and Cultural Organization (UNESCO) also deemed the self-immolation incident a hoax.

§A2.3 Analysis

Below is a selection of facts that reveal how the self-immolation hoax on Tiananmen Square was staged by Chinese authorities for propaganda purposes.[370] These are corroborated by the accounts of at least ten eyewitnesses and six insiders who saw or had advance knowledge of the event.

§§A2.3.1 Victim Liu Chunling Did Not Practice Falun Gong and Died from Blunt Trauma

Running the Chinese Central TV (CCTV) program in slow motion shows that one of the women, Liu Chunling, who in the Xinhua version of events supposedly died from burn injuries, actually received a sharp blow to the forehead with what looks like a metal bar, delivered by a man wearing an army overcoat. She is seen crumpling instantly to the ground and most likely died from that blow. The man in the military coat made no attempt to rescue Liu Chunling.

In the scene where Liu Chunling is beaten to death, her hair was burning. This meant that she could not have been burning for more than a few seconds. However, the police officers started to extinguish the fire from the onset of the flames and would have been able to put out the flames before she was fatally injured.

On February 4, 2001, the Washington Post published a front-page investigative report entitled "Human Fire Ignites Chinese Mystery—Motive for Public Burning Intensifies Fight Over Falun Gong."[371] The article stated that Liu Chunling was not a native of Kaifeng as alleged and that no one had ever seen Liu do the Falun Gong exercises.

§§A2.3.2 Numerous Inconsistencies Surround Wang Jindong

One of the self-immolators, Wang Jindong, supposedly used a green plastic Sprite bottle filled with gasoline to douse himself with the flammable liquid. A plastic bottle filled with gasoline should have been one of the first things to melt in a fire. However, the video footage showed that the bottle was intact between Wang's legs.

According to the official report, the police extinguished the flames in less than a minute. Human hair is highly flammable and will totally burn in just a few seconds. In the video, however, Wang's hair did not burn at all, while his face appeared to be burned to an ashen gray. Despite Xinhua's claims that Wang was covered in flames and smoke, the CCTV footage never shows him on fire or emitting smoke.

The CCTV footage also shows a policeman waiting behind Wang as he sits on Tiananmen Square. Only after Wang shouts some slogans does the policeman cover him with the fire-extinguishing blanket—as if waiting for a signal. If this were truly a life-and-death matter, he would have been covered up immediately.

Finally, while government officials said Wang Jindong was a Falun Gong practitioner and that he was responsible for coordinating the self-immolation, neither the words Wang shouted nor his meditation position were consistent with Falun Gong.

Wang tried to give an explanation in an April 2003 interview with Xinhua: "As I flicked the lighter, instantly the flames engulfed me—I did not have time to sit in the Dapan posture so I sat in the single-leg crossing posture." However, the term "Dapan" is not a part of Falun Gong, and Wang did not sit with one leg crossed in the CCTV video.

Some viewers observed that Wang Jindong sat exactly like a Chinese soldier. According to a reliable source from China, the person in the video was actually a People's Liberation Army officer.

§§A2.3.3 Twelve-Year-Old Girl Sings after Tracheotomy

In a tracheotomy, an incision is made in the trachea and a tube is placed in the throat below the vocal cords so the patient can breathe. The patient cannot breathe through his mouth or nose, and air cannot get to the vocal cords and larynx, so the patient cannot speak. It takes many days for an adult to adjust to this and much longer for a child. If a patient really wants to speak, he has to cover the tube opening, but the voice will be intermittent and unclear.

However, an interview of Liu Siying, the twelve-year-old victim, by Xinhua News Agency depicted the little girl singing and talking to the interviewers loudly and clearly only four days after a tracheotomy. This is medically impossible.

The authorities did not allow any reporters other than those from Xinhua to interview Liu Siying, nor did they allow any of her family members to visit. They threatened her grandmother to such an extent that she was too terrified to be interviewed.

Liu Siying died suddenly on March 17, 2001, when she was ready to be discharged. One of the medical staff who treated Liu Siying said, "Liu Siying died suddenly at a time when her burns were more or less healed. She had basically recovered, and she was ready to be discharged from the hospital. The cause of her death is very suspicious."

§§A2.3.4 Police Had Firefighting Equipment Ready at the Scene

The *Beijing Evening News* reported on February 16, 2001, that "there were three or four police officers putting out the fire on each self-immolator." Altogether, they had about 25 pieces of firefighting equipment.

This story differed significantly from the program broadcast by CCTV, which showed that there were only two police vehicles at the scene. Officers who patrol the square do not normally carry firefighting equipment, and the footage does not show any firefighting equipment on Tiananmen Square itself. The closest building was at least 10 minutes away on foot.

A practitioner in the United States recalled what he saw on the day of the self-immolation:[372]

> *The police forced eight of us college students over to one side of the Monument of Heroes, but we didn't know why. Shortly thereafter we heard an unusual sound less than 10 meters away, and then we saw a ball of fire. The fireball was running.*
>
> *Within a minute a lot of policemen suddenly appeared and put out the fire with fire extinguishers and blankets. Someone was shouting slogans, and for a while the policemen were in a tangle with the burning body. We had no idea what was happening and*

just craned our necks to try to see, but we were driven off a great distance by the police.

One of my classmates said, "Where is that strong gasoline smell coming from?" Another answered, "Certainly it was gasoline that was burning." As we turned back, we saw four people pass by, all drenched with gasoline. No sooner had we grasped what was happening than we heard the sound of the gasoline igniting, and all four people were on fire.

Meanwhile, a large group of police rushed out suddenly from behind the monument, carrying extinguishers, fire blankets, and boards. They quickly began to extinguish the fire and, at the same time, blocked our view with the boards. We were all surprised and exclaimed, 'They've got everything prepared; they were ready for the fire!" "Maybe there will be some coverage on TV tonight," commented a classmate.

The police put out the fires quickly, but we saw no ambulances arriving. Some tourists, including foreigners, took pictures. The police rushed to take their cameras no matter who they were. We could not figure out what was going on and never thought to relate those burning people to Falun Gong.

Another time an honest-looking fellow in my class was stopped by police in the underground passage near Tiananmen Square. They ordered him to read a sentence slandering Falun Gong on a piece of paper they handed him. When he asked why, an officer replied, "If you don't, we will arrest you as a Falun Gong member." He was very scared, so he read it and then ran away.

§§A2.3.5 Falun Gong Prohibits Suicide and Killing

The quote below is from the main text of Falun Dafa, *Zhuan Falun*, published in 1995:

The issue of killing is very sensitive. For practitioners, we have set the strict requirement that they cannot kill lives. Whether it is of the Buddha School, the Tao School, or the Qimen School, regardless of which school or practice it is, as long as it is an upright cultivation practice, it will consider this issue very absolute and prohibit killing—this is for sure. Because the consequence of killing a life is so serious, we must address it in detail. In the original Buddhism, killing mainly referred to taking a human life, which was the most serious act. Later, killing large-sized lives, large domestic animals, or relatively large animals were all considered very serious. Why has the issue of killing been taken so seriously in the community of cultivators? In the past, Buddhism held that lives that were not supposed to die would, if killed, become lonesome spirits and homeless ghosts. Before, rituals were performed to free these people's souls from misery. Without such services, these souls would suffer hunger and thirst, living in a very bitter situation. This is what Buddhism said in the past. (Zhuan Falun, "The Issue of Killing")

The following quote is from one of Master Li Hongzhi's lectures in Sydney in 1996, directly answering a practitioner's question on suicide:

Disciple: My third question is about the issue of killing mentioned in the book. Killing is an enormous sin, so is it considered a sin if a person commits suicide?

Master: It is considered a sin. Today's society is bad and all sorts of strange things have appeared. People advocate for "euthanasia," in which a person receives an injection and dies. Think about it: Why would a person take an injection to die? It's because he thinks that he is in pain. But we think that his pain is eliminating his karma, so when he reincarnates into his next life, his body will be light and free of karma, and he will have great happiness and other things waiting for him. It's of course really uncomfortable when eliminating karma through pain, but when you don't let him eliminate his karma and kill him, isn't that homicide? He leaves [the world] carrying karma, which he will have to pay off in the next life. Which way would you say is the correct one? There is another sin when you commit suicide. Human lives are arranged, and so you will have damaged higher beings' overall, grand scheme of things, which involves your duties to society and the interpersonal relationships you form. If you die, won't it mess up higher beings' arrangements for the overall sequence of things? If you mess up those things, they won't let you off the hook, so suicide is sinful. (Lecture in Sydney, 1996)

Based on these teachings, no genuine Falun Dafa practitioner would consider immolating him or herself. The actors who carried out the staged "self-immolation" were discovered not to be practitioners, and there have been no valid or sound reports of Falun Gong practitioners killing or committing suicide before or after this event.

Appendix 3: 1,400 Alleged Deaths

§A3.1 Overview[373]

§§A3.1.1 Background

Chinese authorities have alleged that "the practice of Falun Gong has led to more than 1,400 deaths" of its followers. Although Falun Gong was widely practiced in China throughout the 1990s, this claim was first made only in July of 1999, after the regime had commenced the persecution of Falun Gong. The claim has been repeated by Party publications and spokespersons ever since.

§§A3.1.2 The Problem

While the burden of proof lies with Chinese authorities, who continue to make this claim, evidence was never furnished. More importantly, no independent investigation was ever allowed. Where individuals have managed to investigate, cases of alleged Falun Gong-induced deaths have been found to be fabricated, with some of the alleged victims never having existed. Nor have such deaths occurred outside of China, where Falun Gong is practiced freely. The claim is also staked on a distortion of Falun Gong's teachings on health and medicine, often depicting the Falun Gong practice as dangerous or unhealthy. However, even on its own terms, the claim fails to hold up to analysis.

§§A3.1.3 Why it Matters

Various misrepresentations of Falun Gong and its members, spawned by Chinese communist officials and publications, seek to discredit the group (portraying it as dangerous, misguided, or nefarious) and undermine support in the free world. Inside China, in particular, propaganda surrounding the "1,400 deaths" has played a central role in fostering disgust and animosity toward Falun Gong among a large segment of the population. Historical parallels from as recently as Nazi Germany suggest that such misrepresentations can have devastating consequences.

§A3.2 Analysis[374]

While there is no accusation by the Chinese Government more haunting than that Falun Gong leads to health problems, mental illness, suicide and death, there is also no claim more deceptive and imaginative. Falun Gong has earned the praise and endorsement of many of Beijing's elite scientists and medical professionals. Several health surveys have found that Falun Gong practice is effective in healing illness over 90% of the time (with a "cure rate" of nearly 60%) and greatly improves mental health and overall quality of life. Falun Gong's enormous popularity has been in large part due to its unprecedented health benefits. In fact, this is what led the Chinese Government to patronize the practice its first four years, before political winds shifted unfavorably.

The alleged "causal" explanation for purported Falun Gong side effects is grounded in one of two fictitious claims. First is the suggestion of some hidden causal link between Falun Gong practice and psychosis or suicidal tendencies. This is a claim for which there is no known medical or legal basis, however, and none has been offered by Chinese officials. Were such a connection to be established, it would quickly grace the covers of medical journals East and West.

Second is the pivotal Chinese government claim that Mr. Li Hongzhi prohibits Falun Gong practitioners from taking medicine, putting them at risk. Examining Mr. Li's teachings reveals that this is an utter fabrication, as he never has prevented—nor could he prevent—practitioners from seeking medical treatment. In banning Falun Gong, the Chinese government is thus "protecting" the Chinese people from something that does not exist.

Were the stakes of the Chinese government's accusations not so high, they might even prove amusing for their fanciful, illogical qualities. Since these claims, however wrong, have found their way into the Western media and been the topic of several English-language Chinese government publications, we offer clarification below.

According to Chinese government sources and state-run media, the official number of deaths attributed to Falun Gong was set at an even 1,400. Despite repeated requests for further information about this statistic, Chinese sources have never been able to say how this number was arrived at.

A Ministry of Public Security spokesperson stated that Falun Gong were to blame for the deaths of these 743 "followers". Even though, in Falun Gong's seven years prior to the persecution, never were any of these alleged 743 or 1,400 cases reported.

§§A3.2.1 The Claim That Falun Gong Induces Psychosis and Suicide

First, consider the claim that Falun Gong "caused" severe mental illness, resulting even in irrational behavior, suicide, and death.

Mental illness is a serious problem facing China today: over 16 million mentally ill patients are distributed throughout all occupations and social groups in Chinese society. The bigger question, however, lies in attributing mental illness to Falun Gong. Can it be expected that none of these 16 million people have decided to practice Falun Gong, regardless of Mr. Li's admonition for mentally ill persons not to?

Given that all Falun Gong materials are available for free viewing or download on the internet, and there is no organization, leadership, or membership, anybody could take up the practice of Falun Gong. However, people with mental illness are unable to live by the principles of Falun Gong and will not experience the health benefits of Falun Gong. Thus, they are bound to suffer the same symptoms and challenges as before.

The Chinese government has also erred in asserting that some of the alleged "1,400 deaths" are Falun Gong-induced suicides. First, it can be said that where there is suicide there is mental disturbance; most likely some form of mental illness, be it common (as in depression) or severe (as in psychosis). Just as there is no known medical basis for asserting that Falun Gong could induce mental illness, there is no evidence that Falun Gong induces suicide.

Nevertheless, the Chinese government has attempted to frame Falun Gong on this matter. On several occasions, letters supposedly by Mr. Li Hongzhi were forged by government offices. These letters have made a variety of nonsensical statements, such as "make sure to come to such-and-such place on this date for the group suicide" or "it is time for us to leave this world." These fake letters have tried to mislead practitioners into suicide–a crime punishable in most nations. Yet on no occasion have any practitioners been reported to have shown up.

§§A3.2.2 Falun Gong's Teachings on Medicine and Medical Treatment

Falun Gong is most accurately called a "cultivation practice" (xiulian), much akin to "self-cultivation" in the West, though it is more generically a form of qigong practice as it includes five gentle qigong exercises. As a cultivation practice, the emphasis in Falun Gong practice is on the improvement of one's xinxing (moral character, or "heart/mind nature"). Cultivation of xinxing is mainly a matter of assimilating to the essential nature of the universe: Truthfulness-Compassion-Forbearance (真善忍). Such assimilation is the goal of cultivation practice, in turn enabling the practitioner to develop his or her wisdom and reach "enlightenment," an aspiration basic to Eastern spiritual practices, such as Taoism, Buddhism, etc.

The goal of Falun Gong is thus not health and fitness, as in conventional qigong practices. Nevertheless, healing often occurs as a byproduct of cultivating xinxing in Falun Gong practice. Hence, many people have been attracted to Falun Gong for its healing abilities.

Mr. Li Hongzhi has made clear on numerous occasions that the goal of Falun Gong practice is not to heal one's ailments. He has been explicit on this matter in both his writings and lectures and refused to admit critically ill patients to his lectures or classes. In the most widely read Falun Gong book, *Zhuan Falun*, Mr. Li states, "I do not talk about healing illness here, and neither will we heal illness here" (p.3). He continues later: "Some people come here just to have illnesses healed. As to seriously ill patients, we do not let them attend the classes since they cannot give up the attachment to having illnesses cured or the idea of being ill... This person is unable to practice cultivation" (p.41).

Similarly, Mr. Li has stated that patients with severe mental illness (psychosis) are forbidden from attending his classes or practicing Falun Gong as they are unable to control themselves. One strict requirement for practicing Falun Gong (and not dissimilar from qigong in general) is that one must have self-control, both mental and physical. There must be mental alertness, and one must be cognizant of where one is and what one is doing at all times. If one cannot meet these requirements, then one cannot conduct oneself according to a practitioner's standard. Mr. Li has been firm: people suffering from psychosis and the like must seek help elsewhere.

A second issue that needs clarification is the relationship between Falun Gong practice and taking medicine. The Chinese government has repeatedly claimed that Mr. Li forbids all Falun Gong practitioners from taking medicine. In the heat of its crackdown on Falun Gong, the Chinese government-run English newspaper *China Daily* ran four articles disparaging Falun Gong and Mr. Li. And for the anti-Falun Gong campaign, forcing "followers" not to take medicine is purportedly the biggest crime. Such reporting completely confuses the issue, however, suggesting cult-like dependency and suspension of personal choice. Never mind that it clearly distorts what Mr. Li has taught and how practitioners have regarded his teachings.

Consider Mr. Li's own words on the issue of taking medicine, as stated in China Falun Gong (the introductory first book). In response to the question, "Do we still need to take medicine while cultivating?" Mr. Li replied, "On this issue, you should think and decide for yourself" (p.138). Also, in a 1997 New York City lecture that has since been read by almost every practitioner, Mr. Li stated, "An everyday person needs to take medicine when he gets sick. But with you being a cultivator, I'm not forbidding you to take medicine either." He also added, "Some people want to damage [Falun Gong], and say things about not taking medicine like, 'We aren't allowed to take medicine once we start practicing this.' Actually, it's not that I don't allow you to take medicine."[375] Nevertheless, the Chinese Government and media have translated such teachings to mean the exact opposite.

Confusion over this matter stems from the fact that so many Falun Gong practitioners choose not to take medicine anymore after beginning cultivation practice. The key term here is "choose." As in every other facet of Falun Gong practice, how one handles one's health is a free choice. Since most Falun Gong practitioners become or are healthy, they choose not to take medicine simply because it is no longer necessary.

§§A3.2.3 How the Chinese Regime Framed Falun Gong

(a) Chinese Authorities Admit Report Was Total Fabrication

Zhang Zhiwen killed her child, then herself, so claimed a Party-controlled newspaper. The article was reprinted by many other news outlets. The only problem is, independent investigators found that Zhang never existed.

Hai Tao, a journalist at *Voice of America* filed this report from Los Angeles: Since the Chinese government started to crack down on Falun Gong in July 1999, all state-run media agencies have started to attack Falun Gong, its founder, and its key members.

On November 28, a special report authored by Li Xingang was published in the newspaper *Xi'an Worker.* The article reported that Zhang Zhiwen, a woman living in the Wei'nan region of Shanxi Province, burned her six-month-old daughter and then committed suicide by setting herself on fire, protesting the government's crackdown on Falun Gong.

This report caused a stir throughout the country and was reprinted by many newspapers in Shenzhen, Harbin, Shanghai, and other places. The Hong Kong Information Center for Human Rights and Democratic Movements investigated and found out that the report was a total fabrication.

The center said, by quoting Chinese officials, that the people, location, time, and the story in that report were all fabricated. An official named Wu of the Weinan Political and Legal Affairs Committee of Shanxi Province testified that there was absolutely no suicide by burning and, moreover, no woman named Zhang Zhiwen existed at all. In addition, many news agencies in China called them for verification and got the same answer.

When Falun Gong practitioners asked the author of the *Xi'an Worker* article why he fabricated the "news," the author's reply was: "I was writing fiction."

(b) Family Denies Mother's Death Caused by Falun Gong

Chinese state-run television widely publicized the death of Ma Jinxiu as one of the "1,400 cases of death due to Falun Gong."

After her husband learned of this reporting, he said, "That's not true. She had diabetes for nearly twenty years and had a stroke twice prior to practicing Falun Gong."[376] Ms. Ma's daughter, Jin Youming, wrote in an article to explain her mother's death:[377]

> *My mom had clearly died from a brain aneurysm. While she was hospitalized, she was carefully attended to and took all the medications and injections her doctors prescribed, but she still died. So why didn't they say that she died as a result of the treatment in the hospital? How could the authorities say that she died from practicing Falun Gong just because she had practiced Falun Gong at one time?*

(c) Suicide Victim's Mother Sets the Record Straight[378]

The mother of a suicide victim tells the truth about her son's death and the coercion faced by her widowed daughter-in-law:

My name is Xia Zurong. My husband and I are both Falun Dafa practitioners. I am the mother of Long Gang, who committed suicide by jumping into a river. His death was reported by Chinese Central Television (CCTV) as one of its "1,400 death cases" falsely attributed to Falun Gong. We live at 70 Shuangqiao Street in Shuangshi Village, the Yongchuan District, Chongqing.

As parents, we would certainly know if our son had a mental problem, and he did, indeed, have a mental problem. At the time he jumped in the river, he was having a psychotic episode, which had nothing to do with Falun Gong. As his parents, we must say what is true. We cannot, against our consciences, watch the government use our son to vilify Dafa.

After our son died, a reporter surnamed Du came to interview my daughter-in-law, asking her to claim that her husband was a Falun Gong practitioner. The reporter wrote on a sheet of paper some words slandering Falun Gong and told her to read them. At that time, my daughter-in-law yielded to their pressure and did what she was told to do. The next day she was given 200 yuan in cash. Those who do evil often use money to buy one's conscience and manipulate one to do evil. My grandson (the child of my dead son) was even taught to slander Dafa. This is how the "news" on TV was fabricated.

ABOUT FALUN DAFA

Falun Dafa, also called Falun Gong, is an ancient and advanced self-cultivation way based on the principles of the universe, Truthfulness-Compassion-Forbearance (真善忍). All the original teachings of Falun Dafa are in the main book *Zhuan Falun*. According to *Zhuan Falun*, the cultivation of one's mind and character is the key to increasing Gong (energy potency).

Falun Dafa also includes cultivation of the body, which is accomplished by practicing the five meditative Dafa exercises and cultivating one's character.

明

Graphs and Photos

May 1992 - July 1999

Falun Gong was first introduced to the
public in China in May 1992.

It quickly spread by word of mouth
because of its principles
(Truthfulness-Compassion-Forbearance)
and outstanding impact on health and fitness.

By July 1999, just seven years later, there
were 100 million people, or just about
one in every ten Chinese,
practicing Falun Gong.

羊城晚报

YANGCHENG WANBAO

1998年11月

10

星期二

农历戊寅年九月廿二

小雪：农历十月初四

今日16版

老少皆练法轮功

8日早上，广东省体委武术协会有关领导到广州烈士陵园等处，观看了5000法轮功爱好者的大型晨练活动。练功者来自各行各业，年龄最大的93岁（左下图），最小的仅两岁（上图）。

据介绍，目前，广东省有近25万人修炼此功法。在练功现场，体委的同志询问了几位法轮功的受益者，他们的修炼故事非常感人。有一位叫林婵英的女士介绍说，她是广州皮革迪威有限公司统计员，原患高位瘫痪，全身70%部位麻木失灵，大小便失禁，修炼了法轮功以后，不久便可以站立，尔后又可以行走。见她现在的样子红光满面，练功的动作灵活自如。

法轮功强调传功不收费，义务教功。

孙璇　晓明　摄影报道

Before July 1999, every day at dawn, many people would go to a park to do the Falun Gong exercises before work or school. The scene was beautiful and serene. Chinese media outlets rarely reported on this phenomenon, however. The above article from a Guangzhou newspaper, titled "People of All Ages Practice Falun Gong," was a rare piece that showed the true situation of Falun Gong.

97.9% Saw Improved Health

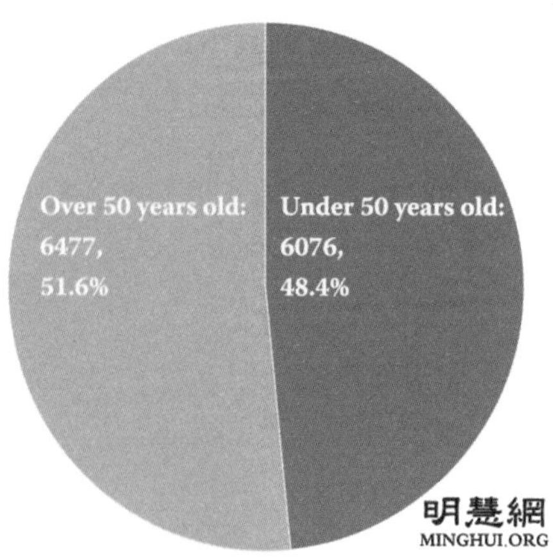

A health survey conducted in 1998 in Beijing, China showed that 97.9% of people who studied *Zhuan Falun*, the main book of Falun Gong, and practiced the five Falun Gong exercises saw their health improve.

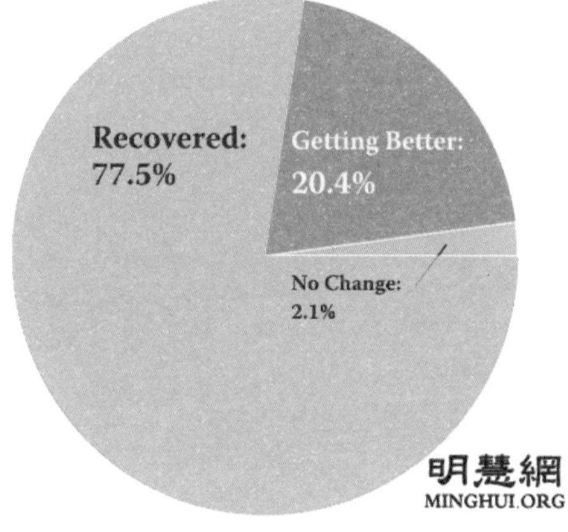

Among the 12,553 practitioners who participated in the survey, 51.6% were over 50 years old, and 48.4% were under 50.

Of the respondents, 10,475 suffered from one or more diseases. After practicing Falun Gong for 2 months to 3 years, 77.5% of those who suffered from diseases had recovered, and 20.4% reported getting better.

Practitioners doing the Falun Gong exercises on Lantau Island, Hong Kong before the persecution began.

Group exercise practice in Guangzhou before the persecution. The banner says "Falun Dafa volunteer instruction site."

People from all walks of life gathered in public parks to do the Falun Gong exercises. The above photo was taken in Chengdu, Sichuan Province in early 1999.

Awards presented to Mr. Li Hongzhi, the founder of Falun Gong, at the 1993 Asian Health Expo held in Beijing.

法 輪 大 法 好

July 1999 - Today

Note: The data in this section include only cases that Minghui.org has managed to report during the ongoing persecution in China.

Due to the CCP's censorship and persecution of Falun Gong, such reporting carries great difficulties and risks. Therefore, these figures likely reflect only a small subset of all cases that have occurred, and many more have yet to be compiled and reported by our teams.

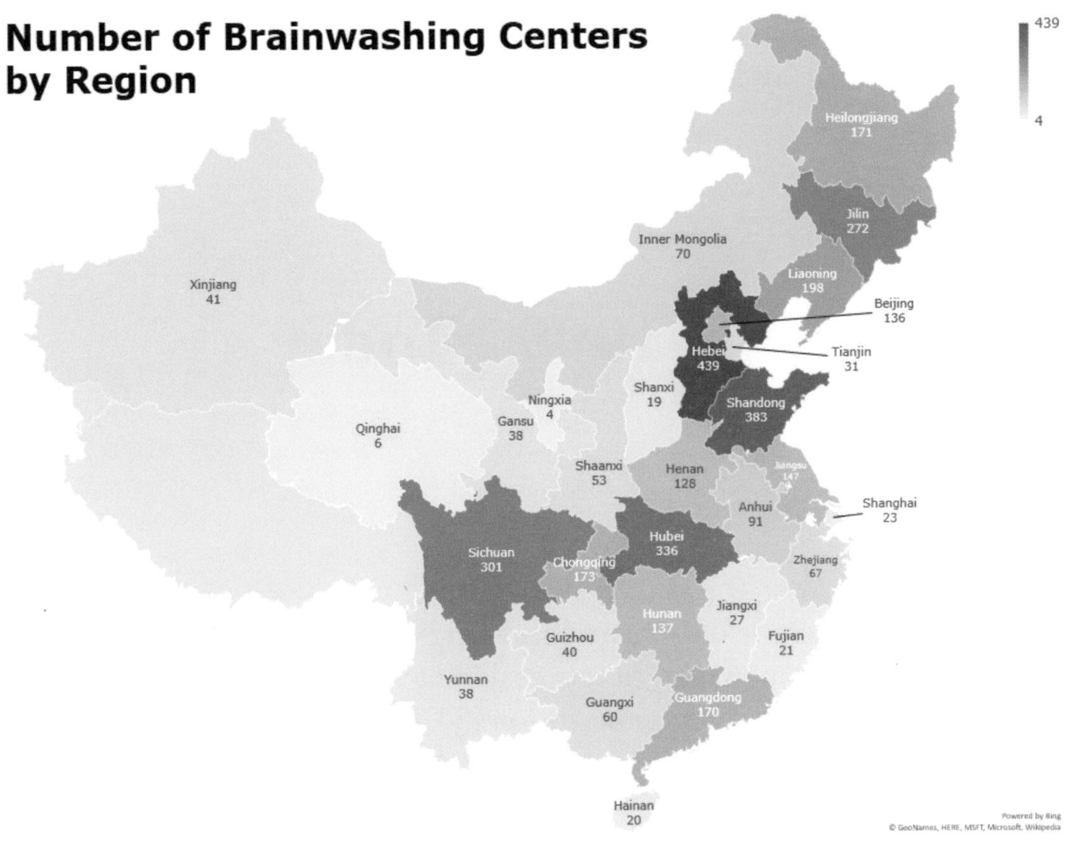
Number of Brainwashing Centers by Region
439
4
Heilongjiang 171
Jilin 272
Inner Mongolia 70
Liaoning 198
Xinjiang 41
Beijing 136
Tianjin 31
Hebei 439
Shanxi 19
Ningxia 4
Shandong 383
Qinghai 6
Gansu 38
Shaanxi 53
Henan 128
Jiangsu 147
Anhui 91
Shanghai 23
Hubei 336
Sichuan 301
Chongqing 173
Zhejiang 67
Hunan 137
Jiangxi 27
Guizhou 40
Fujian 21
Yunnan 38
Guangxi 60
Guangdong 170
Hainan 20
Powered by Bing
© GeoNames, HERE, MSFT, Microsoft, Wikipedia

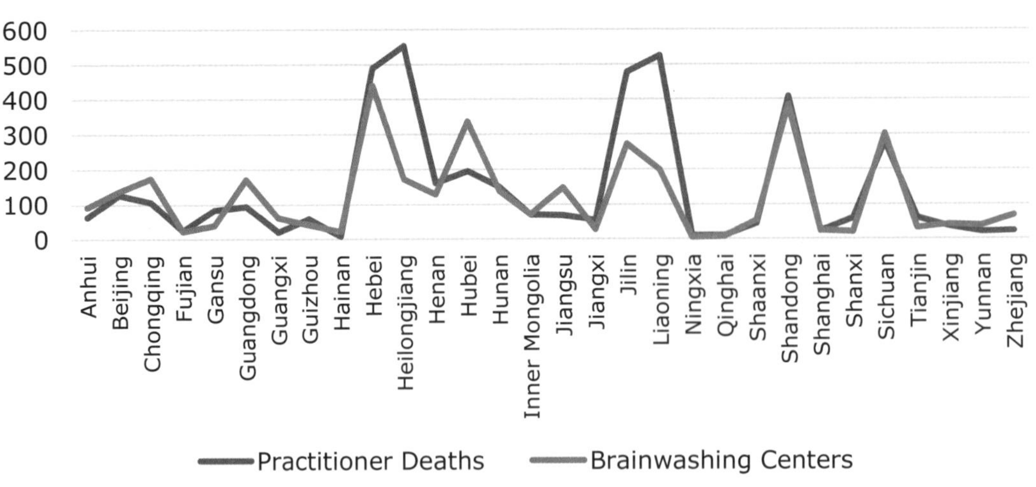
Brainwashing Centers vs. Practitioner Deaths by Region
600
500
400
300
200
100
0
Anhui
Beijing
Chongqing
Fujian
Gansu
Guangdong
Guangxi
Guizhou
Hainan
Hebei
Heilongjiang
Henan
Hubei
Hunan
Inner Mongolia
Jiangsu
Jiangxi
Jilin
Liaoning
Ningxia
Qinghai
Shaanxi
Shandong
Shanghai
Shanxi
Sichuan
Tianjin
Xinjiang
Yunnan
Zhejiang
Practitioner Deaths
Brainwashing Centers

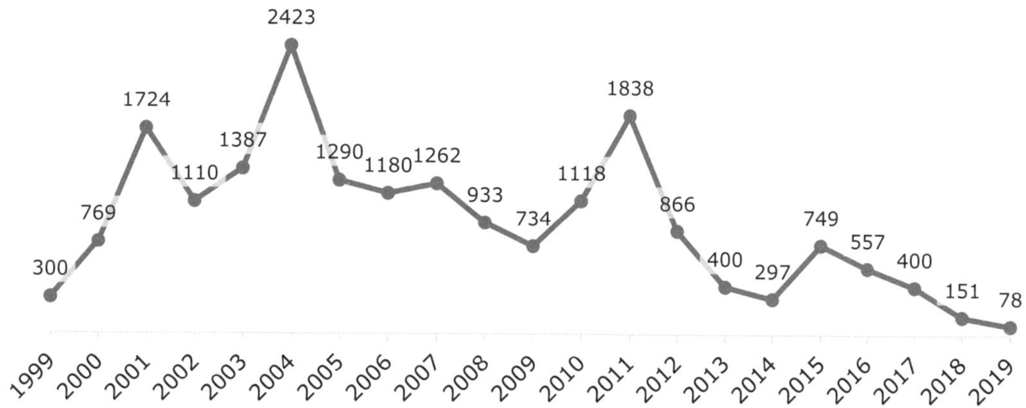
Number of Falun Gong Practitioners Taken to Brainwashing Centers by Year
Documented cases from July 1999 to July 2019
300
769
1724
1110
1387
2423
1290
1180
1262
933
734
1118
1838
866
400
297
749
557
400
151
78
1999
2000
2001
2002
2003
2004
2005
2006
2007
2008
2009
2010
2011
2012
2013
2014
2015
2016
2017
2018
2019

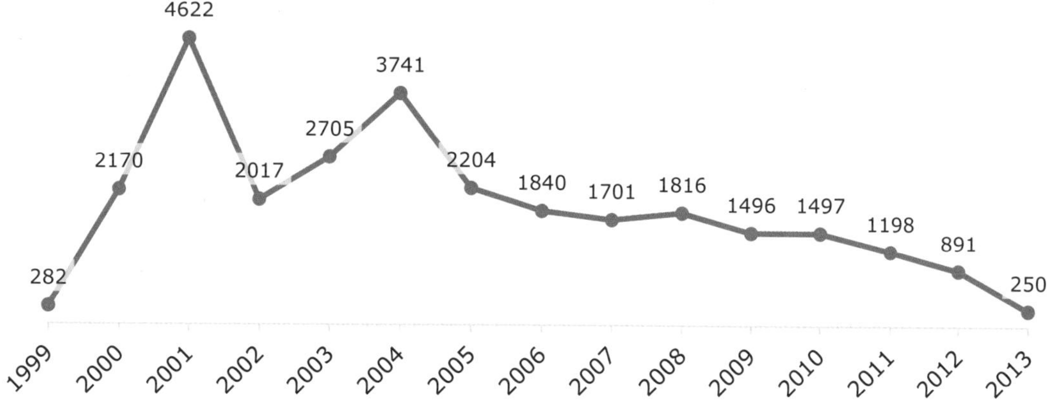
Number of Falun Gong Practitioners Taken to Forced Labor Camps by Year
Documented cases from 1999 to 2013
Note: Labor camps were officially abolished in 2013.
282
2170
4622
2017
2705
3741
2204
1840
1701
1816
1496
1497
1198
891
250
1999
2000
2001
2002
2003
2004
2005
2006
2007
2008
2009
2010
2011
2012
2013

Number of Falun Gong Practitioners Sentenced by Region

Documented cases from July 1999 to July 2019

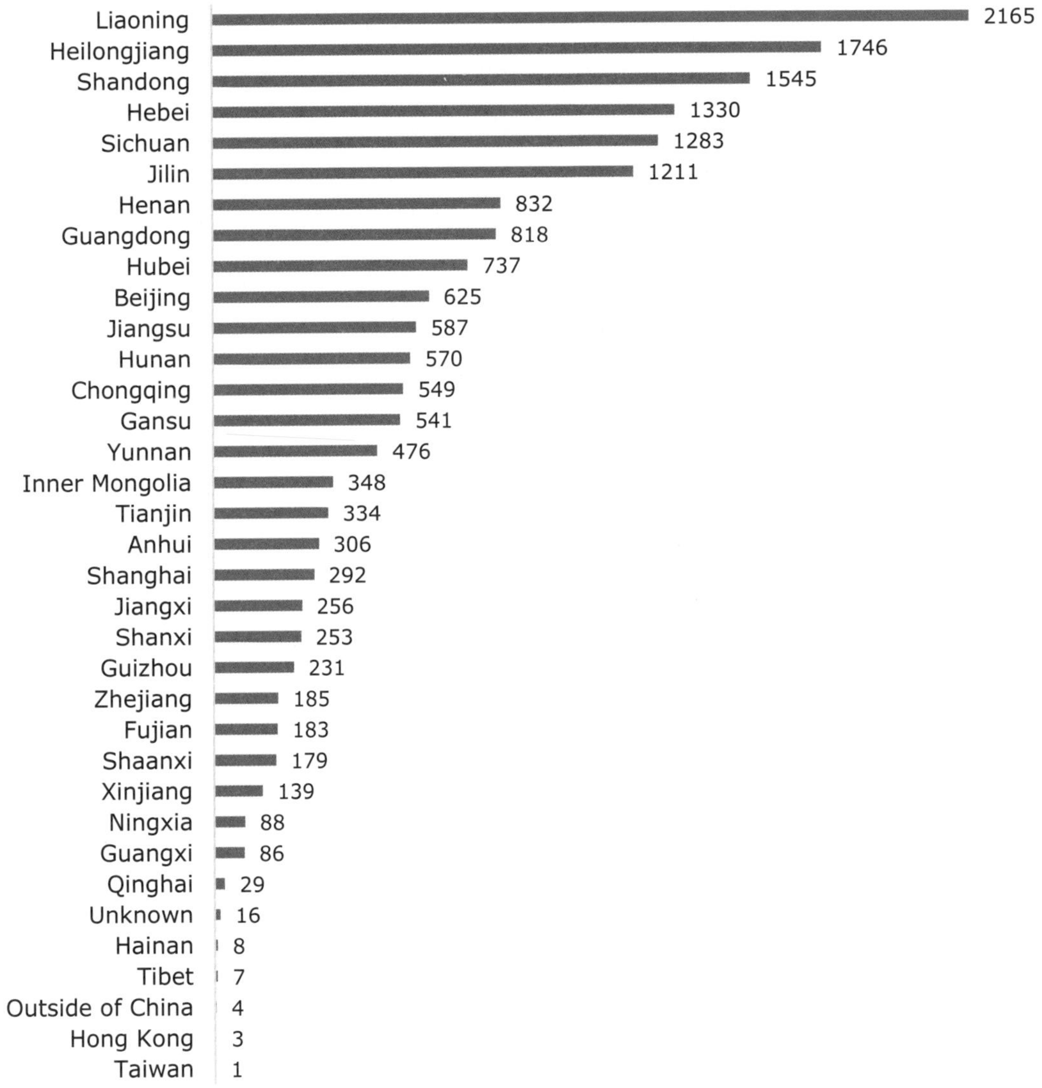

Region	Number
Liaoning	2165
Heilongjiang	1746
Shandong	1545
Hebei	1330
Sichuan	1283
Jilin	1211
Henan	832
Guangdong	818
Hubei	737
Beijing	625
Jiangsu	587
Hunan	570
Chongqing	549
Gansu	541
Yunnan	476
Inner Mongolia	348
Tianjin	334
Anhui	306
Shanghai	292
Jiangxi	256
Shanxi	253
Guizhou	231
Zhejiang	185
Fujian	183
Shaanxi	179
Xinjiang	139
Ningxia	88
Guangxi	86
Qinghai	29
Unknown	16
Hainan	8
Tibet	7
Outside of China	4
Hong Kong	3
Taiwan	1

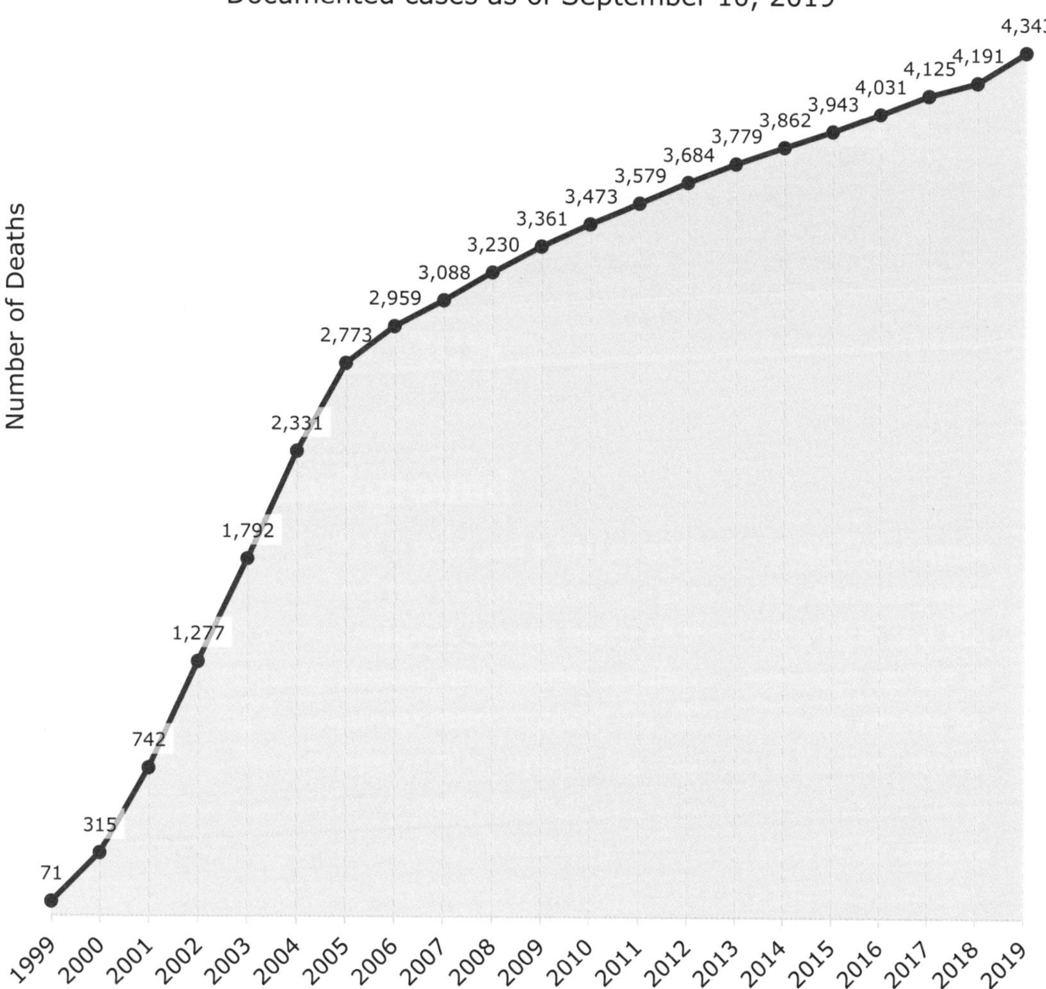
Cumulative Total of Falun Gong Practitioners Persecuted to Death
Documented cases as of September 10, 2019
Number of Deaths
71
315
742
1,277
1,792
2,331
2,773
2,959
3,088
3,230
3,361
3,473
3,579
3,684
3,779
3,862
3,943
4,031
4,125
4,191
4,343
1999
2000
2001
2002
2003
2004
2005
2006
2007
2008
2009
2010
2011
2012
2013
2014
2015
2016
2017
2018
2019

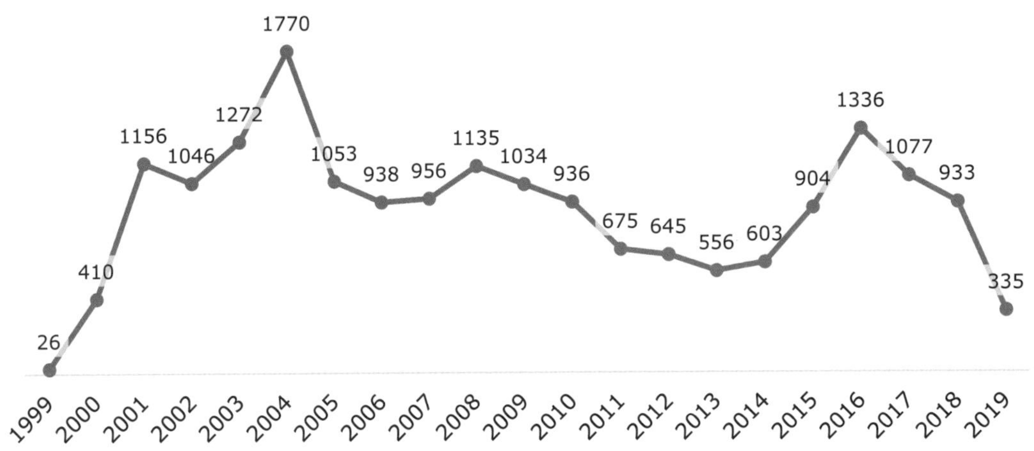
Number of Falun Gong Practitioners
Sentenced by Year
Documented cases from July 1999 to July 2019
26
410
1156
1046
1272
1770
1053
938
956
1135
1034
936
675
645
556
603
904
1336
1077
933
335
1999
2000
2001
2002
2003
2004
2005
2006
2007
2008
2009
2010
2011
2012
2013
2014
2015
2016
2017
2018
2019

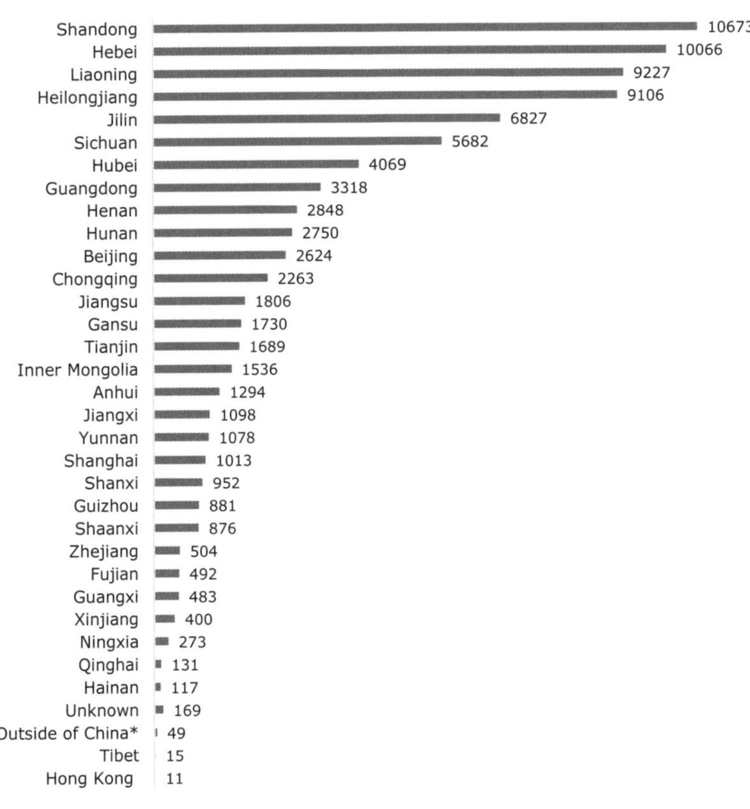
Number of Falun Gong Practitioners
Arrested by Region
Documented cases from July 1999 to July 2019
Shandong 10673
Hebei 10066
Liaoning 9227
Heilongjiang 9106
Jilin 6827
Sichuan 5682
Hubei 4069
Guangdong 3318
Henan 2848
Hunan 2750
Beijing 2624
Chongqing 2263
Jiangsu 1806
Gansu 1730
Tianjin 1689
Inner Mongolia 1536
Anhui 1294
Jiangxi 1098
Yunnan 1078
Shanghai 1013
Shanxi 952
Guizhou 881
Shaanxi 876
Zhejiang 504
Fujian 492
Guangxi 483
Xinjiang 400
Ningxia 273
Qinghai 131
Hainan 117
Unknown 169
Outside of China* 49
Tibet 15
Hong Kong 11

明

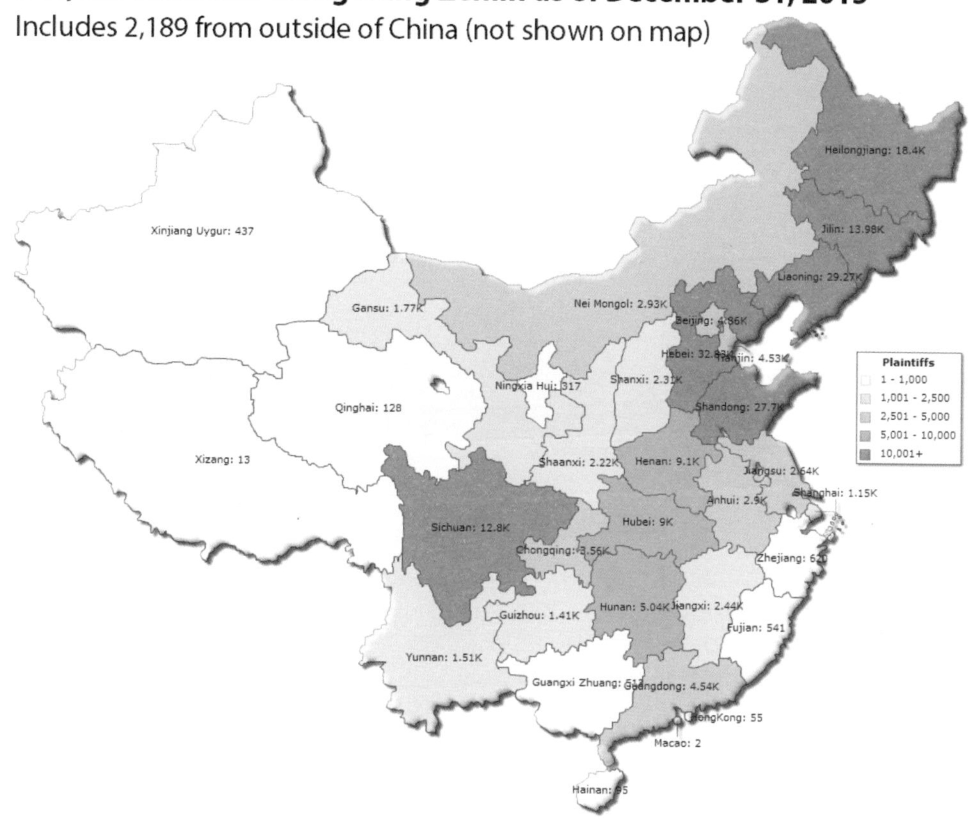

Criminal Complaints Against Jiang Zemin

Cumulative, through December 31, 2015

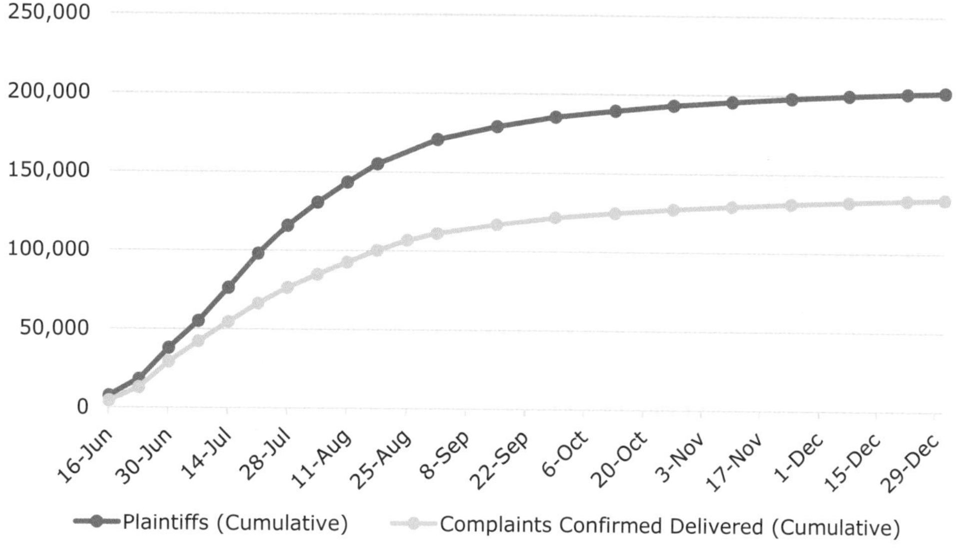

MINGHUI.ORG

After Falun Gong practitioners were beaten and arrested in Tianjin, practitioners lined up outside the national appeals office next to the central government compound in Beijing. They stood on the sidewalk quietly, reading books and waiting for officials to receive them. This peaceful appeal on April 25, 1999 was later mischaracterized by the CCP to justify the persecution of Falun Gong. (See Appendix 1 for details.)

Labor camps were the most convenient facilities in the CCP's persecution of Chinese people and the most reported on Minghui.org. In 2013, Falun Gong practitioners' global efforts brought the labor camp system to an end.

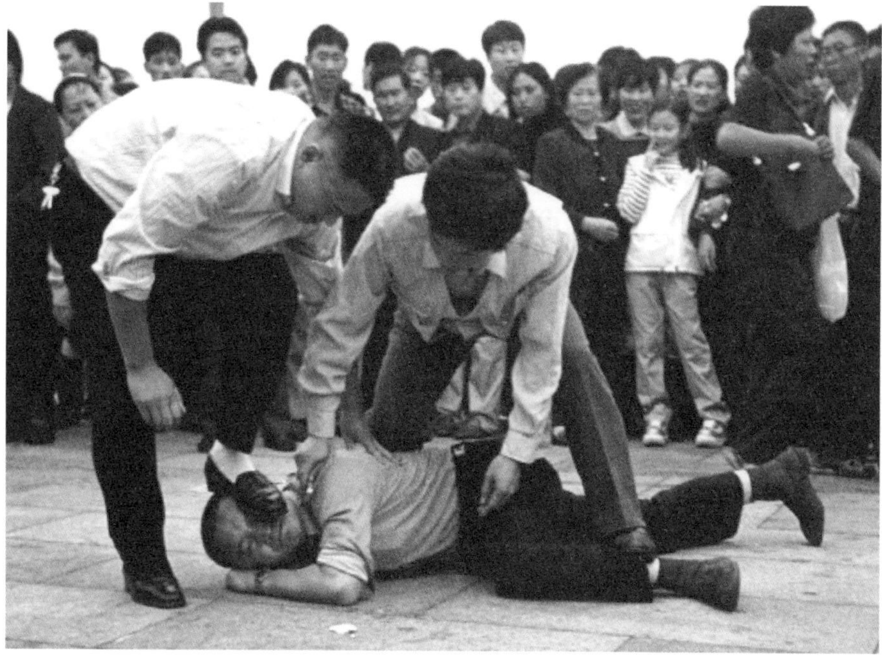

Plainclothes police arrest a practitioner on Tiananmen Square in Beijing. Background: In July 1999, Chinese government appeals offices started arresting Falun Gong petitioners instead of listening to their cases. Left with no place to go, many practitioners went to public sites to tell others how Falun Gong benefited their lives and to expose the brutality of the persecution.

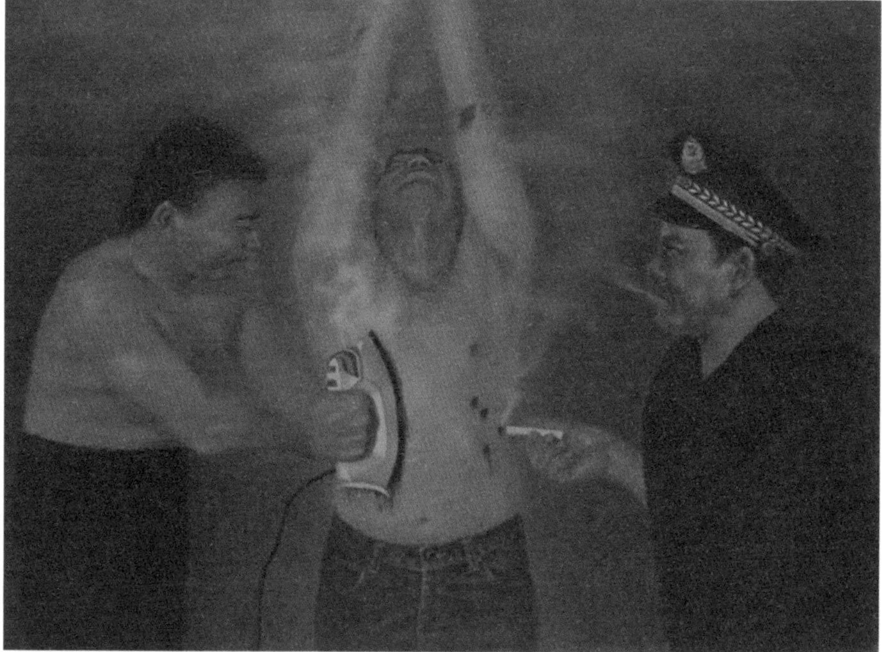

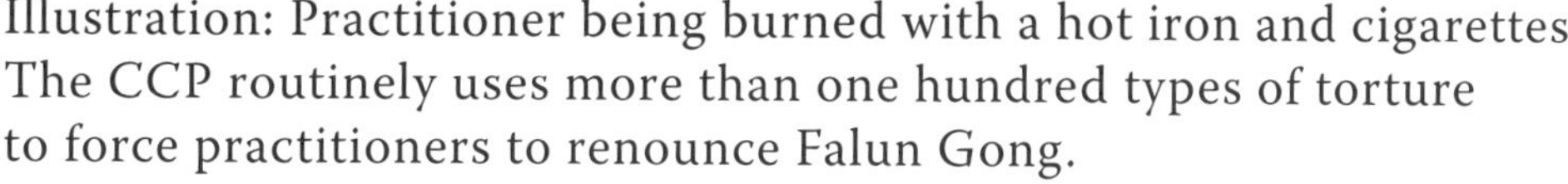

Illustration: Practitioner being burned with a hot iron and cigarettes. The CCP routinely uses more than one hundred types of torture to force practitioners to renounce Falun Gong.

MINGHUI.ORG

Ms. Gao Rongrong, an accountant from Shenyang, Liaoning Province, was disfigured from seven hours of electric shock torture by policemen. Her face was covered with blisters, and her hair was matted with pus and blood. She could only open her eyes a crack because of her swollen face, and her mouth was severely swollen and deformed. The purpose of the police abuse was to force her to denounce Falun Gong. Ms. Gao was killed at the age of 37.

Ms. Gao's two sisters, who also practice Falun Gong, filed a legal complaint against Jiang Zemin—the CCP leader who initiated the persecution—in China in 2015.

Mr. Wang Chan, 39, worked at the headquarters of the People's Bank of China and was highly regarded by his friends and colleagues.

After the persecution began, he wrote a letter urging Jiang Zemin to stop the persecution. With Jiang's personal approval, Beijing police detained Wang for three months at the end of 1999 without giving a reason.

Mr. Wang lost his job. Over the next three years, he traveled to more than ten provinces and established communication channels between practitioners in those areas and Minghui.org, allowing people inside and outside of China to receive real-time updates of the persecution. The Chinese authorities offered a 100,000-yuan reward for his capture.

Mr. Wang Chan was arrested and tortured to death in August 2002.

Ms. Chen Zixiu, a retired factory worker and widow from Weifang City, Shandong Province, was detained in a brainwashing center over the Chinese New Year and beaten to death on February 21, 2000, at the age of 58.

The day before Ms. Chen was tortured to death, she still refused to renounce Falun Gong. Instead, she maintained that practicing Falun Gong was her right.

Her two children tried to seek justice for her, but no lawyer would take on their case.

On April 23, 2000, Ms. Chen's daughter, Ms. Zhang Xueling, 32, accepted an interview with Ian Johnson, a reporter for the *Wall Street Journal*. Ms. Zhang was arrested for "leaking state secrets" and later taken to a forced labor camp for three years .

Ms. Chen Shulan (back row, second from right) lost both of her parents, two brothers, and a younger sister to the persecution. As the sole survivor, Ms. Chen was sentenced twice to a total of eleven and a half years in prison, where torture left her with debilitating injuries.

Practitioners hold banners reading "Truthfulness, Compassion, Forbearance," the core principles of Falun Gong. This form of peaceful protest was a common sight on Tiananmen Square in Beijing after the persecution began in 1999.

In November 2001, while Falun Gong practitioners in over 80 countries were trying to help practitioners inside China to get the word out and to stop the persecution, 36 Western practitioners gathered on Tiananmen Square to tell people that "Falun Dafa is good."

Ms. Yin Liping testifies at a U.S. Congressional hearing on April 14, 2016 as a survivor of the notorious Masanjia Labor Camp in China, where guards allowed male inmates to gang-rape 18 female Falun Gong practitioners, which led to deaths, disability, and mental trauma of the victims.

Falun Gong practitioner Ms. Zhang Yuhua talks to U.S. President Donald Trump on July 17, 2019. Ms. Zhang was one of 27 survivors of religious persecution who were in Washington, D.C. to attend the Second Ministerial to Advance Religious Freedom hosted by the U.S. Department of State.

An unknown person wrote "I agree" in black on a sticker in Qingdao, Shandong Province, that says "All of China [Should] Sue Jiang Zemin." (Photo taken in 2017)

A customer at a farmers' market in Jiamusi, Heilongjiang Province, receives a Minghui calendar. Practitioners in China often give out pamphlets and keepsakes to tell people about the persecution happening around them and clear up the misinformation about Falun Gong propagated by state-controlled media. (Photo taken in 2015)

Examples of Minghui periodicals available online for download, printing, and distribution in almost all the cities in China and elsewhere, including the U.S., Hong Kong, and South Korea.

Falun Gong practitioners brave the winter cold outside the Chinese Consulate in Irkutsk, Russia. Practitioners all over the world have established a presence outside Chinese embassies and consulates to raise awareness of the persecution. (Photo taken in 2016)

Chinese tourists at the Liberty Bell Center in Philadelphia in the U.S. read about the persecution of Falun Gong in China. (Photo taken in 2013)

Practitioners hold a rally in front of the United Nations headquarters in New York on December 10, 2014, Human Rights Day.

People wait in line to sign a petition condemning the CCP's killing of Falun Gong practitioners for organs. Photo taken in Madrid, Spain on October 4, 2014.

Thousands of Falun Gong practitioners gathered for a rally on the 20th anniversary of the Chinese regime's persecution of the spiritual practice in Washington, D.C. on July 18, 2019.

Practitioners in Berlin, Germany hold a march and rally at Pariser Platz in front of the Brandenburg Gate on August 10, 2019.

Greeting cards for the Mid-Autumn Festival sent to Master Li Hongzhi by Falun Gong practitioners in China in September 2019. Each year, Minghui.org receives tens of thousands of greetings to Master Li from Falun Gong practitioners and supporters all over the world on traditional Chinese holidays and May 13, World Falun Dafa Day.

Eighteen of the 36 Swiss lawmakers who signed a joint letter in 2016 to urge the UN High Commissioner for Human Rights to help bring former CCP leader Jiang Zemin to justice for the persecution of Falun Gong.

People practice the Falun Dafa exercises at Union Square in Manhattan on May 13, 2014, celebrating the 15th World Falun Dafa Day.

New practitioners learn the fifth Falun Gong exercise, the sitting meditation, at Tianti Bookstore in Seoul, South Korea in February 2019.

Students at a Tibetan school in India learn the Falun Gong exercises. (Photo taken in 2018)

Participants of an inter-religious activity in Argentina learn the Falun Gong meditation practice on March 3, 2019.

Tianti Bookstore, established in 2007.

Falun Dafa, also known as Falun Gong, consists of the main book *Zhuan Falun* and five meditative exercises. Falun Gong books, the nine-lecture video series, and exercise instruction video have been translated into more than 40 languages. As a non-profit organization, Tianti Books provides tuition-free classes for new students. (Class schedules can be found on Tiantibooks.org.)

ZHUAN FALUN AND THE FIVE EXERCISES OF FALUN DAFA

1

2

3

4

5

明

References

明

References

世界需要真善忍

1 Adapted from https://en.minghui.org/html/articles/2019/3/28/176300.html
2 https://en.minghui.org/html/articles/2019/3/31/176335.html
3 https://en.minghui.org/html/articles/2004/3/25/46394.html
4 https://minghui.org/mh/articles/2004/2/8/66823.html
5 https://en.minghui.org/emh/articles/2004/2/20/45228.html
6 https://en.minghui.org/html/articles/2004/3/26/46395.html
7 https://en.minghui.org/html/articles/2004/4/8/46851.html
8 https://en.minghui.org/html/articles/2014/7/18/2093.html
9 https://en.minghui.org/html/articles/2014/5/7/508.html
10 https://en.minghui.org/html/articles/2014/4/19/254.html
11 https://minghui.org/mh/articles/2014/6/17/293593.html
12 https://en.minghui.org/html/articles/2014/8/2/2351.html
13 https://en.minghui.org/html/articles/2014/5/7/508.html
14 https://en.minghui.org/html/articles/2014/7/1/1861.html
15 https://en.minghui.org/html/articles/2014/6/29/1842.html
16 https://en.minghui.org/html/articles/2014/2/23/145575.html
17 https://www.uscirf.gov/reports-briefs/annual-report/2014-annual-report
18 https://en.minghui.org/html/articles/2015/1/11/147930.html
19 https://en.minghui.org/html/articles/2019/3/23/176241.html
20 https://en.minghui.org/html/articles/2015/3/5/149208.html
21 https://en.minghui.org/html/articles/2000/2/9/8618.html
22 https://en.minghui.org/html/articles/2019/6/9/177990.html
23 https://en.minghui.org/html/articles/2019/3/20/176213.html
24 https://en.minghui.org/html/articles/2018/4/20/169425.html
25 https://en.minghui.org/html/articles/2019/1/31/174829.html
26 https://en.minghui.org/html/articles/2016/3/15/155917.html
27 https://en.minghui.org/html/articles/2018/2/8/167860.html
28 https://en.minghui.org/html/articles/2013/3/18/138548.html
29 https://en.minghui.org/html/articles/2013/3/29/138663.html
30 https://en.minghui.org/html/articles/2017/3/28/162647.html
31 https://en.minghui.org/html/articles/2017/11/20/166463.html
32 https://en.minghui.org/html/articles/2019/5/1/176691.html
33 https://en.minghui.org/html/articles/2019/3/24/176259.html
34 https://en.minghui.org/html/articles/2019/7/9/178379.html
35 http://en.minghui.org/emh/articles/2008/4/14/96420.html
36 http://minghui.org/mh/articles/2008/11/17/189850.html
37 https://en.minghui.org/html/articles/2017/11/5/166297.html

38 http://en.minghui.org/html/articles/2010/5/3/116637.html
39 http://en.minghui.org/html/articles/2019/7/30/178656.html
40 https://minghui.org/mh/articles/2008/1/2/169469.html
41 https://minghui.org/mh/articles/2010/4/6/221088.html
42 https://en.minghui.org/html/articles/2010/11/19/121502.html
43 https://minghui.org/mh/articles/2015/6/14/310859.html
44 https://minghui.org/mh/articles/2016/9/8/334057.html
45 https://en.minghui.org/emh/articles/2008/4/20/96583.html
46 https://minghui.org/mh/articles/2015/10/28/318256.html
47 https://en.minghui.org/html/articles/2015/3/11/149289.html
48 http://en.minghui.org/html/articles/2013/9/26/142412.html
49 http://minghui.org/mh/articles/2016/2/19/324307.html
50 https://en.minghui.org/html/articles/2009/8/26/110323.html
51 https://en.minghui.org/html/articles/2009/10/14/111530.html
52 https://en.minghui.org/emh/articles/2008/8/20/99992.html
53 https://en.minghui.org/html/articles/2019/4/27/176642.html
54 http://en.minghui.org/html/articles/2019/1/28/174791.html
55 http://en.minghui.org/html/articles/2016/10/6/159429.html
56 https://en.minghui.org/html/articles/2016/7/19/157878.html
57 http://en.minghui.org/html/articles/2019/5/15/177495.html
58 http://minghui.org/mh/articles/2008/10/16/187820.html
59 http://minghui.org/mh/articles/2007/10/19/164829.html
60 https://en.minghui.org/emh/articles/2007/4/11/84453.html
61 http://en.minghui.org/html/articles/2019/4/15/176496.html
62 http://en.minghui.org/html/articles/2016/2/21/155645.html
63 http://minghui.org/mh/articles/2012/4/20/255917.html
64 http://minghui.org/mh/articles/2008/9/26/186587.html
65 http://en.minghui.org/emh/articles/2008/8/18/99929.html
66 http://en.minghui.org/html/articles/2017/12/25/166871.html
67 http://en.minghui.org/emh/articles/2007/2/17/82759.html
68 https://minghui.org/mh/articles/2019/4/10/384948.html
69 https://minghui.org/mh/articles/2010/3/24/220327.html
70 https://en.minghui.org/emh/articles/2007/6/5/86470.html
71 https://minghui.org/mh/articles/2018/4/27/364489.html
72 https://en.minghui.org/html/articles/2018/12/3/173492.html
73 https://en.minghui.org/html/articles/2017/1/23/161232.html
74 https://minghui.org/mh/articles/2001/3/25/9322.html
75 http://en.minghui.org/html/articles/2004/2/25/45469.html
76 https://en.minghui.org/emh/articles/2001/5/8/9360.html
77 https://minghui.org/mh/articles/2001/3/4/8702.html
78 https://en.minghui.org/emh/articles/2001/3/9/5796.html
79 https://en.minghui.org/emh/articles/2001/3/9/5796.html
80 https://www.upholdjustice.org/node/85
81 https://en.minghui.org/emh/articles/2005/2/22/57795.html
82 https://en.minghui.org/emh/articles/2004/12/8/55371.html
83 https://en.minghui.org/emh/articles/2005/2/18/57663.html
84 https://en.minghui.org/emh/articles/2004/5/1/47604.html
85 https://en.minghui.org/html/articles/2013/9/24/142375.html
86 https://en.minghui.org/html/articles/2013/9/24/142375.html

87 https://en.minghui.org/emh/articles/2005/4/20/59888.html
88 https://en.minghui.org/emh/articles/2006/1/5/68687.html
89 https://minghui.org/mh/articles/2013/11/13/282322.html
90 https://en.minghui.org/emh/articles/2005/1/17/56650.html
91 https://en.minghui.org/html/articles/2010/2/26/114956.html
92 https://en.minghui.org/emh/articles/2008/7/11/98881.html
93 https://en.minghui.org/emh/articles/2007/2/20/82864.html
94 https://en.minghui.org/emh/articles/2006/11/13/79873.html
95 https://en.minghui.org/emh/articles/2005/2/15/57578.html
96 https://minghui.org/mh/articles/2018/1/12/359542.html
97 https://en.minghui.org/html/articles/2014/10/14/146373.html
98 https://en.minghui.org/html/articles/2018/10/31/173068.html
99 https://en.minghui.org/html/articles/2009/10/23/111780.html
100 https://en.minghui.org/emh/articles/2004/6/7/48974.html
101 https://en.minghui.org/html/articles/2010/6/29/118230.html
102 https://en.minghui.org/emh/articles/2008/9/4/100378.html
103 https://en.minghui.org/emh/articles/2004/3/22/46293.html
104 https://en.minghui.org/emh/articles/2006/11/11/79828.html
105 https://en.minghui.org/html/articles/2015/10/24/153371.html
106 https://minghui.org/mh/articles/2006/10/12/139955.html
107 https://en.minghui.org/html/articles/2019/6/5/177928.html
108 https://en.minghui.org/html/articles/2014/8/23/2640.html
109 https://en.minghui.org/emh/articles/2006/8/4/76337.html
110 https://en.minghui.org/html/articles/2013/12/21/143754.html
111 https://en.minghui.org/emh/articles/2004/11/14/54530.html
112 https://minghui.org/mh/articles/2013/2/3/268659.html
113 https://en.minghui.org/html/articles/2018/9/2/171743.html
114 https://en.minghui.org/html/articles/2006/5/8/73004.html
115 https://en.minghui.org/html/articles/2014/9/7/2884.html
116 https://en.minghui.org/html/articles/2017/10/19/166100.html
117 https://en.minghui.org/html/articles/2004/2/24/45435.html
118 https://en.minghui.org/html/articles/2014/9/28/3472.html
119 https://en.minghui.org/html/articles/2014/9/28/3472.html
120 https://en.minghui.org/html/articles/2013/7/21/141160.html
121 https://en.minghui.org/html/articles/2017/10/19/166100.html
122 https://en.minghui.org/html/articles/2015/8/15/152075.html
123 https://en.minghui.org/html/articles/2018/8/25/171639.html
124 https://en.minghui.org/html/articles/2013/8/20/141621.html
125 https://en.minghui.org/html/articles/2015/9/13/152517.html
126 https://en.minghui.org/html/articles/2019/5/28/177816.html
127 https://en.minghui.org/html/articles/2019/6/16/178099.html
128 https://en.minghui.org/html/articles/2013/11/9/143091.html
129 https://en.minghui.org/html/articles/2014/10/24/146541.html
130 https://en.minghui.org/html/articles/2015/2/1/148189.html
131 https://en.minghui.org/html/articles/2012/4/13/132684.html
132 https://en.minghui.org/html/articles/2015/2/1/148189.html
133 https://en.minghui.org/html/articles/2015/1/10/147911.html
134 https://en.minghui.org/html/articles/2014/11/20/146957.html
135 https://en.minghui.org/html/articles/2019/2/16/175846.html

136 https://en.minghui.org/html/articles/2015/11/19/153730.html
137 https://en.minghui.org/html/articles/2015/11/19/153730.html
138 https://en.minghui.org/html/articles/2015/3/2/149160.html
139 https://en.minghui.org/html/articles/2005/1/19/56709.html
140 https://en.minghui.org/html/articles/2018/7/19/171167.html
141 https://en.minghui.org/html/articles/2010/11/3/121221.html
142 https://en.minghui.org/emh/articles/2008/5/20/zip.html
143 https://en.minghui.org/html/articles/2019/4/13/176478.html
144 https://en.minghui.org/html/articles/2011/8/24/127648.html
145 https://en.minghui.org/html/articles/2004/7/12/50141.html
146 https://en.minghui.org/html/articles/2019/4/11/176455.html
147 https://minghui.org/mh/articles/2017/7/16/351165.html
148 https://en.minghui.org/html/articles/2019/3/19/176195.html
149 https://en.minghui.org/html/articles/2014/8/27/2704.html
150 https://en.minghui.org/html/articles/2003/1/17/31007.html
151 https://en.minghui.org/html/articles/2018/11/20/173324.html
152 https://en.minghui.org/html/articles/2007/11/17/91408.html
153 https://en.minghui.org/html/articles/2013/3/12/138485.html
154 http://en.minghui.org/html/articles/2011/8/24/127648.html
155 https://en.minghui.org/html/articles/2011/8/24/127648.html
156 https://en.minghui.org/html/articles/2015/2/6/148251.html
157 https://en.minghui.org/html/articles/2015/4/20/149807.html
158 https://en.minghui.org/html/articles/2013/3/12/138485.html
159 https://en.minghui.org/html/articles/2018/8/28/171674.html
160 https://en.minghui.org/html/articles/2014/9/7/2884.html
161 https://en.minghui.org/html/articles/2014/9/7/2884.html
162 https://en.minghui.org/html/articles/2019/5/30/177841.html
163 https://en.minghui.org/html/articles/2019/7/16/178460.html
164 https://en.minghui.org/html/articles/2019/6/10/178007.html
165 https://en.minghui.org/html/articles/2019/4/13/176482.html
166 https://en.minghui.org/html/articles/2018/10/14/172851.html
167 https://en.minghui.org/html/articles/2014/7/12/2002.html
168 https://en.minghui.org/html/articles/2016/11/20/160016.html
169 https://en.minghui.org/html/articles/2017/8/1/164866.html
170 https://en.minghui.org/html/articles/2012/5/20/133491.html
171 https://en.minghui.org/html/articles/2018/9/22/172022.html
172 https://en.minghui.org/html/articles/2010/8/14/119242.html
173 https://en.minghui.org/emh/articles/2007/5/1/85127.html
174 https://en.minghui.org/html/articles/2019/6/3/177907.html
175 https://en.minghui.org/html/articles/2016/5/26/157169.html
176 https://en.minghui.org/html/articles/2017/2/23/162277.html
177 https://en.minghui.org/html/articles/2014/11/14/146856.html
178 https://en.minghui.org/html/articles/2018/1/6/167496.html
179 https://minghui.org/mh/articles/2018/1/9/359438.html
180 https://en.minghui.org/emh/articles/2006/12/24/81128.html
181 https://minghui.org/mh/articles/2018/4/4/363722.html
182 https://en.minghui.org/html/articles/2018/11/27/173410.html
183 https://en.minghui.org/emh/articles/2009/4/14/106511.html
184 https://en.minghui.org/html/articles/2019/6/4/177915.html

185 https://minghui.org/mh/articles/2017/4/6/345234.html
186 https://minghui.org/mh/articles/2015/6/23/311257.html
187 https://en.minghui.org/html/articles/2015/6/11/151012.html
188 https://minghui.org/mh/articles/2015/10/3/316996.html
189 https://en.minghui.org/emh/articles/2004/12/3/55202.html
190 https://en.minghui.org/emh/articles/2007/6/4/86417.html
191 https://en.minghui.org/html/articles/2018/1/3/167465.html
192 https://en.minghui.org/html/articles/2017/11/11/166356.html
193 https://en.minghui.org/html/articles/2018/12/17/173660.html
194 https://minghui.org/mh/articles/2017/7/1/350360.html
195 https://en.minghui.org/html/articles/2014/5/2/428.html
196 https://minghui.org/mh/articles/2016/12/26/339387.html
197 https://minghui.org/mh/articles/2016/7/20/331583.html
198 https://en.minghui.org/html/articles/2006/4/22/72310.html
199 https://en.minghui.org/html/articles/2006/4/22/72310.html
200 https://en.minghui.org/html/articles/2016/5/16/157028.html
201 https://en.minghui.org/html/articles/2016/5/16/157028.html
202 http://en.minghui.org/html/articles/2014/5/19/1241.html
203 http://en.minghui.org/html/articles/2014/5/19/1241.html
204 https://minghui.org/mh/articles/2004/8/25/82606.html
205 https://minghui.org/mh/articles/2001/9/19/16732.html
206 https://minghui.org/mh/articles/2000/8/21/2887.html
207 https://minghui.org/mh/articles/2009/12/17/214589.html
208 https://en.minghui.org/emh/articles/2006/3/22/71075.html
209 http://en.minghui.org/html/articles/2016/5/16/157028.html
210 https://en.minghui.org/html/articles/2014/12/29/147492.html
211 https://en.minghui.org/html/articles/2016/5/20/157085.html
212 http://en.minghui.org/html/articles/2016/5/16/157028.html
213 http://en.minghui.org/emh/articles/2007/6/10/86636.html
214 http://en.minghui.org/html/articles/2008/6/9/98027.html
215 https://en.minghui.org/html/articles/2004/6/28/49646.html
216 https://en.minghui.org/html/articles/2006/2/9/70114.html
217 http://en.minghui.org/html/articles/2006/3/15/70824.html
218 http://en.minghui.org/html/articles/2008/6/9/98027.html
219 http://en.minghui.org/html/articles/2012/8/13/134924.html
220 https://en.minghui.org/html/articles/2018/4/30/169541.html
221 https://en.minghui.org/html/articles/2019/4/7/176410.html
222 http://en.minghui.org/html/articles/2019/9/26/180067.html
223 http://minghui.org/mh/articles/2004/7/17/79549.html
224 http://en.minghui.org/html/articles/2007/3/31/84084.html
225 http://en.minghui.org/html/articles/2007/5/23/86003.html
226 http://en.minghui.org/html/articles/2011/11/12/129394.html
227 http://en.minghui.org/html/articles/2011/10/7/128578.html
228 http://en.minghui.org/html/articles/2011/9/11/128024.html
229 http://en.minghui.org/html/articles/2013/3/4/138364.html
230 https://en.minghui.org/html/articles/2002/6/11/23011.html
231 http://en.minghui.org/html/articles/2014/12/21/147390.html
232 http://en.minghui.org/html/articles/2019/4/30/176670.html
233 http://en.minghui.org/html/articles/2006/2/15/69986.html

234 http://en.minghui.org/html/articles/2002/10/19/27715.html
235 http://en.minghui.org/html/articles/2018/12/10/173570.html
236 http://en.minghui.org/html/articles/2003/6/22/37242.html
237 https://www.shenyun.com/spirituality/challenges-we-face
238 http://en.minghui.org/html/articles/2014/3/24/146052.html
239 http://en.minghui.org/html/articles/2018/3/12/169019.html
240 http://en.minghui.org/html/articles/2016/5/9/156604.html
241 https://www.shenyun.com/spirituality/challenges-we-face
242 http://en.minghui.org/html/articles/2010/1/24/114110.html
243 http://en.minghui.org/html/articles/2009/6/28/108660.html
244 http://en.minghui.org/html/articles/2009/3/1/105229.html
245 http://en.minghui.org/html/articles/2017/9/10/165366.html
246 http://minghui.org/mh/articles/2003/11/30/61425.html
247 http://en.minghui.org/html/articles/2015/6/9/150989.html
248 http://en.minghui.org/html/articles/2015/6/5/150920.html
249 http://en.minghui.org/html/articles/2011/3/11/123733.html
250 http://en.minghui.org/html/articles/2011/7/21/126885.html
251 http://minghui.org/mh/articles/2010/7/20/227226.html
252 http://en.minghui.org/html/articles/2010/7/10/118486.html
253 http://en.minghui.org/emh/articles/2007/6/10/86636.html
254 http://en.minghui.org/html/articles/2008/7/18/99068.html
255 http://en.minghui.org/emh/articles/2003/12/10/42984.html
256 http://en.minghui.org/emh/articles/2003/10/15/41280.html
257 https://en.minghui.org/html/articles/2014/5/8/554.html
258 http://en.minghui.org/html/articles/2017/10/11/166023.html
259 http://en.minghui.org/html/articles/2014/11/2/146667.html
260 https://en.minghui.org/html/articles/2014/5/8/554.html
261 http://en.minghui.org/html/articles/2007/8/6/88378.html
262 http://en.minghui.org/html/articles/2007/7/7/87431.html
263 http://en.minghui.org/emh/articles/2007/7/6/87395.html
264 http://en.minghui.org/html/articles/2011/9/6/127880.html
265 http://en.minghui.org/html/articles/2008/6/13/98135.html
266 http://en.minghui.org/html/articles/2007/9/4/89235.html
267 http://en.minghui.org/html/articles/2007/9/4/89235.html
268 http://minghui.org/mh/articles/2005/7/13/106055.html
269 http://en.minghui.org/emh/articles/2004/6/30/49673.html
270 http://en.minghui.org/html/articles/2013/10/16/142771.html
271 https://en.minghui.org/html/articles/2013/11/1/142982.html
272 http://minghui.org/mh/articles/2019/9/9/392266.html
273 http://minghui.org/mh/articles/2019/9/9/392266.html
274 http://minghui.org/mh/articles/2019/9/8/392265.html
275 https://npcobserver.files.wordpress.com/2018/12/PRC-Constitution-2018.pdf
276 https://en.minghui.org/html/articles/2015/5/1/149952.html
277 Rome Statute of the International Criminal Court, https://www.icc-cpi.int/nr/rdonlyres/ea9aeff7-5752-4f84-be94-0a655eb30e16/0/rome_statute_english.pdf
278 http://minghui.org/mh/articles/2016/9/9/334185.html
279 http://minghui.org/mh/articles/2013/4/15/272084.html
280 http://minghui.org/mh/articles/2017/5/29/348800.html
281 http://en.minghui.org/emh/articles/2006/2/13/69911.html

282 http://minghui.org/mh/articles/2013/7/30/277328.html
283 http://en.minghui.org/html/articles/2012/3/22/132332.html
284 http://en.minghui.org/html/articles/2013/7/18/141114.html
285 http://minghui.org/mh/articles/2011/8/19/245367.html
286 http://minghui.org/mh/articles/2019/3/24/383941.html
287 https://en.minghui.org/html/articles/2015/5/25/150749.html
288 https://en.minghui.org/html/articles/2015/11/14/153658.html
289 http://en.minghui.org/html/articles/2014/5/19/1241.html
290 https://en.minghui.org/html/articles/2015/6/14/151073.html
291 https://en.minghui.org/html/articles/2016/5/9/156606.html
292 https://en.minghui.org/html/articles/2016/8/9/158186.html
293 http://en.minghui.org/html/articles/2016/9/4/158548.html
294 https://en.minghui.org/html/articles/2016/5/31/157223.html
295 https://en.minghui.org/html/articles/2016/10/23/159647.html
296 http://en.minghui.org/html/articles/2016/5/8/156581.html
297 http://minghui.org/mh/articles/2015/11/22/319484.html
298 https://en.minghui.org/html/articles/2019/4/24/176604.html
299 https://en.minghui.org/html/articles/2001/11/6/15473.html
300 https://www.epochtimes.com/gb/6/5/12/n1316568.htm
301 https://minghui.org/mh/articles/2004/8/25/82606.html
302 https://en.minghui.org/html/articles/2000/1/3/10733.html
303 https://en.minghui.org/html/articles/2014/4/22/290.html
304 https://en.minghui.org/html/articles/2018/11/6/173152.html
305 https://en.minghui.org/html/articles/2017/7/18/164699.html
306 https://en.minghui.org/html/articles/2000/3/4/8938.html
307 https://en.minghui.org/html/articles/2006/6/17/74550.html
308 https://en.minghui.org/html/articles/2019/4/12/176471.html
309 https://en.minghui.org/html/articles/2008/11/30/102642.html
310 https://en.minghui.org/html/articles/2019/5/5/176736.html
311 https://en.minghui.org/html/articles/2007/7/8/87471.html
312 https://en.minghui.org/html/articles/2011/11/23/129657.html
313 https://en.minghui.org/html/articles/2014/5/9/605.html
314 https://en.minghui.org/html/articles/2019/2/7/175738.html
315 https://en.minghui.org/html/articles/2018/1/23/167683.html
316 https://en.minghui.org/html/articles/2014/3/15/145856.html
317 https://en.minghui.org/html/articles/2010/3/13/115322.html
318 https://en.minghui.org/html/articles/2019/2/17/175854.html
319 https://en.minghui.org/html/articles/2006/5/8/73016.html
320 https://en.minghui.org/html/articles/2013/6/15/140508.html
321 https://en.minghui.org/html/articles/2008/9/6/100425.html
322 https://en.minghui.org/html/articles/2013/11/22/143339.html
323 https://en.minghui.org/html/articles/2018/8/26/171653.html
324 https://en.minghui.org/html/articles/2018/7/24/171246.html
325 https://en.minghui.org/html/articles/2019/3/2/176013.html
326 https://mhpublishing.org/story/spiritual-journey-of-a-software-developer/
327 https://en.minghui.org/html/articles/2019/6/21/178153.html
328 https://en.minghui.org/html/articles/2019/2/18/175866.html
329 https://en.minghui.org/html/articles/2003/12/9/42979.html
330 https://en.minghui.org/html/articles/2003/1/30/31516.html

331 https://en.minghui.org/html/articles/2004/8/9/51185.html
332 https://en.minghui.org/html/articles/2012/1/6/130542.html
333 https://en.minghui.org/html/articles/2003/3/28/33899.html
334 https://en.minghui.org/html/articles/2019/6/1/177876.html
335 https://minghui.org/mh/articles/2019/8/6/391133.html
336 https://en.minghui.org/html/articles/2019/8/1/178675.html
337 https://en.minghui.org/html/articles/2019/7/19/178502.html
338 https://www.theepochtimes.com/pence-meets-with-representatives-of-religious-groups-persecuted-in-china_3032274.html
339 https://en.minghui.org/html/articles/2019/8/8/178815.html
340 https://freedomhouse.org/report/china-religious-freedom/falun-gong
341 https://en.minghui.org/html/articles/2017/2/26/162317.html
342 https://en.minghui.org/html/articles/2013/9/23/142366.html
343 https://en.minghui.org/cc/80/
344 https://en.minghui.org/html/articles/2019/5/17/177657.html
345 https://www.congress.gov/bill/108th-congress/house-concurrent-resolution/304
346 https://www.congress.gov/bill/111th-congress/house-resolution/605
347 https://en.minghui.org/html/articles/2010/3/31/115786.html
348 https://en.minghui.org/html/articles/2019/7/21/178519.html
349 https://en.minghui.org/html/articles/2019/7/24/178567.html
350 https://www.europarl.europa.eu/sides/getDoc.do?pubRef=-%2F%2FEP%2F%2FNONSGML%2BWDECL%2BP8-DCL-2016-0048%2B0%2BDOC%2BPDF%2BV0%2F%2FEN
351 https://en.minghui.org/html/articles/2016/7/15/157833.html
352 https://en.minghui.org/html/articles/2019/5/25/177770.html
353 https://en.minghui.org/html/articles/2019/5/19/177683.html
354 https://en.minghui.org/html/articles/2018/4/1/169235.html
355 https://en.minghui.org/html/articles/2018/4/5/169276.html
356 https://www.declarationofistanbul.org/index.php?option=com_content&view=article&id=267:israel-transplant-law-organ-transplant-act-2008&catid=83:legisl%20ation&Itemid=130
357 http://documents.law.yale.edu/sites/default/files/criminal_code_spain.pdf
358 http://www.quotidianosanita.it/allegati/allegato4671710.pdf
359 http:/en.minghui.org/html/articles/2014/7/23/2191.html
360 https://en.minghui.org/html/articles/2015/6/19/151159.html
361 https://en.minghui.org/html/articles/2019/3/24/176260.html
362 https://en.minghui.org/html/articles/2019/6/18/178116.html
363 https://en.minghui.org/html/articles/2019/5/5/176732.html
364 https://en.minghui.org/html/articles/2019/5/2/176692.html
365 https://chinatribunal.com/final-judgement-report/
366 https://en.minghui.org/cc/86/
367 https://en.minghui.org/html/articles/2010/4/22/116248.html
368 https://en.minghui.org/html/articles/2010/4/24/116311.html
369 https://en.minghui.org/cc/88/
370 https://en.minghui.org/html/articles/2011/10/1/128477.html
371 https://en.minghui.org/html/articles/2001/2/5/4783.html
372 https://en.minghui.org/emh/articles/2004/11/21/54787.html
373 https://en.minghui.org/cc/87/
374 https://en.minghui.org/html/articles/2011/10/1/128695.html

375 https://en.falundafa.org/eng/lectures/1997L.html#_Toc511984051
376 https://en.minghui.org/html/articles/2012/5/15/133372.html
377 https://en.minghui.org/html/articles/2011/10/1/128695.html
378 https://en.minghui.org/html/articles/2002/1/20/17934.html

法輪大法好
明慧網
MINGHUI.ORG

INDEX

A

B

C

D

E

F

G

U

V

W

Other